# The Brotherhood of Oil

# The Brotherhood of Oil

Energy Policy and the Public Interest

## Robert Engler

The University of Chicago Press

Chicago and London

Robert Engler is the author of *The Politics of Oil* (1961). He is professor of political science at the City University of New York.

The University of Chicago Press, Chicago 60637
The University of Chicago Press, Ltd., London

**Library of Congress Cataloging in Publication Data**

Engler, Robert.
  The brotherhood of oil.

  Includes bibliographical references and index.
  1. Petroleum industry and trade—United States.
2. Energy policy—United States. I. Title.
HD9566.E58 338.2'7'2820973 76–56189
ISBN 0–226–20948–2

*For Leland Olds, Robert S. Lynd*
*and Roderick Seidenberg*
Three who cared

After the rising of the 17th June
The Secretary of the Writers' Association
Had leaflets distributed in the Stalinallee
In which you could read that the people
Had lost the Government's confidence
And could only win it back
By redoubled efforts. If so, would it not
Be simpler for the Government
To dissolve the people
And elect another?

*Bertolt Brecht*
"The Solution"

# Contents

|   | Preface | ix |
| 1 | Crude Awakenings | 1 |
| 2 | Traces of Oil | 16 |
| 3 | Political Explorations | 57 |
| 4 | The Rites of Government | 84 |
| 5 | Imperial Energies | 98 |
| 6 | Partners in Development | 146 |
| 7 | Bureaucratic Wastelands | 177 |
| 8 | Planning for New Beginnings | 209 |
|   | Notes | 251 |
|   | Index | 323 |

# Preface

This is a study of the political economy of oil and of the challenge it poses for the American political system. The title has, in the mind of the author, two meanings. At one level, *The Brotherhood of Oil* refers to the network of organizations, primarily private but recently joined by public ones, which function wherever petroleum is sought, found, and used. Much of the study deals with power: the economic power over production, markets, and prices wielded by the merchants of oil, and the political power that flows from such control. The central focus here is upon the giant corporations and their relation to public government and to social forces, primarily in the United States, which are also involved or seek involvement in the shaping of basic energy policies.

At the second level, the title is intended to convey the interdependence of people everywhere whose lives have been caught up in the quest for oil. For many its presence is a condition of nature and petroleum thus far plays a minor role in meeting their own daily needs. Yet this presence links their fates with those for whose mechanized economies oil is the lifeblood. A cutoff from their connection would be, in the words of one State Department official, "the most total challenge that could be launched . . ., something very close to nuclear warfare." The underlying concern at this level is the replacement of policies now responsive to the "bottom line" of corporate statements and the might of favored nations with planning which acknowledges the fraternity of all mankind and encourages directions which are economically just, ecologically sane and politically accountable.

The present book follows from *The Politics of Oil* (New York: Macmillan, 1961),* which had its origin in my interest in the problem of power. The fifteen years since the latter's publication saw the nation move from celebration of what was to be "the American century" to intense examination of the social costs of development. There was angry opposition to armaments, the Vietnam war, discrimination, poverty, urban decay, the shoddiness of goods and the degradation of the environment. The irresponsibility of authority in every institution became a target. A rebirth of populism brought questioning about the corporation and the business system and ultimately about technology and growth. The oil industry and its global operations became increasingly visible.

It was the "energy crisis" of 1973–74 which catapulted the separate aspects of oil policy to the center of public attention. Using this national educational experience as a case study, the book looks backward to trace the efforts of the industry to tie up energy resources at home and abroad. The oil dimensions of foreign policy, from involvement in Asia to the blockade against Cuba, are discussed, as is the permeation of every level of the body politic, from Watergate to the boundaries of policy options for the nation.

Research for the earlier work involved unearthing relatively obscure documents, interviewing corporate and public bureaucrats, seeking out isolated public servants across the country who were trying to preserve what they saw as the public interest. Today the scholar is inundated by materials on oil policy and politics. The challenge this time was one of winnowing and interpreting rather than searching out and organizing basic facts about oil.

But I was eager to see who had learned what from the earlier experiences with oil and what were the outcomes of previous struggles over offshore oil, shale, and natural gas. I wanted to appraise such counterforces as the environmental movement and awakened nationalism. To what extent are they effective in challenging the "first world government" by introducing standards of responsibility other than those of this private government of oil?

---

*Reissued in 1967 by the University of Chicago Press as a Phoenix paperback.

What has been the meaning of such new rallying points as "Santa Barbara," "alternate energy," and the "new international economic order"? And what have been the responses within the house of oil and public government—the new energy timetables, the changing definitions of corporate citizenship and of public policy?

Such questions led to research in New England, Appalachia, the region of the Tennessee Valley Authority, the great plains, the west coast, Alaska, Puerto Rico, Mexico, Canada, Great Britain, and portions of the Middle East. And the trail of oil repeatedly led me back to Washington, to oilmen and their spokesmen defending their versions of the common good, to public bureaucrats wondering how to cope with forces whose resources seemed unlimited set against their own information and mandate, to aroused legislators and their staffs exploring ways to challenge private privilege, to community activists meeting to share experiences in the development of political leverage. This time I found citizens, journalists, ecologists, legislators everywhere aware of the history of oil and of the need for alternatives to corporate stewardship and morality.

I wish to thank Victor Rabinowitz and the Louis B. Rabinowitz Foundation for generous assistance when it mattered most. The Research Foundation of the City University of New York gave travel and secretarial aid at several stages. I also wish to thank Sheri Tierney and Inea Bushnaq for help in preparing the manuscript for publication. The basic writing was completed in December 1975. Certain developments before going to press have been cited in the notes and occasionally in the text.

# 1

## Crude Awakenings

*There are three billion people in the world and we only have 200 million of them. We are outnumbered 15 to 1. If might did make right they would sweep over the United States and take what we have.*

President Lyndon Johnson to American and Korean servicemen, South Korea, November 1, 1966[1]

*The U.S.A. and its 205 million people use all we can get.*

Full page advertisement, American Petroleum Institute, *The New York Times*, April 26, 1971

*We use 30 percent of all the energy. . . . That isn't bad; that is good. That means that we are the richest, strongest people in the world and that we have the highest standard of living in the world. That is why we need so much energy, and may it always be that way.*

President Richard Nixon to Seafarers International Union, Washington, D.C. November 26, 1973[2]

The "energy crisis" of 1973–74 brought the separate pieces of the politics of oil together in a dramatic global collage. A long threatened Arab producers' embargo, launched in protest against United States military aid to Israel in the October 1973 war, triggered the emergency. Paralleling this action was a series of sharp increases in the price of crude oil. Almost immediately every sector of world society was affected. The American people received fresh

1

instruction as to the nature of power over resources in an integrated industrial setting. They also received damning evidence as to the incapacity of their public government to govern responsibly.

This time, however, initial awareness required the prodding of neither the scholar nor the journalist. Sweating out heating fuel deliveries (which, like voltage reductions and brownouts, had begun for some in previous years) and lines at the service station were jolting if fleeting experiences for a people heretofore assured that the consumption of more and more was their birthright. There were layoffs in automobile and petrochemical plants, cutbacks in airline schedules, sharp increases in the prices of food, steel, and other energy-intensive commodities of an already savagely inflated economy. The real gross national product for the first quarter of 1974 showed a decline of 7 percent. Highway blockades by truckers and walkoffs by coal miners resenting soaring fuel costs and allocations emphasized the dependence upon petroleum and showed how a disturbance in its flow could bring people to the edge of violence and martial law. There were even suggestions of a new war between the states. The governors of Louisiana, Oklahoma, and Texas hinted they might cut off shipments of oil and gas to the big consuming regions if the latter continued to resist exploration and refinery construction in their own backyards in order to preserve their beaches and air.[3] The Department of Defense, which early in 1973 had difficulty in buying the 50 percent of its petroleum requirements usually obtained from domestic refineries, now reported that the Arab embargo had cut its foreign supplies drastically and that its stocks were at a dangerous low.[4]

Officially, the immediate events were treated as if they had no history—and at times, as in some of the statements that President Richard M. Nixon made early in the embargo, as if they had no future. Reluctant to apply the term "crisis" he promised a speedy solution of the "problem," with minimum disturbance to daily living and a return to an America which could use energy freely.[5] By November he publicly described the shortage as a "national crisis." But by 1980 his "Project Independence" would bring the United States relief from such worries and from dependence upon foreign supplies—"for all time."[6] The projection bordered on fantasy, given the prevailing patterns of production and consumption. It also suggested an abandonment of less well-endowed industrial allies who had neither the fossil fuel reserves of the United States nor the immediate capability of developing alternative energy sources. Others in the administration promptly tempered this xeno-phobic call with the explanation that the ultimate goal, of course, was Project Interdependence. Appeals for consumer national soli-darity were mixed with admonitions against unilateral attempts, notably by France, and also England and Japan, to negotiate for oil directly with individual Middle Eastern countries. Europeans were also aware that the United States had its own connections through corporate and diplomatic corridors to ensure supplies. Trust abroad in United States leadership remained limited. Nor was it enhanced in Europe by Secretary of State Henry A. Kis-singer's oft-repeated view that world peace was frustrated less by communist intransigence ("We have a generation of experience" in dealing with our enemies, and "with ups and downs we are going to handle it") than by the insecurity of the Common Mar-ket countries (who "have never fully regained public confidence" since World War I) which he saw reflected in their distrust of any American-encouraged unity. "The deepest problem in Europe to-day . . . is that there has been very rarely, fully legitimate govern-ments in any European country since World War I."[7]

The events were also treated as if they had no public handles. Oil and other businessmen were rushed in, and civil servants were shuffled to staff a succession of White House emergency agencies and advisory bodies. Wildly conflicting estimates as to the extent of Middle East imports, the effectiveness of the embargo, and the shortages for the United States, Europe, and Japan were released. Still the world's largest producer, the United States was now im-porting about a third of its petroleum requirements, chiefly from Canada and Venezuela, and perhaps 7 percent from the Middle East. For Western Europe the potential threat was more serious. Under Marshall Plan stimulus it had shifted to oil and become the major market for imports.[8] Giant refineries had been built to ac-commodate the crude now flowing from the Persian Gulf. Both the fields and the refineries were heavily under American corporate control. The entire supply line, including the tremendous profits from each stage of the integrated process, enjoyed the protection of the United States through the Truman Doctrine and related military operations. Eighty-five percent of Europe's oil now came from the Middle East and North Africa. Japan, encouraged by the U.S. occupation to convert from coal, imported all the oil for her booming industrialization: 45 percent from the Arab countries, 38 percent from Iran, and 12 percent from Indonesia, mostly through the Western international corporations. The postwar recovery of Europe and the miracle of Japanese growth had relied upon an un-impeded oil supply refined from crude whose price had been kept stable and free from producing country "interference." Energy relief was a possibility for the United Kingdom once its costly dis-coveries in the stormy North Sea would begin to flow in 1975. In exuberant moments Prime Minister Harold Wilson foresaw a new industrial revolution and even the possibility of a future British minister of energy chairing the Organization of Petroleum Export-ing Countries.[9] But the target of self-sufficiency and even the ability to export were perhaps a decade away. Japan intensified searches in its own waters and on the Asian mainland, but prospects were far less promising.

While the public government of the United States was trying to show its people that it was in command, it continued to delegate the task of ensuring its fossil fuel requirements to the private gov-ernment of oil. The latter determined national need, negotiated with governments of producing areas, and handled global dis-tribution. The corporations accepted responsibility for balancing European needs in face of the selective embargo, paying special attention to the Netherlands, which was singled out by the Arabs presumably because of its sympathies with Israel. At home, alloca-tion policies to alleviate the worst stress were worked out. The government had no program beyond urging the companies to bring in as much as they possibly could.[10] It repeatedly expressed con-fidence that prices would ultimately drop, since the rises were arti-ficial and could not withstand the laws of supply and demand. Energy policies to reduce dependence upon the Middle East and build up domestic alternatives would also help. Spokesmen made clear that political investment in Saudi Arabia could still pay off and that United States economic tactics might speed up the inevitable demise of OPEC. Within this framework, freshly anointed public officials explored alternate schemes for rationing, and raised price ceilings. Throughout, President Nixon reaffirmed his faith in the workings of a free market and his preference for letting the price mechanism (that is, increases) bring forth the needed fuel.

His earlier warnings as to congressional accountability were reiterated. If the legislators remained "distracted by other matters" (the Watergate break-in and coverup); if they ignored his appeals to pass an environmentally contested Alaska pipeline bill, to remove natural gas prices from federal regulation, to authorize more research in coal, to open up public lands and the long-coveted naval reserves for private development, and to relax environmental constraints, then "we will have an energy crisis."[11]

The president pledged United States influence for a peaceful Arab-Israeli settlement as the road to reducing oil shortages. "Both sides are at fault. . . . We're not pro-Israel; and we're not pro-Arab. And we're not any more pro-Arab because they have oil and Israel hasn't."[12] The immediate oil price increases, however, had a history independent from the latest round of Arab-Israeli fighting. They had been initiated by Iran. Like Venezuela, Nigeria, and Indonesia, Iran had no direct stake in an Arab crusade against Israel. Indeed, it remained the latter's chief supplier of crude oil. What the shah did want was for his country of 30 million people to become a powerful industrial and military nation. The road to such modernization was through high oil revenues. In response, Mr. Nixon invoked the memories of the American action against Iran in 1953 and the failure of an Arab embargo after the 1967 war. He hinted darkly "to responsible Arab leaders" as to the consequences of continued price increases and expropriations. "Oil without a market, as Mr. Mossadegh learned many, many years ago, doesn't do a country much good."[13]

Some of his aides were to speculate publicly about retaliation through food cutoffs or even military intervention, should Middle Eastern producers continue to use oil as political leverage and what began as an inconvenience threatened to become the gravest emergency. The American secretary of defense said that the Arab countries ran the risk of increasing public demand for force against them. But as the embargo accelerated, the administration's public tone came closer to the caution and conciliation of its closed dealings with the oil producing nations.[14]

Meanwhile, commercial airlines found the crisis an appropriate opportunity for eliminating nonlucrative flights. (Military sources also speculated that the airlines had duped the Federal Energy Office, which in turn had overreacted to the presumed shortage for that industry: the FEO had diverted jet fuel from military allocations at what the airlines hoped would be preembargo prices. When the airlines discovered that it could not be July at Christmas, that they would have to replace stock at the going prices, "their fuel crisis evaporated as quickly as it had materialized.") The trucking industry renewed its quest for permission to operate longer and heavier vehicles on interstate highways; the automobile and other industries declared their willingness to postpone environmental and safety measures; and the House of Representatives voted, avowedly, for energy conservation reasons, to ban the use of fuel to transport children beyond their neighborhood schools so as to achieve racial balance.[15]

Throughout, the American public was told that the basic responsibility for muddling through was theirs. From the White House came fatherly advice about health habits. On one occasion the president flew to his California retreat on a commercial plane, a gesture which aides promptly hailed as a triumph of democratic leadership, conservation, and public relations. Citizens were exhorted to drive more slowly, to lower thermostats and use less electricity. Year-round daylight saving time and lowered speed limits were legislated to ensure that the seriousness of the shortage and the firmness of the government's management were conveyed to every household.

Yet the confusion continued. If the private government of oil had been deposed from its world throne, as it was beginning to insist, it still claimed the prerogatives of sovereign custodian of national security. The oil companies resisted disclosing information as to crude stocks, refinery runs, and inventories at each of their installations. When Connecticut's attorney general sought figures from the United States Army Corps of Engineers on oil shipments into his state's ports, he was told this was "proprietary information" which could affect competition among the corporations.[16]

Reports of the shortages were countered by pictures of loaded tankers riding at anchor and accounts of underutilized refinery capacity around the country. Companies were cutting imports as a show of resistance against a government allocation program which forced them to share some of their imports at prices which these companies viewed as discriminatory.[17]

The immediate pain—save for the price—was of remarkably short duration. By the spring of 1974 the embargo was lifted. Saudi Arabia, now the world's leading exporter, had restored full production. American energy patterns seemed back to normal. Soon the familiar references to a glut in immediate world oil supplies reappeared in the trade journals. The long run remained uncertain. The only clear data were that Middle Eastern crude prices had more than quadrupled and producer nation incomes had soared: Saudi Arabia's oil revenues moved from $3 billion in 1972 to over $27 billion in 1974, putting her in third place among the nations of the world in monetary reserves. Total petrodollar earnings for the producers were to reach $100 billion by the end of 1974. United States oil industry profits increased 70 percent in 1973 over the previous year. And the energy bills for American consumers rose by 50 to 100 percent within less than a year.

During the emergency, widespread skepticism, cynicism, and anger as to its origins and legitimacy prompted legislators to thunder against "the interests"—albeit uncertain whether those interests were the emerging producers' cartel, the more familiar (if reluctantly labeled) corporate one, or both. Nor was confidence expressed that the federal administration was responding knowledgeably, justly, or even credibly. Citizens feel "somewhat abandoned," Senator Warren G. Magnuson (Democrat, Washington) observed. "If there were an election today," added a New Jersey assemblyman, "they'd throw us all out; I've never seen people so mad."[18] Legislators from oil and gas states found that, at least temporarily, energy was no longer their exclusive fiefdom. Their remedies, so warmly seconded by the president, were not being accepted as gospel. Congressional committees vied with one another for newly discovered jurisdictions over energy. Leasing patterns, government statistics, tax credits, depletion allowance, antitrust waivers, market performance, and corporate-government diplomacy came under review. Every representative seemed to be in search of a bill or a platform, eager to lead if not always quite sure as to directions.

Senator Henry M. Jackson (Democrat, Washington), a presidential contender who chaired two committees studying energy, along with several colleagues challenged and scolded executives of seven major oil companies who early in 1974 had been summoned as a panel to explain the relation of their supply policies to public discomfort. The senators seemed startled to discover how far-reaching and profitable oil was. It was suggested that the corporations had misled the public as to the nature of the shortage. And that Exxon had betrayed the American government by holding back on supplies to the United States military when Aramco was ordered to do so by King Faisal of Saudi Arabia.[19] Another Senate committee, under Senator Frank Church (Democrat, Idaho), was putting together the picture of how Aramco was directed to supply oil to the Arab war effort. The request, Aramco explained, was a matter of state priority, and the company "had no alternative but to comply."[20] Aramco denied that the issue was "corporate disloyalty to the United States," as Jackson had charged. It was responding to a threat from Saudi Arabia that "any deviations" would be "harshly dealt with." Thus the consortium "had no choice but to follow instructions" if it did not wish to be cut off from its crude supply. Its compliance "had nothing to do with patriotism."[21] Saudi Arabia was friendly to the United States and had warned Aramco leaders of the mounting anti-American and anti-Israel sentiments among other Middle East producers. Aramco had briefed every American policy maker who would listen that King Faisal felt that the interests of his country were virtually identical with those of the United States on all fronts, save Israel. But his position was becoming untenable, and he would be isolated from an increasingly militant Arab world. He could not permit this to happen. The oilmen were directed to advise their home government that the political alliance and the economic concessions were both in danger. If United States policy toward Israel did not change, "everything will be lost." This intelligence went largely unheeded when transmitted to Washington, the oilmen felt.[22] Nevertheless, Saudi Arabia had opposed a boycott, had been reluctant to launch the embargo, and had been moderate on price. Once the war was underway, the heads of Exxon, Texaco, Socal, and Mobil (the partners in Aramco) had urged President Nixon not to resupply the Israelis. The Arabs were certain to retaliate. United States influence and penetration, so carefully nurtured over the previous decades, would diminish. With such loss would go control over Middle Eastern oil.

The oilmen also reminded that the king was a strong force against regional radicalism and international communism. Along with Iran, Saudi Arabia could be counted upon to frustrate any attempts by the Soviet Union to build influence or footholds in the region. The Persian Gulf, and Saudi Arabia in particular (160 billion barrels reserve and an ability and readiness to increase a daily production of 8 million barrels), were the United States' best immediate source, and the oil companies were the most reliable intermediaries.[23]

Those with long memories recalled how during World War II, when the armed forces were alarmed about daily shortages, industry leaders operating within the war councils of the United States had torpedoed the proposed public acquisition of the holdings in Saudi Arabia of Standard Oil of California and the Texas Company. (These two were soon to be joined by Jersey Standard and Mobil, which sought both the crude and the control over the abundance which could cause such mischief to world pricing if in the wrong hands and made available to independents.) The oilmen had also blocked the construction of a United States-owned refinery and pipeline in the Middle East. A government Petroleum Reserves Corporation would be "fatal" and "fascist," they had argued. It could shackle "free enterprise," involve the United States in "the new highway of international power politics," and surrender freedom. "Oil in the hands of nationals of the United States is equally available for national security with oil owned or financially shared in by the Government of the United States."[24]

Questions were asked why the Cost of Living Council had permitted domestic crude oil from "older wells" (volume pumped by a producer in 1972), which accounted for about 75 percent of production, to rise a dollar to $5.25 a barrel, and why it had left crude from new wells, which was selling at $10.35 a barrel, free of controls. Less than a year before the crisis the industry had agreed that crude prices of around $4.35 to $4.55 would encourage adequate exploration and production for the domestic market. These increases could not be explained by cost justifications but rather by a response to the arbitrarily set Middle Eastern prices. International prices no longer awaited negotiations. The producers had taken the initiative and were testing as to what was gettable. Resistance by the international corporations was selective and ineffectual; their primary concern was maintaining overall control and synchronization of price-supply patterns. The United States government set no ceiling on these prices.[25]

"We've got politics mixed in this and it shouldn't be there." The hearings were run like a "criminal trial" and "went far beyond the ethics of fair play. . . . We didn't have a chance," said the president of Gulf Oil in reviewing the hearings. "Massacre," concurred Secretary of the Treasury George P. Shultz.[26] To Henry Jackson, such sensitivity to lifting a veil of corporate secrecy in oil suggested how protected the industry had been. "We ended this idea that they are a law unto themselves."[27] He also saw the foundations being laid for a long-circulating reform which was gaining new interest—the federal chartering of oil corporations. Meanwhile, Senator Church's committee had reviewed the history of the industry's Middle Eastern ventures and speculated about the implications of corporations negotiating with foreign governments and the consequences for the national energy crisis.

State legislatures, grand juries, and attorneys general launched investigations and conspiracy suits against oil companies. States and municipalities searched for remedies. One governor, Tom McCall of Oregon, won acclaim for his "even license numbers, even days" measure to relieve queues and tempers at the pump—a sensible, voluntary innovation which also underscored the limits of state power. Even abroad, where the American interest in antitrust has often been viewed as reflective of the nation's trained innocence, in this instance about economics, there was a spate of government investigations into oil corporations' collusive pricing and supply practices.

Once the press discovered energy to be "the mainspring of civilization" and, more important, news, it made room for an energy beat. Radio and television competed with specials and even exposés. The Middle Eastern world received unaccustomed coverage. Places like Abu Dhabi, Iran, and Kuwait were discussed and compared as communities concerned about welfare, development, and changing values rather than viewed simply as ports of call for tourists or corporate employees. Prudhoe Bay, the Athabasca Basin, the North Sea, and Southeast Asia offshore waters began to be mentioned familiarly. Windmills, solar energy, and other alternate energy sources were no longer treated as the hobbies of eccentrics. The record profits of the oil corporations and the embarrassment to executives of the timing of such normally private heraldings were now featured. Scholars and foundations rushed to stake out preserves and launch expensive interdisciplinary projects and conferences. Scientists found funding to pursue energy studies heretofore viewed as idle curiosity. Apocalyptic treatises on the end of Western civilization, of the era of cheap resources and unlimited growth, proliferated. The specter of millions of immobilized cars and trucks, or at least the demise of the big gas guzzlers, received mournful attention. The massive transfers of payments from industrial to oil producer regions invited endless speculation as to the capacity of parvenu colonials—now the principal creditors of Europe and Japan—to handle such wealth "responsibly." Could the astronomical foreign exchange holdings, perhaps $60 billion in 1974 and not likely to be absorbed into their own economies, be recycled into the international payment system so that oil importing countries could continue to finance their deficits? Meanwhile, Kuwait purchased a 15 percent interest in Daimler Benz. Iran acquired a 25 percent interest in Krupp steel works and began negotiations for an equivalent share of the "House of Krupp," the vast overall holding company. There was talk of foreign investers entering Lockheed, Grumman, and other troubled defense corporations. However, foreign government securities, corporate bonds, real estate, and short-term bank deposits were believed to be soaking up much of the surplus. Each report or rumor of Arab or Iranian investment beyond their own borders prompted discussions as to whether the Western world would soon be under new management.

Forecasts of international industrial depression found sobering support in unemployment figures. Nations sought frantically to meet their oil import bills. Inflation intensified and governments tottered. The energy independence of Russia and China, in contrast to Europe and Japan, forced reappraisal of national security assumptions and alliances and of ultimate responsibilities to allies. Although rarely mentioned in the ceremonial hoopla over a new Asian detente, the stepped-up courtship of Communist China by the American government, and more surreptitiously by the international corporations, had a distinct petroleum cast; China's dimensions as a producer and growing exporter were being carefully studied in business and intelligence circles. And a review of traditional positions on Israel, presumed launching point for the oil embargo, was far more visibly underway. Oil-thirsting nations appraised the economic threat behind the avowed determination of producers to bring to the world's notice the grievances of the Palestinian movement, the expansion of Israel's boundaries, and their own cumulative hostility to Western manipulation. Crude oil, recently selling for $2.40 a barrel, was now over $10 and offering political leverage for national and regional assertion.

But the producers, however exhilarated by their economic achievements, were gauging the point at which the West might see its "vital interests" endangered and convert contingency plans into military actions. A new president of the United States, Gerald Ford, warned in 1974 that sovereign nations could not allow their policies to be dictated or their fate decided by artificial rigging and the distortion of world commodity markets.[28] He obviously had in mind the new actions of OPEC rather than the accepted patterns of the "seven sisters," (the seven largest international corporations). Secretary of State Kissenger said that military actions to bring down prices would be dangerous and probably counterproductive; but it would be a different matter if "actual strangulation of the industrialized world" should be at stake.[29] There were also occasional reminders about the immediate relation of oil prices to fertilizer, food, and famine for hundreds of millions in India, Bangladesh, and other oil-poor "developing" countries of Asia, Africa, and Latin America. Pathetic foreign aid and grudgingly offered Western loans were canceled out by such increases. Painful growth gains were lost.

Oil, gas, and utility corporations rushed to the defense in a heavy outpouring of advertisements. Stung by the robustness of the irreverent assaults on their patriotism, they reorganized and redoubled their public relations. Communications had become as important as finding oil, the president of Shell concluded. Breaking precedent, the corporations attempted to answer the charges that the crisis had been conceived in conspiracy. Exxon's chairman announced "we are embarking on the oil industry's version of Project Candor," an unfortunate borrowing of language from the Nixon administration's last stand.[30] The industry made no mention of its campaigns to increase consumption. And it abandoned the unbridled optimism, expressed by a former Exxon president: "We see no saturation point in the demand for oil. We are confidently looking forward to increased and new uses for our products."[31] Now the oil industry emphasized how long it had been warning about the pressures of accelerated demand and the costliness of exploration. (In 1972, for example, the National Petroleum Council advised that the industry could meet the nation's energy requirements, but only with a more sympathetic government policy which abandoned the crippling constraints upon it and with the support of an understanding public willing to pay significantly higher fuel prices).[32] If truth be known, said the industry and its banking allies, profits were not large enough for the capital investment requirements that lay ahead. Where the industry once generated internally 85 percent of such funds, the figure was now down to 69 percent.[33] The premise that the consumer was the chief investor was not to be challenged.

The energy crisis was seen either as the fault of "all of us" or due to conditions beyond corporate control. Advertisements made frequent if somewhat oblique references to greedy sheikhs, righteous environmentalists, profligate consumers, and bumbling bureaucrats lurking in the dwindling fuel pile. Texaco had unveiled the secret new ingredient in better mileage performance—"You." Then it retreated discreetly behind the faithful (and now perspiring) dealer who was "giving you everything he's got." Shell offered on prime viewing time one-minute patriotic glimpses of its adopted American heritage. Mobil was to underwrite modern art and bicentennial concerts, a national town meeting of the air and British television drama. "We think we're adding some gaiety and sparkle to American life," its public relations manager explained.

"And we're also helping ourselves get a hearing with opinion leaders." This "goodwill umbrella" was intended to build enough credibility "to allow us to get tough on substantive issues."[34] Mobil messages defending profits, attacking natural gas regulation, supporting the Alaska pipeline and Sesame Street, and calling for a national energy policy began to appear on editorial pages throughout the country—every Thursday on the Op-Ed page of the *New York Times*. The company tried to demonstrate what it felt was statesmanlike compromise in the public interest by calling for the gradual rather than the immediate removal of controls on oil prices, generally advocated by its industry. And it pleaded for an end to "playing politics" with energy. It challenged politicians to support, as they had done a generation earlier in the case of foreign policy, a bipartisan energy policy.[35]

Official government positions tended to absolve the industry. For example, after the "crisis" seemed to have faded, the Department of the Interior reiterated that utility costs, which for some consumers now exceeded their mortgage payments, "must be laid back on the oil exporting countries. They interrupted our oil supplies into this country and caused the price to remain at a very high level."[36]

Yet, the cries of "rip-off" continued to be heard throughout the land. Proposals for price rollbacks, stringent profits taxes and regulations, divestiture, public development corporations, and even nationalization entered the political dialogue. By 1975 much of the sense of urgency had disappeared from public discussion. The nation still lacked a coherent energy policy. The Congress and the White House continued to fumble. Yet forty-five senators voted for a largely unpublicized bill calling for the breakup of the integrated corporations and limits upon their moving into other energy areas. Had the long-feared tiger of public consciousness escaped from the tank?

The world's greatest industrial power seemed in disarray. Vietnam mocked its military capability, Watergate its political solvency. Now an "energy crisis" threatened the viability of its economy. "Backward" raw material producers were standing up to its sophisticated corporate order. Its own people were discovering national vulnerability and possible limits to growth and power. The complex private government of oil had functioned globally behind a shield of secrecy sustained by a responsive national state. But until now "it had worked," contributing significantly to the gross national product. There had been no independent public oil policy or any continuing review of oil patterns. After all, it had been an article of faith that corporate and national interests were identical. If there was a price, the major costs were borne by a bountiful environment, the less powerful, the remote, the unborn, and a corroded political process. Now it appeared as if the system was serving new centers of power. It was no longer quite so clear that what was good for oil was good for all. The risks and the costs were being thrown right back to that small, privileged minority—the northern-tier industrial people, including the United States—who consumed the bulk of the world's fossil fuels. What had gone wrong? What were the roots of the energy crisis? What were the new imperatives and the new options for the American way of life?

# 2

# Traces of Oil

The fifteen years preceding the 1973–74 crisis had seen a tremendous growth in energy consumption in the United States, and there was a projected doubling for the decade ahead. An expanded labor force, including a great influx of women, meant higher energy usage at home, at work, and en route. There were now 130 million registered vehicles on the roads, an almost 300 percent increase in total horsepower. Neither the automobile nor the petroleum industry showed concern over the inefficient energy conversion of the internal combustion engine, its insatiable thirst, the consequences for air pollution, or the scarring of the landscape. Indeed, along with building contractors, construction unions, lawyer-politicians clearing the rights of way, and other allies, they fervently supported a national superhighway system and the exclusive earmarking of gasoline taxes for more highways. Roads continued to command a lion's share of nonmilitary governmental expenditures, and their untouchability has been a critical component of the mounting fiscal difficulties of cities and states seeking revenues to meet other social needs. Trolleys had been eliminated earlier, with the active assistance of the two big industries.[1] Suburban living required more daily travel and spawned the two- and even three-car family. Yet trains continued to disappear and tracks to be abandoned. Inland waterways, once key arteries for inexpensive commerce and development, were forgotten. Trucks grew longer and heavier, choking streets and making city plans obsolete.

Architectural design and corporate vanity ignored energy factors: glass skyscrapers required intensive cooling in summer and heating in winter. Air conditioning became a must for public and, increas-

ingly, for private facilities and travel. Power gadgetry of every description was made attractive to consumers. Petrochemicals promised "better living" and high energy consumption was equated with
personal liberation.

Industry was the major user of fossil fuels—at least 40 percent,
and electric rates favored the large consumers. Refineries and utilities drew heavily upon natural gas as a boiler fuel. The disposable
economy, with throwaway bottles and accelerated obsolescence,
encouraged greater energy usage. The switch from tin-plated to
aluminum cans, from soaps to detergents, from natural fibers to
oil-based synthetics, the intensified use of artificial fertilizer in agriculture, the race to eliminate chemically every bug—whether harm-
ful or not—all meant that productivity remained the dominant perspective.[2] The replacement of labor, human skill, and experience by
what in corporate accounting was a cheaper substitute—fossil fuel
energy—was also encouraged. Profits were the surest guide. There
was no one to say "no."

The Vietnam war became a major conflagration drawing heavily
on American resources. Then it appeared to subside as the nation
was forced to shift its strategy of direct military involvement while
seeking to maintain its global hegemony. Mobilization of resources
continued. A trillion, five hundred billion dollars were spent for
armaments by the United States in the post–World War II period,
and the new "post–Vietnam" budget showed no letup. The warfare state, like the consumer society, was powered and lubri-
cated by petroleum. The "peacetime" Defense Department demand
ranged from 4 to 6 percent of national consumption. Guns *and*
butter had been the nation's pride, and the United States increasingly drew from all of the world to support this style.

The oil industry continued its growth as molder and beneficiary
of this national destiny. Pipelines became bigger and tankers super.
There were corporate changes and mergers. Eight of the first
twenty-five companies in 1960 had merged by a decade later.
For example, Amerada, once a symbol of the independence so
attractive to North Dakotans, joined with Hess, an aggressive marketer seeking crude oil, to enter the ranks of the integrated; Hess
thus gained a sizable crude supply and a dramatic reduction in its
federal income tax liabilities. Standard Oil of California acquired

Standard (Kentucky), Union Oil and Pure Oil merged, Sun Oil acquired Sunray DX. Atlantic Refining merged with Richfield and then absorbed portions of Sinclair to become one of the largest of the majors (Arco). British Petroleum landed in North America and its highly successful finds in Alaska promised the invader freedom from worries about import quotas. It gradually acquired the equivalent of 25 percent of the common stock of crude-hungry Standard Oil (Ohio). Sohio thus gained access to crude oil. British Petroleum received marketing outlets from it and from Sinclair, as well as the possibility of an eventual 54 percent ownership of the former. Burmah Oil, an international holding company now controlled by the Bank of England, has had a 22 percent interest in BP. In 1974 it purchased Signal Oil, a large American independent on the West Coast, for $480 million. The British government already holds 49 percent of BP in addition to the new 22 percent, but ownership is passive.

Energy became an important base for the conglomerate movement. For example, Tennessee Gas and Transmission Company (Tenneco), a relatively new firm, rose dramatically to become one of America's biggest corporations. It has an extensive network of natural gas pipeline and produces oil and gas throughout the world. In 1967 it acquired Kern County Land, a producing company with assets of $706 million. Other operations are in chemicals, agribusiness, land development, shipping, and packaging.

A separate volume could be written about Occidental Petroleum. Through its Libyan concessions and other holdings it skyrocketed from a net worth of $34,000 in the mid-fifties to become the eleventh largest of American crude oil producers and the largest nonintegrated supplier of crude oil to independent refiners. Taking over Hooker Chemical Corporation it became a leading chemical producer. Its acquisition of Island Creek Coal made it the third largest coal company in the United States, complete with one of the vestiges of exploitative mining life—a network of company retail stores. Meanwhile, Armand Hammer, its peripatetic chairman who confessed that "I would not have known a barrel of oil if I fell into it" and who had entered the oil business because "an accountant friend pointed out that in my tax bracket it would not cost very much even if a venture lost money," promoted billion dollar natural gas, chemical, and fertilizer projects with the Soviet Union.[3] On several occasions Occidental's financial activities have been questioned by the Securities and Exchange Commission. And rumors were commonplace about the scale of political payments used to secure entry into North Africa and Venezuela. But the United States government's Export-Import Bank was not deterred from offering low-interest loans. And the company continues to extend its research into fertilizer and sulphur. It also claims to be moving toward full commercial production of shale on private lands through an in situ process which heats the rock and separates the shale oil within the mountain, thus eliminating many technological and environmental objections. Occidental's record won it numerous corporate admirers. In 1974 Standard (Indiana) declared interest in marriage, noting favorably Occidental's abundant petroleum, coal, and chemicals. There was also the unstated attraction of Oxy's shale activities (and its proclaimed readiness to market shale competitively in Standard's midwest territory). Hammer publicly denounced the proposal: its consummation would violate competition and herald the death of the private initiative that had built America. He seemed unmoved by the possibility of being saved from what Standard's chairman hinted might be a foreign suitor, and sought protection through the courts, Congress, and the antitrust division. Two years later it became known that Hammer was negotiating with Iran for access to the latter's oil for the company's European refineries. Iran would gain outlets for its oil and revenues for its intensive modernization program beyond what it was receiving from the consortium of Western companies marketing its oil. It would also have gained almost 20 percent voting rights if the deal had gone through, making Iran the largest single shareholder in Occidental.[4]

The basic pattern of the oil industry as a private planning system operating on a global scale remains.[5] Oil corporations cluster at the top of the lists of America's largest industrial enterprises. Ranked by assets, they occupy five of the first eight and eight of the first fifteen positions. The seven worldwide giants (five American—Exxon, Texaco, Gulf, Standard of California, and Mobil; and two international—Royal Dutch/Shell and British Petroleum) have assets whose combined worth, at a minimum, is $132 billion.[6]

Oil and gas account for a fifth of America's capital investment. And the overall energy total could go up at least by half if the accelerated development plans discussed during the 1973–74 crisis materialize. A recent projection by the Chase Manhattan Bank estimates the overall capital "needs" of the industry in the noncommunist world in the period 1970 to 1985 to be nearly $1.4 trillion. Of these funds, $810 billion were for searching for new reserves and developing the necessary facilities for refining and distribution. The bank saw $540 billion going for financial needs, including shareholder returns and debt servicing.[7]

Jersey Standard, wishing to be known as Exxon to enable it to market across the United States under a single name (the name change cost an estimated $100 million), has been the standard bearer in sales, assets and income within the industry and the corporate world. Its revenue for 1974 was $46 billion and its worth at the end of the year was listed at $31 billion, a figure which barely begins to describe the total resources and power of its more than 400 affiliates operating in over 100 countries. One must also calculate the present and future value of its reported worldwide reserves of 45 billion barrels of crude oil and 106 trillion cubic feet of natural gas. And these are inadequate guides for determining the market power in the tremendous capital that flows through its hands.

As of 1970 the first twenty oil companies accounted for 94 percent of domestic reserves, 70 percent of domestic crude production, 86 percent of domestic refinery capacity, and 79 percent of domestic gasoline sales.[8] The first four alone account for over 30 percent of each of these operations. The majors own or have interest in 70 percent of interstate pipelines. They own or lease half the world's oil tanker tonnage.

Until the nationalization moves of the seventies, the seven international giants had held at least two-thirds of the world's proved reserves and production, including the Middle East, North Africa, Canada, Latin America, and Southeast Asia. Price was under their control. When there was some upward spiraling because of producer nation pressure, their chief focus was to prevent whipsawing which might upset the "orderly" relations crucial to corporate global planning. Within this framework resistance was rather selective.

As seen in Saudi Arabia, for example, profits moved in tandem with those of the host country. The new higher costs were, in effect, payments to themselves or their subsidiaries which held the concessions.[9] They were able to pass along these "costs" to consumers. Meanwhile, they gained further tax credits and insulation from the American income tax. Thus their ultimate profits rose, as did the worth of their holdings abroad and at home under the stimulus of the overseas increases in price.

The integrated nature of these corporations remains critical for their effective domination of the flow of oil. They are able to shift profits from one stage to another, whether to maximize advantage from import quotas and the different tax laws of host nations or to drive out refinery competition or marketing intruders. They thus mask the nature and profitability of their businesses. The maneuverability was pertinent to the background of the energy crisis of the early seventies. Faced with greater demands for profits, production controls, and participation from the increasingly sophisticated producer nations, the international companies sought to divert more of their own profits downstream to the refinery and marketing phases.[10] It wasn't that they had been giving away their oil. Observers have often been lulled by this corporate poor-mouthing. "Losses" in marketing abroad were often bookkeeping fictions occasioned by sales to themselves at padded prices.[11] Similarly, sales to "independents" at home, rather than being desperate surplus-dumping devices, had become highly profitable strategies for maintaining volume. But now they wanted to accelerate home revenues while also developing price umbrellas for alternative energy sources.

There remains some competition for new reserves and markets. Yet the chief characteristic of the "independents" seems to be dependency at every stage, whether in marketing of crude oil or refined products. Independent producers generally sell to major refiners, independent refiners rely on major producers, and independent marketers draw upon major refiners. They operate at the margins of the industry, often profitably but always on sufferance. In the sixties the abundance of crude helped the "private branders" to expand marketing operations. But by the early seventies the supplies from the majors which independents had taken for granted were restricted and some were forced to close down or restrict operations. Meanwhile the majors reorganized their domestic marketing so as to move out of areas where they were not strong. At the same time, they began to open aggressive self-service and price-cutting chains under new names. Thus they moved to tighten their marketing controls and their system of regional leadership.

The giants continue to share a community of interests which is guarded through patents, banking ties, common capital underwriters and accounting services, interlocking directorships through a third firm, bidding understandings in relation to public lands, recognized territorial prerogatives, crude oil and product exchange arrangements, and price fixing. As a Federal Trade Commission staff report concluded, domestically they operate much like a cartel.[12] Expensive continental shelf drillings are undertaken jointly, as for example in 1974 when Exxon, Mobil, and Champlin Oil were awarded a lease for a tract off Florida in the Gulf of Mexico after a $212 million bid. Once the high prices of crude promised a desired floor for shale, Standard (Indiana) and Gulf successfully bid $210 million for the first shale lands offered by the Interior Department—a tract of 5,000 acres in Colorado containing perhaps 3 to 4 billion barrels of recoverable crude oil. (The second highest bid, $175 million, came from Sun Oil.) Six years earlier Interior had canceled a shale lease sale because the highest bid was only $500,000. Shell, Atlantic Richfield, Ashland, and the Oil Shale Corporation are partners in a comparable project on the second tract offered, for which they bid $118 million. They also began the development—and then suspended operations late in 1974— of the first major American commercial shale oil plant, with Arco as the operator. Capital expenditures had been estimated at $1 billion. The vital interstate pipelines are jointly owned. The Colonial pipeline system, for example, is the nation's largest products pipeline and is owned by a cluster of nine majors. It dominates the flow of petroleum products from Gulf coast refineries to the Southeast and their storage along the East Coast. When the Midwest experienced a severe shortage of heating fuel during the winter of 1972, it was discovered that a considerable amount of fuel had been witheld from its usual market there while the Colonial system was handling and then storing an amount far in excess of its normal requirements, raising basic questions as to the nature of that winter's fuel crisis.[13]

The much fought-over 800-mile trans-Alaska pipeline, billed as the largest private construction project and estimated to cost $7.7 billion, is owned by a consortium of Atlantic Richfield, British Petroleum, Exxon, Phillips, Mobil, Union, and Amerada Hess subsidiaries. The first three own over 90 percent of the forty-eight-inch pipeline, which is expected to bring two million barrels of crude oil a day to the ice-free port of Valdez on Alaska's southern shore, where it will be loaded on tankers, presumably bound for West Coast refineries. (There was speculation that Japan was a preferred destination.) Arco, BP, and Exxon also control most of the Prudhoe Bay proven reserves on the Arctic North Slope—the largest oil field in United States history. These three companies have exploration, production, and shipping agreements which narrowly define the competitive options for other producers and the prices for consumers.[14]

The scale of lease payments often sounds impressive. State and federal officials repeatedly express surprise and gratification at the bids, suggesting a rather limited knowledge or concern as to the potential worth of the public lands being offered. Most of the Prudhoe Bay field was acquired in the mid-sixties for $12 million in lease payments. After Arco's big strike in 1968 there was a new oil rush and perspectives appeared to change.

Excitement in Alaska ran high, and the state treasury took in nearly a billion dollars just from its first round of sales in 1969. To citizens the income meant the beginnings of self-sufficiency and possible tax relief for their financially poor state which might at last be shedding (or trading in) its colonial dependence upon the federal government. Alaska's commissioner of natural resources, an ex-oilman and protégé of developer Walter J. Hickel, was sure he could drive a tough bargain: "Oilmen are tough buzzards and it takes one to deal with them." To the investing corporation, millions and even billions of dollars can be very modest down payments when set against the long-run expectation of the return on each barrel at every stage of the delivery, ultimately, of perhaps 20 percent of the total United States crude oil and at least 10 percent of the total natural gas resources.[15]

Banks remain significant if elusive centers for orchestrating common outlooks and circumventing antitrust prohibitions against interlocking directorships. A sustained effort during the early seventies by Democratic senators Lee Metcalf (Montana) and Edmund S. Muskie (Maine) to identify the leading stockholders in major corporations revealed how far ownership is concentrated in the hands of a few banks. The actual owners are often camouflaged or not identified in the reports corporations are legally required to submit to regulatory agencies. Of the eighteen large oil companies queried, four gave the information sought. Mobil, for example, indicated that the top thirty stockholders held 29 percent of the shares of common stock. The three largest, accounting for 14 percent through nominees, were banks (Bankers Trust, Chase Manhattan, Morgan Guaranty). Atlantic Richfield's first thirty stockholders held 26 percent, with Chase Manhattan and First National City holding through nominees 7.2 percent. In both cases only four stockholders held as much as 2 percent each of the stock. Control over a small bloc of voting stock—10, 5, or even 2 percent—in a widely held company can convey significant influence over corporate policies.[16]

Exxon and Standard of California volunteered a minimum of information. The former's president explained that although he was sure the inquiry "had a substantial purpose in the public interest," he would not identify them on principle since the relation between company and shareholder is a "private one." He did indicate that the thirty largest shareholders were intermediate holders, mostly nominees of banks. "The real owners are not disclosed to the company."[17]

Three oil corporations—Occidental, Signal, and Getty—failed to respond. And six—Texaco, Gulf, Standard (Indiana), Phillips, Union, and Cities Service—refused on grounds of confidentiality. The general counsel of Texas wrote Senator Metcalf that such information would be divulged "only upon a showing of proper purpose in accordance with applicable provisions of the law. No such purpose is indicated by your letter."[18]

To Metcalf, long the most persistent Senate critic of the private power industry and a careful student of the modern corporation, these information gaps handicap stockholders, government officials, and citizens in their ability to make private and public decisions. He has repeatedly called for an overall investigation of economic and financial concentration: "No one knows who owns America."[19]

While protecting the notion that oil is a private business is a first principle when dealing with the "outside" world, within the empire of oil the cardinal principle in the search for increased profits and security is control over price. Vigilance against competition and abundance can never be slackened. The maintainance of a delicate balance between supply and demand remains crucial. This has meant caution about levels of imports: it helps explain the earlier secret agreements with Canada to keep down imports and the rejection of Venezuelan proposals for preferential treatment for her oil's entry in return for a guaranteed supply. (As the United States began to look beyond her own borders for up to a third of her petroleum needs, Canada and Venezuela were judged politically the reliable foreign sources.)[20]

The underlying principles for private world order in oil which began in 1928, when the international oil corporations initiated complex agreements to share and regulate production and marketing so as to minimize competition and maintain price, have remained basic guidelines.[21] Adjustments have been made for dealing with the newer overseas corporations, and increased attention has been paid to guiding the abundant sources of supply which became so threatening with the opening of the Persian Gulf and, more recently, the North African reserves.

Of central concern was the heightened national consciousness in the regions of greatest productivity and promise. Older ruling groups, avaricious and politically beholden to the West, had surrendered control over land, resources, and even political sovereignty to foreign concession holders. As had been true for state "conservation" laws within the United States, petroleum laws and arrangements had often been drafted by corporate lawyers and diplomats. The recognition of shared grievances, such as modest development of vast tracts, arbitrary pricing, double bookkeeping (as for example when treating royalty payments as part of the income share of producing countries but as costs in computing tax obligations to home countries), and minimum reinvestment gave strength to demands for more equitable relations with the multinational corporations. The latter, in turn, had to devise new strategies for anticipating and accommodating such pressures while preserving their global eminence.[22]

Libya, for example, especially attractive because of the low sulphur content of its crude oil and proximity to Europe, became a major producer in the sixties. Learning from the experience of others, it had diversified its concessions. Many majors had contracts, but preference was often given to smaller companies who were eager to produce, willing to take care of receptive public officials, and uninterested in long-term planning to protect the life of an oil field. Libya recognized that the worldwide reach of the cartel members involved tying up reserves and then accepting new production only most judiciously, rather than maximizing immediate returns. To the giant corporations, Libyan crude could come on stream only if the overall flow from Middle Eastern sources was restrained. Hence their planning involved the political determination as to which host countries would be amenable to keeping production restrained (and reserves understated). Meanwhile, the giants were to maintain strong although carefully monitored output in Saudi Arabia and Iran, the two largest producers, who seemed most securely in the American orbit.

In contrast, newer entries on the world scene such as Occidental and Bunker Hunt had to elbow their way onto the market. Occidental built a 150-mile pipeline and a Mediterranean terminal within a year after its Libyan discoveries. Price cutting, dealing with independent buyers, and other brash stratagems inevitably became sources of conflict with the old order. Occidental was also to discover that its eagerness had not purchased the unshakable gratitude of Libya and the emerging new order. For despite its shrewd sense of history when bargaining, Libya was increasingly troubled over an income tax yield per barrel of crude oil lower than in other producing countries which had been able to tie their revenues to negotiated posted prices rather than to falling market prices. Such disparities were also a threat to the fledgling attempts at price solidarity among Persian Gulf producers.

In its formative years, the Organization of Petroleum Exporting Countries seemed more successful as a forum than as a counterforce. Sparked by Venezuela, Saudi Arabia, Iraq, Iran, and Kuwait as founders in 1960, it ultimately included Qatar, Indonesia, Libya, the United Emirates, Algeria, Nigeria, Ecuador, and Gabon. OPEC was able to place constraints upon the corporate habit of cutting prices without consultation and without appreciation of a producing nation's economic dependence upon a predictable flow of oil revenue which often had become its chief source of income. A unilateral price cut for Venezuela in 1959 and a sharp one for the posted prices in the Middle East triggered by Esso in 1960 and emulated by its brethren, despite their trepidation as to likely repercussions, were to be the immediate catalysts for OPEC's formation. It sought to orchestrate production levels to keep a floor under crude prices so as to protect members who were bearing the brunt of declining or fluctuating crude prices and of impaired purchasing power due to inflation. A greater voice in price determination was seen as essential if they were not to remain colonial victims of the steadily rising prices of the finished goods they imported from the industrial nations. These concerns were to lead to demands for protection against unilateral dollar devaluation and for an indexing system which would link the prices of crude to those of critical manufactures. Despite historic conflicts and often conflicting perspectives among its members, OPEC sought to affirm a one-for-all and all-for-one spirit. It pledged resistance to corporate sanctions against or preferential treatment for any one member, practices which so often in the past enabled the private government of oil to play off one producer against another.[23]

The imagery, the language, and the precedent at times suggested international class conflict against oildom. But the working focus was more on price than on power. It had taken OPEC a decade to gain a raise of a few pennies per barrel. There was a stated commitment to the needs of consumer countries for a regular supply and of the corporations for a fair return. The consequence was often cooperative, if not collaborative. The multinationals, selectively loyal to the free market model and ignoring their own joint holdings and intimacy, initially had piously rejected collective bargaining with the producer countries. Yet their painstakingly constructed mechanisms for global planning at moments seemed antiquated for containing all of the exploding developments of the sixties. The price stabilization sought by OPEC need not be inimical to corporate objectives; given the militancy of several of the producers (such as Iraq, Libya, and Algeria), along with the more volatile possibilities of sabotage (including strikes) and openly political appeals for socialism and regional integration—all of which had been taking place—OPEC could be a moderating force. Agreements, implemented by OPEC, could prevent leapfrogging efforts by "irresponsible" nationalists to escalate demands and repudiate previous commitments.

By 1971 the corporations (and their mother countries) were openly working together to defend their "consumer" interests and were now insisting that OPEC commitments be binding on all members. Producer income was maintained through so-called tax payments (royalties) paid by the corporations and based upon artificially high "posted prices" rather than upon actual market prices. Under this agreement producer countries were pacified—through the United States Treasury—since taxes paid overseas could be written off against taxes due the United States once income returned home. And corporate treasuries were further fattened since royalty increases abroad still meant greater tax credits, just as crude price increases assured profit increases.[24]

Libya remained a leading troublemaker. A revolutionary government which came to power in 1969, under Colonel Muammar el Qaddafi, took advantage of growing European dependence upon its crude, as well as the shutting of the Suez Canal after the Arab-Israeli war of 1967 and the disruption of the Trans-Arabian Pipeline, to breach the more cautious OPEC incremental demands over price, income and corporate investment. The telling tactic was a sharp cutback in production, heretofore more familiar when applied by the multinational corporations. Backing this move was a proclaimed willingness to forego oil revenue rather than let its national directions be determined unilaterally by international corporate forces. Libya also had assurance from its somewhat uneasy producing brethren that they wouldn't betray the unity of their cause by stepping up their own production.

Production cutbacks were also used to force 51 percent government ownership of Libya's largest producer, Occidental. This pattern was soon repeated with other companies operating in Libya. Some, including BP, Shell, Texaco, Standard Oil of California, Atlantic Richfield, and Bunker Hunt, were fully nationalized. The action against the company headed by the son of H. L. Hunt was described by Qaddafi as a "strong slap" in the "cool arrogant face" of the United States.[25]

Occidental discovered how cold it could be outside of the seven sisters or even the more embracing brotherhood of oil. The other giants refused to ally themselves with the maverick, either by reducing their own offtake from Libya or by supplying Oxy, whose Libyan crude was its chief source, with replacement for any Libyan oil now denied to it. This stance was a signal to the producing nations in their probing of corporate responses to future producer actions.

As the increased participation, profit-sharing, and nationalization moves began to sweep the producing areas, many corporate assumptions had to be modified. Price determination was no longer the corporations' exclusive prerogative. In countries such as Iraq and Indonesia they were evolving into contractors for the national corporations. The Western corporations could not assume their concessions were inviolate. Iraq, for example, revoked most of hers; by 1976 its oil industry was completely government-owned. Nor was the West to remain the only source for equipment and experts; Iraq drew technical assistance and loans for development from the Soviet Union. Perhaps most significantly, Western oilmen were on notice that they had to view producing countries somewhat differently. The latter, whether militant socialist or galvanized feudal, were not on earth to be wards or oil reservoirs for the West. There was nothing so crippling in their genetic structure or so esoteric in the economy of oil that automatically excluded their nationals from understanding and involvement. Increased employment and even training of local labor, however, had not necessarily led to sharing in decision-making. The earlier takeover and operation of the Suez Canal by Egypt had been, as oilmen then sensed, a critical turning point.[26]

Empires which survive have to adapt—without losing sight of their underlying purposes. The oil companies' focus was on maintaining their access to crude supplies in these regions (while stepping up access to alternative sources) and ensuring that the producer states and their new national companies respected the business value of orderly marketing. Iran, it will be recalled, had nationalized its oil fields and refinery in 1951. But the foreign consortium which ultimately replaced the deposed British Petroleum Company secretly decided and divided allowable offtakes among each of the corporate participants in harmony with their global requirements. Extreme deference was shown to the sovereignty of the country and the majesty of the shah (so recently restored to his throne through the CIA). But levels of production were technical business matters deemed not worthy of royal attention. And so while the shah focused on plans for national development, the economic limits for these aspirations were quietly set by the Western merchants who were integrating Iran into their world calculus.[27]

Keeping all the dominoes upright and in line was a never-ending occupation. Now Saudi Arabia had to be appeased lest it feel that its cash ambitions would be slighted because of Iranian production. The Aramco partners, who of course were also in the Iranian consortium, had comparable discreet agreements for keeping down production and penalizing corporate transgressors. During the sixties they educated Saudi Arabia (again without providing too many details) on the importance of preventing surpluses of crude oil from appearing on the market. (One of the unprogressive teaching devices of the industry had been the sharp cutting of crude prices paid to the producing countries). Saudi Arabia had taken over 60 percent of Aramco and was moving to absorb the 40 percent still in American corporate hands. Under the newer arrangements, the corporations had to negotiate for the privilege of buying back the crude oil now owned by the producers or gaining access to products which might be refined in Saudi Arabia by new partners, such as the American owners of Aramco and Petromin, the government company. But transportation, refining, and marketing were still largely in old corporate hands, and so most of the oil flow remained under their control. Successfully holding regional output within global production targets, all the while balancing the sometimes conflicting needs of the individual corporations and the desires of the individual producing countries who were developing ambitious growth plans dependent upon soaring national income, and discouraging direct dealings among producers, independent corporations, and consuming nations—activities of this kind summoned all the negotiating talents of the private government of oil.[28]

Exxon's annual report for 1973 offers fascinating data for speculation about this negotiating ability in relation to the "energy crisis" of the same year. During the last quarter of 1973, after the outbreak of the Yom Kippur war and the ensuing embargo launched by the Arab OPEC (founded in 1968 by Kuwait, Libya, and Saudi Arabia and intended to give all its Arab members a more political and activist oil lever to supplement OPEC), Exxon's worldwide production and other offtake dropped to the level of the same period in 1972. But during the first three quarters, production in Saudi Arabia and elsewhere had run considerably higher than during the comparable period in 1972. Thus, "production for 1973 as a whole averaged 6,718,000 barrels a day, still a record, and 9.3 percent over 1972."[29] This rate was intriguingly close to targeted production for the entire year.

Direct negotiation between consumer and producer nations, either individually or collectively, could undermine the system. Before the 1973 embargo the American government was repeatedly admonished that such attempts would "create a hostile atmosphere" and invite reprisals rather than rational compromise. The Japanese were warned by the chairman of Exxon against the temptation to bypass their connection: "There is no evidence that such supplies will be any less costly than oil obtained through the international companies. . . . A consuming country which seeks privileged access to the oil of a producing nation encourages other consuming nations to look for the same sort of preferences. This would create an atmosphere of intense competition for oil by consuming countries."[30]

The new national companies formed by many of the producer nations posed additional hazards for corporate world order. Were they to step up direct sales to independent refiners or to governments, they could undermine supply and price patterns. Were they not to accord the international companies primary right to buy oil, or were they to expect them "to pay the same price as every Tom, Dick or Harry," then the internationals would be in difficulty.[31] Were they to implement the oft expressed ambition to become integrated when they grew up, or at least become marketers as well as producers, then the private government of oil might encounter the competition and price cutting it had always sought to preclude. Why not then an Arab tanker fleet or pipeline? The National Iranian Oil Company (by the end of 1974 ranking third in sales of all non-United States industrial corporations, behind Royal Dutch/ Shell and British Petroleum) explored teaming with Ashland or

Shell in a marketing venture in the United States. Was the lion soon to be roaring attention to its royal wares across the road from the tiger?

But on the optimistic side, from the corporate perspective, was the awareness that, once producing countries become so involved, sheikhs and shahs might not only be held accountable for clean restrooms; they might also find it to their national advantage to behave in harmony with the prevailing rules of the game so as not to upset price—perhaps uniting as one big People's Oil and then joining the seven sisters in a new World Petroleum Institute of state and corporate capitalists. Or each national company, governed by short-run profit considerations and acting within a more primitive entrepreneural framework, might set aside blood vows of loyalty to fellow colonials, to OPEC, and to price floors. It would then take up the more earthly pursuit of wheeling and dealing in markets wherever they could be found. A potential disturbance to orderly marketing but not an unfamiliar one with which the global corporations could not cope. Then too, downstream investment would shift capital away from the domestic development pushed by the producing countries; their new capital intake was liberating, but the needs and aspirations of some quickly devoured this income. Their overseas holdings opened the door to possible retaliation, with such investments becoming hostages, should consumer resentment intensify.

There were also the more inventive prospects of an Arab common market, focusing on regional industrial planning and technical assistance teams which could, among many projects, build refineries for new industries which would absorb some of the petroleum within the producers' own world.[32] The separate Arab OPEC was to create a network of financial and technical institutions for the development of an indigenous industry capable of providing the basic services, from exploration to ship building, essential to an operation free from western control. There was also some help from the newly affluent producers to other developing nations who were savagely set back by the leap in oil prices; aid was channeled through the International Monetary Fund and the International Bank for Reconstruction and Development (World Bank) as well as through direct loans and agencies such as Kuwait's own Fund for Arab Economic Development and Iran's aid programs. Oil credits were extended to India and Bangladesh by Persian Gulf exporters. Libya and Venezuela also launched aid and investment programs for their hard-pressed regions. These efforts were often downplayed in the Western press and viewed with some resentment as discriminatory in non-Arab developing countries. There was also frank fear among industrial powers such as the United States that OPEC members would press for voting power in the International Monetary Fund and the World Bank commensurate with their new wealth and contributions. Such representation would weaken the Western hold over these agencies and the ability to shape modernization in a capitalist mold, including financial discouragement of third world countries from developing petroleum and other resources under national rather than corporate agencies.[33] Yet OPEC was still a producer cartel before it was an agency for international justice. Bitter memories and noble visions notwithstanding, there was inconclusive evidence that any new global redistributive ethic would determine its disposition of petroleum in the immediate future.

OPEC had established the legitimate rights of its members over their oil. And it saw such action as the vanguard for all raw material producers of the third world. It insisted it had no apologies to offer for any disruption within the industrial world. The latter had modernized and built empires on the exploited energy of other peoples. These more "advanced" countries had done so while imposing few constraints upon the administered prices of finished goods and upon the ambitions of their corporations. In 1973, before the great price takeoff, Aramco was making for its American shareholders (Exxon, Socal, Texaco, and Mobil) a profit of about $1.25 on a barrel of oil costing about 12 cents to lift and selling for $3.30.[34] OPEC also had to shoulder the continuing business responsibilities for maintaining effective control over its 85 percent of the world's oil exports in face of a worldwide recession and lowered consumption that followed the "crisis" of 1973–74. There were full storage tanks, idled and slowed-down tankers, closed-down pipelines, and reduced refinery runs. Production was lowered by most of its members. In the best tradition of a cartel, prices were cushioned and price cutting or dumping discouraged, although specific sanctions against straying members were limited.[35]

Fortunately for the Western industry, the business acumen that more money could flow from less oil, if properly managed, found support among producers, including Libya and Venezuela. The latter had doubled its oil revenues in 1974 despite a 15 percent reduction in exports. Yet it had long recognized that oil might not be forever. It was eager to reduce dependence upon a dwindling resource in favor of more diversified and long-run economic development. There was a broadly supported commitment to total nationalization. But with it went compensation, rather than outright seizure, although the billion dollars received was considerably less than the international companies believed was their due for takeover of installations. And there was an awareness that the corporations might still be needed for technical assistance—"Venezuelans can get the technicians, but not even Moscow will share the technology," claimed one foreign oil executive. Gaining access to world markets which had been so intricately bound to corporate operations might make independent entry difficult, especially for the multiplicity of refined products which had constituted half of Venezuelan exports. Corporate-producer cooperation would continue, although under new terms. This sophistication about world order that A. A. Berle had so admired was in contrast to United States governmental policy when it sought to retaliate in its trade policies against all OPEC members, even though Venezuela had not been party to the 1973 boycott.[36]

It also appeared that the international corporations would not be paying the educational bill for their unruly disciples. Higher prices would be passed on to consumers, as would payment of compensation for the loss of tax credits where the giants were now purchasers rather than payers of royalties (disguised as taxes). Also passed along through increased prices was the payment of compensation for the cutting of their classic but no longer sacred "right"—the domestic depletion allowance. As added comfort in the wonderland of energy pricing, the worth of now "inexpensive" domestic production rose to meet the new overseas "competition."

Such managerial foresight and recuperative strength required the sympathy and occasional direct assistance of the United States government. As always, the State and Justice departments were predictably supportive of corporate needs for cooperation. For the primary fear of United States policy makers was not of high oil prices, whether charged by international corporations or by state capitalists, but rather of revolutionary upheavals which might expel American influence and access. Such specters dampened any temptation for active military intervention. Putting upstart producing nations in their place through force, regardless of immediate success, might only emphasize to masses in the Middle East how tenuous were the power and independence of their kings and shahs, despite impressive economic leverage and new-found arms and deference from the West. Overthrowing Mossadegh and then supporting the oil corporations in the conning of the shah (and the American people) may have been "imperatives" to the national security managers. But from a longer perspective they were not victories which could be sought too often if the objective was the orderly flow of petroleum. Given this imperial perspective, the international oil corporations remained the preferred agents.

Back home the federal government gave additional support to the industry's quest for a more lucrative United States market. Federal pricing regulations had as their avowed intent the minimizing of energy shortages and the stability of prices for the consumer, while also promoting competition and preventing unreasonable profit. The administration had frozen all domestic crude oil in 1973 at $4.25 a barrel. This was an increase of about a third and close to what the industry not much earlier had signified would bring forth adequate production. Shortly before the October war the government lifted the controls from all oil production over the level of 1972. It thus allowed a market price of over $10 a barrel as incentive to produce "new oil." The average cost of production was about a dollar a barrel, although in some fields it might go up to $2. All oil from stripper wells, those producing less than 10 barrels a day and accounting for about 13 percent of domestic production, had also been exempt by congressional action. Meanwhile, the industry pressed for a removal of all ceilings on production up to the level of 1972 ("old oil"). Some officials, including William E. Simon, who then headed the Federal Energy Office (later to be the FEA), favored a ceiling between $7 and $8. The compromise figure that emerged from the Cost of Living Council was $5.25. No economic analyses of the cost of production and their relation to original capital investment were offered for the increase. No new expenses were involved, and the actual cost of lifting such oil was under a dollar a barrel. Staff of the Cost of Living Council had argued that the price increase wouldn't produce any significant rise in production immediately. As additional incentive, for each barrel of "new oil" produced one barrel of "old oil" was released from controls.[37]

Thus a new weighted average price of $7.35 for domestic oil ($5.25 for "old" and $10 for "new") meant a direct price increase of approximately $10 billion during 1974. Independent refiners and marketers found themselves further pressed since they generally had to buy new and stripper well oil. The integrated companies had easier access to the price-controlled crude. Nonbranded gasoline was becoming more expensive than that of the majors. Coal and intrastate natural gas prices also quickly responded to this invitation to inflation. An administration economically illiterate, factually empty-handed, and readily cowed by industry's ideological rhetoric and political influence, accepted the argument that such price enticement would stimulate sufficient new production and secondary recovery at home to help free the economy from dependence upon imports and the exploitative talons of the unfeeling, profit-hungry "Arabs." Higher prices would also discourage consumption, thus cutting down imports and weakening OPEC, it was claimed. There was little reliable knowledge as to the actual reserves likely to be developed. Correlations between price and production remained equally murky. And there was no assurance as to where this new consumer-provided capital would actually go.

Crude oil production in the United States continued to decline in 1974 and 1975. "New oil" was being produced very slowly. Consumer prices continued to rise; gasoline was selling for around 60 cents a gallon late in 1975, an increase of some 20 cents in the two years. Consumption of fuel did decline, in part because of the recessionary impact of the oil crisis. OPEC imports increased, and the United States was paying out $24 billion, three times what it had paid in 1973. And to keep up with the rising OPEC prices the administration pressed for an import tax of $3 per barrel which would be passed along to the consumer to discourage his consumption. To stem a world surplus and to maintain its new price levels, OPEC cut back production by almost 25 percent. The American government, in turn, counseled the new men of power to be sensitive to the explosive and possibly tragic global implications of their pricing. (After all, as Walter J. Levy, a leading oil consultant to the corporations and the American government had reminded, they come from "relatively primitive and unsophisticated societies" with unstable governments. Their new accumulation of wealth and power was "obtained so to speak like manna from heaven," and at least for the time being was not accompanied "by any substantial contribution in political, managerial or technical competence.")[38] The government then negotiated with OPEC to guarantee a permanent floor under their prices. All price controls on domestic production of oil and natural gas were to be removed so as to allow a free market to reign. By mid-1975 the price in the United States for noncontrolled oil was $12.50 and for imported it was $14.50 per barrel. The overall strategy was clear and working: "cheap" domestic oil prices were approaching the level of the new and expensive world market prices "politically" set by OPEC and maintained by the corporations and the American government. The industry did not gain the complete decontrol of all domestic prices which it sought, with the backing of the president. After considerable political seesawing, an energy bill was passed in December 1975 which provided for a moderate rollback for the average price of domestic crude and placed ceilings on "new" and stripper well oil. But it opened the door to gradual price increases and the removal of all controls in 1978. Throughout, President Ford scolded the public for "squandering" energy and not realizing that the still higher prices certain to come were "a very small price to pay" for what he saw as long-term solutions to energy and the maintenance of a free economy.[39]

Control over crude oil is never simple, but it continues to require unending vigilance, as John D. Rockefeller had realized. But the other stages must also be dominated if the industry's integrated system is to function effectively. New pipeline and refinery construction is appraised most cautiously to ensure the "orderly flow" of petroleum. There has been very limited refinery construction in the United States, despite the sharp increase in demand. Not one major new refinery was constructed on the East Coast in the fifteen year period prior to 1973. Much of the self-celebrated industry investment went into overseas facilities, where the markets and profits appeared more attractive. Yet refinery capacity was not the immediate cause of the 1973 "energy crisis." Just before the Arab-Israeli war, refinery runs in the United States were under capacity, despite the availability of sufficient crude and the abundant evidence of rising demand. This reflected the majors' resistance to government controls over the price of heating fuel oil, their concern over the vigor of independents, and their "conservative forecasting," an industry euphemism for underestimating demand and then underproducing fuel oil so as to strengthen price. Some companies cut back on their allowed imports, thus helping to bring about reduced inventories and a fuel oil shortage in the winter of 1972–73 which they had previously assured the government would not happen. At the same time the industry resisted increased quotas for finished products, arguing that there was sufficient refinery capacity. Then, with government price encouragement, they built up fuel oil production, with the result that there was a gasoline shortage by mid-1973. All of this happened before the cutoff by the Arab producing nations.[40]

Announcements of new refinery expansion and construction followed the increasingly favorable prices after the "oil crisis" began and the government had lifted the oil import quotas. These were followed by quiet cancelations of what had been labeled "press-release refineries," presumably because of "the difficulty of assurances of crude supply," the leveling off of demand, and the resistance of major suppliers to government programs for fairer allocation of crude oil among refiners. Some of the giants made clear they had no intention of losing money on their expensive imports by supplying, at average weighted prices, competitors who were often independents but also included majors such as Texaco and Arco which had received allocations. Instead they cut off imports, reduced refinery runs, and directed crude to foreign refineries. Gulf, denouncing the mandatory program as confiscatory, filed suit to challenge the validity of the program and in turn was indicted for violating FEA requirements.[41] Meanwhile, supply available to American consumers tightened.

Few of these events reflected the characteristics of a genuinely competitive industry. As an independent marketing executive testified, one reason he could not believe that the energy crisis was real is that "you wouldn't catch these 23 top executives of the largest oil companies in the world asleep at the same time," so that the shortage would "creep up on them to the point that it became critical to their business." His conclusion was that "it's designed, carefully designed."[42]

One may not have to prove "conspiracy" to see historic roots of the crisis and the patterns of collaboration of the presumably competing companies. When there is a miscalculation, such as not taking into full account the switch of northeast utilities from coal to the more environmentally favorable low-sulphur oil, or when there is an unpredicted curtailment, as happened, for example, when the industry's private timetable for getting Alaskan oil flowing was set back by the native claims and environmentalist actions, and possibly some corporate misgivings (the pipes were stacked, the route surveyed), then the tightly wound mechanisms for the control of oil can easily lead to temporary consumer shortages.[43] Had the Saudi Arabian oil minister been prescient in a discussion three years earlier over the industry's spare productive capacity outside of the Persian Gulf? He had told the senior vice president of Exxon: "You know the supply situation better than I. You know you cannot take a shutdown."[44] By the spring of 1974, there were reports of a "surplus" in world crude supplies, idle tankers and shortly afterward, full intrastate gas pipelines in search of out-of-state sales.[45] And although pump prices were up 50 percent and more, gasoline stations were beginning once more to offer gifts and even price cuts as inducements to the wary motorist.

The corporations know that popular usage of the term "reserves" is misleading. "Proven reserves" apply not to any absolute geological limits as to what is in the ground, but rather to petroleum considered recoverable at the going market price, employing current technology. Hence the exodus of many exploratory operations from the American continent during the sixties was clearly related to what was seen as the more lucrative overseas operations. From the perspective of the giants of the industry, the regions of the world are a cluster of natural storage basins. Reserves are to be staked out, not developed, until there is no threat to the long-run control by the corporations from the expanded supply and the price is right. Reserves are money in the bank. The major task is to ensure that their worth increases. And that in the interim they are not expropriated. Meanwhile, the corporations must continue to pursue new sources.

If the oilmen rarely succumb to the periodic hysteria over petroleum's immediate disappearance, they are mindful that fossil fuels have ultimate limits and are essentially nonrenewable. Alert to the interchangeability and potential threat of alternate fuels, the corporations have broadened their activities in coal, shale, tar sands, uranium, natural gas, and even the so-called nonconventional geothermal and solar sources. Gaining water rights for the newer processes of recovery and conversion is also important, since many of the known methods require tremendous reservoirs. They now view and often describe themselves as "total energy" corporations. "Energy" sounds more basic and neutral—like water or air—and, they hope, is less likely than "oil" to arouse public questioning or be placed in a political context. But although the core of the industry remains oil, this change is not simply public relations affectation, the apparent disinterest of the Antitrust Division of the Justice Department in such expansion notwithstanding.

In the 1960s, oil corporations moved into the coal fields. A much lower capitalized industry than oil, coal had declined to about 20 percent of the nation's energy usage. It remained the most abundant of the fossil fuels, perhaps three-fourths of the total fossil fuel reserves in the United States. (The U.S. may have a fourth of the world's coal supply.) And by narrow economic standards it was the cheapest of the fossil fuels. Gulf bought Pittsburgh and Midway Coal; then Continental Oil took over Consolidation Coal (the nation's largest noncaptive coal company); and Occidental acquired Island Creek Coal, the third largest. Standard Oil (Ohio) now controls Old Ben. Exxon has become one of the largest holders of coal reserves as well as a producer. Seven of the fifteen largest coal producers are now oil companies. Oil controls 25 percent of coal production and at least 30 percent of coal reserves. Only two of the top ten coal companies remain independent; the rest are owned by oil, mineral, or industrial corporations. Competition within the industry is minimal. Since the takeover, coal prices have risen markedly and there has been difficulty of access for some users.[46]

The oil companies have coveted the great coal fields of the western plains, where it is believed over half of the nation's recoverable coal—often low in sulphur content—is to be found in thick seams and close to the surface. In the eyes of the oilmen, the American West bore certain attractive similarities to the Middle East: huge tracts in the hands of a few owners, mostly government, as contrasted to the smaller holdings in Appalachia. Some 80 percent of this coal is on Indian and federal lands. Lease prices have accelerated rapidly where once leases could be obtained for a dollar. Sun Oil, for example, won a lease of over 6,000 acres in Wyoming with a bid of $505 per acre. Atlantic Richfield is the second largest leaseholder on the public domain. El Paso Natural Gas, Continental, Shell, Sun, Gulf and Kerr-McGee are also major leaseholders.[47]

The industry envisions a tremendous expansion of electricity generated by coal-fired steam turbines and a network of huge gasification plants for the transmission of gas eastward. Industry and government have often been quite secretive as to where these plants are to be located. "For competitive reasons" is the usual explanation. They obviously fear adverse community reactions and the demand for public hearings. A "highly confidential" study by the American Gas Association located 176 sites for commercially feasible coal gasification plants.[48]

Most of these coal fields have not been developed. The industry justification is that it is waiting for the development of Western power plant markets and also the technology for conversion into oil and gas. A less kind conclusion is that, in familiar fashion, it is waiting until the price is right, that is, until all governmental intervention in natural gas pricing has been eliminated.

Strip mining of the public and private lands in Montana, North and South Dakota, Wyoming, Utah, Colorado, New Mexico, and Arizona is seen as the most profitable method for extraction. This raises a host of unresolved questions about job safety, reclamation,

and the long-run impact on the people of the region. North Dakotans, for example, may have been unsophisticated about the oil
takeover.[49] But they have had more time to ponder the second age
of coal. Reserves in the state, mostly lignite which has a low heat
value, are second to Wyoming in size and are found under roughly
a third of its territory. Was pollution being exported westward?
Would the prairies soon be dotted by mining camps and trailer colonies? Would economic life soon be controlled by absentee eastern
capital?

Reflecting in 1972 about the options to forestall a likely shadow
of desolation, North Dakota's governor argued for strong federal
controls, but confessed; "I am not one who is anxious to turn this
nonreplaceable resource into cash. . . . We have left the efficient
recovery of most of our natural resources pretty much to the economic laws of profit and loss. And in so doing we have skimmed
the cream and profit only to leave the loss and waste to future
generations."[50]

The industry remains wary of shale, the largest untapped source
of hydrocarbon energy. Geological estimates of western reserves
are repeatedly revised upward: conversion of the organic matter
—kerogen—in the rock through tremendous heat into 2 trillion
barrels of low-sulphur petroleum has become a prudent estimate.
Yet the corporate approach has been less than exuberant. Perhaps
too much of a good thing, with 80 percent on the public domain.[51]

There has been accelerated buying up of private shale lands and
securing of water rights. The majors now control the bulk of these
lands. And they are interested in gaining a good foothold on the
public lands. Originally, some were obtained at nominal cost by
prospectors and speculators. Then the integrated companies began
to seek "modest" development acreage. Shell, for example, wanted
50,000 acres—which would yield perhaps 150 billion barrels of oil.
As the Interior Department became sensitive to the obvious giveaway implications, it refused such leasing. Meanwhile, there was a
flurry of somewhat suspicious claims for other minerals on the
shale lands, the granting of which further clouded decision-making
about shale oil.

Research and development have been minimal. One gets no
sense of the members of a great competitive industry racing to be

first. Union Oil, a pioneer, found a crude-oil daddy in Gulf Oil and ceased its shale activities. The government's experimental facilities near Rifle, Colorado, representing $15 million expenditure, remained idle until turned over to Interior in 1962 under pressure from western congressmen. Interior then leased the facilities to the Colorado School of Mines Research Foundation. With a promptness uncharacteristic of shale history, the foundation subleased them to Mobil, Humble, Phillips, Sinclair, Standard (Indiana) and Continental. (The president of the School and the Foundation had been an oil company geologist who served on Interior's Oil Shale Advisory Board and urged release of public shale lands for private commercial development: "Government should now stand aside and let the free enterprise system, which has created this magnificent country, operate.") The research was quite modest and the companies withdrew after a few years.[52]

One small operation, the Oil Shale Corporation (Tosco), stuck at the search for successful shale oil production. It subsequently become partners in the Colony Development Operation with Atlantic Richfield, which made clear its long-run interest in developing secure domestic sources as demand rose and imports became insecure.

The technological obstacles and economic risks have been greatly exaggerated. Initial investments, which sound high, become modest set against the anticipated returns. There are no exploration costs. The essential mining character of the process may have discouraged some oilmen, and there is a search, including through underground nuclear explosions, for a workable way of retorting the shale in the ground. An *in situ* process, such as Occidental has been working on, using simple explosives to create chambers in the mountains, would bypass the expensive and ecologically destructive mining. The problem of subsidence persists, however. But the Occidental approach would considerably lessen the estimated water requirements, which could be further cut were refining to take place near marketing areas where sources of water may be more plentiful.[53] Then, too, there has been some concern as to what the United States government would eventually do with its reserves. Nonintegrated companies have generally been discouraged by the recognized difficulty of gaining entry into markets, especially during a period of crude oil abundance. But there is agreement that the technology exists for production at competitive prices. And the energy crisis brought new oil up into the $10 a barrel range, several times what the most cautious oilman used to say was needed to protect an infant industry.

Interior finally opened a number of 5,120 acre tracts (the Mineral Leasing Act of 1920 restriction) for limited leasing for prototype production programs, and the oil consortia slowly moved in. Gulf and Standard (Indiana) took one tract, with perhaps 4 billion barrels of recoverable oil, for $210 million. (Interior had anticipated as acceptable a bid of under $10 million but subsequently was reluctant to disclose the exact figure.)[54] Phillips and Sun took a tract. Colony Development also acquired a tract and moved toward the construction of the first full-scale commercial shale oil operation.

It remained unclear as to why the major corporations had to await public leasing, since they had adequate private acreage to support shale plants. They obviously were most interested in the most accessible shale, repeating the familiar pattern of leaving more costly operations for another generation.

But they had not been idle on the political front: a pattern was being set for the proper governmental climate. Smaller companies were effectively frozen out by Interior's quest for initial high bids rather than high royalty payments. Rents before production were very low. Royalties would work out considerably below conventional oil leases. And, of course, such payments were business expenses, deductible from income tax. Any "extraordinary" environmental costs encountered were to be credited against royalties, thus giving the taxpayer the bill for repair of his own property. Oil shale was given a 15 percent depletion allowance on the final crude oil rather than the mined shale. And the industry continued to pressure for a full 22 percent—"Why discriminate against this form of oil?" In addition, in Colorado the industry gained a full 27.5 percent depletion allowance, low tax assessments and exemption from any state severance tax.[55]

To environmentalists, the Interior Department's impact studies were inadequate appraisals of the tremendous residue from mining to be dumped into nearby canyons. They were also wary of the diversion and increased salinity of precious water to the possible detriment of agriculture and vegetation. And they lamented the despoliation of another magnificent region.[56]

Thus the energy industry tightened its grip over this great resource, acting to tie up as much of the public domain as possible on its terms before ideas for public development within a public energy planning framework could gain momentum. As far as actual production, it has moved most cautiously, determined that shale oil remain within its private profit timetable, otherwise known as orderly development. In October 1974 another stage of a now familiar scenario emerged: Colony Development announced the suspension of plans for its commercial shale plant. "The Colony venture has proved a technology for extracting oil from shale and is confident that it can satisfactorily resolve the environmental concerns. . . ." But inflation, tight money and the absence of national energy policy which would assure shale a secure place were blamed.[57] "The shale industry, at the moment, is a dead issue," Arco's president declared shortly afterward at an American Petroleum Institute meeting. And a Union Oil vice-president said that if the United States government was interested in developing shale oil it should consider offering price supports for it; the price "would have to be higher than the price for imported oil" if the shale oil was to be competitive with imported crude.[58] At the very same time Standard Oil (Indiana) ran full-page advertisements alerting the public to its expensive purchase of oil shale rights as a new source of billions of barrels of oil—"and no foreign power can turn it off." In 1976 the Interior Department suspended its prototype oil shale development program. This action, avowedly because of "environmental, legal and technical problems," was taken at the request of Standard (Indiana) and the other corporate leaseholders who sought postponement of their payments due the government.[59]

In Canada, comparable decisions were being wrestled with by Synacrude, owned by Gulf, Cities Service, Exxon, and Atlantic Richfield subsidiaries (the latter was to pull out because of the high cash flow and fear it would not be allowed to export; it was replaced by the Canadian government and two provinces which together acquired a 30 percent equity). The consortium was seeking to extract oil from the Athabasca River tar sands, generally conceded to be among the richest known reserves. It also sought the assurance of the Canadian government that it could sell at "internationally oriented prices" rather than the much lower controlled domestic prices.[60] In the wings, skeptics noted neglected ecological warnings. There was also the recognition of a returning "surplus" in world oil supplies and the specter of untrustworthy Arabs reducing prices. To fend off such familiar nightmares the industry obviously would have to await a better security blanket from its own private arrangements and the mother countries.

Looking ahead to the growth of nuclear power for electricity— in optimistic moments when it dismissed the critics who fear health and safety consequences—the Atomic Energy Commission envisioned up to 50 percent of generating capacity by the year 2000— the oil companies have sparked a new uranium boom. The lone prospectors with their Geiger counters are now replaced by the big energy corporations who are drilling deep in the search for the increasingly valuable ore. In 1974, Exxon paid a Navajo tribe $6 million for prospecting rights, with the latter also receiving an option to be a partner in development. Gulf has large ore deposits and is also active in research, exploration, fuel preparation, reprocessing, and building reactors. Gulf and Shell are partners in a domestic and an international corporation, manufacturing nuclear reactors. Atlantic Richfield, Getty, Exxon, Continental, Sun and Standard (Ohio) are among the oil companies involved in one or more stages. Kerr-McGee remains the largest single producer, controlling over 25 percent of the nation's uranium milling capacity. It is one of the two companies which convert uranium oxide into uranium hexafluoride ($UF_6$), a compound employed in the uranium enrichment process. By 1970 the oil industry controlled one-half the uranium ore reserves and accounted for over half the drilling.[61]

For a long time the industry appeared to be avoiding wind, solar, and geothermal energy, perhaps because they theoretically could be found everywhere, could be developed through smaller, decentralized institutions, and hence would not be easy to control. But the companies have been bidding on government lands where there are promising possibilities for geothermal exploration which might enable them to tap the heat in the molten rock of the earth's interior and convert it into electric power. At the first offering of federal lands, Shell bid $4.5 million for two tracts. Signal, Union, Standard of California and Occidental also submitted bids. Other companies actively exploring in the west include Getty, Gulf, Phillips and Sun. Federal limits on acreage and inadequate tax incentives for drilling have been cited by the industry as factors in the slow development.[62] Union Oil has been a partner with Pacific Gas and Electric in the one operating commercial geothermal field in the United States. Exxon, Shell, and Gulf are among the companies active in solar research.

Natural gas, the second largest source for domestic fuel consumption (32 percent), has long been part of the oil industry. Integrated companies control over 70 percent of the reserves and production. Exxon, Shell, Amoco, Gulf, Phillips, Mobil, Texaco, Union, Atlantic Richfield, and Continental are the first ten producers of natural gas. They can be found among the top positions in each of the six major areas where natural gas is produced. In southern Louisiana, where one-third of the nation's gas is produced, four of these companies control 97 percent of uncommitted reserves.[63]

The industry's unswerving objective remains complete freedom from federal regulation at the wellhead of the price of gas sold in interstate commerce. Gas prices in new fields have escalated under special regional and cost rulings of the Federal Power Commission. But the industry felt frustrated in 1968, when the Supreme Court and the FPC rejected its arguments that rates were not producing new reserves and failed to grant the higher pricing sought.[64]

Industry talk of gas shortages then accelerated. Pipeline buyers and consumers have been told more gas may not be forthcoming, that reserves have not kept up with the demand for this low polluting fuel. Meanwhile, there has been increasing use at much higher prices in producer states, for intrastate sales—a third of the total —are not under federal control. Half of the supply goes to industrial plants and electric utilities as boiler fuel. The oil industry itself makes the largest single use in its refineries.

From the industry's perspective the comparative cheapness of natural gas has made it too attractive to consumers and the rate restrictions too unattractive to producers to encourage adequate exploration. The familiar solution is to end rate uncertainty by letting gas be subject to what one sympathetic commissioner has called "the discipline of the free market."

But the free market in energy remains a myth. Much of the activity of the majors is pooled. There is no effective competition among producers. Pipelines, which pass along to consumers all costs, are ineffectual bargainers; at times they are buying gas from themselves. The energy industry has access to adequate capital, should it choose to expand production.

Much of the talk about shortages is misleading and some of it is plain dishonest. Natural gas is certainly not unlimited, and there is every reason to begin to use it wisely. Demand remains high, reserves are largely uncharted and some geologists are concerned that the nation may be nearing peak production levels. The industry, which has spent millions to persuade consumers to switch to gas, has continued to drill to locate probable reserves, while reluctant to list these as proved or to develop what it finds.

The energy industry wants rates which will provide "incentive" rather than meet costs and a fair return. The issue is not present unprofitability but the expectation of what it might get in the future for reserves now in the ground. Companies had been asking for a 75 to 80 cents per thousand cubic feet minimum. Deregulation could easily reach that target, tripling the price at the wellhead which averaged 25 cents per thousand cubic feet in 1973. (During the sixties, costs of production were averaging under 20 cents, and in 1971 the FPC proposed fixing the nationwide wellhead price through 1977 at 26 cents per thousand cubic feet.) To the American Petroleum Institute the increase to the householder would be "minor," perhaps 16 to 32 percent—an understated projection which ignores all the industrial costs which would be passed along. Yet the producers would gain over $10 billion a year, in addition to an overnight leap in the worth of their proven reserves of at least $150 billion.[65]

The cry to get natural gas "competitive" with other fuels, including oil and imported liquified natural gas, means to bring it up to such prices. No mention is made of the artificial pegging of oil prices by the industry, by the United States government, and now, by the overseas producing nations.

Meanwhile, the "energy emergency" provided the justification for review of rates on gas already committed to consumers and for rounds of new rate increases. In June 1974 the FPC established a national wellhead floor for "new" gas of 42 cents a thousand cubic feet, with provision for subsequent upward adjustment. And in December 1974 it fixed the uniform price of natural gas at 50 cents, explaining that "it is in the best interest of the consumer to pay the higher price for gas which is necessary to induce expanded exploration in production efforts than it is for that same consumer to pay even higher prices for other fuels, if substitutable." It thus continued to frustrate by administrative ruling what the Supreme Court has interpreted as legislative intent and FPC responsibility under the Natural Gas Act of 1938, namely "to protect consumers against exploitation at the hand of natural gas companies." The energy corporations have said that the 15 percent rate of return on capital now allowed is inadequate. President Nixon and then President Ford still favored deregulation. William E. Simon, secretary of the treasury and former federal energy administrator, supported a ceiling of 75 cents to a dollar—the price of unregulated intrastate natural gas![66] By mid-1976, rates of $1.42 for "new" gas had won FPC approval.

Such rulings and declarations do little to ensure additional interstate supply. If they provide incentive, it is for producers to keep reserves in the ground. The General Accounting Office estimated that two-thirds of the price increases between 1970 and 1973 went to the interstate pipelines rather than gas producers.[67] An American Gas Association official concluded that conservation, as the immediate hope for control over supply, was working. But, alas, the "curse" was that "profits have dropped alarmingly because of it." The consumer was getting his reward through assured supply. Now, as if to ensure that consumers would not get off the administered inflationary hook by conserving, "the utility company must be rewarded for its prudent energy management by assurance that rate relief will be granted to cover the lowered consumption."[68] Reviewing the overall situation, the attorney general of Connecticut concluded that the major oil companies "have simply held a gun to our heads and said, 'We won't supply natural gas until you let us set whatever price we feel like charging.'"[69]

Monopoly control over technically alternative fuels—oil, coal, gas, and uranium—reduces the freedom of electric power companies, manufacturing industries, metallurgical processors, and residential space heat users to choose from competing sources. The giant utilities find their options increasingly shaped by the private government of oil. But adjustment clauses in many states have allowed them automatically to pass along fuel increases without regulatory review. Such escalation, totalling an estimated $6.5 billion in 1974, helped diminish zeal for searching for alternative fuels. And the clause provided a bonus for companies which passed along "market prices" for coal (the source of over 45 percent of the nation's electricity) but had their own mines.[70] Once more the American consumer is asked to foot the bill for increases which, as the advertisements and monthly bill enclosures coyly explain, are "beyond our control."

Even the TVA falls under the influence of big oil. Built for the people of the United States as a yardstick for low-cost power, as its river sources have become fully utilized it has turned to coal for 80 percent of the electricity it generates. As a major coal consumer it finds itself unable to obtain coal competitively and is forced to negotiate with oil-owned coal companies. From 1970 to 1975 the prices it paid for power plant coal increased between 300 and 400 percent; where $5 per ton was an average price in 1970 and $15 in 1975, it anticipated for the immediate future prices stabilized at around $25 per ton. In process it has raised its rates sharply since 1968. Further complicating this pattern has been TVA's willingness to use strip-mined coal.[71]

The oil and gas industry has continued to diversify beyond energy boundaries. Fertilizer plants, pesticides, chemicals, synthetics, large-scale farming, cattle feeding, real estate developments (for example, Gulf's new town of Reston, Virginia), and motel networks are a few such areas of its broadening domain.

In 1973 Mobil sought to acquire CNA Financial Corporation, a large holding company with interests in insurance, financial services, and real estate. This plan was dropped, but in the following

year it declared its interest in the money-making talents of the
Marcor Corporation. Marcor owns Montgomery Ward, the fourth
largest retail merchandiser in the country, and the Container Corporation, the largest producer of paperboard packaging. Atlantic
Richfield had been eyeing the copper and aluminum business for
some years as part of its strategy to diversify its natural resource
holdings. Anticipating major revenues from its Alaskan oil, which
would be available for profitable reinvestment, it began to buy
into the Anaconda Company. Gulf Oil explored taking over Ringling Brothers–Barnum and Bailey Combined Shows, suggesting an
unconscious identification with rulers of an earlier empire.

Both defenders and critics of the industry wondered how to
reconcile such ambitions with corporate claims that mammoth
profits are essential if there is to be sufficient capital reinvestment
for meeting the nation's energy needs. Mobil's chairman assured
shareholders that gaining control of Marcor could add to the corporation's overall strength. The more than $800 million it would cost
reflected no loss of faith in the oil business or intention to withdraw from it. "We cannot, however, ignore the many charges that
have been directed at the oil industry by politicians and some segments of the communications media, nor the fact that more than
3,000 bills have been placed before the Congress with the intention
of inhibiting the oil industry in one way or another." Meanwhile,
there were congressional calls for explanation and for antitrust
action against Mobil.[72] Gulf's board decided to abandon its circus
fantasies, presumably because of the poor timing and image.

The handwringing advertisements of the American industry—
some now suggesting they spend more than they earn—might lead
one to suspect that the oil business operates as a public service or
what the chairman of British Petroleum has described as a "tax
collecting agency" for public governments. But a survey of its international activities quickly dispels such notions. One finds oil
corporations engaged in joint ventures exploring and staking out
reserves on every continent and beneath every sea, searching with
a giant improvised ice cutter for a northwest passage for a possible
tanker route, encouraging National Science Foundation research
on the Antarctic, making geological surveys for intercontinental
pipelines, expanding the size of supertankers to bypass Suez and

circle the globe, looking for harbors deep enough to berth them, probing the unclaimed ocean beds that comprise 70 percent of the earth's surface, and then fighting legally and politically to extend the accepted definition of the continental shelf to include its seaward edge (the junction of the submerged continent with the bottom waters of the ocean floor). Scottish nationalism, French-Canadian separatism, Latin American development, Puerto Rican independence, Cuban isolation, Samoan sovereignty, Nigerian and Indonesian civil strife, Israeli boundaries, Indian balance of payments, Soviet-American detente, Japanese-Soviet economic pacts, Chinese-American rapprochement—each is an important oil component placing it high on the agenda of corporate deliberations. Each suggests the global dimensions of the political economy of oil.

The dream of "another Persian Gulf" is always present in the industry's overseas involvements. Southeast Asia provides a useful illustration. Amidst the genocidal battles of the Vietnam war, American oil companies and the United Nations Economic Commission for Asia and the Far East, with some American government participation, were separately engaged in geophysical reconnaissance on the continental shelf off the coast of Vietnam in the late 1960s.[73] The region had long been an object of oil affections, as had all of Asia, as reservoir and market. Royal Dutch/Shell had its start in the Netherlands East Indies. Caltex and Stanvac also became producers there. Once the Indonesian republic shed its colonial rule after World War II, such corporate entanglements were discouraged as imperialist. By 1967 the Sukarno regime had been overthrown, with the help of the American CIA, and there was a more hospitable climate for foreign investments. The companies were now interested chiefly in offshore drilling. The technology for such operations had improved. And there was a ready Japanese market for the low-sulphur fuel. Union, Cities Service, Gulf, and Atlantic Richfield were among the companies to join in the search. Production-sharing contracts (rather than concessions) were made with Pertamina, the government corporation. Oil became the leading earner of foreign exchange.[74]

Industry sights extended along the coast of Korea, Japan, and China as well as the Philippines, where the American corporations dominate drilling and marketing. The continental shelf under the

Yellow, East China, and South China seas are viewed most hopefully. Bountiful findings are anticipated here or in the broad sweep from the Bay of Bengal southeastward across the Malay peninsula to the Gulf of Siam and across the South China Sea through the Java Sea and Indonesian and New Guinea waters to northern Australia. Gulf Oil is the largest foreign investor in South Korea. Shell, Texaco, and Standard of California also have concessions and there is increasing activity in the waters between South Korea and Japan. Gulf, Caltex and Standard (Indiana) are among the majors holding concessions on Taiwan, in partnership with the Nationalist government.

Singapore's proliferating refineries and international oilmen have given it the familiar tempo of an oil town. David Rockefeller has predicted the industry might be sending $35 billion into the region in the coming decade, and the blossoming of Chase Manhattan branches in Southeast Asia lends credence to this prophecy. Major oil companies, including Gulf, BP, Continental, Union, Amoco, Tenneco, and Phillips have been drilling in the Gulf of Siam off Thailand. Exxon and Shell are among the companies active off Malaysia.

To the South Vietnamese, their fossil fuel future is "spectacular." President Nguyen van Thieu's government, aided by American oil consultant Walter J. Levy, framed petroleum investment laws which included assurances against nationalization. Tracts were opened on the continental shelf and bids actively solicited. In July 1973, leases were awarded to Shell, Mobil, Exxon, and Canadian and Australian interests.[75]

These new technological and regional frontiers for oil exploration sometimes obscure what may be a more significant thrust of modern capitalism—the penetration into the developed industrialized nations. Here is where one now sees the heaviest American overseas investment and expectation. The European Economic Community, for example, enabled American capital to leap over trade barriers, furthering the transnational corporate expansion which the Marshall Plan had done so much to promote. By 1970, direct investments exceeded $70 billion, with Europe, Japan and Canada being the major centers. Building refineries, pipelines, marketing networks, and resort areas have been highly lucrative ventures for the oil companies, for the consumer market is larger and growing at a faster rate than in the United States. When oil leaders speak of their use of profits for investment, they rarely mention that the great percentage is going in such directions— where the greatest profit awaits them.[76]

The oil corporation thus is the prototype of the much-discussed "multinational" corporations—most of which are American-controlled and based. Highly accomplished profit gatherers, they relentlessly roam the earth in search of reserves, markets, profits, and sympathy. As they see it, they are bringing to the United States the energy base for wealth, progress and comfort; upon the rest of the world they bestow the magic of modern technology and its management.

During the period 1968–72, seven United States companies (Exxon, Texaco, Mobil, Standard of California, Gulf, Standard (Indiana), and Shell (American) accumulated net profits of over $44 billion. These companies managed to pay less than $2 billion in United States federal income taxes during the same period. Paying at an effective rate of 5 percent or less was made possible through the skillful use of a range of tax advantages, including the depletion allowance, tangible and intangible drilling and development costs, and the foreign tax credit system.

In 1973 the worldwide earnings of the first thirty companies increased 71 percent over the previous year, although sales volume increased about 10 percent. The six leading American international oil corporations had gross revenues of $50 billion and net profits of $6.7 billion. Their combined federal income tax bill came to $642 million. Gulf reported $800 million, Mobil $843 million, Standard of California $844, Texaco $1.3 billion and Exxon $2.4 billion income after taxes. British Petroleum's profits climbed 332 percent to $760 million, although its sales volume declined from 1972. Royal Dutch/Shell approached $1.8 billion. Amerada Hess had a tenfold increase in net earnings, and Occidental had an almost sevenfold increase.[77]

Aramco almost doubled its profits for its four American parents (Exxon, Mobil, Standard of California, and Texaco), who still held 75 percent control in 1973—their concessionary oil worth perhaps a trillion dollars. In figures made public for the first time,

Aramco's auditors estimated the gross income at $8.7 billion. Of this, $1.1 billion went as royalties and $3.9 billion as taxes to Saudi Arabia, leaving the world's largest producing company with profits of $3.2 billion. Dividends to the American companies totalled $2.5 billion. (In 1972 the comparable figures were $4.6 billion gross income, $0.6 billion royalties and $2 billion taxes to Saudi Arabia, and $1.7 billion profits. In 1971, the figures were $3 billion gross income, $0.4 billion royalties and $1.3 billion taxes to Saudi Arabia, and $1.1 billion profits). The increase of dividends over a five-year period was 350 percent, a percentage comparable to Saudi Arabia's increase in royalties and taxes from the same operations. Aramco felt these figures exaggerated its earnings since they were based on "posted" prices rather than the actual market prices. But the higher posted prices meant higher taxes for Saudi Arabia and hence greater tax credits for the Americans and lower tax payments to the United States. What appeared unshaken was the profit of $4.50 in 1974 ($1.25 in 1973 before the embargo, then $2.00) on a barrel of crude oil costing less than 15 cents to lift.[78]

A United States Treasury Department study indicated that the major oil companies averaged higher earnings in 1973 than in any of the preceding ten years. The average rate of return on stockholders' equity was better than 15 percent.[79] Oil profits have been about a fifth of the total of all major corporations in the United States.

The companies were quite busy explaining why they were not embarrassed; the profit figures were "bloated by inflation" resulting from "the selling of inventory at the new prices," were "currency translation gains," were the "long overdue" results of "an extraordinary year," were "needed for expansion" and for purchasing "oil which will cost us more next year," and reflected "a general realization that oil as a commodity is no longer readily available to meet world demand."[80] Meanwhile, first-quarter profits for 1974 were averaging 80 percent over the first quarter of 1973. By the end of 1974 they had turned downward and the net income for the full year for the top twenty-nine oil corporations of the west came to $16.4 billion, an increase of 40 percent. Total revenues, mostly from oil, were $244.5 billion, an increase of 90 percent over 1973.

The worldwide rate of return on average invested capital was over 19 percent, an amount which even Chase Manhattan conceded was "within the range considered necessary to generate and attract the funds for high-risk capital intensive industry such as petroleum." But it expressed disappointment over the American rate which was lower (14.6 percent) than that which prevailed outside (23.9 percent).[81]

All these earning figures depend largely upon industry presentations, and without a full breakdown of separate operations and accounting practices it is difficult to know exactly what they reveal beyond enormous profitability. Several of the 1973 reports were unduly modest, according to some financial analysts. Exxon, for example, confirmed that it was holding back substantial funds, which normally would be included in profits, for what it explained as anticipated Middle Eastern fuel price increases and possible taxes should the government remove a foreign tax credit.[82] And none of the reports gave a true indication of the economic power of the corporations from their total cash flow, which includes depreciation and depletion in addition to net income. These corporations continue to command physical and financial resources greater than those of most industries and many nation states.

Nevertheless, the drive to mass new capital and expand operations "without interference" intensifies. The corporate message to the American people becomes more urgent every day: without such freedom to grow, the industry which pumps the nation's lifeblood will decline, and with it Americans will enter a new historic era, no longer first citizens of the world.

# 3

# Political Explorations

The years since 1959 obviously had not been unkind to the private government of oil in America. Its vistas were increasingly global. But it continued to make political investments to ensure the support of public government and opinion at home.

Dwight Eisenhower's administration in 1953 had shown complete deference to private enterprise and profit. What oil wanted it generally received. The president himself had been an admirer of wealth and its possessors. It is now known that his much beloved farm at Gettysburg was paid for by several oilmen, one of whom was W. Alton Jones, the chief executive of Cities Service.

The energy industry's close-knit relations with government remained basically secure under his successors. Crude industrialists may have been patronized or snubbed in the social whirl of Camelot. But their legal and banking spokesmen encountered few problems of access. The policies of John F. Kennedy's administration posed no threat to oil's interests in such areas as taxes, regulation, and foreign policy, however much at variance were the lifestyles and rhetoric of the new frontiersmen and the oil entrepreneurs. The depletion allowance remained untouched. "We have studied that matter at some length. We probably have not studied it enough. I do not know how to study it enough," Secretary of the Treasury C. Douglas Dillon, was to confide.[1] (Dillon was a director of Chase Manhattan and heir to the investment banking holdings of Clarence Dillon, of Dillon, Read, and Company.) Lyndon Johnson of Texas, the most effective congressional spokesman for the domestic oil industry, was chosen vice-president. The secretary of the navy was oil lawyer John B. Connally, who reinforced the ties to

southwestern oil and gas interests while broadening his own international oil connections. The partnership of business and government was accepted and the Kennedy claim that the nation's problems were essentially administrative ensured ideological harmony.
The much celebrated Keynesian conversion of the economically
conservative president was readily shared by corporate sophisticates
as helpful for keeping the system going. Oil, of course, remained a
prime beneficiary of the welfare state. Secretary of State Dean
Rusk told the nation's leading businessmen that they had two fundamental roles in carrying out American foreign policy: "First,
business is the key factor in maintaining a dynamic domestic economy. Secondly, business must expand its present important role
in the world economy. The dynamism that has been central in the
development of the United States must now be employed on a
global scale."[2]

Lyndon Johnson made it to the White House, his openly expressed fears about the likely cost to his career of his oil loyalties
notwithstanding.[3] To allay suspicion, there was a much publicized
shifting of formal policy responsibility for petroleum from the
White House, where it had been, back to the Interior Department.
There was little likelihood, however, that control over so sensitive
an area would be abandoned to "apolitical" bureaucrats. His populist sentiments kept him attuned to the "little" oilmen from back
home. But the new pipelines from the Southwest that carried natural gas east also brought new oil and gas conglomerate influences
to Washington. Johnson's political alliances in Congress and his
ambitions as a national leader combined to keep him receptive to
the voices of the entire industry and to the continuation of existing
programs and vacuums.[4]

Nor was the taint of oil an impediment for Richard Nixon. The
disclosures of private oil financing for his senatorial office had
failed to derail his vice- presidential and presidential career. Ironically, President Eisenhower, who had explored dumping his running mate in the 1952 campaign, had speculated about replacing
him as a second-term vice-president with oilman Robert B. Anderson, who was also close to Lyndon Johnson. Anderson, secretary
of the navy and then of the treasury, was central to byzantine oil
intrigues and reportedly had sought a million-dollar income through

special oil privileges as compensation for the sacrifice of holding further public office. Fees for his services, in part linked to the price of oil while he was in office, were imaginatively arranged through a financial pipeline involving oilman Sid W. Richardson and a Standard (Indiana) subsidiary.[5] Anderson was now free to apply his expertise to matters of national interest such as oil imports, Alaskan naval reserves, the Iranian consortium, and the Cuban blockade, while awaiting the higher call that never came.

In retrospect, Nixon's slush fund, his "Checkers" speech defense, and his part as vice-president in blocking a full-scale investigation of oil money in congressional politics triggered by Senator Francis Case's disclosures during the 1956 natural gas fight provided a modest but accurate preview of ethical standards to prevail during his tenure in the White House from 1969 to 1974.[6]

Throughout his campaign, in speeches and private meetings, Nixon made one thing perfectly clear to the oil industry—his complete reliability on specific issues of concern (including antitrust, regulation, foreign expropriation, and, of course, the depletion allowance) and his general deference to wealth and power. In return he received heavy campaign backing from corporate leaders, the independents and newer entrepreneurs. As always, Rockefeller, Mellon, and Pew family contributions provided the solid foundation.

Once elected, he insisted that basic energy decisions, including those dealing with the mandatory oil import program, belonged in the White House. For a while, Peter M. Flanigan, an investment banker from Dillon, Read and Company with tanker investments, imported liquified natural gas interests, and oil ties and sympathies, was considered the "man to see" in the executive office on oil matters, including the keeping down of oil import quotas despite rising demand. Governor Walter J. Hickel of Alaska was nominated as secretary of the interior. This was at the urging of oilmen, including Robert O. Anderson, chairman of the board of Atlantic Richfield who was also Republican national committeeman from New Mexico and a substantial contributor. Arco was eager to have Alaskan oil flowing. Hickel was an ambitious developer who had been a natural gas utility executive and held oil leases. John B. Connally, increasingly active as a business consultant to oil corporations since his service in the Kennedy cabinet and as governor of Texas, and also a counsel for International Telephone and Telegraph, was later to join Nixon's administration as secretary of the treasury.

Nor was it to be overlooked that the incoming president and his attorney general, John N. Mitchell, came from a New York law firm (Nixon, Mudge, Rose, Guthrie, Alexander, and Mitchell) that had been representing El Paso Natural Gas, a giant pipeline system dominating the West Coast and closely linked to major oil, coal, and gas interests. El Paso had been negotiating with a host of federal agencies for clearance to import liquid natural gas from Algeria to the East Coast. This quest raised tangled questions concerning relations with a "third world" nation which had nationalized American oil interests, the impact on the Federal Power Commission's ability to maintain the lower prices of domestic natural gas, and the safety of the new tankers required. El Paso had also long been involved in complex antitrust litigation, resisting court attempts to lessen its monopoly control by divestiture of some of its acquisitions. Once in office both Nixon and Mitchell made clear their disdain for such actions. The Justice Department immediately dropped an El Paso merger suit. The law firm had also been retained by Atlantic Richfield in connection with its complex takeover of Sinclair Oil, which coincided with the accession to office of the new administration.

In the spring of 1971 the president reported to his attorney general that "we have a situation . . . Connally has spoken to me about it . . . where the business community . . . believes that we're a hell of a lot rougher on them in the antitrust than our predecessors were." The two agreed they didn't "give a damn about the merits" of the immediate situation (the pursuit of the case against International Telephone and Telegraph), but the issue was, in Mitchell's words, "political dynamite."[7] The attorney general previously had assured Harold S. Geneen, chairman of ITT, who had been bringing pressure against the antitrust division through the White House staff and Vice-President Spiro T. Agnew, that Nixon did not believe in a bigness is badness policy or that mergers were necessarily against the public interest.[8] The president, mindful of

his loyalties to oil, could not forget that antitrust lawyers had testified before the cabinet task force that the imports control program
helped eliminate competition and served to fix prices. He warned
his associates against "letting all those bright little bastards" in the
antitrust division "who hate business with a passion" run around as
"God damn trust busters," prosecuting people, "stirring things up
at this time. They have raised holy hell with the people that we,
uh, uh—well, Geneen he's no contributor. He's nothing to us. I
don't care about him . . . Fifty years ago maybe it was a good
thing for the country. It's not a good thing for the country today."[9]

In this spirit, Nixon and Mitchell were also to squelch a probe
into the antitrust implications of the projected Alaskan pipeline
which was to be controlled chiefly by the three giants dominating
the North Slope reserves. They were also readily persuaded by
corporate arguments against an alternative Canadian route which
would have brought the oil to the energy hungry Midwest. At the
end of 1972 a publisher of energy journals could report to members of the petroleum industry that never in his twenty-one years in
Washington had he seen a more favorable climate in the executive
branch: "Having the Nixon Administration act as your spokesman
canot help but spread the energy message across the land. . . .
Government officials . . . have been the best press agents the industry has had in a long time. Many newspapermen who wouldn't
take your word about the time of day, much less about industry
affairs, are willing to quote government officials who are saying
the same thing you have been saying for years."[10]

By the time of the Watergate investigations of 1973 there was
also disquieting evidence suggesting several political "firsts": a
president in the White House setting up a parallel personal governmental system, not only on the make, but also on the take.

Early in 1969, within a month after entering office and after a
victory without campaign debts, the president's men were looking
for cash. Such unencumbered sources as industrialist Howard E.
Hughes and oilman J. Paul Getty were prime targets. A confidential
memorandum from the president's administrative chief of staff,
H. R. Haldeman, to the president's chief domestic adviser, John
D. Ehrlichman, suggested the tone that was to prevail:

> Bebe Rebozo has been asked by the President to contact J. Paul Getty in London regarding major contributions. Bebe would like advice from you or someone as to how this can legally and technically be handled. The funds should go to some operating entity other than the National Committee so that we can retain full control of their use. . . . The President has asked him to move quickly.[11]

Fifty thousand dollars in cash was sought as a first installment, supposedly as a budget for social functions at the White House during the next six months. Some of the staff were to advise that this particular use was inappropriate. Herbert W. Kalmbach, the president's personal lawyer, testified that in addition to the 1960 contacts, Rebozo arranged for him to see Mr. Getty in Europe about funds for the 1970 congressional campaigns. Charles G. (Bebe) Rebozo, a Florida business promoter and a personal friend of Nixon, collected and disbursed money for "administration-connected projects," the president's reelection campaign, and for the purchase, maintenance, and improvement of Nixon's private homes. Rebozo recalled he had been asked to make an appointment for Kalmbach with Getty for the 1972 election. Given the intrigue, the cash specifications and the "laundering" that was to take place to confuse original sources, it became difficult to sort out when funds were intended for the party, when for presidential politics, and when for personal use. Nixon himself had confided to a defender that "I have never cared much about money."[12]

In the 1972 campaign Mr. Nixon renewed his pledges to maintain a favorable climate for oil. Under the leadership of former attorney general Mitchell, who had directed his 1968 campaign, and former secretary of commerce Maurice H. Stans, the Committee to Re-elect the President (CRP) and a related Finance Committee operated independently of the normal Republican National Committee channels and vigorously solicited funds. They received at least $5 million from oil sources, including illegal cash contributions of $100,000 each from Gulf, Phillips, and Ashland. Other funds came through Amerada Hess, Pennzoil, Marathon, Texas Eastern Transmission and the related Brown and Root, Getty, Edwin Pauley, John and Clint W. Murchison, Jr., and a host of less well-known independent producers. Jake L. Hamon, the first independent producer to have headed the American Petroleum Institute, gave $25,000. Armand Hammer of Occidental contributed $100,000, part of which was funneled through a former governor of Montana who was an Occidental vice-president and who served as Nixon's campaign manager in the West. The owner of an oil company in Greece gave $25,000. Representative Les Aspin (Democrat, Wisconsin) compiled a list of 413 persons in the oil business who gave $5.7 million to the president's war chest. Much of the money was rushed to Washington in April 1972, two days before a new federal disclosure law ending confidentiality of contributors was to go into effect. Some of the financing of the Watergate plumbers' activities behind the break-in into Democratic party headquarters came from southwest oil interests. Money was routed through a Mexican bank to William Liedtke, president of the Pennzoil Corporation and a presidential fundraiser. Some $700,000 was then delivered to CRP via a Pennzoil plane.[13]

Investments in politics are unique neither to oil nor to the Republican party. In the case of oil, this acumen has a long bipartisan history at all levels of the political process. The opportunities for political brokers seem limitless in this environment, and every administration has its Bobby Bakers, although few end up in the penitentiary. Secretary to the Senate majority and close to Lyndon Johnson and Robert S. Kerr, Robert G. Baker handled campaign needs, oil money, and committee assignments for the faithful without losing sight of the main chance.[14]

If Johnson, Kerr, Sam Rayburn, and Tom Connally were no longer in Congress to champion oil and gas regions, the industry still did not lack for advocates. For example, from his vantage point as chairman of the Senate Finance Committee, Russell B. Long is able to fend off unfriendly taxes while protecting profits and imports quotas (even warning about the possibilities of war with Canada). Long thus protects the interests of Louisiana's producers and also his own family holdings in oil and gas. His income has come chiefly from oil. In 1968, thanks to the depletion allowance, the tax-free portion of his royalties was alone greater than his Senate salary. During the energy crisis Long argued that "we must allow domestic producers to receive at least as much for new discoveries of crude oil produced here as is being paid to foreigners who ship oil to us."[15] Three members of the Senate Finance Committee—Long, Robert Dole (Republican, Kansas, and formerly National Republican Chairman) and Mike Gravel (Democrat, Alaska) received a reported minimum of $210,000 from oil sources for their 1974 campaigns. A fourth member, Lloyd Bentsen (Democrat, Texas), who had defeated liberal Democratic Senator Ralph Yarborough in the 1970 primary and then Republican Representative George Bush, founder of a multimillion-dollar oil drilling firm, in the election, received a reported $135,000 from oilmen in 1974 for his presidential campaign.[16]

The two senators from Alaska, the newest big oil state, play the traditional role of equating industry and state goals. Mike Gravel sees the segregation of Alaska's tremendous reserves (estimates range from 10 to over 30 billion barrels) for the military establishment as subverting the civilian economy: "The soundest policy would be to turn these reserves over to the Secretary of the Interior who would then permit their exploitation by the private sector as is being done on other public lands. . . . Let the oil industry produce oil and let the Navy sail the sea." Gravel and his colleague had no trouble in equating the pipeline sought by the corporate giants with their state's development. If private enterprise promises a road free, "you should get down on your knees" in gratitude, Republican senator Ted Stevens advised constituents and environmentalists worried about the possible adverse impact of such construction.[17] Stevens, who had represented large oil companies and had been on the legal staff of the secretary of the interior during the Eisenhower regime, was quickly placed on the Committee on Interior and Insular Affairs when he reached the Senate in 1968 —as was Gravel. The latter was responsible for an amendment pushed through the Senate (Vice-President Agnew was recruited for the deciding vote) which exempted an inadequate environmental impact statement, paid for by the oil industry and issued by the secretary of the interior in defense of the proposed Alaskan pipeline, from subsequent judicial review. This action subverted the intent of the National Environmental Policy Act. It shut the door against critics who feared the ecological impact of the pipeline and doubted the integrity of the administration in its negative appraisal of an alternate Canadian route.[18] Gravel's ardent support of industry positions led some of his fellow senators to suggest privately that the pipeline seemed to end in his office.

Expectations of specific returns for campaign contributions vary. Only infrequently can one prove venal intent in settings where the line between "corruption" and normal business and politics is so murky. One can still encounter the crudest understandings and tradeoffs, supposedly more appropriate to the less sophisticated stages of capitalism. For example, in 1963 and 1964, the Colonial Pipeline Company, owned by major oil companies and operated by veteran oil executives from their ranks, paid $110,000 in cash through the Bechtel Corporation to municipal officials in New Jersey. What were sought and received were rights-of-way and building permits for storage tanks, without the public hearings required by law, so that Colonial might complete the $400 million pipeline. The oilmen, through their counsel in court, saw themselves as part of a young corporation which had "lost its way." Innocent victims of a shakedown, they acceded because of their determination to prevent the "national disaster" that might have followed in the wake of the Cuban missile crisis if the pipeline was delayed further and the country exposed to the menace of Soviet submarines. To the involved municipal officials of Woodbridge, acclaimed as an "All-American City" by the National Municipal League and *Look* Magazine, it was an ordinary political contribution to the local organization: it certainly was not to be misconstrued as payment for services rendered in circumventing public opposition to an oil tank farm. To the prosecution, whose indictment was upheld in the court, it was a case of "corrupt public officials met and joined . . . by big businessmen . . . equally corrupt for their own reasons."[19]

At the national level, Amerada Hess executives, including lifelong Democrat Leon Hess (the principal stockholder in Hess who had been treated well by the Interior Department under Secretary Udall and President Johnson when he was seeking preferred treatment in the Virgin Islands) and corporate associates gave $250,000 in the 1972 campaign, according to a contributors' list kept by Rose Mary Woods, Mr. Nixon's longtime personal secretary.[20] Shortly after the election, the company received increased import allocations which it had been seeking for its refinery in the

Virgin Islands. An earlier move by the Interior Department to revoke a special import license was ended.[21] Occidental, whose chairman contributed $100,000, and Texas Eastern Transmission, whose executives gave $30,000, were interested in White House support for negotiations to import liquid natural gas from the Soviet Union.[22] Occidental was also in difficulty with the Securities and Exchange Commission in connection with its sale of securities to the public. Standard Oil of California, whose chairman contributed $50,000 in cash, was involved in litigation with the navy over drilling on and around the Elk Hills reserves; another member of its board, a former deputy secretary of defense, gave $89,000. The Greek oil company garnered a $4.7 million contract to refuel the United States Sixth Fleet.

Ashland Oil (Kentucky), the nation's largest independent refiner and marketer of petroleum products, with reported assets of $1.5 billion and profits of $113 million in 1973, siphoned at least $800,000 to political campaigns between 1967 and 1972. Orin E. Atkins, the chairman, explained to a stockholder that "there was a good business reason" for giving $100,000 in cash to CRP, and, "although illegal in nature, I am confident it distinctly benefitted the corporation." Mr. Atkins insisted before Senator Sam J. Ervin Jr.'s committee investigating these campaign activities that his company was not seeking any particular privilege.

> I think all we were attempting to do was to assure ourselves of a forum to be heard. Were we a larger factor in our respective industries (refining, marketing, chemicals, coal), we could expect to have access to administrative officials in the executive branch of Government with ease, but being a relatively unknown corporation, despite our size, we felt we needed something that would be sort of a calling card, something that would get us in the door and make our point of view heard. . . . Sort of like water wearing away a rock; you present your view and hope a little bit of it will rub off.

He admitted his associates at the time "were more concerned about the income tax aspects of the situation than we were about the contribution aspects. I guess we had our priorities in the wrong sequence."[23]

The oilmen had rejected funneling so large a sum of cash through the familiar device of padded expense accounts. Instead, they decided to contribute through one of Ashland's African subsidiaries in Gabon. The money was withdrawn in cash from a Geneva branch of the First National City Bank ("The Swiss, being a more sophisticated financial society than ours, I believe are used to dealing in such numbers and it does not excite anybody's curiosity if you walk in and ask for $100,000"). It was then flown to Mr. Stans, who deposited the cash in his desk drawer. The payment was carried on Ashland's books as an investment—in land.[24]

According to the final report of the Ervin committee, three days after the contribution Ashland officials met with officials of the Office of Emergency Preparedness on the subject of obtaining greater supplies of crude oil. "There is no evidence that the meeting and the contribution were connected."[25] As subsequently unfolded, Ashland's involvement offered what one SEC official described as a "textbook on how to make payoffs." There were complex borrowings from foreign banks "for exploration," which ended up as unlawful political payments, including some $500,000 in cash to officials and "consultants" in Libya, Gabon, Nigeria, and the Dominican Republic. A sum of $125,000 from a Canadian subsidiary went into Canadian elections. These were presumably to support its aggressive search for overseas crude and for possible refinery projects. There was also at least $100,000 from the Central Intelligence Agency, much of which was kept in cash in the company safe together with its "political" funds, suggesting that Ashland was also providing a cover for an agent abroad carried on the books as an oil executive.[26]

Claude C. Wild, Jr., formerly an attorney with the Mid-Continent Oil and Gas Association and Gulf's vice-president for government relations, delivered $100,000 in two payments after conferring with Attorney General Mitchell and Secretary of Commerce Stans while they were still holding office. The money came through Bahamas Exploration Ltd., a Gulf subsidiary. He explained that, since other corporations were also giving, he wanted his company to be treated in an equal way, and wished that someone would "answer my telephone calls once in a while." Wild also made modest contributions for Gulf to Democratic presidential hopefuls. ("Republicans always cost you twice as much as the Democrats. They ask for twice as much.") Cash in the amount of $15,000 went to Representative Wilbur Mills, then chairman of the powerful House Ways and Means Committee which guards all tax measures and which had been unusually zealous in easing corporate pain after the depletion allowance lost its once inviolate political support. The solicitation was handled by a mutual friend, formerly with the American Petroleum Institute, who later explained that "he never suspected it was corporate money." According to Stans, Mills had also received a $25,000 loan from Gulf the previous year. The Ashland investigation unearthed a $50,000 contribution to Mills. Wild also said Senator Henry Jackson, chairman of the Interior and Insular Affairs Committee, which oversees the Interior Department, arranged a meeting to discuss his financial difficulties and received $10,000. Jackson also received a secret $225,000 contribution from Leon Hess. Wild reported to his company's senior vice-president at the July 1972 board meeting that there was no need to respond to further solicitation since Gulf had already given at the office in Washington. The government relations office operated with an annual budget estimated at $2 million (not including the campaign offerings) and with a national staff of some forty persons. Wild said that his colleague must have assumed that the money came from Gulf's Good Government Fund, which had been established by the company's legal counsel to receive contributions from employees.[27]

Once these dealings were exposed, B. R. Dorsey, Gulf's chairman, announced that they were undertaken without the knowledge or approval of the board of directors: his company was not seeking favors, nor did it have any activities under federal scrutiny. "There was enormous pressure in the political system and the fact that others apparently also yielded is evidence of this. The pressure was intense and at times it was thought to be irresistible by our Washington representatives. Nevertheless, the pressure should have been resisted, whatever the consequences." Dorsey pledged a tightening of the corporation's accounting system.[28]

The Securities and Exchange Commission later charged Gulf with falsifying reports to conceal a $10 million fund for political payments between 1960 and 1974 which was channeled through the Bahamas company. In a consent decree Gulf agreed to refrain in the future from such alleged violations.[29] It also appointed two Gulf directors and Wall Street lawyer John J. McCloy to review the charges. McCloy had been chairman of the board of Chase Manhattan, president of the World Bank, and board chairman of the Ford Foundation. He had also represented each of the seven international oil companies, among others, and his ties to the White House helped him guide his clients through the troubled antitrust waters during the confrontations with OPEC.[30] The review committee found that the total of Gulf's political giving, legal and illegal, domestic and international, exceeded $12 million. It described the Bahamas company, originally organized for exploration purposes, as "a vehicle for accumulating cash with which domestic political payments were made and for recording changes resulting from transfers of funds abroad for political purposes."[31] Further revelations by a former "legislative coordinator" who had served Gulf in Washington for many years indicated that cash contributions were delivered regularly, "maybe four or five or six times a year," and discreetly, in sealed envelopes to the offices of some fifteen senators and congressmen of both parties, as well as to candidates. Among the recipients between 1960 and 1972 were Senate Republican leader Hugh Scott (Pennsylvania), who was on an annual retainer and who continued to ask for funds after the preliminary Watergate exposé of Nixon campaign funds made Gulf want to pull back; Senator Howard H. Baker, Jr. (Republican, Tennessee), who was vice-chairman of the Senate Watergate investigation; Senator Daniel K. Inouye (Democrat, Hawaii), also on the Watergate committee; Senator Russell B. Long (Democrat, Louisiana); Senator Mark O. Hatfield (Republican, Oregon), a member of the Senate Interior and Insular Affairs Committee, who received $10,000 at the request of the ambassador from Kuwait, where Gulf had its largest overseas holding; five 1976 presidential hopefuls—Senator Lloyd Bentsen, Senator Henry Jackson, Senator Hubert H. Humphrey (Democrat, Minnesota), Governor Milton Shapp, (Democrat, Pennsylvania), and Senator Fred R. Harris (Democrat, Oklahoma)—and Representative Gerald R. Ford (Republican, Michigan). Senator and then Vice-President Lyndon B.

Johnson (Democrat, Texas) was one of the earlier recipients, having been given $50,000 in cash. No mention was made of the modest corporate benefactor; recipients were told that the offerings came from Mr. Wild.[32]

Nor were local political matters slighted. Gulf gave a $10,000 "thank you present" to an official of the New Jersey Turnpike Authority who had been helpful in the negotiations for the route of the Colonial Pipeline, of which Gulf was an important owner.[33] The majority leader of the Pennsylvania House of Representatives, K. Leroy Irvis, was on annual retainer, although the review committee expressed some confusion as to whether it was for his legal advice or his public relations talents. He helped Gulf gain a reduction in its real estate tax assessment in Pittsburgh. And his standing with the black community made him especially valuable.[34] (In 1971 Gulf submitted the lowest bid to supply oil to the city of Dayton, but its bid was rejected by the city council because it had not reported the number of blacks it employed in the area, as required by municipal law.)[35] According to Representative Irvis, as reported by the committee, he tried to make Gulf understand the relationship between domestic racial tensions and events in Africa, where Gulf had substantial holdings. In Texas, a lawyer who represented Gulf in antitrust matters and before the elected Texas Railroad Commission (the regulatory body which has been critical in determining the price and supply patterns of domestic oil and gas) "made payments to any Commissioner who faced opposition in an election. He recalled having made payments to all Commissioners save one since the early 1960's." The attorney general of Texas subsequently filed suits against Gulf and Phillips, charging the former with operating "a systematic program of surreptitiously making campaign contributions to candidates for public office in the state . . . all of which was patently illegal."[36]

According to W. W. Keeler, retiring board chairman of Phillips, the chief executive officer was "in charge of the ethical standards of a corporation."[37] Keeler, who had also been active in the American Petroleum Institute, the National Petroleum Council, and the Military Petroleum Advisory Board and had served as chairman of the National Association of Manufacturers, sustained Dorsey's interpretation of events. When asked by the Senate Watergate committee about his frequent contacts with Stans while the latter was in the cabinet and about his presumed role in contributing Phillips funds and coordinating oil contributions from other companies, he first invoked the Fifth Amendment against possible self-incrimination. After the case had been disposed of, Keeler told the committee that he was courted assiduously by Stans and that he did consent to talk to a number of executives. Keeler "had no alternative" but to give substantially. He turned over $100,000 in cash which "had apparently been obtained (from foreign transactions) for the specific purpose of use for political contributions" and which were kept by a senior company officer. According to Keeler, Stans expressed dissatisfaction with oil's performance in the 1968 election, feeling it had been much more magnanimous in other campaigns (Keeler and Phillips admitted to contributing $50,000 to $60,000 for congressional candidates in 1970 and 1972).[38] The SEC subsequently charged that the officers of Phillips had made false entries on the company's books to divert nearly $3 million through two Swiss corporations into a secret political fund and had paid out $585,000 in cash to candidates for federal offices during the previous decade.[39] The Special Report made to the company, much less revealing than the one filed by Gulf, indicated that Phillips had spread its contributions rather widely. Payments were in cash, records were casual, and corporate sources presumably were not disclosed. But individual amounts were generally quite modest, as if not to encourage any of the politicians too much. (Senatorial candidates were often given $1,000 or even less, although candidates from Oklahoma, where Phillips is based, generally received more. Some representatives, including Gerald R. Ford, received more than $1,000, but most received less. Candidates for the state legislatures in Oklahoma, Texas and Alaska were watched carefully, with the payments reported "typically ranging from $100 to $200.") One interesting item was a $50,000 cash contribution, delivered personally by W. W. Keeler to Richard Nixon in the latter's apartment in 1968. Mr. Keeler had not mentioned this in his earlier statements and Mr. Nixon had repeatedly denied he had ever personally received such contributions. "I have had a rule. . . . I have refused always to accept contributions myself. I have refused to have any discussion of contributions. Before the election, I did not want any information from anybody with regard to campaign contributions." Another oilman, Clint W. Murchison, Jr., also recalled giving $5,000 in cash in 1968 to Mr. Nixon's secretary, after being told by Nixon that the money could be given either to him personally or to Miss Woods.[40]

Ashland, Gulf, and Phillips were each fined $5,000 and the three principals $1,000 each for violating federal campaign laws in the 1972 capers. There were no prison sentences since the charges were brought in as nonwillful misdemeanors. Had they been "willful," they would have been felonies and the perpetrators liable to up to two years imprisonment. Tim M. Babcock, former governor of Montana, pleaded guilty to a misdemeanor and received a four-month prison sentence for his part in arranging the illegal Occidental cash payment to the 1972 Nixon campaign. Armand Hammer was fined $3,000 and placed on probation for one year because of his age (77) and health. (He could have been sentenced to a three-year term.) Babcock subsequently was spared from serving his sentence since, as the court explained, he was only the legman in a case where the principal remained free.

Wild, with Gulf since 1958, was dropped only to reappear on the payroll as a consultant "on an emergency basis" concerning pending proposals to end the depletion allowance as well as government actions relating to petroleum allocations and contracts with foreign producing companies. His successor had been most eager to have his services. "Wild's 1972 and 1973 diaries . . . confirm Wild's frequent dealings with important government officials as well as with the senior management group."[41] Questions from within Gulf and also from outside made Wild's new stay tenuous. A suit by the Project on Corporate Responsibility, the Council for Christian Social Action of the United Church of Christ, and several individuals, representing thirty-seven shares (Gulf had 372,000 shareholders), charged Wild and the Gulf officers with losing good will for the business and wasting corporate funds for the purpose of corrupting public morals. But from August 19, 1974, through April 10, 1975, Wild received $93,000 in compensation, in addition to his early retirement benefits of $2,300 per month. The former vice-president subsequently was charged with using money from Gulf's Committee for Good Government (he had been administrator of its fund) to pay back to Gulf $25,000 in settlement of his liability to the company, as stipulated by the first suit. He pled the Fifth Amendment rather than elaborate about political activities before the SEC. Further investigation by the special Watergate prosecutor's office led to Wild's indictment by a federal grand jury on two felony counts of making illegal campaign contributions.

The McCloy committee debated the responsibility of B. R. Dorsey, chairman of the board and chief executive officer. The latter, along with the executive vice-president, repeatedly insisted that they had no knowledge of the clandestine contributions prior to being informed by Wild during the Watergate investigation in July 1973.

SENATOR SYMINGTON (Democrat, Missouri, at the Senate hearings on multinationals): How would he be able to have these millions of upon millions of dollars without your knowledge as president of the corporation?

MR. DORSEY: . . . In 1960, or maybe the year before . . . an arrangement was made by the people that were running the company at that time, to where these funds could be made available for those political purposes, and the authorities were established and the mechanism was established, and it simply was like any other authority that gets established in a company. And there are thousands of authorities, if not hundreds of thousands. And this one kept right on going and everyone that was involved in it, quite apparently from the investigation that has been made since, was acting within his authority and within the authorities that had been given to him, and it simply went on until it was revealed in 1973.

SENATOR SYMINGTON: How was it expressed on the balance sheet you would sign when you put out your earnings statement to your stockholders? . . . Did you put it under the heading of miscellaneous?

MR. DORSEY: Miscellaneous expense.

SENATOR SYMINGTON: And there were no questions about what this miscellaneous expense was for?

MR. DORSEY: Senator, this was a relatively small amount of money. During this period of time I think the company did some $60 or $70 billion worth of business in that 15-year period, and $10 million is not really a very large amount of money, it does not stand out.[42]

The McCloy committee concluded that Dorsey was

not sufficiently alert and should have known that Wild was involved in making political contributions from an unknown source. Although it is too much to ask the chief executive of an enterprise of Gulf's magnitude to police questionable activities of all corporate officers, particularly where the source of information may be no more than rumor and conjecture, the activities of the company's Washington lobbyist, widely regarded for his influence there and in close touch with top management, should not have been so lightly supervised. If Dorsey did not know of the nature and extent of Wild's unlawful activities, he perhaps chose to close his eyes to what was going on. Had he been more alert to the problem, he was in a ready position to inquire about and put an end to it.[43]

Strong pressures from the directors representing the Mellon family interests, believed to control 20 percent of Gulf stock, forced Dorsey and three other top executives to resign. Sources inside the board described the tense, prolonged sessions, where each director had lawyers standing by, as "an experience none of us has ever gone through before, and we hope never to again." Any "Ford-type pardon settlement" (a reference to President Ford's generous terms for the departure of Richard M. Nixon) which would have released Dorsey from further liability in litigation concerning the illegal giving was ruled out as part of a determination to "calm shareholders' nerves." Sister Jane Scully, president of Carlow College (which had received Gulf contributions) and the first woman director on the board, voted with the five Mellon representatives. "I felt enormously sympathetic to Bob Dorsey. He is a good and decent man, a fine person. But it was imperative the corporation restore its own sense of rectitude."[44] His replacement, another chemical engineer with a reputation for running a tight organization, was brought in from the presidency of Gulf's Canadian affiliate. From 1960 to 1974 Gulf Oil Canada had given $1.3 million to national and political groups in Canada. Such payments were not considered illegal there, according to the affiliate's general counsel, and they were made under the control of the Canadian company's board of directors.[45]

The corporate delinquencies had minimal effect on the careers of the Phillips board members, who were overwhelmingly reelected despite the SEC investigation, the consent decree and some pointed stockholder questioning. Keeler, who at sixty-five had stepped down from office early in 1973 and from the board the following year, after forty-one years with Phillips, was required to return to the company $82,000 for the fine, legal expenses, and loss of interest incurred in the illegal expenses, in addition to a $1,000 he had received as cash reimbursement for tickets purchased for a political fundraising dinner. His salary had been $300,000, his stock holdings in Phillips were estimated at $3.4 million, and his annual retirement benefits were slightly over $200,000.[46] W. F. Martin, the new chief executive, had known of the political activities, was a defendant in the SEC suit, and with Keeler and several other officers had made a $150,000 settlement with the company which released them from further claims that might be made because of their part in the illegal disbursements. The special committee appointed by the board and reporting to the shareholders and to the SEC recommended that Mr. Martin be retained.

His involvement commenced several years after the fund had been created and amounted for the most part to acquiescence in a program which had been earlier instituted by his superiors. Beginning in about 1967 or 1968, Mr. Martin was given the responsibility of monitoring payments made to the Swiss corporations . . . and was involved, at the direction of his superiors, in the transfer of cash from Switzerland to the Company headquarters. Although Mr. Martin was aware of the use of the cash fund, he did not take part in the making of contributions therefrom.

In its recommendation to the board, the special committee further said:

While they are not to be condoned, Mr. Martin's activities with respect to the fund were in keeping with a standard of conduct which unfortunately pervaded many aspects of our national life during the years in question. During those years evasions of the election laws by one device or another were quite widespread. Mr. Martin was aware of that pervasive practice. There is no doubt that he believed, albeit mistakenly, that the making of political contributions was in the best interests of the Company, and that it could turn out to be detrimental to the Company not to do what various other corporations evidently were doing.

The Special Committee met with Mr. Martin and was impressed by the sincerity with which he expressed his intention to avoid future violations of the election laws and to implement firmly the policies which have been established to avoid such violations by the Company. The standards of business conduct represented by those past violations of law are totally unacceptable as the basis for conducting any aspect of the business of Phillips Petroleum Company, and Mr. Martin clearly recognizes this proposition and agrees with it without reservation. The Special Committee believes that Mr. Martin is a most effective chief executive officer of the Company and finds no impediment to his continued effectiveness in that office by reason of his past participation in the program of unlawful political contributions. To the contrary, the Special Committee recommends as a matter of business judgment that it would be contrary to the best interests of the Company and its stockholders to interrupt Mr. Martin's employment or to take any action with respect to it which would distract him from or handicap his continuing performance.[47]

The board concurred. A subsequent class action stockholders' suit led to an expansion of the board, from eleven (with eight of them insiders) to include up to 60 percent independent outsiders. There were also the requirements that in the future Phillips's nominating committee for candidates for board membership be composed of independent outside directors and that outside directors should select the firm to review the company books. In 1976 a federal grand jury indicted the Phillips company, Martin, Keeler, and another former president on charges of conspiring globally to conceal the political slush funds and thus defraud the Internal Revenue Service. The three men pleaded not guilty. And once more, by unanimous decision, the Phillips board affirmed its support of its chief.[48]

Further disclosures about Ashland's illegal activities led to another corporate plea of guilt and a new fine. The SEC consent decree and the report of the company's special committee amplified the original disclosures, confirming that no records were maintained (funds were often kept in a company safe) and that most contributions were made on the authority of chairman Atkins.

Ashland's top officers were required by their company to reimburse it for some of the illegal payments. (Atkins, who earned $314,000 a year, was asked to return $175,000 over a six-year period.) But its board concurred with its special investigating committee that to terminate their positions would be punishment out of proportion to the acts chargeable and not in the best interests of Ashland; these men had acted toward what they had believed were the legitimate concerns of the company, candor was shown during the investigation, the payments involved were "relatively modest," the officers were "still young, vigorous, and effective . . . likely to be of continuing benefit to Ashland if . . . retained," and their leadership during the period under question had brought Ashland a growth in its net income averaging 18 percent per year.[49]

Each of the companies was refunded its $100,000 by CRP. As a spokesman explained, "we don't accept illegal contributions."[50] During the 1972 campaign Maurice H. Stans had indicated that he wanted $400,000 (at another meeting he said "at least $200,000") from each company he solicited. His style in searching for contributions, according to a former campaign associate, included emphasizing to the executive of a polluting company the troubles he had as secretary of commerce in making the Environmental Protection Agency, whose head "didn't understand the system that we businessmen are here to preserve," loosen up on regulation so as not to take the country "right over the cliff." He would then tell the potential giver that the substantial assessment being suggested was insurance against Democratic Senator Edmund S. Muskie or George McGovern presiding over the White House. A letter from Stans to over 150,000 corporate officials, including the "*Fortune* 500" list, stated not too subtly that "our committee's records of the combined contributions from you and your associates will maximize recognition of your group's support of the President." To Stans, the only wrongdoing of the Finance Committee may have been some "unintended technical violations." As for the concealment of sources, "privacy was a right of the contributor which the committee could not properly waive. The right to live without undue intrusion is a long-respected benefit of the

American system." Stans, who saw himself as an "innocent victim" of Watergate, later pleaded guilty to accepting and inaccurately reporting illegal contributions, and received a $5,000 fine.[51]

The Gulf lobbyist's expressed terror at the prospect of his company relegated to the "bottom of a list" or "blacklisted" seems as ingenuous as the assertion of his board chairman that Gulf wanted nothing from the government. While bigness is generally most respectful of bigness, and the function of government in support of the interests of oil is generally clear, corporations do wish to ensure smooth entree whenever the need may arise. The McCloy report dated Gulf's contemporary political militancy, which it labeled as shot through with illegality, to 1958. The company had seen itself "kicked around, knocked around by government," increasingly subject to attack by public agencies, unlikely to get effective support from the State Department in connection with its overseas expansion program, and denied a fair public hearing. It then announced its intention of becoming increasingly active to gain "muscle" in practical politics. Joseph E. Bounds, a retired executive vice-president, told the review committee that the original idea for an "off-the-books" political fund had been developed by the then chairman of the board, William K. Whiteford. Whiteford had informed Bounds and Archie D. Gray, then senior vice-president, that he had checked with top management in other major oil companies and had learned that all of them had set up similar arrangements. Described by the committee report as "dynamic and colorful," Whiteford had been emphatic, according to Bounds, that "knowledge of this arrangement should be kept from 'the Mellons' and the 'Boy Scouts' in Gulf." Dorsey, a chemical engineer whose lifetime career was with Gulf, was considered one of the Boy Scouts. While there was some internal scuttlebut about little black bags being transported regularly to and from the Bahamas, the practice continued unchallenged, despite changes in directors and comptrollers. Bounds had become increasingly uncomfortable with the vulnerability of the Bahamas arrangement, but was told "that was what he was getting paid for and he had better do it or be fired." He eventually received a transfer to the West Coast and early retirement. The Bahamas front was terminated at the end of 1972, and a new corporate vehicle, Midcaribbean Investments

Limited, was created. It arranged with Gulf Marine and Services Company, Ltd., another subsidiary, for the handling of the former business of Bahamas Exploration. The new connections were assumed to be more effective in keeping the cash transfers unrecorded and unobserved. These transactions continued until the disclosure in August 1973 of Gulf's illegal contributions to the Finance Committee to Reelect the President.[52]

Meanwhile, a flurry of written codes of ethical standards have been emanating from board rooms, joining the declarations on social responsibility and corporate citizenship. Oil companies obviously are not abandoning the political arena. Sun, Atlantic Richfield, Texaco, Standard of California, and others have become leaders in a corporate movement to build networks of political action committees, legally sanctioned by the new Federal Election Commission, for soliciting and distributing funds from employees, executives, and shareholders for political causes and "citizenship" programs. Sun Oil sought voluntary, unearmarked contributions which would go into a fund whose managers would be picked by the corporation. First priority would be for friends of the industry. Employees could also contribute to candidates through automatic payroll deductions. But the company assured that "we lean over backwards" to avoid any feeling of compulsion among workers. "We're just trying to encourage them to participate." As a Phillips spokesman explained when discussing company-sponsored "social" activities: "We don't tell employees how to vote but we do give them both sides of issues. In issues concerning Phillips, we help the employees to understand that what's best for our company is best for them."[53]

At the same time they have resisted dissident stockholder pressures for ending all corporate contributions—or at least for open information about them. For example, a stockholder proposal before the annual meeting of Socal recommended that:

Within five days after approval by the shareholders of this proposal, the management shall publish in newspapers of general circulation in the cities of San Francisco, Los Angeles, Chicago and New York, and in the *Wall Street Journal*, a detailed statement of each contribution made by the Company, either directly or indirectly, within the immediately preceding fiscal year, in respect of a political campaign, political party, referendum or citizens' initiative, or attempts to influence legislation, specifying the date and amount of each such contribution, and the person or organization to whom the contribution was made. Subsequent to this initial disclosure, the management shall cause like data to be included in each succeeding report to shareholders.

The supporting statement explained that

this proposal, if adopted, would require the management to advise the shareholders how many corporate dollars are being spent for political purposes and to specify what political causes the management seeks to promote with those funds. It is therefore no more than a requirement that the shareholders be given a more detailed accounting of these special purpose expenditures than they now receive. These political contributions are made with dollars that belong to the shareholders as a group and they are entitled to know how they are being spent.

The board urged stockholders to vote against the proposal, pointing out that in the previous year owners of almost 63 million shares (out of 85 million) had rejected an identical proposal:

It is the policy of the Company to support worthwhile political causes when it believes that such support is in the best interests of the Company and its stockholders. All political contributions are carefully reviewed by management and are made only if determined to be legal and proper business expenditures.

In management's opinion, these political contributions do not warrant the special treatment called for by the stockholder proposal, which would be time consuming, expensive and serve no constructive purpose. In management's opinion, this proposal is not in the best interests of the Company.[54]

Speculating about the possible relationship between Nixon's subsequent reluctance to leave the protective confines of the White House and an estimated $60 million campaign kitty raised from American industry, I. F. Stone observed that "it would shake investor faith in American capitalism if it turned out that so many of our biggest corporations indulgently gave away all that quid without some quo."[55]

As stockholder suits demanded further accountability from the corporate stewards, Gulf subsequently asked each of the political recipients to return the tainted funds, a request which could be quite embarrassing to politicians who prefer not to notice such campaign details and often make explicit to their staffs that they do not want to know the sources of funds.[56] Even during the televised Watergate hearings, when public curiosity and outrage, if not surprise, were high, the Ervin committee had been cautious in going beyond its immediate mandate concerning Nixon's presidential campaign and pursuing the matter of contributions to congressional colleagues. The reticence was understandable, considering that every member of the panel save Senator Ervin had been mentioned as a recipient. According to Ervin, Minority Leader Gerald Ford had "moved heaven and earth" to block a Watergate investigation in the House before the 1972 election, as sought by Representative Wright Patman (Democrat, Texas), by "persuading every Republican on the House Banking and Currency Committee to vote against subpoenaing Mitchell and Stans." One awaits a congressional response to John J. McCloy, who found it "just as improper" for politicians to accept illegal corporate money as it was for the companies to give it.

> Why is it that the people who are offenders in terms of corporate money received can hold themselves out as able to become the President of the United States. . . . The statement "I didn't know these were corporate funds" doesn't wash when you're talking about cash in sealed envelopes [sometimes in motels, in men's rooms, and behind barns]. . . . We've heard nothing from the Senate about purifying itself. There's a double standard here. It's the hypocrisy that bothers me.[57]

When the Senate Ethics Committee moved to look into such charges against members, its chairman was Howard Cannon (Democrat, Nevada)—another Gulf beneficiary. In 1976 the committee, in closed session, voted to drop its investigation of Republican leader Hugh Scott and the other senators alleged to have received funds from Gulf. Cannon explained that there was insufficient corroborative evidence. Senator Edward W. Brooke (Republican,

Massachusetts), the lone dissenter from this decision, insisted that his colleagues had not conducted a thorough investigation, never calling Wild or opening the sealed financial statements submitted annually by each senator.[58]

The "post-Watergate morality" difficulties of so many of the Nixon team were encountered by John B. Connally. Connally had been viewed by Nixon as ideal presidential timber and a possible successor after his conversion to the Republican party. After leaving his post as secretary of the treasury, he continued to advise the president on energy matters. Well-versed in manipulating the levers of power, he traveled the world in multiple capacities; he was on retainer from Armand Hammer (Occidental) and Bunker Hunt (son of H. L. Hunt), who held concessions in Libya jointly with British Petroleum, and was on the board of Brown and Root, helping these clients in their dealings with Libya, Saudi Arabia, and the Soviet Union while carrying out global missions for Mr. Nixon. Connally was subsequently indicted on charges of conspiring to commit perjury and obstruct justice and of accepting a bribe in the form of campaign contributions while secretary of the treasury, in exchange for recommending to the president that price supports be raised. Ironically, the ensnaring commodity was milk, and the source the dairy industry.[59] Connally was acquitted, partly because the government's major witness was a dairy lawyer who was an admitted perjurer and who had arranged to plead guilty in return for the dropping of other charges. Connally reaffirmed his desire to participate in public affairs: "I've seen the system work . . . and it has made me more deeply committed to preserving the system."[60]

One of the character witnesses for Mr. Connally was Robert Strauss, chairman of the Democratic National Committee. In 1970, Mr. Strauss had received $55,000 in cash from Ashland Oil. But he escaped prosecution for receiving what he insisted he thought was a personal contribution from Ashland's president, thanks to legislation pushed through in 1974 by Democratic leaders which reduced the statute of limitations on violations of the Campaign Spending Act from five years to three. Representative Wilbur Mills was another beneficiary of such timely reform.

A confidential message from presidential counsel John W. Dean III to the White House staff in 1971 introduced further insight about the rules of the game as applied under Nixon:

> This memorandum addresses the matter of how we can maximize the fact of our incumbency in dealing with persons known to be active in their opposition to the Administration. Stated a bit more bluntly— how can we use the available federal machinery to screw our political enemies.

Grant availability, federal contracts, litigation and prosecution were suggested as legitimate instruments.[61]

The vindictiveness of the executive office had been channeled into domestic surveillance of the antiwar movement, black militants, political dissent, and critical journalists. The restoration of what the Nixon ardministration solemnly referred to as "law and order" clearly applied to the streets, not to any crime wave from corporate suites. But was there an extortion racket being run out of 1600 Pennsylvania Avenue? To suggest that the business system might be a target and oil singled out was ludicrous. Yet given the range of billion-dollar involvements where government help or hindrance was vital, there was always reason for caution on all fronts, especially when, from corporate perspective, the amounts involved in such protection were petty cash.

# 4

# The Rites of Government

Public government's role has remained consistent over the years: to support the oil industry's management of production, that is, to help keep prices up and profits secure. When the key sources for petroleum were domestic, public policies for prorationing and "conservation" provided the legal price-fixing. Once the vast supplies from overseas entered world trade, their potential for sweeping away these domestic props was readily appreciated. The persuasive talents of segments of domestic oil (and coal), employing pressure from the outside and advocacy on the inside by such industry figures as oilman secretary of the treasury Robert B. Anderson, were brought to bear upon the White House. "National security" was the selling point. First voluntary and then mandatory federal import controls were put into effect, without direct legislative approval.[1]

This government intervention in what was still described as the free market continued from the time of Eisenhower through the presidencies of Kennedy, Johnson, and Nixon. It gained the support of most of the industry since it served to stabilize prices and crude oil allocation patterns within oildom, while keeping what was still lower price oil from abroad in check. Aided by American tax subsidies, some of the newer oil companies were finding Middle Eastern and North African oil. But the quotas helped prevent American consumers from having access to such potentially competitive supplies. The cost to the latter in the form of inflated heating and gasoline bills has been estimated at $4 billion to $7 billion annually, in effect, a tax of at least 4 cents on each gallon authorized by public government and collected for the coffers of private government. The American government and the industry were thus coalescing to maintain an embargo (like "cartel" an unacceptable term when applied to American practices) to keep Middle East oil prices very low, but unavailable to the United States.[2] American consumers, meanwhile, remained innocent about mounting Arab grievances and an imminent, predictable, and preventable crisis in their own economy.

As Americans discovered at the time of the energy scare in 1973, this protective device never fulfilled the public policy promises of its corporate proponents. Inefficient investment in low-yield wells was further subsidized while prorationing tended to hold back the more productive wells. Domestic production did not accelerate. Refinery construction in the United States was slowed down while giant new plants were built in the Caribbean which promised, at least in the short run, greater freedom from import, environmental, community, labor, and tax constraints. Mergers among refiners accelerated, intensifying the difficulty of independents in obtaining predictable crude supplies. Heating oil markets came under the further control of major companies. Petrochemical and other corporations using crude oil as feedstock saw themselves as victims pushed to building overseas where supplies were cheaper and more available. Foreign manufacturers gained advantages: Japan, for example, could purchase middle eastern oil far more cheaply than could the United States. That was because, as chairman M. A. Wright of Humble, the principal domestic operating affiliate of Jersey Standard (now Exxon) explained, "in the foreign circuit . . . there has been tremendous competition" from "people in the producing business for the first time" who needed outlets.[3]

Draining America first was to lead to claims of dwindling reserves and an ultimate need for more imports. The allocation of import rights among refiners generated windfalls to many and cynical suspicions about other possible beneficiaries, including Secretary of the Treasury Anderson. It also invited tremendous pressure upon the executive branch as corporations and legislators vied for special treatment for their regional operations. Its administration was "riddled with exceptions" blatantly unrelated to national security.[4] A modern-day Lincoln Steffens could write a *Shame of the Nation* just investigating expediency, and favoritism relating to refinery proposals or rejections. Separate chapters could be developed covering the Johnson administration's approval, presumably for economic development reasons, and sometimes as backdoor liberalization of a troublesome import control system, of Phillips and Commonwealth Oil refineries in Puerto Rico, a Hess refinery in the Virgin Islands, and an independent refinery in Hawaii.

Occidental's request to the Department of the Interior in 1968 for an import quota revealed how the interplay of corporate objectives defined local as well as national economic options. The maverick company was eager to develop a domestic market for its newly found crude oil in Libya, and also for Venezuelan oil which it hoped to be able to obtain through concessions, or later, drilling contracts. It sought to build a huge tanker terminal and refinery in a foreign trade zone to be created at the deep natural harbor of Machiasport, a fishing village in Maine. The refinery was to sell fuel oil and gasoline in New England at prices which Occidental claimed would save consumers at least $22 million annually. As an added inducement it pledged a payment of 20 cents for each barrel of quota allocation it received to be made to a New England Marine Resources Foundation which would conduct oceanographic research and education under the aegis of the six governors of the region.

To Occidental, the proposal was an economically and politically shrewd route to tremendous profits from its abundant Libyan crude and from the subsidy inherent in the quota allocation. It also provided an opportunity to minimize its tax liabilities to the United States government by writing off its mounting Libyan royalty and tax payments against tax obligations which would be incurred in the American operation. The foreign trade zone was an essential first step for the plan, since the refinery capacity was far greater than any expected quota allocations for New England and was to be served by 300,000 ton tankers. Since such zones are considered to be outside of the country and hence free of customs, crude oil could be brought to the refinery and then shipped abroad at favorable competitive cost. The portion of the refined oil intended for New England consumers would be imported under the quota allocation. Occidental would move into the ranks of the integrated domestically, with all the privileges.[5]

The promise of more energy at lower prices was tempting to the region. It had no coal or petroleum production. Nor were there any great refineries or federal power projects, despite the size of the market. Harnessing its tides and winds was the province of dreamers. Nuclear power was the only alternative on the horizon. There was widespread resentment against what were generally felt to be high and discriminating electric and heating oil costs. A regional refinery might help, while giving independent terminal operators and fuel dealers leverage for dealing with their existing big oil company suppliers. Strong environmentalist fears were expressed about supertankers along the treacherous coast and about harm to the fishing and tourist trades. There was also concern that Maine was not prepared to handle harsh changes in a cherished way of life certain to follow. But the prospect of industrial development spurred by the port and of employment in a depressed section was persuasive. Ending the import control system might have been a simpler way of bringing cheaper oil to the Yankees. But no one was offering that choice. The six governors and the entire congressional delegation of New England, sometimes prodded by the aggressive public relations of Occidental, endorsed the proposal.[6]

To corporations such as Mobil, Exxon, Shell, Gulf, Union, and Sinclair, crude oil to supply a refinery on the scale contemplated would breach the carefully maintained controls over imports. And if the overall amount of oil allowed into the country was not raised to accommodate Occidental, other importers would have their quotas reduced. Coastal and Great Lakes states such as Maryland, Virginia, North Carolina, Georgia, Louisiana, and Michigan might be encouraged to demand comparable zones and import permits. Industry planning whereby Middle Eastern and North African oil were intended for European and Asiatic markets would be upset. Cheap foreign oil and the nightmare of competition would return on Armand Hammer's tankers to haunt domestic producers and their multinational brothers.

The corporations, both independents and majors, mobilized against Maine's application for a foreign trade zone. What was normally routine procedure and approval by the Foreign Trade

Zones Board (an interdepartmental body under the secretaries of commerce, treasury, and the army) became a case study of the permeation of oil in politics. Oil state politicians, including Governor Hickel of Alaska and Senators John G. Tower (Republican, Texas), Gordon Allott (Republican, Colorado) and Fred Harris (Democrat, Oklahoma) were recruited to voice their opposition. Louisiana and Texas oilmen requested Representative Hale Boggs, Democratic whip and soon to be House majority leader, to testify at hearings in Maine before the board's examiners. Boggs proposed that the mission would appear bipartisan and less disloyal to fellow Democrats in New England if he was to be accompanied by a Republican. His nominee was Texas representative George Bush, an oil millionaire, sympathetic to industry positions and later to be chairman of the Republican National Committee. Boggs's oil contact promised to arrange the team through a Humble Oil vice-president. According to Boggs, an Occidental representative, accompanied by officials from its newly acquired Hooker Chemical plant in his district, then offered him campaign funds to dissuade him from appearing. Occidental denied such interpretations and suggested that it was Boggs who had set up the meeting as a ploy for big oil.[7]

After many delays the Maine hearings were finally held, and the examiners found Maine to be a qualified applicant. But on the eve of the hearings the board announced there would have to be additional hearings in Washington. Once the application was back in the safer confines of the capital, every stratagem was employed by the industry to kill the proposal and by the administration to postpone action. The executive branch was under great pressure and the bureaucratic response was to shuttle the issue back and forth in secrecy. Instead of ratifying the findings of their examiners, the cabinet officers in the outgoing Johnson administration continued to discover new reasons for not reaching a conclusion. In the closing days of the regime it was announced that the issue was too important to be dealt with apart from the larger question of oil imports policy and that, given the limited time remaining, further action should be deferred to the next administration. Investigating these roadblocks to Maine's request, Senator Thomas McIntyre (Democrat, New Hampshire) found what he described as a "secret government" about which he had known very little until the Machiasport project, but which he now concluded in some respects "dwarfed the military-industrial complex. . . . The Board appeared firmly within the secret government's control. . . . Some Board officials had such close personal ties with the oil industry as to appear themselves almost a part of the industry." Grateful to the Senate for being alerted to their moral oversight, the three cabinet members disqualified themselves from the case because of oil ties and stockholdings. Now there was no Foreign Trade Zones Board.[8]

Secretary of the Interior Stewart Udall was also under fire since his department was formally responsible for the imports program. The oil network that pervaded Interior, reinforced by the full political apparatus of the industry and such bodies as the Interstate Oil Compact Commission, pressed against the granting of an allocation.[9] Any action to be taken was scheduled to come after the zone decision. Mr. Udall's previous exemptions were viewed with hostility by oilmen who detected a less than one hundred percent belief in the program's national worth. Their earlier opposition to such bypassing of import controls through foreign-trade zones, sought by petrochemical companies in their efforts to gain feedstock, had led the secretary to prohibit such arrangements. This decision would have to be reviewed. But the secretary was also reluctant to confront the industry head-on and deal with Occidental's request. The Democrats were loath to appear subservient to oil interests, but did not feel they could politically risk taking the lid off controls. President Johnson had to leave Washington because of Vietnam, but he was determined not to be discredited on oil. Meanwhile, the industry, whose stalling tactics had reflected a strong interest and involvement in the election, expectantly awaited the arrival of the new Republican administration.

President Nixon's more open commitment to oil was reassuring, as were the specific campaign pledges to block Machiasport. The application of Occidental and Maine were still pending before Interior, now headed by Walter Hickel, and before the Foreign Trade Zones Board, now chaired by the new secretary of commerce and party fundraiser Maurice H. Stans. The majors assumed the now tattered application from Maine would be disposed of. But a committee of alternates to the three new secretaries gave their approval,

and Stans promised a final ruling. He then reversed himself and
said that the larger issues would have to be reviewed.[10] President
Nixon was facing pressures for the zone and refinery from the New
England Republican delegation. But for how long could the national pressures for more oil be deflected by selective exemptions
from national policy?

If "national security" was the overriding justification for import
controls, it seems strange that there was never developed any clear
public definition of desired levels of production or any mechanisms
either for ensuring reserve capacity or for actually setting aside
petroleum reserves. Presumably the natural workings of the marketplace would take care of these concerns. But state prorationing
authorities, chiefly Louisiana and Texas, still controlled domestic
production levels, and their judgment as to adequate pricing remained the arbiter of national need and consumer bills. Given the
ultimate dependence of their practices upon the international policies of the integrated oil corporations, the latter were in fact
calling the signals as to the national economy and security.

Demands for change mounted. Legislators were becoming bolder
in relating seasonal scarcity, the difficulty of getting approval for
foreign trade zones, and high prices to import policies and to a
pervasive private government unaffected by transitions in power in
the formal government. Acting on the advice of leaders from the
American Petroleum Institute and the corporations, President
Nixon appointed a cabinet task force, headed by the then secretary
of labor George P. Shultz, an economist, to review import policies.

Word soon began to spread that the emerging staff study was
devastatingly thorough, that the majority would declare the program a failure which kept prices artificially high, and that it should
be replaced by a differential tariff system. The National Petroleum
Council quickly advised the secretary of the interior and the president that such a change would be calamitous for national security.
The American Petroleum Institute sent out distress signals. Visits
and appeals by oilmen were made to the president and his aides.
The Interstate Oil Compact Commission—its sensitivity to charges
that it was a political agent for the domestic industry outweighed,
as always, by its sensitivity to fluctuation in the price of a barrel
of crude—mobilized member governors to add their voices. Repre-

sentative Wilbur Mills advised the staff not to tinker with such matters. Cabinet officers Hickel and Stans, along with John N. Nassikas, the chairman of the Federal Power Commission, insisted that the quotas were effective. In their subsequent dissenting report they expressed fear that the new proposals would lead to inadequate prices for domestic oil, impairing security and wrecking the economy. Keeping the quotas but raising imports as needed would provide opportunity for a gradual reduction in prices while avoiding "major shock to the oil producing and refining industries, to their stockholders and landholders, and to the states dependent upon them for tax revenues." Attorney General Mitchell, as ever alert to the politics of policy making, warned his colleagues: "Don't box the President in."[11]

Early in 1970 the majority, with Shultz as spokesman, reported as the industry had been warned they might, and as an advance copy, leaked to Exxon, had confirmed.[12] The underlying premise was that the preeminent position of the United States in the world depends in large part on the uninterrupted flow of oil and its products to its armed forces and civilian economy. It recommended a transition to a preferential tariff system. The tariff would compensate for an anticipated drop of about $1.30 in the wellhead price of domestic crude oil once the insulation of import controls was removed. It would provide a shield of about $1.45 against the Middle East and $1.25 against Latin America. Most future imports were to be drawn from the presumably politically secure Western hemisphere. Imports of low cost crude oil from the volatile Middle East would be limited to 10 percent of United States demand—clear deference to the market concerns of the multinationals as well as rising Arab nationalism. The task force projected for 1980 a 27 percent dependence on imports, at current domestic prices, barring major synthetic breakthroughs. It had studied previous oil cutoffs (such as Suez) and worked out contingency models for political oil embargoes, partial and complete, from the Middle East and North Africa. One basic calculation showed that even at $2.50 a barrel domestic price, a drop from the current $3.30 but higher than the $2 Middle Eastern oil delivered to the East Coast without import quota, the United States could satisfy all import requirements with oil from the Western Hemisphere.[13]

The report assumed that the neighbors to the north would respond to the absence of a tariff on their oil and share the enthusiasm for integrating Canadian and American oil planning. It also assumed that Venezuela, the largest Latin American source, would respond to the preferential treatment. More of its oil would move into the United States, the price being attractive in contrast to what it might get in the world market, but competitive for the American scene. No consideration was given to the fact that "Canadian" and "Venezuelan" oil was largely in the hands of a few international corporations who refine and distribute through their integrated systems. (Esso and Shell together controlled three-fourths of Venezuelan production.) As John M. Blair, then chief economist of the Senate Antitrust and Monopoly Subcommittee, pointed out to Shultz, some of these provisions might solidify the power of these corporations. The latter were busily expanding refinery capacity in the Caribbean, with Esso and Shell having half the total. Latin American exports were thus likely to be the more profitable finished products which would then flow to the marketing outlets of the giants. The consequence would be the further cutting off of independent refiners and marketers from supply as well as the cutting off of moderate-size companies who in the sixties had developed production in the Middle East and North Africa from the American market.

The task force and Secretary Shultz saw many positive gains for responsible public policy. Oil prices would go down. The benefits of the tariff, perhaps a dollar a barrel, would go to the United States treasury rather than to the corporations. Some marginal producers would be eliminated. But a measure of efficiency and competition would be introduced into the domestic industry. Anticipating the cries of the industry about investment needs, Shultz quietly suggested that if the corporations found diminished ability to generate internally as much capital for expansion as they would prefer, then they might have to return to an older business practice and go to the capital markets. "It seems to me that in the kind of free market system we have, the desirable situation is that new investment is tested in the marketplace, so to speak, against its alternative uses."[14] In effect he was challenging the prevailing assumption that the consumer should continue to be an investor, paying in the price of his fuel not simply for its cost and a reasonable profit but also for its replacement. But an investor without any rights and, as the energy crisis briefly illustrated, without the assurance of the supply for which he had already paid. Not even the trinket, the shiny piece of glass or the half of a coupon for an elusive bicycle (profusely celebrated in corporate advertisements and paid for by the less than enthusiastic dealer), which had emphasized the motorist's treatment as a native, remained at the service station as inducement and consolation.

The effectiveness of the rigid market-demand prorationing in the key oil states, which had been sustained by import quotas, would be ended. There would then be less reason for Alaska to be fitted into that structure and have price management masquerading as conservation laws. And a related staff study indicated that the industry was grossly exaggerating the likely costs of Alaskan oil and its need for protection.

The proposal also plunged into a thorny conflict over the outer continental shelf. The adjoining states, notably Louisiana and Texas, had been integrating production on federal leases into their state production controls. This had been done with the tacit consent of the Department of the Interior despite periodic prodding from some members of the department and from the Justice Department. Such acquiescence negated much of the political conflict and the Supreme Court decisions which had placed these offshore lands in federal hands. The majority of the task force recommended that the secretary of the interior move to free this production (excess capacity totalled 500,000 barrels a day) from state controls and that only genuine conservation considerations prevail in any federal prorationing that might be introduced. Thus, federal rather than state controls would operate in matters affecting national well-being.[15]

This assertion of federal primacy offered the president a weapon for challenging any price increases he might consider unwarranted or inflationary and for adjusting supply levels he considered too low: he could increase production from shut-in wells on federal lands. The import quotas, in contrast, had been administered as a two-edged sword against the consumer. They protected domestic prices against the world oversupply which prevailed in the 1960s.

And when domestic crude prices were increased by the industry early in 1969, no attempt was made by the Oil Import Administration or the president to raise quotas. Once again the private government of oil was safeguarded by public government from the possibility of a free market.

The report was uncomfortable for the industry, even if by itself it posed no fundamental threat to the power of the international corporations. To the contrary, in relation to irritants such as Machiasport, it pointed the way to narrowing the arena, all too characteristic of American political life, for special pleading and bargaining between crude industry upstarts and politicians without firm loyalties which were enfeebling big oil's higher purposes.[16] But the report did suggest points of vulnerability of import controls and directions for a full-scale challenge to the rule of private law.

If the industry was outmatched in economic analysis, it had, however, been doing the political homework necessary for survival in an imperfect world. White House advisers and congressional delegations were fully prepared, spelling out the possible consequence for seats from oil producing states, including the candidacy of George Bush in Texas, and even the loss of control of the Senate if such theoretical defenses of the amorphous consumer were to be implemented. President Nixon was persuaded to ignore the heretical document and its central recommendations. A new committee was appointed, chaired by Brigadier General George A. Lincoln who headed the White House Office of Emergency Preparedness. It had the same cast of cabinet members, except that the realist Mitchell replaced Shultz and his old-fashioned illusions about private enterprise. Presidential aide Peter Flanigan rejected the cynical suggestion that the administration was procrastinating. As for industry pressure, "the President had a policy of not meeting with people to discuss the oil import problem and that includes Governors of oil producing states, . . . businessmen and . . . groups of Senators and Congressmen."[17]

The new committee wasted little time on scholarly analysis. Its report upheld the workings of imports policy and was warmly received by the president.[18] Nothing in the record of oil shook his faith in the performance of "private enterprise" and the judgment of its captains, not even an inequitable subsidy program which was already giving signs of being a major contributor to the "energy crisis" soon to follow. In the eyes of oildom, the Nixon administration was on stream.

Meanwhile, brownouts were becoming a new feature of urban living. Midwesterners faced severe heating fuel shortages in the winter of 1972–73. New Englanders continued to fret about tight fuel prospects for the winter and the absence of any refineries in their energy-expensive region. Import allowables were adjusted upward. Liberal importation of residual fuel (a low-priced, heavy fuel byproduct of refining) from the Western Hemisphere for the East Coast was continued.

The administration and industry spokesmen (at times their speechwriters seemed to be cribbing freely from the same National Petroleum Council and American Petroleum Institute sources) assured the nation that the program was working and the supply flow adequate. In the "first presidential energy message," in June 1971, Mr. Nixon identified increased demand since 1967 and recent environmental standards as the troublemaking new factors. The United States had grown great through cheap energy which did not reflect true social costs. Higher prices would elicit abundant and clean energy. The government could help accelerate energy production through such measures as opening up the public lands for corporate leasing and development. There were also cautious references to such alternate possibilities as oil shale and coal gasification. For the longer pull, science and technology would point the way: nuclear energy and the fast breeder reactor were "our best hope" for securing the blessings of a high-energy civilization. Little was said about reappraising the American way of consumption. No mention was made of the role of import quotas. There was a hint, however, that the United States was now receptive to letting Canada step up shipments from her western provinces.[19]

Technically self-sufficient, Canada was sending about half of its oil southward while also supplying its own markets west of the Ottawa Valley. The eastern provinces brought in cheaper oil from Venezuela and then, increasingly, the Middle East and North Africa (often paying less at the pump than New Englanders for oil landed in Maine and shipped "in bond" across the northeast corner of the United States to Montreal). In apparent violation of the earlier overland imports exemption and without congressional review, a secret agreement had been negotiated by the foreign offices of the two nations whereby the Canadian National Emergency Board unofficially was to keep a lid on Canadian oil exported to the United States. The pull of higher United States prices kept pressure on the quota which was raised somewhat and made official in 1970 through a presidential order. The explanation was that voluntary controls were breaking down, creating "inequities" within the United States and impairing national security.[20] Domestis oil producers had resented the competition, and giant refineries had not welcomed the crude becoming available to Midwest independent refiners. There was disappointment and anger over Canada's reluctance to limit its own imports for its East Coast and to join in continental energy planning satisfactory to the United States. The "energy crisis" was almost upon the nation, yet planning for maintaining scarcity still held sway.

As late as the end of 1972 the National Petroleum Council was still urging the retention of the oil import control program to protect the nation and the industry against the menace of "unrestricted imports." Speaking soberly of the national need to balance energy supply and demand, it saw three policy options for the nation in the period 1973–85: greater reliance upon imports, restraints upon demand growth, and increased emphasis on development of domestic supplies. Greater imports dependence meant vulnerability and balance-of-trade problems. While more efficient use of energy would be desirable, "restrictions on energy demand growth could prove expensive and undesirable. Among other things, they would alter life-styles and adversely affect employment, economic growth and consumer choice. Despite possibilities for extreme changes or revisions in existing social, political and economic institutions, substantial changes in lifestyle between now and 1985 are precluded by existing mores and habits, and by enormous difficulties of changing the existing energy consumption system." The best option was to boost domestic supply—through government encouragement of private enterprise and higher prices. Reserves of oil and gas "are sufficient to support a substantial increase in production. . . . Coal is abundant. . . . Domestic uranium resources . . . are adequate" and there are rich oil shale deposits. "No major source of U.S. fuel supply is limited by the availability of resources to sustain higher production."[21] But only a few months later, in April 1973, Texaco and Exxon publicly called for the end of import limitations, explaining this reversal on the grounds that the demand situation no longer required them.[22]

That same month, the president formally acted to end import quotas. Domestic demand was outrunning available supply. Texas wells were no longer shut in by the state Railroad Commission. The world was still floating on a sea of crude oil costing pennies to lift from the ground. (*U.S. Oil Week* estimated that Gulf's Kuwait oil then cost 8 cents a barrel to find and pump into tankers, $1.24 royalty to the Kuwait government—50 percent of the $2.48 posted price—6 cents or less to transport to Philadelphia, 63 cents to refine and add lead. With the new tariff of 10.5 cents a barrel, the total cost at the refinery gate came to $2.11, or 5 cents a gallon. Meanwhile the price services were posting just under 17 cents a gallon for regular gas at the refinery gate.)[23] For independent refiners, paying for overseas crude oil at the posted prices, the costs would be more. Meanwhile, product prices were moving upward. Imports would remain under the control of the giant international companies; their tightly concentrated and synchronized refinery capacity in the United States was counted upon to help keep this oil from engulfing the American market and inviting destructive price wars. Exxon and its sister corporations now explained that governmental protection from the perils of the world market was no longer essential. World crude prices were beginning to reverse their downward spiral of the previous decade. Overseas oil prices were overtaking domestic prices. The immediate prospect for profits was very heartening.

# 5

# Imperial Energies

The global perspective of the major oil corporations has found a generally sympathetic response in the executive branch of the American government. The containment policies of the 1950s seemed primitive and even counterproductive for ensuring world stability. Direct military intervention and the counterinsurgency so glorified in the 1960s became too costly and ultimately unworkable without the support of local populaces. They appeared to be more successful in mobilizing sentiment, first abroad and then at home, against an imperial reach than in making the world safe for the American way of life.

Military and foreign aid had other longer run consequences. As President Kennedy observed, "too little attention has been paid to the part which an early exposure to American goods, skills and American ways of doing things can play in forming the tastes and desires of newly emerging countries."[1] Similarly, seaports, airports, highways, telephones, and hydroelectric projects helped create a physical climate for American trade and investment. In some places, the "green revolution" transformed small-scale subsistence family operations into commercial agriculture dependent upon international petroleum.[2] Discussing American programs to help the people of Thailand develop their own strength (while also serving as a base for the war against North Vietnam and Laos), Ambassador Leonard Unger in 1969 disclosed the presence of oil companies. American business was catching up with the Japanese and becoming the major source of investment. Three oil companies, two rubber factories and one tin smelter were among the corporate entries.

There is one very, very large development that may take place. Nobody knows at this point whether it will prove out or not. That is oil exploration that is going on in the Gulf of Thailand . . . not only from Thailand but also from Malaysia, Indonesia and so on, but it is very important in the case of Thailand and there are six companies, five of them American that are now carrying out explorations and presumably with some pretty good hopes of finding something there.[3]

Segments of the anti-Vietnam war movement quickly speculated that perhaps at last they had a tangible explanation for why the United States was so immovably bogged down in Asian jungles, even intensifying its efforts as more of its own people were turning against the war. United States officialdom bristled at such crude economic determinism. Reports of large deposits "have absolutely no effect on United States policy," said Secretary of State William P. Rogers.[4] The State Department found "the idea that the United States would expend 40,000 lives and billions of dollars so that the scant natural resources of South Viet-Nam could be exploited by American commercial interests . . . repugnant," as were imputed correlations between the rate of withdrawal of troops and the gaining of offshore drilling rights. "That it is even advanced is evidence of the irresponsible nature of some element of the anti-war movement in this country."[5]

The thesis was simplistic, perhaps grounded more in frustration at an inability to find either justification for involvement in the war or leverage for ending it than in historical evidence. There were not major oil investments in Indochina at the outset of American military engagement. War contracts for the petroleum industry were substantial, and the permanent mobilization sustained civilian buying power for energy-intensive equipment, stimulated by the industry's campaigns to have high consumption by each car and household equated with good citizenship. But the arms buildup was not directly decisive for the industry the way it was for so many industries and so much of the economy. B. R. Dorsey, chairman of Gulf, which had lower sales than some of the other sisters supplying the armed services and their contractors, said that "we've been attacked as part of the military-industrial complex, but we sell about one percent of the total product we make to the U.S. Government. And we don't know what they do with it."[6]

Many within the business community became openly disaffected in the closing years of direct troop involvement. And the giant corporations, impatient with the disruptive side of such conflict, increasingly characterized themselves as forces for worldwide peace and development. An article in the *Aramco World* suggested that since corporate leaders were truly "men without a country" as they strove to overcome irrational nationalist constraints and integrate the world, their corporations should be seen as "peacemongers" rather than "warmongers".[7] But there are no records, save perhaps in the files of the Federal Bureau of Investigation, of how many oil executives marched in demonstrations or funneled funds to peace groups or used their easy access to the highest reaches of public government to express their doubts. It would be enlightening to know who did raise questions, when, in what contexts and with what responses.

There is evidence that the heads of the global oil corporations, chiefly technicians by training and preference, "went along". Distrustful of ideology—save for a few oldtime independent producers, they pride themselves on being practical men who can get things done. They are primarily absorbed in their trade, whose essential character, ironically, is political. As always they want to stake out oil reserves everywhere, and there is a special urgency to have alternatives to Persian Gulf sources. They feel they need a stable political environment at home and abroad if the planning so central to the oil business is to function effectively and freely. The global management of oil required governments able to maintain law and order, policed if necessary by American or American-trained and equipped indigenous forces. Uninformed about history and uncomfortable with ideologues, they applaud or accept the prescriptions for such a climate eloquently conjured up by statesmen, generals, and academician-strategists of the court—as long as they work. European oilmen are wont to view their American colleagues in oil as "provincials." In places like the Middle East, the latter's frontier excitement over technology for development and their directness about profits made them more attractive than the oil diplomats with their national encumbrances, forked tongues, and inability to turn a valve. The lives of the big oilmen were within big organization, and big organizations depend upon accommodation for survival. Thus they could have second thoughts about messy and inconclusive combat in Vietnam. They could line up for contracts with the communist bloc and with third world socialist nations—as long as agreements, orderly marketing, and their take were respected. One cannot show that the oil corporations were central to decision-making about Vietnam. In the immediate sense, then, it is likely that the United States neither entered nor withdrew its military presence "because of oil investments."

The righteous rebuttal of the State Department was disingenous. The historic moral fervor of the American nation for extending civilization and in process defining its own character had been inextricably joined to an economic imperative for expanding its domain and finding markets. Contemporary policy makers have been ignorant about other peoples' history and impatient with their nationalism. Keeping underdeveloped countries, which also happened to have desired raw materials, from falling into communist clutches would help keep their people free and Western society strong. Once integrated into an alliance, both they and their protectors would be secure from communist subversion masquerading as national liberation and from external conquest. Overseas investments were indispensable components of the national mission. It was the civic duty of the corporations to find oil and markets. And in turn, the developing countries were told again and again by Democratic and Republican secretaries of state that it would be "wise and prudent" for them to put out the welcome mat for the Yankee corporate emissaries.[8] If approaches were resisted, if demands were unreasonable, if contracts were broken, property threatened or confiscated, then the oilmen were to run to the White House. And they did. There they found sympathetic listeners, often their own colleagues or bankers, lawyers and politicians with whom they had been dealing all their lives, ready to take appropriate remedial action.

An inquiry from J. W. Fulbright, chairman of the Senate Committee on Foreign Relations, prompted a somewhat obfuscating denial as to United States assistance in the original seismic searches off the coast of Vietnam during the late sixties. But shortly after-

ward the State Department acknowledged the traditional relationship of encouraging private investments to help economic development in southeast Asia.[9] And in a speech on January 21, 1971, to
the American Chamber of Commerce in Saigon, in which he was
enumerating the impressive gains of pacification and Vietnamiza-
tion in bringing the people along to political and economic matur-
ity, Ambassador Ellsworth Bunker spelled out the symbiosis between the objectives of the government of oil and the governments
of the United States and South Vietnam:

> Though aid from abroad is vital to Vietnamese plans for achieving
> greater prosperity, ultimately the most important condition for those
> plans' success will be the Vietnamese ability to make better use of
> their own resources, both internally and externally. Therefore, an
> effective strategy must be designed to further participation in foreign
> trade and to attract private investment from abroad. All of you here
> today can help to forge and further this strategy. I think you may
> also serve your own economic best interest, as well as America's and
> Viet-Nam's, by convincing other American companies of the merits
> of doing business here. The recent petroleum law and the new invest-
> ment law now before the upper House indicate the Government's
> desire to create a flexible long-term investment policy which will
> serve Viet-Nam's interests while at the same time it creates an eco-
> nomic climate foreign investors will find attractive.[10]

It wasn't, then, that the oilmen were innocents who just didn't
know. They had backed a series of cold warrior presidential candidates who elevated these themes to high national purpose. In
their dual capacities as business statesmen and party donors, oilmen were privy to endless off-the-record briefings by Defense and
State Department secretaries affirming the oneness of business and
national security. The global strategists spoke passionately of the
need to contain Communist China by being strong on its perimeters ,which must be controlled by friendly regimes.

More likely the oilmen were listening to the beat of a somewhat
different if not unrelated drummer. "A mention of China brought
a gleam to Mr. Dorsey's slate-colored eyes." His company was a
major investor in Taiwan, Korea and Okinawa; it had concessions
to explore off Korea, Taiwan and Japan. "We're optimistic there

might be tremendous reserves of petroleum there and if there are, then they're on the continental shelf of China. . . . Down the road the Chinese might well ask the Americans, or foreigners, to come in for exploration." With the emergence of the People's Republic of China from isolation and subsequent movement toward rapprochement with the United States, this was a distinct possibility for corporate planning. Meanwhile Gulf was "strategically located" to move chemical products and petroleum into mainland China.[11]

The United States' interest in the economic dimensions of Southeast Asia was not new. And the possibility of rich oil fields had long been discussed. There was also concern about the implications of Japan's intensified search for a fuel supply independent of Western corporate control. A Vietnam "peace" settlement in 1973 made it easier for the oil companies to get on with exploration. It also improved their relations with other oil-producing third world regimes which had found it embarrassing, although profitable, to be fueling imperial expeditions of the United States government. Once the corporations settle in, generally with assurances of protection from the mother country, the latter has a stake in a stabilized setting for their continued presence. Some of the oil companies prospecting in Thailand and South Vietnam quickly sought nationalization insurance from the United States Overseas Private Investment Corporation which had replaced AID.

There has been drilling and the companies have found oil. But the post-Vietnam political climate has been too unsettled. There has been a fear that concessions made by the corrupt client government in Saigon would be repudiated because of their link to the United States' effort to turn the civil war back to the Vietnamese, with South Vietnam's own soldiers doing more of the direct fighting and their own oil paying more of the bill. There was a distinct possibility that the existing production and marketing facilities would be nationalized despite the careful draftsmanship of American consultants. Had the grand strategy of the cold warriors backfired, the oilmen more used than using? In 1975 the rigs moved on, and further operations were postponed until conditions might be more favorable for Western technological dynamism. Hanoi was eager, and secret negotiations were undertaken with the companies who wanted to recoup their initial investments.

What was still required, however, was a clearing of the political air, including lifting of the trade embargo by Washington and steps toward the recognition of North Vietnam.[12]

Détente with the Soviet Union was also agreeable to the multinationals. The two powers were increasingly respecting each other's sphere of influence and interests in common. The United States welcomed maximum leeway in protecting its oil lifeline in the Persian Gulf; silence if not assent on the part of the Soviet Union (and China) could be reassuring, notwithstanding the latter's verbal identification with those presumed to be under the iron heel of Western imperialism. The Russians once more were welcoming American technology for modernization of fertilizer and chemical plants and other sectors of the economy. In return, there was promise of access to Siberian natural gas and the building of major pipelines—of interest to the energy-seeking United States and such companies as Occidental, El Paso, the Bechtel Corporation, and Tenneco. (Russia is believed to have a third of the world's proved natural gas reserves; the U.S. perhaps 14 percent.) The way was to be smoothened by generous low-interest credit arrangements through the Export-Import Bank. Gulf Oil signed an agreement to help Russia develop for its Far Eastern markets the offshore oil around the island of Sakhalin, with financial help to come from Japan. And the two governments sought bilateral agreements whereby the USSR could sell oil to the United States at favorable prices and comparable in value to the grain being received (perhaps a billion dollars annually), without the former's offending or undercutting OPEC and without the latter's appearing to abandon the cause of Western unity.

But a letup in the cold war meant no necessary reduction in armaments or the internal security apparatus of the two states. Pleas by the United States Navy for a formidable armada to protect the sea lanes for the new supertankers became more eloquent as it pointed to an increasingly active Soviet fleet. The ships and submarines of "our primary potential adversary" were venturing into heretofore off-limits seas. Once "a coastal defense and interdiction force, Soviet fleets operating increasingly in the Indian Ocean, have begun to edge out the United States in the seas around Japan," former secretary of defense James R. Schlesinger warned, "and in certain respects have become a match for the U.S. Fleet in the Mediterranean, formerly an American lake."[13] The United States Army showed renewed interest in desert warfare, as if to be prepared for the eventuality of conflict in the Middle Eastern oil regions.

Nor were the developing nations to misunderstand the new internationalism. Détente meant that it would be more difficult to play off the great powers one against the other. The United States was not turning soft on communism, at least not where oil was at stake. In 1970, oil accounted for 30 percent of all American overseas investments, 40 percent of all American investments in underdeveloped areas, and 60 percent of American earnings from the latter regions. Oil companies had long since recovered their investments in Latin America, Canada, and the Middle East. Much of their investment was local earnings and capital gathered in the producing areas rather than capital from the United States. One study of the Middle East estimated that from the time of their involvement up until 1960, the major oil companies had gross receipts of $32 billion; approximately $6 billion went for costs of operation and $10 billion went to the local governments. The balance, $16.3 billion, went to the oil companies, which reinvested about $1.7 billion in their local oil operations and transferred the remaining $14.6 billion abroad. Almost every study of Latin America and the Middle East reinforces this picture of the nature of corporate investment and the direction of corporate profits. They suggest, as noted earlier, how far the great investments the corporations so often refer to should rather be understood as the expectation of great profits.[14]

Economic independence in these countries, whether championed by socialists or military nationalists, was not viewed lightly by corporate and United States government leaders. The United States Information Agency has tried to deal with what it has described as "one of the principal problems" in Latin America—creating a favorable climate for corporations when "so often foreigners see huge American investments as a sign of imperialism." It has prepared pamphlets for distribution in Ecuador by Texaco and Gulf, with no sponsor's credit indicated, contrasting the menace of public control and "communist solutions" with the blessings of private development. When J. W. Fulbright expressed bewilderment as to why United States taxpayers were picking up the bill, he was reassured by the deputy director of the USIA that "there are many instances . . . where private companies have been exceedingly generous giving us materials which they already had for their own purposes or helping us to defray costs of seminars or a variety of other things where they have used their own resources, to do what they considered to be in the interests of their company as well as of their country."[15]

Food shipments to India were held back by the Johnson administration until that country's government, which was seeking public development of fertilizer, accepted the terms for marketing and pricing of fertilizer sought by Standard (Indiana). Exxon's recurring battles with Peru were reinforced by the United States cutting off of aid in 1964, when Peru pressed for participation in the International Petroleum Company subsidiary. In the dispute between IPC and Peru, which had a long history generally unknown to the people of the United States, the State Department and the embassy in Peru generally identified with the company, accepting its facts, figures, legal interpretations, and positions. What the United States viewed as a "hands off" policy of refusing to involve itself in the substance of negotiations meant that "in effect we placed American policy in Peru in the hands of the negotiators for IPC. For if they didn't agree there would be no aid." The suspension of aid hurt a poor economy and the chances for sustaining moderate popular government in a setting that had been dictatorial for so long. Argentina, Brazil, Ceylon, and Indonesia have had comparable experiences in relation to American loans. Latin Americans have learned that aid programs do not come without strings. Nor would the World Bank or the International Monetary Fund, heavily influenced as they are by United States capital, view as sound those national plans which sought funds for the public development of petroleum. The "energy crisis" stressed once more that, despite the warnings to developing people against wasting precious earnings by building up their own industry when there were already available private worldwide systems ready to serve them, they could ill afford not to develop their own resources.[16]

American efforts to isolate Cuba, after a brief period of ambivalence followed by the abortive Bay of Pigs military intervention in 1961, were officially defended as responses to Soviet entanglements and to her revolutionary intentions for the hemisphere. Yet it is clear that Cuba's taking over of Shell, Esso, and Texaco refineries (built under most favorable terms during the Batista regime), the seizure of the records of exploration companies and increasing the government's percentage from 10 percent to 60 percent, and even the authorization of service stations to sell other brands than those of their company so as to create outlets for a small nationalized Cuban refinery, were tangible and troubling precedents for the United States government and the international oil companies. Lacking water power, coal and petroleum, "in order to turn on an electric light" Cuba has to rely upon imports, and, from the State Department perspective, "whoever supplies petroleum to Cuba in a sense controls Cuba or makes it highly dependent."[17] The Cuban demand that the companies refine Russian oil obtained through barter, in place of half of their usual imports, as a way of paying the companies money owed to them by the Cuban government, threatened the "orderly marketing" of their own oil brought in from Venezuela. The companies indicated concern over the technological difficulties in running lower-quality Russian oil without seriously damaging their refineries. It has been suggested that the basic fear of the oilmen was that if they went along, there would be comparable demands elsewhere.[18]

Philip W. Bonsal, the last United States ambassador to Cuba, and no admirer of the Castro regime, has written that it had been his judgment that the companies should accept this arrangement while contesting the action in the Cuban courts. If no satisfaction was achieved, then the United States could file a diplomatic claim against Cuba.

However, on the afternoon of Saturday, June 4 [1960], I received a visit from the chief executive in Cuba of a major American oil company who had just returned from Washington. He said that he was calling me at the request of the Assistant Secretary of State for Inter-American Affairs, Mr. Rubottom, in order to bring me up to date on

recent developments with regard to the Guevara demand that the refineries in Cuba handle Soviet crude oil. After confirming my impression that until very recently the companies' position had been that of
going ahead with the operation under protest and attempting to secure recognition of their rights through the Cuban courts, he added
that this position had been predicated on the assumption that the
United States government would not wish to take a stand on the
matter. This assumption had now proved to be contrary to fact.

My visitor went on to tell me that on the previous day representatives of the two American companies with refineries in Cuba had
been summoned to the office of the Secretary of the Treasury, Robert Anderson, [the Texas oilman] and had been informed by the Secretary that a refusal to accede to the Cuban government's request
would be in accord with the policy of the United States government
toward Cuba and that the companies would not incur any penalties
under American antitrust laws should they take a joint stand in this
matter. They were further told that the situation was being discussed
in London with the Shell company along the same lines. My infor-
mant added that there had been a representative of the Department
of State present at the meeting conducted by the Secretary of the
Treasury. He concluded that the companies had decided to conform
their policies to that of their government and that they would refuse
the Soviet crude; they understood that the Anglo-Dutch company
would follow suit—as indeed it did.

Shortly afterward, the three companies, in separate communications, "so as to give the impression of company decisions independently arrived at," informed the Cuban government they would
not refine Russian crude oil.[19]

The United States move, together with the suspension of sugar
quotas, had been intended to strangle Cuba economically, to "make
plain to the people of Cuba . . . that the present regime cannot
serve their interests," and to accelerate Castro's downfall.[20] Instead, this direct challenge to the revolution guaranteed the taking
over of the three refineries and the adoption of Cuba by the Soviet
Union. The latter then sent Cuba her full crude oil needs and
technicians. Red oil went through the refineries, possibly without
corrosive effects on the Western machinery.

The corporations, quite naturally, prefer political regimes that
are good risks for long-run investments. Then they can be "good

citizens," rocking no boats, absorbed primarily in the first order of business—the quest for profit. Obviously their welcome depends upon relations with those in power.

"Oil is where God put it," Gulf's vice-president for advertising and public relations explained to a church conference whose members had been challenging the company's continued operations in Portuguese Africa. Liberation movements were struggling to overturn "the last colonial empire," and in response the churchmen were organizing a boycott against Gulf products, including the turning in of credit cards. Angola was a vital source of oil. "That's why we're there. It's tough enough to discover where the new oil reserves are. It would be impossible to find sufficient reserves if we limited our search only to those nations with whose political philosophies we agree."[21] The company's management and board had "spent many long sessions in analyzing Gulf's operations in Angola from all points of view, the humanitarian and the moralistic . . . as well as from the business standpoint. . . . We have concluded that Gulf's presence in Angola is in the best interests of the Angolan people and our shareholders."[22]

"Oil is where nature put it," said Gulf's chairman to the shareholders in a secularized version of the same message. "We've found it in Angola. And as long as the oil is there and we are welcome, we are staying."[23] While the critics "sit in parish headquarters and worry about world problems . . . stirring up these problems," the corporation's subsidiaries were doing business in seventy "free world" countries.[24] They were "guests of those governments and as a matter of policy and self-interest, we do not engage in public debate about their political systems. . . . As a legal corporate entity, an international company must remain politically neutral. As corporate and personal citizens of the United States, we seek to do business only with those nations whose government our own government recognizes."[25]

Gulf's job was to find oil for the progress of mankind. Oil "only becomes a natural resource when somebody turns it into capital." Gulf's capital was creating jobs, education, skills, and real progress for the people; only by improving the economic base would there be any substantial change in government.[26] "Recent history has shown that territories gaining the greatest volume of foreign investments have been among the first to become self-governing."[27] If Gulf withdrew from its contract, it would "simply leave the government with all the revenue from a well-established oil field—which it is fully capable of operating or could contract to another country. In either event, the government would not be deprived of revenue. In fact, its revenue would increase substantially."[28] The officers and directors of Gulf thus concluded that they did not "have the right to attempt to intrude in the strictly political affairs of any foreign country." To succumb to church or other pressures would violate the code that multinational companies "must remain nonpartisan abroad" and would transform them into "international political tools."[29] Meanwhile, the company opposed a stockholder resolution calling for a full airing of its involvement in Angola, arguing that "the real purpose of the resolution is to enable the organization which has submitted the resolution to use the forum of the Corporation's proxy statement and annual meeting to promote such organization's social and political views concerning the present government in Angola."[30] And it threatened legal action "to obtain redress for the damages done to the Gulf Oil Corporation and to the reputation of its principal officers" by the dissemination of the church resolution against Gulf.[31]

No information was volunteered as to Gulf's secret funds, used for bribery and campaign contributions. As later brought out through the Securities and Exchange Commission, these included $5 million in cash to foreign politicians and parties between 1966 and 1972.[32] "As a matter of pragmatism," over $4 million of this went to President Park Chong-huii's ruling party in South Korea, where Gulf had a $350 million investment. Most of the giving took place during an election year when Park won by a very slim majority. "The company never asked for nor received anything in return for the contributions," chairman Dorsey explained, "except, perhaps, the unfettered right to continue in business." One concern was the possibility of reunification with North Korea and a communist domination of the peninsula which might make an American petroleum presence tenuous. "As the biggest foreign investor, we could play an expanded role," Gulf's chairman suggested, "although the opposite could happen too."[33] Such trepidation has been shared by the United States government. Its bases, nuclear weapons, and $12 billion in aid, along with its support of Japanese economic penetration, are crucial to the maintenance of the repressive regime. They bear testimony to the cold war determination to quarantine the Chinese revolution and to the perspective that Korean nationalism is subordinate to Chinese and Russian expansion.

About a half million dollars of Gulf money went into Bolivian politics in the years immediately preceding the 1969 nationalization of the company's holdings. Money was also given to a group in Beirut for a public relations campaign in the United States press aimed at creating a better understanding of Arab positions. Investments were also made in Italian politics by Gulf and Mobil, although these were quite modest in contrast to those of Exxon. In the period 1970–73 Mobil Oil Italiana, with records falsified, gave nearly $2 million to the Socialist, Social Democratic, and Christian Democratic parties. When asked in 1973 by a shareholder at a shareholders' meeting about the exact amounts, Exxon's chairman had replied that "I don't think we want to give that information." This record was also concealed from internal auditors "in the belief that it was too sensitive for them to know," Emilio Collado, Exxon's executive vice-president was to explain. But the corporation subsequently admitted to giving over $50 million to Italian politics from 1963 to 1972, including at least $12 million to the Christian Democrats, $5 million to the Social Democrats, $1 million to the Socialists, and $86,000 to the Communists. There was evidence to suggest that the U.S. State Department, the CIA, and the American Ambassador to Italy had some knowledge of these activities. Secret bank accounts, "adjustments" in bank interest rates, inflated prices, dummy invoices, and kickbacks were among the devices used, in the words of the company's controller, "to further the democratic process." These practices also defrauded the Italian government of taxes. The company's general auditor concluded that "bogus documentation and false accounting were accepted by many levels of management [and so] it was virtually impossible under the circumstances to verify the validity of specific transactions. . . . The entire control system was rendered ineffective." And there were disclosures that, when some years ago auditors had become aware of the unusual activities, their concern was more about value than values: "We were unable to obtain infor-

mation on these payments sufficient to enable us to have the level
of payments reviewed by those who are knowledgeable of 'prices'
to be paid for specific favors, or to ascertain that the favors paid
for had actually been received." An Exxon special committee ultimately concluded that there were "errors in business judgement"
rooted not in lack of devotion to duty but in the "trusting nature"
of the men at the top who had assumed that their own commitment to high ethical standards prevailed throughout their empire.[34]

Mobil defended its contributions "to support the democratic
process of government" in Italy and Canada "as legal and accepted
practice." Gulf gave $1,400,000 to Canadian politics over a fifteen-
year period. Imperial, the Exxon affiliate in Canada, initially had
balked at disclosures of amounts and recipients: "We feel that it's
a private matter between the company and the political parties."
What did emerge was that Imperial gave an average of $234,000
a year to Canadian parties at the federal and provincial levels over
a five-year period. The chairman explained it was company practice
"to assist in the support of the political system in Canada," but "it
would not be reasonable to expect Imperial to support political
philosophies that would be detrimental to the company."[35] Not to
be outdone, Occidental was charged in a Texas court suit by the
former general manager of its Venezuelan subsidiary with having
paid more than $3 million in campaign contributions and bribes to
officials and candidates in that country, including its chief OPEC
representative. Chairman Hammer's initial response was that the
accusation was groundless and the court lacked jurisdiction. The
chief accountant at the SEC, familiar with minor payoffs to customs officers, construction unions and other officials, to cut through
red tape, admitted "he never dreamed executives of major corporations were running around the world with briefcases full of cash."[36]

Reviewing the "sorrowful chapter" in his company's history ("I
was basically ashamed of what was going on"), Gulf chairman
B. R. Dorsey explained that at the time the company's leaders,
only a few of whom were aware of these activities, felt they had
no choice. Gulf's joint ventures with the Korean government were
expanding, encouraged by United States government AID loans,
investment insurance, and overall military-economic assistance. The
political pressures in Korea "left little to the imagination as to what

would occur if the company would choose to turn its back on the request" for funds to support what he recalled was described as a "struggling young democracy . . . trying to have democratic processes." But he was able to bargain down the suggested giving. Neither the U.S. Embassy nor the State Department were advised of these doings. Gulf's reticence was rooted in what Mr. Dorsey saw as a lifetime's experience of oil multinationals such as Gulf having had "damn little interest" shown in their welfare and even being discriminated against by the United States government in their overseas activities—"they were sort of like motherless children."[37]

The chairman's deepest anger seemed reserved for newspaper leaks of the specifics of the Gulf admissions before the SEC and a Senate Foreign Relations Subcommittee "in callous disregard" of confidentiality. These were "disastrous" to his company, placing it in an untenable situation in the seventy countries where it had investments; they were also "seriously detrimental to our nation" since the countries and leaders involved in the payoffs were allies.[38]

Mr. Dorsey hoped the United States Congress would make overseas political contributions illegal so as to bolster the corporate will to resist solicitation and extortion, a plea which roused the curiosity of Senator Richard C. Clark (Democrat, Iowa):

SENATOR CLARK: You have already violated both American law and Korean law. What would one more law mean to you in this respect? Why would that help you?

MR. DORSEY: I am not speaking to the U.S. matter, I am speaking to the foreign matter.

SENATOR CLARK: You violated U.S. law in your contribution to the Committee to Re-Elect the President.

MR. DORSEY: Are you saying I am a rascal and no matter what—[39]

American interests in Africa had been limited. A stable continent meant one that did its share in withstanding the overseas influence of international communism, protected sea lanes, and kept resources accessible. European colonial powers were clearly more reliable than liberation movements. At the time of the October 1973 war, over 70 percent ($2,254 million) of U.S. direct investment in Africa was in petroleum.[40] Gulf was the largest American investor in Angola, claiming to have spent over $200 million since it first began exploration in 1954. Its major discovery came in 1966. Other energy companies there include Texaco, Mobil, Standard of California, Sun, and Tenneco. In the mid-sixties, as Lisbon saw its finances being drained by its massive armed actions (complete with napalm and the corraling of people into strategic hamlets) against the increasingly vigorous liberation movements, it actively began to court foreign investors to open up its African "provinces," as it preferred to call Angola, Mozambique, and Guinea. All mineral resources were considered in the "public domain," that is, under the jurisdiction of metropolitan Portugal and not of its colonists. Mineral and petroleum company activities heightened, as did the dependence of the home country upon the revenues from its colonies for a "defense" budget primarily aimed at its own people. In 1971 Gulf appointed a former Portuguese ambassador to the United Nations and the United States, not an oilman but a staunch defender of his country's imperial mission, as chairman of Cabinda Gulf, the Angola subsidiary.

To Africans and others sympathizing with the colonists' struggles for independence, the oil companies and the Portuguese police state were partners in repression.[41] In 1970 President Nixon and Secretary of State Rogers reaffirmed their commitment to the right of self-determination for the people of the Portuguese territories and encouraged "peaceful progress" toward that goal, with private investment playing an important role.[42] In addition to such benedictions, the United States also gave economic and military aid to Portugal. It trained military personnel and maintained air base privileges in the Azores. Portugal was a member of the North Atlantic Treaty Organization, and a NATO naval standby command center was located near Lisbon.[43] American military supplies to Israel went through the Azores during the Middle East war of 1973, while oil supplies from Cabinda (Gulf) met all Portugal's needs enabling her to withstand an Arab economic boycott. Portugal had been repeatedly censured by the United Nations General Assembly for its discriminatory treatment of its African subjects, and for subordinating to alliances with foreign monopolies and their home governments the people's "inalienable right . . . to self-determination and independence and to the natural resources of their territories."[44] Portugal and South Africa cast the two negative votes. The United States, along with a primarily Western bloc, abstained. Meanwhile, Exxon, Sun, Amerada Hess, and others continued to negotiate with Portugal for exploration concessions. Subsequent successes of the resistance movements were to trigger an overturn of the mother country dictatorship, swift decolonization, and civil war in Angola. United States policy makers (with China) opposed a Soviet-backed faction while clinging awkwardly to positions which suggested that the prospects for human freedom on the Iberian peninsula and in Africa were of less clear priority than the fate of military bases, cold war postures, and crude oil sources. Daniel P. Moynihan, U.S. ambassador to the United Nations, predicted that if the United States backed down, "then the Communists will take over Angola, and thereby considerably control the oil shipping lanes from the Persian Gulf to New York."[45]

Gulf was eager to continue its operations in Angola, from which it derived about 8 percent of its overseas profits. The warring factions were eager to have the $500 million annual royalties. The company's payments, greater than the estimated $30 to $50 million CIA funds going to groups aided by South Africa, were ending up in the treasury of the government in Luanda established by the Soviet-armed and Cuban-aided Popular Movement for the Liberation of Angola. For a brief period Gulf put its payments in escrow, as suggested by the United States government, until there was a government "recognized by the world community." The Luanda government was ultimately accepted, sometimes uneasily, by many Western European and African countries. As the United States was forced to reappraise its hard line position, Gulf, which insisted that "we would have no trouble working with any government in Angola," received a green light from Washington and Luanda to prepare to resume drilling.[46]

A comparable situation has held in South Africa. Caltex, (overseas subsidiary of Socal and Texaco), Mobil, and Exxon dominate refining and marketing. And now many majors and independents are busily searching onshore and offshore for oil supplies to end the country's dependence upon the Middle East. To South Africa, self-sufficiency in oil would end a drain of $200 million a year and also provide immunity from third world wrath and United Nations boycotts. The companies see themselves bringing economic stability. They do not support apartheid any more than they condone bribery; they follow the laws and the customs of their hosts. The boundaries of good citizenship for a multinational are not always easy to draw. The best paying and the supervisory positions are classified for white "skilled" workers. Mobil employment advertisements call for "European" truck drivers. Mobil and Caltex, along with other American corporations, are contributing members of the South African Foundation which lobbies in Europe and the United States to develop better understanding of South African ways and needs, including apartheid and investment.[47]

In Nigeria a civil war during the late sixties left the corporations wavering as to the proper, i.e., profitable, course. Close to American and European markets, and without any need for Suez transit, Nigeria had become the sixth largest oil-exporting country since the discovery of oil in 1956 and nationhood in 1960. British Petroleum and Shell had the major operations in the former British colony, where the crown had owned all subsurface minerals. Eager to see rapid development, political leaders had encouraged foreign investment, offering assurances against nationalization. Gulf, Mobil, Sun, Texaco, Standard of California, Phillips, Brown and Root, and Italian and French government oil companies responded. Oil became the nation's largest source of foreign earnings.

When war broke out between the federal government and the Ibos in the eastern region, some of the companies were able to maintain exploration and production. There were differences among them and some thought they could live with either side. At one point, the newly proclaimed republic of Biafra, where most of the oil was, seemed to be a plausible host nation. But the secessionist forces could not hold, federal troops recaptured the seized BP-Shell installations, a tanker blockade by the Nigerian government was becoming effective, damage to facilities was mounting, and oil production and income had plummeted. Then too there were new discoveries in the federal region and its offshore waters. And the British government was reluctant to jeopardize its Nigerian supply by having its corporation back a chancy Biafran rule. The course for most corporations was clear.

Nigeria was to demand better terms for its concessions (influenced by the Libyan settlement), and it also spoke of local incorporation of foreign firms which troubled the Americans who foresaw loss of their United States tax privileges. It moved towards fuller shares in the concessions. But it did offer greater security, including protection from guerrilla forays. The United States maintained economic aid to Nigeria; AID activities in the eastern sector were suspended. Public sympathy for the plight of Ibo refugees grew. Early in 1969 Mobil sponsored a visit to the United States of a Nigerian official to help counteract strong pro-Biafran sentiment. Once the strife ended, oil production made a quick recovery, and corporate activities stepped up, as did the intimacy of the partnership with government.[48]

The global corporations still welcome tax favors from home, along with diplomatic assistance, the military might—more for the caution it introduces in the calculations of other nations than for its use—and the occasional services of the Central Intelligence Agency or the United States Information Agency. The State Department remains an understanding and reliable ally. It will be recalled how the department had been instrumental in launching the provincial American industry on its international career. State had cleared the way for concessions and investments through an "open door" policy and then diplomatically had helped slam the doors shut once its "motherless children" were safely inside. Wherever the flag was needed—Iraq, Kuwait, Saudi Arabia, Iran, Indonesia, Mexico, Peru, Venezuela—there the State Department has intervened in support of corporate objectives against foot-dragging or questioning host countries and against meddling European nations championing their own oil interests. Back home it worked within the highest reaches of the national security apparatus to protect the industry from antitrusters, revenue agents, and downright enemies. Unaware of the sophisticated ways of the world outside and of how the nation's security rested upon the corporations teaming up for the common good with the full trust and power of their government behind them, such zealots wanted to institute lawsuits which would damage or destroy the painstakingly constructed house of oil. State used all its persuasive talents against such actions, which it argued would only discredit the corporations abroad and play into the hands of the Russians and of growing nationalist, often Soviet-inspired, movements seeking to expel the United States.[49]

As the producing countries grew restive with their percentage of the take from their own oil, the companies sought United States help for keeping the lid on the kind of profit sharing developed in Venezuela. State worked through the National Security Council and the Treasury Department to devise a 50-50 formula for increasing Saudi Arabia's share. The added revenue would emerge through a foreign tax credit system, discussed earlier, which shifted income tax payments by Aramco from the United States to the Saudi Arabian treasury. This model was then recommended by Exxon and Mobil for adoption wherever their brethren were under pressure:

> With its 50-50 slogan, it is attractive alike to governments and the public. Its central idea can be easily understood by the man in the street and it makes an immediate appeal as something essentially reasonable and fair. For these reasons it is a strong formula from a public relations standpoint. Also, it provides a firm basis on which to stand and therefore may be considered as perhaps the most stable formula available.[50]

A major attraction was that the bill for this public relations and the security of Aramco was picked up by American taxpayers, without their knowledge or representation.

To the State Department this was a small price for preventing the menace of communism from enveloping the Middle East to disrupt the flow of oil and impede European and Japanese economic recovery. Such measures kept in power friendly governments appreciative of their role in supplying the West through American oil interests. The corporations deserved all the support of their home government, for as the State Department said in a policy paper discussed with the oilmen, they "helped protect and preserve overall U.S. interests in the area, e.g., removal of the sources of Communism and attainment of overall U.S. policy objectives such as economic and political stability, increased standards of living and the development of Western orientation and democratic practices."[51]

The subsequent fall in the market price of crude was to threaten the legal justification for the tax credit which was based on artificially pegged posted prices "In effect," a staff analysis of the Senate Subcommittee on Multinational Corporations noted, "producer company income taxes had become taxes on sales, not on profits"; thus it became more difficult to justify company payments to the producer countries as eligible for credit as income taxes. Yet the original ruling was maintained. The international oil corporations were accumulating capital while paying United States income taxes at a rate averaging under 5 percent. In 1972, for example, Gulf paid 1.2 percent of its worldwide net income, Mobil 1.3, Texaco 1.7, Socal 2.1, and Exxon 6.5.[52]

The Internal Revenue Service is periodically under pressure to audit the modest returns and also to review the relationship between the posted prices system and the tax credit as applied in the Middle East. The mounting costs of the Vietnam war and the welfare programs of the "great society" were added catalysts for questioning such blatantly inequitable taxation and privileged administration. In 1967 Secretary of State Dean Rusk was reminded by John J. McCloy, who represented the big companies, as to the history and rationale of this arrangement and also about the proper function of his office:

I believe that the Department of State has a particular responsibility to make known to the Treasury Department the implications of its proposed attack on crude oil prices because the present system . . . was recommended to the oil companies and to the foreign governments involved by the Department of State and the Treasury Department. If the oil companies did not provide the necessary revenues by paying substantial taxes to producing countries large amounts of direct foreign aid might well be required.[53]

The government was suitably impressed. For 1974 Mr. McCloy's clients accumulated $16 billion of such credits.

Over the years the State Department came to accept that the industry had grown up and was now the best instrument for protecting the energy base of the nation. It abandoned its network of petroleum attachés and retained a minimum of independent experts at its command. The oil industry dealt directly with the two central sources—Saudi Arabia and Iran, keeping the State Department generally informed, but the need for direct involvement was no longer assumed. Industry objectives and national policy were interchangeable, two halves of the same whole. This mutuality was seen preserving both the economic well-being of the American people and their ideological commitment to the separation of economics and politics. As the department explained:

> It has generally been the practice over the years, and one that has been sought by both companies and the governments, that the basic relationships of an individual company to a foreign government are the exclusive province virtually of those two. The United States Government becomes involved only when there is some general problem that involves a number of companies or when there is a very special problem involving the security of people or a nationalization problem in which legislation is triggered.[54]

In this context the State Department plays the part of an international law firm. Its clients are the oil corporations, that is, the American people. As Richard J. Barnet has suggested, secretaries such as Dean Acheson and John Foster Dulles have functioned as bargainers negotiating from strength, gaining from adversaries maximum advantage while conceding as little as possible, appropriate qualities for pursuing a cold war or defending a corporate empire.[55] An Arthur Dean and a John J. McCloy, their counterparts who generally remained in the "private" sector but who also have moved in and out of public policy areas, shared similar characteristics, emerging from the same legal setting and often (as Dulles and Dean) the same firms.

Occasionally the oil firms are in need of guidance from their home country. After World War II, for example, the government cautioned the Aramco partners, under pressure from Saudi Arabia, that higher oil prices to Europe and Japan would undo the objectives of the Marshall Plan. They were reminded of the treatment which guaranteed their favorable entry into Europe. "It is ECA policy in every transaction an American oil company must be involved," Secretary Acheson explained. "Deliveries from sources other than the United States and possessions will be eligible only if made by American owned and operated companies." Although the corporations differed among themselves as to specific strategies, depending in large part whether they had an abundance of crude for their refineries or were crude short, they understood the benefits of low cost oil to the people of Europe. Caltex appraised the possibilities of "widespread reaction that we are squeezing and taking advantage of them in their desperate straits" which "might produce political consequences of very far reaching effects in the European nations, including representations to our own government, which would be embarrassing to us." The wisest course, Exxon concluded, was "to avoid anything which would look like monopolistic abuse. . . . Foregoing localized high returns would not be serious enough to interfere with satisfactory aggregate returns." It would be an investment in future relations.[56]

To ensure the implementation of this planning, the United States employed both the carrot and the stick: legal actions by the European Cooperation Administration to force back prices and the tax credit privilege to satisfy the cries of producer nations.[57] Such intervention notwithstanding, the basic pattern of industry autonomy was set. As the senior vice-president of Exxon summed up:

> Although in earlier years, the U.S. Government had participated actively, during the sixties there was little need for it to do so. The fact is that, up until 1970–71, there was no need for the Government's active involvement or intervention. Oil was flowing in ever-growing quantities at low prices. The American companies were participating effectively in the worldwide growth of the industry not only to their own benefit, but also to that of the U.S., of other consuming countries, and of oil producing countries. Moreover, the record plainly shows that the companies were able, through negotiations, to arrive at mutually satisfactory accommodations with equitable results for oil consuming countries.[58]

Natural resources had been mustered, technology harnessed, capital allocated and national needs served through private initiative. No public monolith had been required, just the occasional guidance of an understanding foreign office. The genius of the American political system appeared to have been applied successfully to global as well as to domestic arrangements. The "first world government," the private government of oil, was in complete command.

The immediate events culminating in the "energy crisis" of 1973 jolted the State Department and its industry co-sponsors, leaving them bewildered as to the missing factors in their global cleverness. Blaming the Arabs for the embargo was, in some respects, more than hastily improvised public relations. It was also a gut reaction, reflecting an inability to comprehend what had gone wrong, and not simply in relation to Arab price controls and the embargo. Neither State Department geopolitics nor corporate computers had sufficiently reckoned with the cumulative intensity of historic forces symbolized by OPEC. What were treated as fissures in a structure in need of patching, or roughness in an engine requiring tuning, were fundamental challenges to the principles underlying the private world order. A quarter of a century earlier, a State Department paper posing alternative tactics for keeping the lid on the Middle East had said: "No absolute values are available in determining how the benefits from oil development should be divided. The problem is a philosophical one to determine in what proportion benefits should be divided between oil companies producing oil, people living over oil reservoirs, consumers using the products and governments."[59] Realists didn't dwell on ethical questions, however. And there was no need to discuss the factor of power in the equation since it was understood who ought to be and were the philosopher-kings.

As the showdown with the OPEC nations approached, the State Department hovered nervously in the background. Eager to be helpful, it didn't seem to have found too much it could do. It had been kept informed as to the broad diplomatic policies of oildom. It knew a great deal about the delicate balancing of production in the different Middle Eastern and North African countries. But it had concluded that generally it would be wisest if it wasn't privy to all the details, lest it be held accountable by Iran, Saudi Arabia, or possibly the American public, for the secret agreements within the industry to keep production down. When the issues promised to explode beyond corporate-producer negotiating channels, as when Iran wanted more offtake by the consortium to finance its military and economic ambitions, or sought oil at cost for its own national marketing, then State would urge the companies to try harder but without, of course, tipping their hand to the shah as to how Iranian production related to that in other countries and how it was fitted into global patterns. "Details on inter-company arrangements are still tightly held by the companies," James E. Akins, the State Department deputy director of the Office of Fuels and Energy (and later ambassador to Saudi Arabia) advised a representative in Teheran, "and should not be revealed to the Iranians."[60]

State was engaged in a balancing act relating to its own multiple responsibilities. United States policy saw Iran as an important military bulwark against Soviet aggression. It also wanted to keep Iranian oil flowing to the West, as it had during the attempted 1967 Arab embargo. Yet it was the pressure for military modernization —and the high cost of arms from the west—which provided a basic incentive for higher oil production. From industry perspective it was desirable for the United States to arrange alternative sources for financing. Meanwhile the oil companies and the State Department agreed that the shah's appetite for arms needed restraint. At a meeting in 1966 with the department, executives of Exxon, Mobil, Texaco, Standard of California, and Gulf expressed the hope and then received assurance that the American and British ambassadors would do whatever they could "to keep the lid on", while also probing in Teheran and then keeping the oilmen posted about Iranian diplomatic intentions.[61]

In all such dealings the United States was to stand ready to serve as a "good broker" where negotiations were difficult. It would remind the world that the corporations were American citizens in good standing. It would reassure first Saudi Arabia and then Iran that the United States would never discriminate against loyal friends. It would caution the oil companies against letting "the shah get his hands on" restrictive covenants among the companies. It would keep an eye on antitrusters who might want to play up such agreements, although it was confident that "they couldn't get very far" because of the exemptions given the oil companies when they patriotically agreed to enter the consortium. But if the term "restraint of trade" did circulate, "it could complicate our already distressing problems in Iran." But throughout, the State Department was pledged not to interfere in the business of oil, that is, how production was allocated throughout the world—the substantive issue at the heart of industry power and of much of the tension among producers.[62]

The State Department also kept a trained eye on oil companies at home who were not always convinced as to the undivided dedication to national security of their more successful international brethren. A number of them, including Standard (Indiana), Union, Continental, and Sinclair, were refusing to accept that the Middle East was already spoken for and were casting covetous glances at concessions in Iraq. The Iraq government had canceled some of its agreements with the Iraq Petroleum Company, the international consortium in which Exxon and Mobil were the American partners, because of unsatisfied grievances that it was keeping production below the growth rate allowed in the Middle East. There were charges that the company was plugging wells and not reporting findings. James E. Akins later conceded that the companies had not been investing in Iraq for years. "In fact they are disinvesting (although this is a very sensitive point and would be denied to the Iraqis). They are taking as much oil out of Iraq as they can while it is still there to take, but there is no question of growth or new facilities."[63]

When the newly formed Iraq National Oil Company sought other companies for developing the concessions, the State Department promptly interceded. It admonished the crude-hungry companies against such actions to gain access to Iraq's underdeveloped fields. Corporate negotiations over the canceled concessions would be weakened, and the intruder risked legal action by the older interests. The health of American foreign policy in the Middle East was at stake. Also threatened, incidentally, was international corporate control over Middle East production, for such intervention could only result in more oil being brought into the market than the planning of the giants viewed as desirable.

The staff report of the Senate Subcommittee on Multinational Corporations summarized what happened next:

When it appeared that Sinclair was on the verge of making an offer to the Iraqis, Arthur Dean, the attorney for the American IPC companies, asked Under Secretary Averill Harriman to have the Department urge Sinclair not to proceed. In a meeting with State Department officials the American participants in IPC described the IPC bargaining position as one of take it or leave it. The Department subsequently persuaded Sinclair against making a deal with the Iraq Government. Again in 1967, when the Iraq Government sought bids from foreign national oil companies such as ELF and ERAP (French), the Japanese and ENI (Italian), the State Department was asked to intervene with the foreign governments to protect the IPC position.[64]

Thus the State Department helped keep Iraq's potential income down and its oil from flowing to consumer regions. It had pressured American companies and had, at the instigation of the international oil corporations, threatened economic retaliation against foreign consumer countries whose national corporations tried to muscle into big oil territory. "After careful consideration of the dangers of alienating the government of Italy we have gone to great lengths to support Iraq Petroleum Company against depradations by ENI."[65] One further achievement, rarely mentioned in State Department releases but not atypical in the history of its petroleum-soaked cold war, was Iraq's welcome of the Soviet Union's entry into its fields. This was followed by the export of Iraqi oil to Eastern Europe.

The State Department sought to play its customary supportive role in protecting corporate involvement in Libya. But the patterns were more complex and the benefits of the assistance more ambiguous. The growing dependence of Europe upon its low sulphur oil had given Libya confidence, and much of its production was in the hands of independents eager to expand rather than modulate its volume. The United States had less leverage with a fiercely nationalist regime willing to defy its power and forego oil revenues, if necessary. Libya's posted price demands, first from Exxon and then Occidental, were higher than other OPEC nations had dared make them. The companies resisted. But Occidental was under the double pressure of a government-ordered cutback in what it could lift and a refusal by Exxon and others to replace such oil. When in 1970 Occidental finally conceded a sizable increase in price and in tax rate, the majors did not mourn. But the industry was split, and all the producers could see this. The companies then expressed some alarm over the impetus for new demands everywhere. They now sought to act collectively, sharing oil where needed and only bargaining with all of OPEC for a simultaneous settlement.[66]

Big oil was not adverse to higher prices. Indeed, properly arranged they could mean only higher profits in Europe and Asia. And as imports became more necessary back home (it was only time before the controls would be eased or removed), the price consequences could only be beneficial. What was disturbing was a succession of unilateral actions which might remove price initiative and production allocation from the jurisdiction of the corporate planners.

The State Department was then called upon to reinforce the counterstrategy before the Justice Department for the right to erect a "safety net," whereby producers would protect one another against producer government retaliation through cutbacks, and to negotiate in unison, backed by such industry bodies as a London Policy Group. State was also requested to appeal to the more amenable Persian Gulf producers "to moderate their demands" and "to engage in fair bargaining practices." The department had taken the position that the Libyan demands were reasonable and that the industry would do well to concede gracefully what it could not forestall. The State Department had also recommended, at the urging of Iran, separate negotiations with the Persian Gulf and with the North African and other countries. Ostensibly both positions weakened the resistance of the multinationals. John J. McCloy said that "we weren't too much impressed, if I may say so, by the attitude of the U.S. government." It is quite possible, however, that State's presumed blundering meant that it was taking the initiative for the industry. Whether deliberate or not, the result was new high prices and new profits for all concerned.[67]

In the fall of 1973, Libya nationalized 51 percent of the fields controlled by a number of the giants, including Mobil, Exxon, Shell, Arco, Texaco, and Standard of California. The affected companies immediately warned other companies from buying such "stolen oil," at least not until fair compensation had been arrived at. The New England Petroleum Corporation (Nepco), the largest single supplier of fuel oil to utilities such as Consolidated Edison in New York, was warned by Texaco and Standard of California of legal action if it continued to purchase oil from the Libyan

National Oil Company. A tanker contract was canceled by Calso, and Nepco had to find alternative transport at several times higher rates. The new costs were passed along to consumers. The State Department advised it against using Libyan oil, suggesting the harm to American policy that would result; according to Nepco, the telephone call from State came a half hour after comparable messages from the two majors. Another importer who had also purchased Libyan petroleum found himself pressed by the corporations, again with the support of State, and decided it was expedient to go along. The Libyan crude was resold to Eastern Europe.[68] Thus American homes were insulated from the dangers of burning nationalized fuel. It was at this time that President Nixon delivered his warning to the Arab world about their likely loss of markets and other consequences if they raised prices, expropriated installations, or otherwise sought to emulate the actions of Iran a generation earlier.[69] No specific mention was made of a return of the CIA. Not long afterward Libya completed its moves to gain 51 percent participation or complete nationalization of all oil holdings.

Once the 1973 embargo and the parallel price escalation were in motion, public shock within the United States over their apparent impact demanded a show of responsiveness by the political process. Government and industry leaders both recognized this. Thus the president took to the air to assure the people that the situation was in hand, there would be no havoc, and their energy future would be bright "for all time," if the industry-favored proposals for strengthening domestic sources of supply were enacted.[70]

The oil corporations, meanwhile, admonished the State Department and the White House against attempting to force down prices by international consumer-producer confrontation or drastic cuts in consumption. Such efforts were not likely to succeed: the resources and cohesiveness of the OPEC nations would allow them to outwait such responses. Besides, oildom's immediate fear then was neither of high prices nor of participation nor even of nationalization. Public government's contribution should remain keeping "an atmosphere of cooperation," explained the chairman of Standard of California. "Who owns certain assets is not the important thing. The international oil companies still have a role to play in the Persian Gulf. The important things were access to oil and the incentive given us to go on producing it and developing new fields."[71] Oilmen debated the safest course for the protection of their supply lines but tended to agree that public government should keep out of direct negotiations on oil with the producing countries. Instead it should lend complete support to the private corporations in the new delicate power relationships and maneuverings. The latter obviously had to accept OPEC as partners in a still highly profitable relationship. What was to be avoided was a junior partnership where they lost control of the critical decision-making at the heart of the private government of oil. Fortunately, the State Department understood and concurred.

> We should be very careful in taking any action which might fundamentally alter the present market orientation of the oil industry. A market economy may not be perfect, but, like democracy, it seems preferable to the alternatives. A situation in which governments are negotiating directly on price and supply might permanently preclude any reduction in price brought about by the market forces of supply and demand. . . . It is not our policy . . . to negotiate prices intergovernmentally because we do not know . . . that we bring to the bargaining table more than what the companies do.

The Treasury Department had a comparable view of its limits: "unless we understand exactly what is taking place during the process of negotiation we really are entering into the process after it has all been concluded. We do not have the expertise, I believe, in the government to understand the intricacies of foreign trading operations of these individual companies."

Asked whether the State Department should not be the agency to protect the public interest during corporate negotiations with the producing countries, "to see what is negotiated has something to do with benefits to the average citizen of the United States, consumers, as well as the company," the acting assistant secretary of state for economic and business affairs defined the perimeters of public authority.

> That depends on what your criteria are for making that kind of judgment. I do not think we are in a position or in the business of making judgments on questions such as price except in particular circumstances or where there is an opportunity to exert influence. On that

and questions of equity interest or other kinds of arrangements or questions of compensation we make rough kinds of judgments but we are not in the position to judge that a particular transaction or the details of a particular transaction are or are not in the public interest. We do not have that kind of mandate. We do not have that kind of authority. We do not have that kind of government. We do not have that kind of economic system. You may not like that but that is the way it is.[72]

While the American government worked for a diplomatic settlement of the Arab-Israeli conflict, it continued to depend upon the international corporations to handle the "business" arrangements. Oil was procured from sources the companies judged most expedient, with some taken from non-Arab countries to compensate for the embargoed oil, and then allocated by them among the consumer nations. Corporate patterns of distribution and shares of world market were respected, as were the complicated categories of most favored, preferred, neutral, and embargoed consumers set by the Arab nations. Cuts in volume were prorated to minimize injustice to any one country. Beyond the urging "to bring as much as possible," there was no government instruction. Nor was there any public policy for dealing with world prices, unless the reiterated faith in the ultimate workings of the free market could be so considered.[73]

The Arab nations also relied upon the corporations. The latter had operations in the various OPEC countries and were ready instruments for the decreed cuts in production. They also still provided the needed markets. The oilmen were invaluable agents for administering the embargo and for policing all shipments and the ultimate destination of OPEC oil. In a cable to Exxon, Mobil, Texaco, and Socal (the four shareholders) which spelled out the embargo requirements of the Saudis, President Frank Jungers of Aramco reported that the Saudis were "entirely aware that this program would be very difficult to administer, but they are looking to Aramco to police it."[74] Since—as George Keller, vice-chairman of Socal and a director of Aramco, noted—Aramco "operates the port for its shareholders, is the one who has the computer programs and the clerks and the rest to do such a thing," it served as the "clerical arm . . . and . . . as a practical matter I see no alternative other than to cut off supplies to those parts of the free world to which we were permitted to continue supplies. Obviously it was in the best interests of the United States to move 5, 6, 7 million barrels a day to our friends around the world rather than to have that cut off."[75] Aramco was required by Saudi Arabia to stop all sales to the United States military and to turn over information from the four companies about all Saudi Arabia crude refined by them for the United States armed forces. Aramco reported that the Saudis were very pleased with its performance, regarding the company which handled the backbone of its economy as the nation's greatest asset; for the short run, the cutback might hurt Aramco's business, but there would be rewards in the future.[76]

The justification for compliance was that companies such as Aramco no longer had options. Before the October war and the embargo, King Faisal had warned the oilmen that "time is running out with respect to U.S. interest in Middle East, as well as Saudi position in the Arab world." If the companies did not get their own government to change its position regarding Israel and give full support to the Arab cause, "you will lose everything."[77] Aramco, now seeing itself somewhat as a "hostage," had to demonstrate its full cooperation. Otherwise Saudi Arabia would nationalize, and then the United States would be totally cut off from a major Middle East source. The companies did not want to lose the advantage of access and the privilege of working out special agreements which would give them favored treatment in the buying back of oil now controlled by the producing countries. The oilmen also urged the diplomatic representatives of the United States to raise their sights. The immediate tension could be of limited duration, while America had long-term needs which would increase. Saudi Arabia remained an ally; if such areas of contention as Israel policy and Palestinian rights were to be reviewed, its vast reserves could allow an easy doubling of production in the future. (At least one participant, the chief engineer of Standard of California, has suggested that Aramco welcomed the cutback on production during the last quarter of 1973, since earlier in the year it may have been taking oil at too great a rate for the health of a major field.)[78]

The oil corporations no longer were arbiters of the price of overseas crude. Nor could they be certain of their position at a bargaining table. But their integrated character still gave them the means for keeping the oil, and the profits, flowing.

They retained the backing of the United States as the chosen mechanism for national oil security. When the secretary of state sought to develop an alliance of industrial nations to withstand a future embargo, there was no suggestion that the corporations would be removed from their pivotal position or might be a factor in the hostility of the producers. The American diplomats tended to share the fear of a governmental voice in pricing and to accept the corporate view of the national value of their profits. There was minimum urgency to develop a national energy policy independent from that of the industry. The State Department seemed to have learned little from the crisis. If it clung to any guiding principle, it was that the proper function of government remained to create the most favorable climate for private investment abroad.

Enjoying the general blessing of the American government, corporations, banks, and consultants swarmed to the huge contracts under the national development plans of the newly affluent producers. El Paso Natural Gas was to build liquid natural gas plants in Iran, which in turn was gaining nuclear plants from France while loaning the latter $1 billion for a uranium enrichment plant in which Iran was to have a 10 percent interest. (The shah was also to advise American business to "become a little more aggressive and dynamic".)[79] Iraq, vocally hostile to Western capitalism, enlisted Brown and Root's talents for offshore terminals. Bechtel's engineers were to appear almost everywhere. Egypt was encouraged by American diplomacy to see the United States as a friend and to moderate its positions. Major corporations, including Exxon, Mobil, Standard (Indiana), and Atlantic Richfield were encouraged in turn by the Egyptian government to accelerate exploration and development activities, while assured not to worry about any antibusiness actions.[80] Shell was to build a billion-dollar petrochemical refinery in Saudi Arabia. The high technology promised development most rewarding for the egos of rulers, the careers of middle-class technocrats, and the exports of the industrialized West. Such projects could employ more of the petroleum locally, including for fertilizer. But while national plans varied, it was less clear that these priorities would improve the lives of great numbers whose immediate needs were for food, work, and land. And despite all the expressed alarm over the new $25 billion bill for imported oil, the United States was to enjoy a slightly favorable balance of trade. The United States Treasury Department, meanwhile, had minimum difficulty in persuading the fiscally conservative government of Saudi Arabia how prudent an investment were United States bonds.

Oil and the State Department have also been bedfellows during the search for public policy on the frontier issue of creating an international law of the sea. Here there have been strong competing forces, and the industry has not been able to assume that its goals would be accepted automatically, even by the State Department, as equivalent to the national good. After great bureaucratic controversy and the opposition of oilmen, who previously had blocked United States support for any study by the United Nations, in 1970 President Nixon pledged United States backing for international administration to develop and protect the seabed for all mankind. The industry was quickly reassured through State as to the true meaning of the diplomatic rhetoric intended for global consumption. Narrow coastal rule over natural resources by nation states and broad licensing authority to exploit all of the ocean under a kind of international mining code, with appropriate genuflection toward historic freedoms of the sea for all and toward contemporary ecological morality, would work out to the oil industry's best interest. International authority over 90 percent of the seabed would preclude the industry's having to deal with some hundred coastal states, each with its own rules, demands, and whims. Creeping annexation of the sea would be minimized, and expropriation by any one revolutionary regime unlikely. American technology and national strength would ensure that its oil companies predominated.[81] But the captains of oil have been wary of tightened controls over the exploitation of the deep sea going beyond the traditional prohibition against claims of sovereignty and the requirement of reasonable regard for the rights of others. And the evolution of genuine United Nations or international authority over the tremendous reserves of oil and gas known to be on the continental shelves of the world is a distinct threat. Oil corporations prefer dealing unilaterally with states whose sovereignty extends to the outer limits of the submerged continents, and have lobbied among foreign countries and their delegates to the United Nations for support of this position.[82] In the United States the corporations would then be able to continue the reassuring relationship maintained with the Department of the Interior, which was responsible for such leasing. They have warned that the United States cannot afford "the abdication" of jurisdiction over its own shelf, perhaps 10 percent of the world's total. "Geology supports the position," the National Petroleum Council adds, in a burst of geopolitical fervor.[83]

Significant among the many complications (fishing, hard mineral interests, passage in international straits) has been the United States military perspective. To the latter, submarine travel and surveillance missions by "scientific oceanographic" ships (the Russians lean toward "fishing trawlers") are facilitated by the most restricted definition of the continental shelf and of coastal state jurisdiction: "To keep ourselves in a position where we can fulfill our military obligations and the obligations of this country for its own national security . . . [we] feel it is extremely important to maintain as wide a breadth of freedom of movement throughout the world outside of the land masses in existing countries as is possible. And, of course, a large part of our deterrent at the moment rests on the use of underseas ships."[84]

While oil, the military, and other forces were wrestling within the executive branch to formulate the "national interest," the State Department fended off Congress and the United Nations by explaining that it was still too early to define precisely the machinery for international policy, and that the nation was keeping its "options open." "Nevertheless, exploitation must go forward during this period, and there should be due protection for the integrity of investments made in the exploitation of natural resources in areas which might subsequently be determined by international agreement to be beyond the boundary."[85] The oil corporations, meanwhile, were busily going forward.

At the Law of the Sea conferences, members of the United Nations have sought to hammer out general principles and create new institutions for enforcement. The United States and its allies (and the Soviet Union and its allies) preferred not to have such general debates since they are outnumbered by the "third world" states. The latter tend not to share American enthusiasm for multinational oil corporations, nor are they convinced that the United States Navy is necessarily a peacekeeping force in their behalf. Their own interests have been far from harmonious, and accommodation has been elusive. There is no assurance that they would be model stewards. Some have been hostile to any proposals which require them to surrender profits now or in the foreseeable future from their coastal oil in return for some equitable distribution of all marine resources under a yet-to-be-established international authority in which they will have a voice. Some, in the best state capitalist tradition, have sought protection for emerging commodity monopolies and cartels. Some have favored absolute sovereignty over territorial waters. Landlocked states fear that the naturally and the technologically privileged will solidify their hold over marine resources. Pollution of the sea and "waiting until all the environmental facts were in" were the luxury of the "haves." Industrial growth took precedence.

The United States has come to accept a twelve-mile limit to territorial waters and two-hundred-mile economic resources zone, as advocated by a growing number of nations. But it has insisted that there must be guarantees of unimpeded passage (for tankers and warships) in international straits and a respect by the individual states for international obligations regarding such matters as pollution. At each of these conferences the American delegates have emphasized to their colleagues the uniqueness of the search by 150 nations for a global authority to regulate the resources of over two-thirds of the earth's surface. The objective in creating the new future was justice—a turning point in history. But, it was added, the nations lived in the "real world" and had to be reasonable. It was "much too easy" for so many delegations to criticize the multinational corporations. The United States relied upon private enterprise for its essential commodities. If its delegates were to initial a treaty and recommend ratification by their government, there would have to be full assurances of secure and attractive conditions for private investment. Enforcement of the new authority's regulations against any recalcitrant company should

be by the individual nation: "not all the governments have a per-
fect record in the world in controlling multinational corporations,
but they will probably be more likely to take effective action than
the Authority." Nor should the private corporations be expected to
turn over all basic and valuable data about their operations to an
unproven authority, as "we know they do . . . in sovereign states."
The projected authority provided a first opportunity for all the
people of the world—industrialized and developing—to learn how
to live with the new world that was being born. But "justice does
not necessarily mean excessive redress for past grievances." The
United Nations General Assembly and its Law of the Sea conferences would not create the new organization "if it is to be struc-
tured and negotiated in such a way as to turn the tables on the
industrialized states."[86]

The search for consensus has continued. Oilmen have appreciated the zeal of the State Department in protecting them from
being forced to walk any plank at such less than hallowed convo-
cations. But the international executives often feel they have out-
grown their parent country and that they are expected to contribute more than they receive, including information to the CIA,
whose reciprocal offerings are often viewed as of dubious worth.
The constraints of multiple obligations which political leaders are
forever bemoaning seem plodding and national loyalties transitory,
set against their own fast-moving and cosmic dealings. Each day's
cable traffic and computer printouts reinforce the pride that the
oilmen are functioning on the frontiers of global integration. At
the outset of World War II the president of Caltex stressed the
need to appear pro-British and anti-Japanese because of Caltex
Chinese and British business, while the parent California company
"must take as strong a pro-Japanese position as possible" to maintain its Japanese trade. Texaco reluctantly dropped its board chairman because of his Nazi associations. Jersey Standard defended the
national gains from the elaborate restrictive arrangements with Germany's I. G. Farben, once these became public. But officials explained that the "company cannot constitute itself judge of the
rights and wrongs of international problems." Behind their planning to protect patents and corporate understandings was the belief that "technology has to carry on—war or no war."[87]

As industry's "one world" involvements have become pivotal for growth and profits, the search for a neutral island base without any encumbering national flag, described in a vision by the chairman of Dow Chemical in 1972, becomes more compelling:

> We appear to be moving strongly in the direction of what will not be really multinational or international companies as we know them to-day but what we might call "anational" companies—companies without any nation, belonging to all nationalities. . . . With the blossoming of a true world economy these multinational bees, whether they are American or British, German or French, Russian or Japanese, will be establishing more hives in the farther fields.

No longer would the corporation with complex international holdings and ownership be obliged to conform to the dictates of the United States government when operating abroad; nor would it remain, "through no choice of its own, to some extent an instrument of American foreign policy. In many nations the American corporation is seen . . . as an arm of what is called American 'imperialism.'" Once "nationless" it could be more effective in dealing with burgeoning nationalism and could operate as a citizen of the country in which it was doing business.[88]

If the drawn-out Vietnam war was justified in part to help keep Asia open and "free," it also slowed up exercise of that freedom by oil companies with one eye on Middle Eastern pressures and the other on Asian opportunities. Some of the most attractive sea-bed and island prospects are in waters between Taiwan and Japan contested by the People's Republic of China and Japan as well as by the Nationalists. The United States, which administered these islands (Senkaku) after World War II as part of Okinawa, has turned them over to Japan under the peace agreements, although the United States Navy continues to patrol the area. To Communist China these actions are an infringement upon its claims to Taiwan and to territorial sovereignty over the continental shelf. Determined not to let oil muck rapprochement, the United States has publicly warned its roving oil citizens that it would be inadvisable for them to explore in such troubled waters and that it would not intercede should their ships or rigs be seized.[89]

Companies such as Gulf have been restive under these constraints. "No oil company will withdraw from that part of the
world until oil has been found and we've forced a resolve." Finding oil would be a catalyst in the resolution of boundary and coastal line claims by the involved nations, one official reasoned, invit-
ing a showdown with the United States as well as the People's
Republic. But the American government has favored the idea of
aiding the Chinese develop their potentially vast reserves. It has
encouraged sales of sophisticated equipment and has sought to
open the door for corporate collaboration.[90] The Chinese appear
cautious about any technological transfer which will upset their
planning for balanced growth and self-reliance. They are interested
in development on their own terms, while aware of the economic and
political gains from exporting oil to such neighbors as Japan. Meanwhile, China relies upon coal for 85 percent of its energy needs.

To the international oil corporations, moral and political sensitivity toward Israel within the United States makes their activities
in the Middle East more difficult than if they could be truly transnational—pledging allegiance to no flag save that of private order
and profit. While they generally have been quite discreet in their
public utterances since the days of the conflict over the recognition
of Israel, the open hostility to that country among Aramco employees is well known. Aramco and other oil companies have been
leading backers of such groups as the Middle East Institute in
Washington and Americans for Middle East Understanding. The
latter, which is tax-exempt, seeks to promote understanding of
Arab culture and political positions, as well as the plight of Palestinians, among church, educational and business leaders. Free sub-
scriptions to its newsletter, *The Link*, have been promoted by the
company magazine *Aramco World*. American Near East Refugee
Aid, which is especially concerned about the needs of Palestinians,
has had substantial financial help from Gulf and Aramco.[91] In the
months preceding the October 1973 war, King Faisal stepped up
his warnings to the oilmen that they must inform the American
public and government of their "true interest" in the area. Aramco
cables summarized his feeling that continued unequivocal support
of Israel by the United States would mean not only the loss of the
oil concession but "was allowing the Communist/radical elements

in the Arab world to take over and sway the opinion of the Arab populus against the U.S."[92]

The code of public silence was breached in July 1973 by Standard of California, over half of whose worldwide production has been in Saudi Arabia as an Aramco partner. In a letter to stockholders and employees, its chairman reviewed the growing national requirements for imports—possibly 45–50 percent by 1980—the desirability of the prolific oil fields of the Persian Gulf, and historic cordial relationships with the Arab people.

> The development of their oil fields has been a story of mutual cooperation and benefit, reinforcing bonds of friendship between our two peoples that were forged decades before.
>
> There now is a growing feeling in much of the Arab world that the United States has turned its back on the Arab people. Many are said to feel that Americans do not hold in proper regard the national interests of the Arab states, their long history of important contributions to civilization, their efforts to achieve political stability and to develop sound and modern economic structures.
>
> All of this is occurring at a time when the Arab states—because of their vast reserves of crude oil—are becoming increasingly important to the future welfare of the Western world. The Arab states —and Iran—hold the key to the energy resources which fuel the industrialized nations of Western Europe and Japan. They represent the only major source to which the United States can look for any substantial increase in its crude oil imports to meet our needs.
>
> It is highly important at this time that the United States should work more closely with the Arab governments to build up and enhance our relations with the Arab people. . . .
>
> It is in the best interest of all of us who are citizens of the United States to urge our Government to work toward conditions of peace and stability. We must acknowledge the legitimate interests of all the peoples of the Middle East and help them to achieve security and a dependable economic future.
>
> Looking forward to the energy needs in the years ahead, it is in our mutual interest to encourage a United States government course which recognizes the importance of these objectives to the future of all of us—a course which above all seeks a peaceful and just settlement of conflicting viewpoints.

No mention was made of Israel.[93]

This statement was paralleled by private discussions between other Aramco partners and State and Defense departments and White House officials. The senior vice-president of Aramco reported that the people in government were attentive but did not, on the whole, see the need for drastic action, some feeling that King Faisal was "calling wolf." Nor did they believe that the United States could or would do much, if anything, to affect the Arab-Israeli conflict.[94] There was also a flurry of corporate advertisements suggesting that America reappraise its foreign policy if it wished to meet its oil needs. These efforts coincided with mounting pressures upon Aramco from Saudi Arabia and were beamed as much toward the Arab world, where Aramco reported they received excellent press and radio coverage, as toward the American public. They came at a time when the Defense Department was hinting about the possibility of showing a strong hand if the oil producing nations were to use an embargo to weaken the American economy and security. Once the war was under way, James E. Akins, now U.S. Ambassador to Saudi Arabia, in a "private eyes only" message, urged the Aramco partners to "use their contacts at the highest levels of USG [U.S. government] to hammer home point that oil restrictions are not going to be lifted unless political struggle is settled in manner satisfactory to Arabs."

Six days after the war began and before the oil embargo was imposed, John McCloy, representing the four Aramco shareholders, relayed a joint memorandum to President Nixon, warning against new military aid to Israel. The "free world" industry was operating without spare capacity. OPEC price demands, if acceded to, would seriously disrupt the balance of payments position of the West. "Any actions of the U.S. government at this time in terms of increased military aid to Israel will have a critical and adverse effect on our relations with the moderate Arab producing countries." Crude oil production for the United States would be cut back. Japan and Western Europe, critically in need of Middle Eastern oil, would expand their Middle East supply positions "at our expense. Much more than our commercial interests in the area is now at hazard. The whole position of the United States in the Middle East is on the way to being seriously impaired, with Japanese, European and perhaps Russian interests largely supplanting United States presence in the area."[95] Increasingly sensitive to re-sentiment in the Middle East over corporate publicity which appeared to emphasize how much was being spent "to lift 'these animals' up to a civilized level" (an angry reference in a speech by the foreign minister of Kuwait), Aramco recommended that the American oil industry "should be making special effort henceforth to accentuate positive aspects of Arab development and avoid appearing patronizing or superior in public statements and written PR."[96] Meanwhile, United States military support for Saudi Arabia and Iran, the largest producers on the Persian Gulf, remained important factors in keeping their leadership in power and, hopefully, pro-American.

Increasingly fearful that an energy crisis might spill over into an abandonment of Israel as well as into anti-Zionism and anti-Semitism, friends of Israel and organized Jewry countered with their own public relations and lobbying campaigns. They were troubled by government acquiescence to an intensified Arab boycott against businesses which dealt with Israel or had "Zionist tendencies," especially now that oil affluence offered such lucrative market and contract possibilities. Their central theme was that an energy crisis and Arab-Israeli conflict were separate issues, and that a resolution of the latter, even on terms most desired by the Arab leadership, would not change the oil situation. "The reason for the present oil shortage," argued the American Jewish Congress, "is economic greed by the Arab oil sheikdoms."

> It has nothing to do with political events in the Middle East. . . . The interests of the people of the United States and those of the oil-producing monopolists are not the same; as regards oil, they are contradictory. The American people want additional energy supplies at the very moment that Arab potentates are curtailing petroleum production in the interests of greater profits. . . . Israel is merely a convenient excuse. . . . It is much easier and safer to blame "Israeli imperialism" than to admit to a policy of ruthless monopolistic exploitation. . . .
>
> It is untenable and unacceptable for the public policies—and who knows—one day perhaps the domestic policies as well—of densely populated, complex and highly industrialized societies like the U.S. and Western Europe to be at the mercy of a handful of small sheikdoms and feudal kingdoms. Surely no nation can collaborate in the

surrender of its own sovereignty by the distortion of its national policies.[97]

The anxiety was intensified by a statement made by General George S. Brown in response to the question whether the United States would use force in case of another oil embargo. The chairman of the Joint Chiefs of Staff confided to a university audience that "Jewish money" owned American banks and newspapers and that Jewish influence keeps weapons flowing to Israel, despite the military's belief that the demands were more than could be realistically supported, with the "Jewish lobby" saying, "Don't worry about the Congress. We will take care of the Congress." Shortly after the furor and the disclaimers and reassurances that followed this disclosure, the military leaked a story that shipments of tanks to Israel were seriously depleting American strength.[98] Throughout, the State Department conveyed its sympathies to the oilmen. The two commiserated with one another about the constraints of domestic politics which they felt overruled State's professional judgment and the industry's commercial dedication, making increasingly difficult their common task of developing an overall Middle Eastern policy which would secure the flow of oil and protect the national interest.

Such experiences have convinced the companies that, however much they appreciate its availability for running interference, it is preferable not to have too close an identification with the United States government and the encumbering requirements of its national politics. Yet to go it alone also has pitfalls in a world increasingly demanding of global planners in whose reveries oil was to transcend all boundaries, including that of ideology.

The United Nations poses a special hazard. As militant third world countries have moved toward a numerical majority, great power domination and oil industry protection can no longer be assumed. Evidence of "neocolonial intervention" meets instant hostility. In 1972, for example, Salvador Allende Gossens, the constitutionally elected Marxist president of Chile, charged before the General Assembly that international corporate interests (International Telephone and Telegraph and Kennecott Copper) had "dug their claws into my country." Together with world banking

institutions and the United States government they had sought to
thwart his election, strangle the Chilean economy, and generally
subvert his regime because of its actions to recover the nation's
basic resources.[99] The economy had been heavily under American
economic control and the Overseas Private Investment Corporation had a commitment of nearly $500 million in investment guar-
antees against expropriation.[100] Nationalization of American copper interests had won unanimous support in the Congress, with
left and right joining in singing the Chilean national anthem after
the vote.[101] Allende was overthrown in 1973 in a military coup
which enjoyed considerable support from United States corporate
and political leadership. One of the intermediaries between the
CIA and ITT was John McCone. The former utility and oil construction executive, with financial ties to Standard of California,
who had also been head of the AEC and then the CIA, was then
a director of ITT while remaining a consultant with the intelligence
agency. In meetings with the CIA he had explored plans to create
economic chaos in Chile and also had conveyed ITT's offer of $1
million to help stop Allende. McCone took such steps, he was to
point out, because of his concern lest the rights of corporations as
citizens be jeopardized, as might the interests of American taxpayers, who, after all, were underwriting the OPIC guarantees.
The international relations director of ITT, who previously had
been in the State Department for thirty-five years, further explained
that there was an obligation to the people of Chile and the Western
Hemisphere, as well as to stockholders, "to not have another Cuba
in Chile."[102] A CIA director subsequently admitted that at least
$8 million was spent to "destabilize" the economy and make im-
possible the development of a socialist society and a popular government. As Secretary of State Henry A. Kissinger was reported
to have said in 1970 to the top security advisers of the United
States, "I don't see why we need to stand by and watch a country
go Communist because of the irresponsibility of its people."[103]
President Gerald Ford later justified such clandestine operations as
"in the best interest of the people of Chile and certainly in our
best interest."[104]

The Allende appeal prompted discussion about comparable
penetration of the developing world by ubiquitous oil corporations.
It led to the appointment by the United Nations Economic and

Social Council of a "Group of Eminent Persons" to investigate the role of the multinational corporations (most of the major ones were oil and American-based) in the development process and international affairs. There was also concern within the industrialized countries. Labor, for example, feared the export of jobs. Canada and the European Economic Community were concerned about their inadequate control of the investments from the "American challenge." And there were many questions about the impact of the control of some $268 billion in short-term liquid assets by these corporations in banks. A United States Tariff Commission study concluded that movement of only a small portion of the holdings, because of such factors as interest rate differentials and currency revaluation, could produce massive monetary crises globally.[105]

Corporate leaders attested to the benign influence of their enterprises as engines for growth. The president of the Royal Dutch Petroleum Company, for example, expressed understanding of the developing nations' fear of impairment of economic independence and the focus upon the foreign investor as the visible manifestation of the growing interdependence within the world economy. But he insisted that the giant corporation "had no privileged position in a political sense."

> The foreign investor can do nothing without the consent of the sovereign state. He is subject to prevailing company laws, tax laws, labour laws, foreign investment or exchange laws, and to endless others, including zoning, industrial and anti-pollution regulations. He will seek compatibility in the given environment and will conform even to unwritten laws, as the success of his operation depends on his being fully acceptable. The State holds firmly the power to reject and . . . the history of oil companies over the last dozen years amply bears this out. The multinational enterprise has proved adaptable and amenable to change, it is not a static phenomenon, and individual governments have the power to restrain or mould its activities within their boundaries to the mutual advantage of themselves and the company concerned.

He also saw competition and decentralized operations in the hands of local subsidiaries imposing constraints upon absentee control.

But despite such assurances, a generally critical report followed. It called for monitoring of the transnational corporation, the possibility of world taxation policies, codes of conduct, and possible United Nations technical aid to help the developing countries in their economic bargaining with the corporations.[106] Officially the United States welcomed the contribution to "thought-provoking discussion." But it deplored the assumption of an adversary relationship between the economic power of international corporations and the political sovereignty of host countries. Restrictions against corporate investment in natural resources were seen as discouraging the infusion of capital and the transfer of technology necessary for growth.[107]

One of the two Americans appointed to the UN panel was Jacob K. Javits (Republican, New York). Sensitive to the interests of the business and banking community, Senator Javits had sponsored legislation creating the Overseas Private Investment Corporation. (OPIC). The bulk of OPIC's support had gone to the big projects of major corporations. Gulf Oil was the largest single contract holder although the oil industry was not the dominant user of this subsidy. In 1973, the insurance portfolio of this United States agency contained $754,000 in convertibility risks, $2.1 billion in expropriation risks, and $2.1 billion in war risks. Corporations were also able to gain insurance against political risks in ventures made under contract with socialist countries.[108] To Javits, the multinationals have been, in the main, a major force for progress and peace. Their critics' misunderstanding of "economic realities" was based on a handful of abuses and unsubstantiated charges that the corporations favor domestic groups welcoming their presence, work against those advocating social reforms, and serve as instruments of home country foreign policies. ITT actions in Chile were admittedly reprehensible, resulting in the company's being denied OPIC insurance compensation on its $100 million coverage of its book value investment of $160 million. But, Javits felt, such behavior was atypical. Ignored were "numerous examples of oil-producing countries forcing their foreign policy objectives on oil-consuming countries through multinational corporations headquartered in those same consuming countries." Any "suffocating surveillance" of the corporations could only boomerang against the developing countries. Home countries could not be expected to keep out of disputes between the corporations and the host countries as the report recommended. On the contrary, while against mandatory termination, the senator saw it as "entirely proper . . . for a home country to review its aid program . . . in the case of a country that has expropriated unfairly the property of home country nationals." Nor could such countries expect developed countries to grant them soft, long-term loans or the international lending agencies to meet balance-of-payment difficulties caused by the use of their scarce capital for nationalization of oil and other multinational corporation property.[109]

Such defense was encouraging to corporate leaders who sought international cooperation but instead found their goals misunderstood and their flanks beleaguered. But how adequate could such protection be against the intensified pressures of people who doubted the contribution of giant private enterprise for their futures and who viewed them as exploiters rather than as collaborators in development? However global the ambition and grasp of the oil corporations, the United States was still their major base. An earlier intervention of the American government had replaced domestic industrial chaos with a self-governing order. It had thus successfully integrated the corporate and the political, using its power to ensure that the planning of the emerging private government was binding upon the American political economy. In the immediate future, security still required a home government appreciative of oil industry contributions and needs.

# 6

# Partners in Development

Within the United States, the energy industry continues to draw support from a federal bureaucracy that is sympathetic, captive, innocent, or incompetent. Central responsibility for managing energy and natural resources for the benefit of the people has rested with the United States Department of the Interior. Its jurisdiction and activities touch upon a great many areas critical for the development and conservation of energy. Its functions range from the gathering of basic energy information and the supervision over public lands to the administration of oil import policies and the stimulus of research for alternative fuels. With respect to the management of publicly-owned mineral resources, it is expected to assure the orderly and timely development of resources, protect the environment, and secure for the public a fair market value return on the disposition of its resources.

To a disturbing extent Interior's performance has been most consistently shaped over the years by the assumption that it is holding public lands (up to one-third of the land area of the United States and the continental shelf) for disposal to private claimants. It has found itself uncomfortable in dealing with broad questions of public policy for energy. And conservation has often been, both historically and at present, an afterthought.

Interior's working perspective thus has kept it a partner in development, responsive primarily to the needs of the private government which controls energy. It is an ineffectual guardian of the public domain and insensitive to the long-run public interest in the development, use, and conservation of energy resources. In many respects it serves as the first line of defense of private indus-

146

try, and its personnel act as the "fifth column" within public government for keeping prices up, profits secure, and private controls of energy insulated from public accountability.

As administrator of American offshore leasing activities, Interior has opposed internationalization of seabed resources. It has "worked hand in glove with the oil companies who made it clear that, insofar as offshore operations were concerned, they preferred doing business in the same old way, namely bilateral negotiations with individual governments."[1] When the Senate Committee on Foreign Relations held hearings on United States policy for ocean space, Interior personnel sat at the elbow of industry, acting, noted Senator Claiborne Pell (Democrat, Rhode Island, a leader in this area who had also encountered the alliance when representing the United States at the United Nations), "as a lawyer for the petroleum interests."[2]

The Interior Department remains beholden to the profit mechanism as the surest guide for the development and allocation of resources. In 1975, when weighing accelerated leasing of the outer continental shelf as opposed to limiting energy use, Interior reasoned that "as long as the total cost per barrel of OCS oil is less than the price of oil, it is better to increase OCS production by one barrel than to conserve an additional barrel through mandatory conservation measures."[3] As long as the government gets a percentage of the revenues from the leasing of public lands for oil and gas, few other questions are encouraged. The Treasury received over $20 billion in oil revenues from the federal domain during the two decades preceding the 1973 energy scare. Interior itself has been a direct beneficiary; it gained over $500 million from the outer continental shelf for use for departmental programs, lending further weight to the charge that it functions more enthusiastically as a promoter of land sales than as a defender of the public trust and a regulator of private forces.

During the outcry over the oil blowout in the Santa Barbara Channel in 1969, it became apparent that Interior had never developed the knowledge and will to appraise the ecological implications of such drilling. Its primary public concern had been the revenue it obtained for the federal treasury. (The successful joint bid by Gulf, Texaco, Mobil, and Union for the parcel on which Union's ill-fated offshore drilling platform was to be located brought in $61 million; total industry payments in the 1968 channel leasing came to over $600 million. And there was a one-sixth royalty on the market price of each barrel of oil.) The year before the blowout Interior had vigorously opposed the creation of a series of marine sanctuaries along the Santa Barbara channel and the entire coastline. The intent of the legislation was to halt offshore drilling until a master plan was developed which recognized conservation, recreation, fishing, navigation, and aesthetic factors as well as oil drilling. Interior argued that it had developed adequate procedures for coordinating multiple perspectives for resources development and it was taking every step possible to regulate operations and placement of oil drilling platforms to avoid pollution. Thus, "this prohibition is undesirable because it would restrict the recovery of valuable and needed minerals and would also curb a substantial income to the Federal Treasury from bonus bids and royalty payments."[4]

The oil industry was ready to drill and Interior officials were eager to resume leasing, despite the organized resistance of coastal communities fearful of ecological and aesthetic consequences. Local officials who felt rushed by Interior were assured there was nothing to fear, at least technologically. Shutoff devices had been perfected and were foolproof. The assistant secretary of the interior also warned them that the industry, having invested millions in exploring the channel, "probably would raise a lot of flak" if federal leasing was further postponed.[5] During the cleanup of the oil slick, the president of Union told how the industry had prepared for accidents and how his company had quickly closed in the well. The seepage then came through the sands or fissures in the earth's crust. The fault was in Mother Earth, "who is always teaching us new things." It was not reasonable to expect "mere human beings" who depended on her geological "uniformity" to anticipate an uncontrolled flow of such magnitude. After watching attempts to gather up the oil, he realized that neither Interior nor industry had the proper apparatus for the ocean. The desecration of the offshore area was unfortunate, but "we should give this thing a little perspective": in contrast to the Long Beach crime and accident rates, no one was killed. Union, which spent an estimated $10 million on the cleanup, would not drill where it was not in the best interests of the people in the community and the country. The federal government had no investment of any consequence in this joint venture; yet its rate of return was already gigantic, and its overall income once the structure had been depleted would be greater than that of the four operating companies.[6] To the oilman, as to Interior, the people were obviously getting something for nothing.

"Santa Barbara" provided a rallying point for a new generation of environmentalists, often recruited from the prosperous and the "apolitical" or conservative. Earlier, the fears of their predecessors could be described publicly by an oil association official as "products of an active imagination linked to an uninformed mind."[7] In a similar vein, a major company executive had once warned at a national conference on pollution that "it is not just idle talk that industries do very definitely assess the air pollution control policies of a community, among other factors, before deciding on the location of a new plant or the expansion of an existing one."[8] But it was not longer judicious public relations to express such views, however strong the feeling against California's "no growth kooks" and national "ecology freaks." To counter the enthusiasm of the "environmental extremists," the industry's Western Oil and Gas Association subsidized university research (a major grant of $240,000 went to the Allan Hancock Foundation of the University of Southern California), which was then used to bolster company claims that the episode was exceptional and that there was "no irreparable damage to sea life on the beach."[9] The oil companies also underwrote a publicity campaign for the city, initially costing $70,000, to help revive a falling tourist trade by emphasizing the beauties of the area and insisting that its beaches, above the high tide line, were as good as ever.[10]

Studies of full chemical and biological damages to the sea bottom and marine life were played down.[11] To the industry, marine sanctuaries, state or federal, were "detrimental." The nation's real goal, said the American Petroleum Institute, "should not be preservation . . . but proper development and use. The U.S. resources are not so vast that we can much afford [the] luxury of dedicating areas to non use." Then too, governmental limits as to where drilling can take place "permanently impair the innovative economic process whereby many individuals making individual decisions assure the most productive development of resources."[12] Nor was governmental exploration a quicker, more productive, or less expensive solution, the president of Humble Oil explained for the benefit of any converts who might be tempted to equate such socialist notions with the public good. "One of the great things about the system we have in this country is that anybody that wants to has the opportunity to get into the business. That takes capital, large amounts of capital," but if all activities were in one organization, the knowledge, experience, and different ideas of "countless companies . . . constantly competing with one another" in the chase for oil would be lost.[13]

To preserve this spirit and also energy self-sufficiency for America, in 1974 the Nixon administration let it be known that it was preparing about 1.6 million acres (reduced from 7.7 million) for leasing along the southern California coast. It was assumed that the sales might bring in $1 billion to $2 billion for the government. The state's Coastal Zone Conservation Commission, created in 1972 through a hard-fought and industry-opposed referendum, sought a delay in lease sales until it could complete its conservation plans supportive of the stringent environmental standards adopted by the state's voters. This stance was supported by the state legislature and many local governments. But a representative of the Interior Department told the commission that his agency would not honor the request. "To stop the world until those studies were done would mean we wouldn't hold any of the (outer continental shelf) lease sales that we have planned. We may lose a year's time in the effort of an entire industry." When Arco presented plans for additional wells, without indicating the onshore facilities that would also be needed, the state opposed this piecemeal approach which cumulatively would make a mockery of coastal planning. When Exxon sought to build a $20 million oil-processing and storage complex near Santa Barbara for its offshore production, the state commission said that to minimize the despoliation of the coast through the proliferation of such installations it preferred consolidated facilities. Exxon's initial rejoinder to the denial of a permit was that rather than comply with such public planning it would handle processing out at sea beyond the state's jurisdiction. And it would use tankers rather than onshore pipelines, thus creating new environmental hazards in the transfer of oil. Interior, meanwhile, made clear that the company objectives had its support.[14]

This attitude was consistent with long-standing bureaucratic responses in Interior to the concept of public hearings. As another official had advised in an earlier controversy over drilling in California, Interior "preferred not to stir the natives up any more than possible."[15] These governmental reactions have paralleled the attitude of the industry, which has repeatedly opposed public hearings on such matters. As the vice-president of Gulf Oil's exploration and production department stated in 1969:

> Gulf is concerned about the possibility that public hearings . . . may be unduly prolonged by enabling persons or organizations having no real or substantial interest in a proposed lease sale to unduly delay leasings of the outer continental shelf. This could be detrimental to the proper and timely development of these mineral resources by creating so much delay as to discourage Gulf and other companies from participating in these lease sales.

Leasing stipulations designed to protect the environment and other resources "could be considered so onerous and uncertain as to discourage the exploration for and development of these mineral resources so vital to the national economy and defense."[16] The spokesman for another company added that public hearings "would divert attention from important concerns involving national defense and anticipated fuel needs and provide a forum largely devoted to an emotional attack on the oil and gas industry." There was no need to intervene to change prevailing patterns, another executive assured: "The past history of the industry in cooperating with the government in the conservation of natural resources and protection of the natural environment is evidence of good faith and concern. Along with this record is a history of efficiency that we feel will be lessened by impediments that could be placed in the way of future operations by well meaning but less than knowledgeable individuals."[17]

Industry and Interior thus appear to have shared an interpretation of the public which excludes full disclosure of all the facts about leasing plans, motives, timetables, and alternatives; adequate time for participation by noninvesting citizens, experts, and environmentalists not on the corporate payroll; and meaningful coordination of planning at all stages of the exploration and leasing process with local, state, and regional agencies. Santa Barbara officials have protested that the two allies have tapped a special provision of the Freedom of Information Act to deny them the raw geological and geophysical data pertaining to projected drilling, including wells by Humble Oil of unprecedented depth and technique in the channel. In a Kafkaesque situation, the community would be asked to comment. But the solicitude for corporate privacy subverted the intent of the National Environmental Policy Act, whose passage had been spurred by the Santa Barbara spill.[18] Interior's assumption that the community involvement criteria of the law are met at the time of the drafting of environmental impact statements ignores the underlying decisions about energy development and leasing and the nomination of tracts made prior to such review. It excludes thoroughgoing analysis of the overall impact, including that of the extensive onshore facilities which may accompany offshore operations, and the social changes and costs in the daily lives of the immediate populace. Such participation comes too late for any open exploration of the premises, objectives, alternatives, and likely results of the national program for energy self-sufficiency and of the place of the specific plans for the outer continental shelf in this framework. No questions are asked about precisely how the resources from these public lands will be placed into the overall operations of the private government of oil. No mechanism is offered for reconciling the conflicts between development and regulation in the mandate of the secretary of the interior.

The actions of the Department of the Interior thus support a widespread suspicion that environmental impact statements are pro forma. Similarly, the spirit and intent of the Coastal Zone Management Act calling for federal actions to be consistent with state plans are undercut, for the decision to lease offshore resources "automatically locks the state and local governments into a program which must accommodate the growth caused by oil and gas processing plants onshore."[19] The proclaimed urgencies of the "energy crisis" and of "national security" have served as convenient escape hatches for the basic commitments for development already made before the communities were so informed. Such grievances have become the basis for complaints filed by the state of California and by a number of Long Island (New York) communities in United States district courts against the secretary of the interior.[20]

The outer continental shelf is believed to be one of the major sources for oil and gas yet to be developed. Both industry and Interior now see it as the key to meeting the nation's energy needs in the immediate decades ahead until the newer techniques for energy are ready.[21] To the industry, the new caution shown in the leasing of the more than 800,000 square miles of outer continental shelf in the federal domain since the passage of the National Environmental Policy Act is an "unwarranted overprotection of the environment."[22]

A coordinated advertising campaign hammers away at the beckoning energy from the sea: "the possibilities are out of sight. . . . The whole East Coast needs more natural gas. Let's not let millions of people suffer from an energy shortage while just beyond the horizon, out of sight, gas just sits there—on the Shelf." Consolidated Edison announces curtailments of natural gas sales and says pointedly that "every Con Edison gas customer has a vital stake in this offshore area being opened for exploratory drilling at the earliest possible date." Mobil, which cites the University of Southern California study to argue that environmental damage was minor and temporary, dismisses the judgments of those who "make a real bugaboo about offshore drilling." It warns that "the choice is clear; more offshore oil and gas, or greater dependence on high-cost, politically insecure oil."[23]

The oil and gas industry publicizes its readiness to invest in these activities. It radiates confidence in its ability to respect the birds, the fishes, and all of marine life and to master the technology for minimizing blowouts and spills. Indeed its multicolor messages suggest nature flourishes under its benign stewardship: oil derricks stimulate fish to spawn, just as road building projects have opened up forage areas and migratory routes for moose. Should, perchance, there be a spill, the American Petroleum Institute has studies on spills and beach cleanup and it offers literature for the rescue of waterfowl who have been incapacitated. And if international underwriters now refuse to insure offshore operations against the uncertainties of pollution damages, corporations such as Exxon will provide their own.[24] Should the "unanticipated" occur, those with specific damages have recourse, the industry reminds its critics. Claims from the Santa Barbara spill ran into the billions. Thus, Union, along with Gulf, Texaco, and Mobil, ended a legal battle by making a $9 million out-of-court settlement with the City of Santa Barbara, the state of California, Santa Barbara County, and the city of Carpinteria. In an earlier and separate settlement the companies paid $4.5 million to beachfront property owners who had filed $105 million worth of claims in a class action suit. Each company was also fined $500 after pleading guilty to one count of criminal pollution. The municipal court dismissed 342 other counts stemming from the Santa Barbara blowout, explaining that the companies had already "suffered sufficiently" from the civil judgments against them.[25]

Oilmen tend to play down the caution of scientists and the warnings of the Council on Environmental Quality that it is the routine production of oil and gas that presents considerable environmental risk.[26] Despite the public alarm over tanker disasters such as the crash of the *Torrey Canyon* off the coast of England in 1967, the attention called to the thousands of less dramatic spills routinely occurring each year, and the potential for mammoth spills by the more vulnerable and largely untested supertankers several times the size of the once-considered gigantic *Torrey Canyon*, the industry has emphasized approaches to biological toxic damage that are more clearly cosmetic than curative. Dumping and loading practices by tankers and refiners, long ignored by the industry, have also been major factors in making oil one of the major ocean pollutants. (The charter system, the "flags of convenience" registry—by 1971 over 80 percent of all tanker tonnage owned by members of the American Petroleum Institute was under foreign flags—and uneven enforcement all help to obscure responsibility and shift pollution costs to coastal communities. The *Torrey Canyon*, for example, was owned by a "Bermuda" corporation, on long-term charter to Union Oil and on a voyage charter to British Petroleum.) The consequences have been vividly described by Thor Heyerdahl who crossed the Atlantic in 1970: "Clots of oil are polluting the midstream current of the Atlantic Ocean from horizon to horizon. . . . During the 27 days of sailing so far, oil lumps in varying quantities have been observed every day. . . . It is entirely possible that the pollution area spans the entire ocean, from the coast of Africa to the coast of tropical America."[27]

Much emphasis is placed by the industry on the higher costs for such exploration and drilling. Less mention is made of the tax subsidies they tap and of the much greater anticipated production per well, making overall offshore costs less than those of onshore production. That the corporations are eager to stake out these coastal waters is clear. But the production and pricing plans are not spelled out for the public or the government. One can only conclude that these will be integrated into the larger timetable of the industry, with controls over prices and allocations for this new oil and gas from public lands set privately and shielded by the myth of the marketplace, while the Department of the Interior looks on from the sidelines.

The corporations have generally taken the lead in indicating the regions they want to see the department open, then suggesting tracts which should be put up for leasing. Under the thirty-two lease sales between 1954 and 1973, bonus payments received by the federal government totalled $9.8 billion and royalty payments $1.4 billion. Lease sales were reduced and then stopped for a few years after the 1968 sales when the department reviewed industry interest in the outer continental shelf, national energy needs, and its own casual policies.[28] A new leasing schedule was developed, although environmental considerations were still largely ignored until the Santa Barbara disaster blew ecology into the political arena. Meanwhile, investment capital and drilling rigs went overseas for the friendlier and more profitable explorations.

Under the Nixon administration's "project independence," leases for ten million acres were to be put up for sale in 1975—more than the total acreage leased in the previous twenty-year history of the program. In 1974, the undersecretary of the interior instructed the Bureau of Land Management and the Geological Survey that

he wanted a "firm leasing schedule laid out that definitely includes
. . . ten million acres leased in 1975—not just 10 million acres
offered" and that sales were to include both Alaska and the Atlantic.[29] The most promising leasing for a future supply of oil and
gas, as seen by the industry and Interior in the latter's *Draft Environmental Statement* released late in 1974, was in the western
part of the Gulf of Mexico, southern California, the Cook inlet of
Alaska, and the frontier areas—new to drilling—of the Atlantic
and the Gulf of Alaska. The 1,400 page mandatory report assembled available and generally familiar findings about the offshore
and onshore environment.[30] It conceded that "sooner or later a
major spill will occur where there is significant development of
offshore exploration and production. . . . We are certain that
thousands of minor spills will occur." A major spill would cause
massive destruction to flora and fauna, but there would be a natural recovery if the ecosystem was healthy. No estimate as to the
time needed for a biological recovery was ventured. "In those
areas where the ecosystem is already stressed, however, as is the
case in many areas within the coastal zone, a single catastrophic
spill could well create effects that are far beyond the natural recuperative powers of the ecosystem."[31] And there was no discussion of the cumulative effects upon the environment of a series of
energy projects, each of which separately may have posed only
"negligible" hazards.[32]

Throughout, the statement acknowledged the large gaps in scientific knowledge which limited the ability to analyze and predict
the impacts of outer continental shelf development.[33] But the prospects of lessened dependence upon foreign imports was welcomed.
While conservation and alternative energy sources were referred to
as policy options, there was minimum effort to link the outer continental shelf leasing to analytic discussion of alternative energy
growth rates for the nation, to a comprehensive view of energy
planning, or to the *Project Independence Report*, a Federal Energy
Administration evaluation of the energy situation and possible strategies for the period up to 1985 released the following month
(November 1974).[34] To Interior, the magnitude of the nation's
energy demand gave the American people freedom for "maintain-

ing general well being, guaranteeing national security, and providing assistance to the less well developed nations."[35]

To local officials in California, the Department of the Interior showed minimum interest in appraising the environmental unknowns and the full social costs of offshore development to their communities. As a drilling engineer warned, the emphasis was upon dealing with spilled oil—assuming that polluting the ocean was necessary—rather than upon technical training and legal requirements for preventing or minimizing blowouts.[36] Standards of drilling performance remained tied to corporate definitions of economic feasibility. The scales were tipped toward drilling, despite high environmental risk and likely opposition at public hearings. The head of the U.S. Geological Survey had told Californians in 1970 that, "the die is cast" and that they might as well get used to the idea of increased oil production.[37] The "catch 22" cynicism of the federal concern for local participation was summed up in a statement by Secretary of the Interior Rogers C.B. Morton.

> Some critics have suggested that new leases should be delayed until coastal states can complete detailed plans for accommodating such onshore developments. I do not believe such delay is necessary or wise. . . . We must move ahead with new offshore exploration as soon as possible—if only to determine the full extent of these resources. We cannot afford to wait for action by the states, which have only just begun to establish mechanisms for coastal zone planning. And it is not necessary to wait, because no onshore effect will be felt until several years after a lease sale. Moreover, state and local governments can hardly do any detailed planning for onshore impact —until the exact location of oil and gas reserves are determined by actual exploratory drilling. . . . Let's get on with the job, together.[38]

Meanwhile, an internal memorandum within Interior suggested that the number one priority in filling the information void under the National Environmental Policy Act concerned the political climate rather than the ecosystem.

> *Reaction analysis and identification of local political and community power structure.* Identify the local and community power structures,

examine the official and unofficial local opinions toward offshore drilling. This need is emphasized by the public remarks presently being made by many area politicians and local interest groups. The unofficial analysis of the feelings of the community power structure is important in that most decisions are formulated at this level. The identification of the composition of community power structure will assist in educational thrusts towards these officials at a later time, with a possible softening of their present opposition to offshore oil development. Estimated cost: $50,000.[39]

The Department of the Interior still lacks adequate knowledge as to the extent and worth of the potential oil and gas. In place of careful, publicly accountable exploratory work, its limited surveying resources have led it to rely extensively upon the geophysical data gathered by industry. In the fiscal year following the Santa Barbara spill, the budget for the U.S. Geological Survey's reconnaissance of the outer continental shelf was kept at about $1.2 million, a quarter of what the agency had sought; in contrast, a major company then may have been spending anywhere from $10 million to $30 million a year to gather and interpret offshore geophysical data.[40] The Geological Survey purchases seismic data from oil corporations, who gather the information jointly and make it available to the government on a proprietary basis without industry interpretations and without disclosure for use by the public. The Geological Survey also purchases "speculative surveys" from private seismic companies who offer these findings on the open market.

To Interior, the most reliable advance information "is what people are willing to lay on the line to pay for it."[41] Estimates of the potentially recoverable oil on the Atlantic shelf have fluctuated dramatically. Geological Survey figures dropped from 114 billion barrels to less than 16 billion as the intensified leasing began— coming close to a National Petroleum Council calculation.[42]

Presale underevaluation by Interior is often startling. Tracts evaluated at a minimum of $25 per acre have elicited bids of $77 million and $92 million. A presale evaluation of $11.9 million drew a high bid of $212 million. Because the yield could not be gauged, it became impossible to relate potential production to national energy goals, assuming there were such publicly defined plans. After reviewing the record, Representative John D. Dingell (Democrat, Michigan) concluded that the agency would be "better off with a dice or a dart game." He added that he now understood why Interior was not startled at the magnitude of its miscalculations in shale leasing: the problems there were "kid stuff" and paled by comparison to the underevaluation of the outer continental shelf. Interior either was unaware or simply did not care. "The United States is the only country in the world that sells the public's resources without knowing what it is selling."[43]

Within Interior, the defense is sometimes made that, after all, it cannot do all these tasks independently—it is not in the oil business. A report of the General Accounting Office has raised "serious questions of conflict of interest" about the individual staff of the U.S. Geological Survey. A review of 1974 financial disclosure statements showed that 22 percent held stock in or received pensions from the private oil and mining companies which held leases whose value and operations are supervised by the agency.[44]

Interior has also lacked criteria, resources, and incentives for thorough environmental impact studies and for the meticulous supervision of preliminary exploration and their relation to outer continental shelf drilling. Its purchased data reflect interest in production, not ecology. Environmental impact studies seem routine rather than analytic. It has taken the political spotlight and court actions of ecological groups to counter some of the pressures of industry and its White House allies and to impress upon the agency the obligation to respect the full intent of the National Environmental Policy Act.

Until prodded by critics, Interior seemed untroubled by joint ventures among the major corporations and by the complex interlocks of producers and pipeline systems. In an effort to stimulate bids by smaller companies who had been discouraged from trying, Interior finally announced in the fall of 1975 what it called "a fairly revolutionary change," wherein it would not accept joint offshore bids by the largest companies for oil and gas leases.[45] It has generally accepted a bonus rather than a royalty bidding system, although the former accelerates the concentration of control of offshore oil in the hands of the majors to the exclusion of smaller companies who have the economic incentive to produce oil as soon as possible. Interior has ignored a Justice Department investigation of the antitrust implications of such joint ventures bidding in the Santa Barbara channel in 1968.[46] A California legislative study charged that five major companies worked together in violation of antitrust laws to divide production and bid jointly for the right to operate lands in the state domain: "In the production of crude oil (and the pipeline system) the companies act as though they were one gigantic California oil company forever exchanging information about production policies and making joint determination about how much to produce."[47] In a September 1972 lease sale, four companies provided 86 percent of the bonus money; 96 percent of the leases went to eight majors and joint ventures dominated by majors. In a December 1973 sale, four majors provided over 60 percent of the bonus money, and 83 percent of the leases went to eight companies.[48]

In sworn testimony in 1974, the chairman of Standard Oil of California described how major corporations met periodically to organize joint bids or, if these fell through, bidding agreements concerning state-owned oil. One meeting involved Humble, Atlantic Richfield, and his own company.

> You just put the number on the table—that is, on this parcel we want to bid $32 million. They come in and say, "No, we want to bid 34." This one comes in and says, "No, we want to bid 60." And then we would look at the geology jointly. Not all of it. And the experts would talk to the likelihood of finding $20 million or $40 million or $250 million or a billion. And this is not too precise, obviously. If we decided that we wanted to bid 32 [million] we tried to bring them down. If they are below us, bring them up. And sometimes they bring us up, and we try and reach a concurrence. If we can't . . . , then the one that wants to bid the high number is free to come out and bid completely by himself. That is part of the procedure.

The companies were not free to bid what they wanted if their negotiations for a joint venture were unsuccessful. "They can't go higher" than the top figure of the deliberations. What this shows, concluded a legislative consultant discussing the chilling of bids, is that "at best, when the offshore bids are opened, they are being opened for the second time."[49]

Interior's lease management efforts have been quite modest. Inspections are often inadequate. It never fully investigates reasons given by the corporations for shutting in leases; it has been casual about renewal of leases which have not been producing, and it has never canceled a lease for "wrongdoing."[50]

Meanwhile, U.S. Geological Survey statistics support the contention that there is speculative withholding of offshore production. Although new wells were being completed at a rate of 300 to 400 per year, completed shut-in oil-producible zones rose from 953 in 1971 to 2,996 in 1972 and 3,054 in 1973. Active oil wells declined from 5,704 to 3,814. A recent study has suggested that reducing flow from producing wells, slowing down drilling activities on wells nearing completion, and shutting in associated gas wells are further speculative tactics open to the industry.[51]

An intensified leasing program ignores the question of adequate drilling and pipe supplies, which creates further limits on all producers, especially the independents. Expanding leases beyond the capacity of immediate drilling and production could also lower the prices paid. There is also evidence that the major corporations now wish an extension from five years to ten years of the time requirements for development and also larger lease blocks. They would thus tie up more lands obtained in a presumably cheaper market.

In such a context, accelerated leasing of the outer continental shelf seems best designed to serve not a national energy policy but the major corporations eager to lock up potential resources which otherwise might fall under more stringent public controls or become part of a nationalized program which the energy crisis helped move into the arena of the politically discussable. Oil and gas will not be produced for some years under the present policies. But public options become considerably narrowed as corporate greed is once more given first priority in the name of consumer need. Accelerated leasing makes it more difficult for such a public agency, left with less desirable public lands, to serve as a yardstick experiment for providing the public with adequate and fairly priced energy developed with respect for generations yet to be born.

Even when the cash nexus is the chief criterion, the Interior Department is deficient. It has been eager to see federal lands leased. Yet it consistently underestimates their worth, despite the eagerness of coal brokers and energy conglomerates caught up in the coal rush. It seemed unaware that values for western lands were sky-rocketing in anticipation of the coal revival. For example, Mobil bid $441 an acre for a 4,000-acre coal tract in Wyoming; the U.S. Geological Survey had estimated its worth at $35 an acre. Similarly, Interior had anticipated receiving $5 million to $9 million for the 5,000-acre oil shale tract in Colorado. The winning bid from Gulf and Amoco was $210 million.

Federal coal leases often have been granted at very low prices and without competitive bidding. There may have been one offer and it was accepted. A review by the United States comptroller general's office of the leases granted in four states showed that 72 percent had one bid and 15 percent had two.[52] Interior has been certain the cause has been disinterest in coal. If there were evidence of collusive bidding, perhaps an advance agreement on upper limits, the department would not know about it—it's not in its field.

The department "traditionally played a reactive role," an internal report acknowledged.[53] Leasing generally has been "on the basis of industry expression of interest."[54] The government has rarely taken the lead in deciding which offshore or onshore area should be opened first. There has been no overall energy development or land use planning—at least not with a public perspective and public participation. Coal production requirements—the law speaks of "diligent development" and "continued operation"—have been unenforced. Energy corporations have held coal leases for many years at minimum annual rental. Several studies have shown about 90 percent of all leases on public and Indian lands to be inactive, most never having been put in production. The comptroller general generously recognized that "some of the lessees may not have had sufficient time to fully develop a mining operation and begin production." Some of the leases were held for over forty years, many for over twenty.[55]

These leases have been bought for speculation, evolving "from a privilege and a mandate to develop public resources to as negotiable a commodity as private land." Or they are being held for the future plans of the energy industry. Public resources are thus being banked in private industry accounts. The Bureau of Land Management in Interior has never moved to cancel a lease. Since these do not expire as long as there is coal in the ground, "coal leases are forever."[56] Renewal of the twenty-year lease in the past was "absolutely automatic if the lessee desired renewal." And, as the comptroller general also noted, the government's royalties on production have been quite low and until recently were not adjusted to varying extraction costs or the market value of the coal.

Reclamation requirements in the past have been modest, and the department has never faced up to the full physical implications of strip mining or to the impact upon the lives of people in the "new west," certain to emerge. Interior chafed under the environmental codes established in 1970 and has been casual about enforcement. Until very recently the department developed no thoroughgoing appraisal of how well the leasing concept was serving the public, either for maximizing fuel and revenue from the public domain or for larger environmental and regional objectives. Early in 1973, the secretary of the interior announced a moratorium on leasing so that his associates might begin to review the direction of the program and possible planning goals. The energy crisis conveniently intervened in this belated bow to the ecology movement, lending support to the industry view that this was no time to go soft on development. In 1975 the comptroller general reported that Interior was still not overly responsive to its earlier recommendations for greater diligence in setting leasing terms and development and reclamation standards. A year later the congress overrode the opposition of the energy industry and its bureaucratic allies, along with a veto by President Ford, to pass legislation to encourage bidding by smaller companies, to limit speculation by requiring lessees to initiate commercial coal production within 10 years, and to increase public royalties.[58]

Interior has granted leases and allowed corporate drilling in the buffer zones which ring the naval reserves in Elk Hills, Teapot Dome, and Alaska. These zones were intended as protection from siphoning. It thus undercut the United States Navy's efforts to prevent Standard of California from draining the oil at Elk Hills which had been set aside for national defense needs. The Office of Naval Petroleum and Oil Shale Reserves has found itself repeatedly under pressure to allow more oil to be taken by the California corporation which holds a portion of the reserve. Socal has also operated the reserve for the navy and owns the pipeline connected to the field. In 1970, President Nixon, ever responsive to California oil interests, proposed legislation which would provide oil from Elk Hills as compensation for terminating some oil leases in the troublesome Santa Barbara channel. This exchange would have opened up the reserve to increased production by both the navy and Standard Oil of California.[59]

The oil industry had long looked forward to the time when the stigma of "Teapot Dome" would fade sufficiently to allow the Alaskan naval reserves (NPR-4) to be transferred to the Department of the Interior. Although individual companies, such as Arco and BP, were concerned about improving their own crude supplies, there was no industrywide eagerness among the giants to unleash substantial new production in the twenty five years following World War II. Arctic sources could magnify what oilmen regarded in the sixties as their surplus supply conundrum. They would compound the task of placating politically clamorous regions while moderating liftings elsewhere. Exxon, which was to buy into the Prudhoe Bay discoveries of Arco, did not share its partners' sense of urgency. Critics within the industry speculated that the dramatic search for a tanker route through the northwest passage was a "slow boat" way of buying time in its commitment to the pipelines. What was generally desired was to have the naval reserve cornucopia, the size of the state of Indiana, together with the even vaster federal lands in Alaska, under a management clearly responsive to overall industry planning. Interior was the preferred instrument. Exploration of NPR-4 had ended in 1953, under orders of then secretary of the navy Robert B. Anderson, just as deeper drilling was about to begin.[60] By now the industry and Interior had strong geological evidence to support the "hunch" about the North Slope that was to lead to Atlantic Richfield's discoveries in 1968 just eastward of the reserve in the Prudhoe Bay area. Both were echoing the old refrain that "naval reserves" were an anachronism, given the nature of modern warfare. Proposals for intensive naval development of oil and shale in the reserves were repeatedly sidetracked. One such plan, as late as April 1973, "disappeared in the White House without a ripple."[61] Meanwhile there were pressures, from the new state government, among other sources, to restore the naval reserves in Alaska to the public domain (and thus to private leasing) and to get substantial leasing under way on the federal lands and then on the lands being chosen from the federal territory under the generous terms of Alaskan statehood.

There were other stumbling blocks to integrating Alaska into the private government of oil. Prevailing mythology had depicted "our happy natives" content to hunt, fish, and tell folktales during the long winters. But more perceptive observers reported anger, "Eskimo Power" sentiments, and rifles in the remote villages of the original inhabitants. And there was sympathy for their cause among knowledgeable people in the "lower 48." Leasing had been frozen in response to the growing unwillingness of Eskimos, Indians, and Aleuts—who constituted about a fifth of the state's 300,000 population—to accept white definitions of "legal title" and white disposition of their ancestral lands. The industry and state leaders feared that the natives might claim lands already leased to industry or earmarked for the projected pipeline south from the North Slope. Western senators were also uneasy over the possible precedent for their own Indian inhabitants: what if they should be inspired to reopen old questions as to what had happened to their ancestral lands. Recognition of native claims was often begrudging, more readily accepted as welfare than as right. But resolution of the issue was imperative; without terminating their claims, no leasing could take place.

The naval reserves appeared to offer an expedient device for compromise. Calls for dealing with native claims were accompanied by demands to end naval rule over the reserves. A Federal Field Committee for Development Planning in Alaska, which prepared a thorough and sympathetic study, *Alaska Natives and the Land*, recommended that all of the Alaskan lands, including the naval reserves, be leased to industry by Interior and that compensation to the native people come from these funds. (Joseph Fitz-Gerald, who headed the committee, moved on to direct community relations in Alaska for Atlantic Richfield.)[62]

In all this, Interior's primary perspective remained getting the navy out, the fields leased, and the giant pipeline built. It showed minimum sympathy for native claims, especially royalty sharing,

and seemed unperturbed over the state's filing for lands traditionally Eskimo. It shared the frustration of the industry which
had already purchased pipe and was ready to build when the new
ecology movement placed a national spotlight on the pipeline and
tanker route, slowing down and modifying corporate planning for
the unprecedented project across fragile tundra, uncharted wilderness, and then turbulent seas along beautiful coastline. Legally required to weigh alternatives, Interior placed primary reliance upon
the judgment of the involved corporations and the State Department that this route was preferable to a much discussed proposal
that the pipeline run further eastward through the Mackenzie River
valley in Canada, and serve the American Midwest where the needs
were clearer. Many criticisms, including some from within the department and also the Alaskan government, were withheld, played
down, or ignored in its initial environmental impact statement.
There was even to be distortion of the Canadian government's
position. And in familiar fashion, Interior was reluctant to have
public hearings once its more comprehensive impact analysis was
released: such procedures only gave more time, ammunition, and
publicity to those not convinced that the pipeline was in the national interest. Segments of the industry were opposed to having
this crude enter Midwest markets. And there was frank unease
over the possibility that once-reliable Canadians might assert their
nationhood by seeking participation in decisions over its use.

Early in 1974 the deputy director of the naval reserves program
resigned from the navy in protest against the Nixon administration's willingness to use what he felt was an industry-manufactured
crisis to draw upon reserves intended for wartime needs. He also
had resisted as a bad bargain for the public the swapping of Elk
Hills and Santa Barbara leases. "I have written my last lie" to
subvert the intent of the law establishing them. He did not oppose
the private profit system: "I have no quarrel with the fox whose
natural, and not reprehensible, hunger makes him want to get into
the chicken coop. My quarrel is with the faithless hired hand, who
would accept the farmer's pay and still leave the door to the coop
open."[63] In 1976 Congress approved the Nixon-Ford administration's quest for commercial drilling in the California and Wyoming
naval reserves. Jurisdiction over the Alaskan reserve was to be
transferred to the Department of the Interior the following year.

Interior generally serves as an industry watchdog on Capitol Hill, testifying against any proposals which might upset its cozy junior partnership with the energy industry or chart independent courses for public energy policy. As the bills calling for worker safety, land protection, and intensified research on alternate fuels poured in during the early 1970s, Interior could be counted upon to explain why they were not needed, why the states or a healthy, unfettered private industry were the nation's best recourse. It has mirrored industry's fear of zealous or uninformed neophytes, such as the Environmental Protection Agency which was established in 1970, being asked to watch over mining activities and thus displacing the "paramount expertise" of the Bureau of Mines, the Geological Survey, and the Bureau of Land Management. The latter two are described as "best suited" to guide state efforts in mine area protection and reclamation. The states are hailed for their regulatory efforts, thus ignoring the widespread agreement that they generally are limited in scope and weak in enforcement. Some states have competed for "development" by holding regulation or enforcement to a minimum.[64]

The department has defended strip mining as safer and more efficient than deep mining, despite growing evidence of the dangers in strip mining. Meanwhile, its Bureau of Mines generally was casual in the enforcement of safety standards during the years when it had this responsibility. Critics, including those from the United Mine Workers, felt this laxity was not unrelated to the agency's serving as a repository for political hacks. In rebuttal, the director of the Bureau of Mines has insisted that "the mining industry has demonstrated its capacity for working within the confines of regulations directed toward environmental improvement."[65] No mention is made of the intense coal and oil lobbying for accepting mine disasters as "acts of nature" and for as narrowly defined as possible "realistic reclamation" rather than the restoration of the landscape. Nor is mention made of the failure of the Bureau of Land Management to file the environmental impact statements concerning coal land leasing, as required under the National Environmental Policy Act.

Both the Bureau of Mines and industry speak confidently of proper reclamation methods. Yet, as Senator Gaylord Nelson (Democrat, Wisconsin) has noted, "far too frequently what has passed for reclamation in the past has been a 'green lie,' revegetation and regrading of the most cosmetic sort."[66]

At times, Interior has been carried away in its advocacy. It has described the beneficial effects of surface mining in exposing groundwater sources for livestock and wildlife and in creating small ponds. This water, "and the spoil piles themselves, frequently provide a pleasant topographic change in areas of virtually flat land." Mine access roads built for the massive equipment are seen as possibly bringing tourism for spectacular views of the mountains and valleys where much of the strip mining has taken place.[67]

A study by the Bureau of Reclamation and a group of electric utilities recommended sites for a network of giant power installations which would tap the coal and water of some 250,000 square miles in the North Central states.[68] The proposal for minemouth thermal plants feeding long-distance extra-high-voltage transmission lines recognized the need for planned development. Environmental impact questions, however, dealing with topsoil and water loss, the pollution of the air and river basins, and the larger physical chain reactions, were outside its pale. The fears of Westerners that strip mining and coal gasification, while bringing a temporary construction boom, may ultimately leave their states a colonial wasteland were sidestepped. Only later did a federal-state task force respond to outraged citizens of the earmarked areas and seek to assess the full social costs while placing such energy development in a larger resources framework. Oil and gas companies, meanwhile, were pushing ahead with their own timetables.

The Department of the Interior has shown limited interest in research in deep mining technology, reflecting the responsiveness of federal budgeting to industry orientation. The president of Consolidation Coal (Continental Oil) has stated that "for all practical purposes coal mining technology for deep mines is obsolete."[69] Yet there are still vast quantities of deep-seam coal in Appalachia, despite the turning to strip mining there, and also in the western lands beneath the much sought-after surface coal. Concern has been voiced that, in the short-run race to blast and gouge with giant machinery the "cheaper" coal from the western plains the corporations may be causing gas or ground water to flow into seams once recoverable by deep mining, making these underlying strata unsafe or inaccessible.[70]

Once interest did revive in coal research, the contracts went chiefly to the integrated energy corporations rather than to independent coal companies. And despite the rhetoric of the Nixon administration about the crucial role of coal, the amounts were quite modest when contrasted to the appropriations for nuclear work. One projection of Interior's Office of Coal Research is for massive coal-based energy producing complexes throughout the country which would produce electricity, fuel gas, pipeline gas, and synthetic oil. Such coal conversion complexes would occupy over a thousand acres and would cost about $450 million each. There is no discussion as to what might happen to existing communities or what life in the new areas would be like.[71]

In 1971 modest legislative proposals for a new Coal Gasification Development Corporation, jointly managed and funded by the government and industry, were aired. It was to search for the best methods for manufacturing substitute natural gas from coal and then to construct and maintain first pilot and then full-scale commercial plants. Interior quickly voiced its opposition. It recounted, rather selectively, the history of its past efforts and told of its own plans. The new proposal would upset current arrangements with the American Gas Association and also with the National Coal Association. In August 1971 the government entered into a cooperative agreement to develop coal gasification processes: $20 million a year public money and $10 million from the gas association and its members for a four-year period. This ratio was in keeping with the formula in the president's June 1971 energy message that government finance the larger share of pilot plants and industry the large share of demonstration plants. Hollis M. Dole, assistant secretary for mineral resources, explained: "In the very high risk area . . . of developing the process . . . it would be in the best interest of the people of the United States that the government do this. Then when we go to the demonstration scale plant, which still has a high element of risk, but not nearly as high, that the industry, those who are concerned about supplying an adequate natural gas base to our country, should take the bulk of the cost."[72]

Mr. Dole also warned that the legislative proposal further fragmented the government's efforts for energy policy. It was a plausible point, except that the basic fear was not of unwieldy administration but that the new research and development corporation was to be accountable directly to the Congress and the president rather than to a proposed Department of Natural Resources, which was intended to replace Interior as part of the overall energy strategy of the Nixon regime.

Some of these patterns of ignorance about the public domain relate to budget, some to the narrow, technical backgrounds of Interior's personnel, and some to the limits of a bureaucratic system where the passive route—"we just work here"—is always the safest. Viewing energy as a commodity rather than a resource and the industry rather than the public as its first client by now comes quite naturally to the department. For example, in 1968, as Richard Nixon was about to enter office, the deputy administrator of Interior's Oil Import Administration, T. C. Snedeker, wrote to the major oil companies and trade associations asking for support for his promotion to head that agency. He described how he had favored the majors' position on strict controls over imports, had opposed the exemptions granted to the newer oil companies, and wanted to return the program to its basic principles. "Any support you may give me in this behalf, either through Members of Congress or through other individuals, will be greatly appreciated."[73] And the following year when John Ricca, the deputy director of the Office of Oil and Gas (and a former Aramco official), was asked at a Senate appropriations hearing why there was no consumer equivalent to the National Petroleum Council within Interior, to balance the latter's interest in high prices, he explained that his agency's pricing responsibilities were "to study and examine the effects that prices have on the health and welfare of the industry primarily and not from the consumers' standpoint."[74]

In such a setting it takes a sustained effort for a civil servant with integrity to develop an awareness of the built-in assumptions guiding the day-to-day work of his agency. The feelings of isolation and powerlessness support one another. And "whistleblowing" takes courage, especially in a setting where so few alternative signals for a genuinely public policy have come clearly and consistently from the president or the Congress or political groups.

The "revolving door" tradition ensures a steady interchange of personnel between industry, industry-oriented universities, oil law firms, and the government.[75] All are carefully screened by the industry. Biographies of members of Interior's Oil and Gas Office continue to indicate that most have had oil ties. In 1971, for example, the highest-ranking staff were technicians with long previous service in corporate vineyards: Aramco (15 years), Shell (14 years), Mobil (15 years), Sohio (13 years), Pure (5 years), Humble-Esso (10 years), Atlantic (18 years), Esso (16 years), Caltex (27 years). Of the four remaining members, one came from the navy, one from the CIA, one from the Federal Power Commission, and one had been in various Interior posts.[76]

Recent heads of the office have come from Continental Oil and Aramco. A former head became a lobbyist for Sinclair Oil, another went in a similar capacity for Lone Star Gas. A third moved on to the American Petroleum Institute. (It was not very far to go, since the trade association had left New York for Washington; presumably it was now more important to be near government than the banks. The API now had a greatly expanded budget and a large staff, headed by Frank Ikard, a transplanted Texas congressman and former member of the House Ways and Means Committee close to chairman Wilbur Mills. Also joining the API was Charles J. DiBona, White House energy adviser in 1973.)

In contrast, David B. Brooks, a geologist and economist, found himself eased out of the Bureau of Mines in 1970 through a reorganization initiated by Assistant Secretary Dole. His crimes as chief economist included an emerging public philosophy in his research on imports, coal, oil shale lands, and helium. In each area he was discovering that the energy industry was subsidized to the disadvantage of the taxpayer, the consumer, and the worker. His study on oil import quotas, which was submitted to the president's task force, found a $5 billion annual excess charge to consumers. A report on helium policy doubted the public gain from paying gas companies to extract helium only to stockpile it underground in quantities good for eighty years ahead. A study on mine safety

challenged the industry-bureau party line on its high costs and the
implied premise that "accidents will happen," especially when men
are careless. The Budget Bureau then asked Brooks to head its
natural resources and environmental planning. But at the last minute it withdrew the offer. A post at the Appalachian Regional Commission for which he was uniquely qualified was similarly vetoed
from above. Despite his recognized competence he was thus blacklisted in the federal bureaucracy. Brooks subsequently found employment directing mineral resources research and later energy
conservation for the Canadian government.[77]

At the same time, John F. O'Leary, who had been appointed
during the Johnson administration, was fired as director of the
Bureau of Mines, most directly because of his stubborn support of
mine safety enforcement. An economist and career administrator
with extensive fuel policy experience, O'Leary had shaken the
passivity of the bureau and its historic collaboration with the coal
industry by his novel insistence that it "represent the public interest
rather than the industry alone." One perceptive observer of the
coal scene concluded that he was the first man to hold the post
who understood that the bureau was not to be "just the Washington office of the coal industry." Although a moderate in his be-
liefs about the speed with which safety standards could be imposed,
he was sharply critical of the record of his agency. Rejecting the
cries of the coal operators that they could not afford the newer
health and safety standards, he pointed to their profits in recent
years and concluded that it was an industry "designed for production economy and not for human economy, and there's going to
have to be a change of attitude on that." Shortly afterward, Hollis
M. Dole, ignoring the appalling annual fatality record and the
shocking inspection pattern, insisted that the coal mines were
"healthier and safer now than ever before." Secretary of the Interior Walter J. Hickel, who later admitted that the safety records
kept at the bureau were a travesty since they mirrored the doctored
industry versions, said he removed O'Leary under instructions from
the White House. Meanwhile, the mineral resources responsibilities
under Dole were reorganized along commodity lines. The intent,
explained an Interior manual, was to give the public agency "a
close and confidential relationship" with industry.[78]

The federal government remains honeycombed by a network of energy advisory bodies composed of leaders of the major corporations and trade associations, along with the usual decoration of "independents." These advisers define the acceptable bounds of policy alternatives, police their implementation, and in effect become the makers of public policy. They thus undercut the legislative process and distort responsible administration.

The National Petroleum Council, within the Department of the Interior, is the largest, most active advisory group. It is openly treated as a "partner" of the Office of Oil and Gas and serves as the official pipeline between government and industry. In 1971 the NPC claimed to operate on a private budget of about $500,000. This figure provided no clue as to the worth of the staff and resources of the many cooperating companies. It also draws support from the American Petroleum Institute, the private source for most government petroleum data. The latter, which is the central oil trade association and is dominated by the majors, operates with a budget of at least $15 million from its members and with access to the files and aid of the industry.

In contrast, the Oil and Gas Office had a direct government appropriation of $775,000 for thirty-eight employees and an additional $128,000 for nine field employees. To Hollis M. Dole, who as Interior's assistant secretary of mineral affairs served as the government cochairman of the NPC, "you couldn't find a better example of an industry advisory committee serving the public interest." Its members worked without public compensation and produced "monumental" reports.[79] One ambitious study was its *U.S. Energy Outlook*, published in 1972, whose cost the NPC estimated at $6 million. Many of its not unfamiliar proposals were to be incorporated into the Nixon energy plan the following year.

Proposals for broader representation, including from consumers, are met with objections such as those voiced in 1971 by John Ricca, acting director of the Office of Oil and Gas, that their presence would inhibit the oilmen. Transcripts were available, but NPC meetings were not opened to the public (before a 1972 law required them to be) because "if you start opening the door to the people, then the first thing you know, the whole place gets packed and you do not have space to conduct your business."[80]

The same protective spirit has prevailed in the Geological Survey, which brought in 23 oil executives to draft antipollution standards for offshore drilling. Until challenged in 1974, it privately circulated proposed regulations on continental shelf drilling to the Offshore Operators Committee, composed of industry representatives, so that they might react before any orders were publicly announced.[81]

There are other advisory groups which provide even more direct control for the industry and for the assumption that only oil and gas men are qualified to deal with energy. The coast guard, which enforces offshore safety and environmental regulations, created a seventeen-member Offshore Operations Advisory Committee chaired by a Texaco official. All seventeen committee members were from industry: thirteen from oil companies, two from oil well drilling companies, and two from charter ship and helicopter companies serving rig operators.[82] When in 1975 the coast guard issued regulations concerning the construction and operation of oil tankers in coastal waters, including the controversial conclusions not to require double bottoms and to require segregated ballast only on larger tankers, its findings came directly from an API-dominated "study group" which the coast guard had appointed. Of the eleven members, six—including the chairman (Exxon)—came from major oil companies, one was an independent tanker operator, one represented the American Institute of Merchant Shipping, and three were from government.[83]

Once the environment became a national political concern, President Nixon created by executive order in 1970 a National Industrial Pollution Control Council within the Department of Commerce. It was to advise the president and the new Council on Environmental Quality on plans and actions of federal, state, and local agencies involving environmental quality policies. As the president explained, it would allow the close coordination of the public and the private sector, enabling the business community to employ "the same energy and skills which have produced quantitative gains in our economy" to help chart the route to a better environment. The heads of Exxon, Atlantic Richfield, Consolidation Coal, Peabody Coal, Bechtel, and many utility, mining, paper, chemical, and rubber corporations—the leading industrial polluters—were appointed. There were no parallel advisory bodies from other segments of the society. And there was no representation from labor or from environmental or consumer groups on the new council. When consumer representatives sought admission as observers, they were turned away.[84]

The council was able to defuse fundamental criticisms of the wastes and hazards of the industrial system, labeling them uninformed or the products of righteous mischiefmakers. It could transform sectarian corporate defenses into the nonpartisan pronouncements of business statesmen. As sales were threatened, even after manufacturing smaller (but expensive) cars, the automobile industry began to resist its role as punching bag for ecologists and declared that pollution problems could not be legislated out of existence "any more than the laws of nature can be overruled." The oil companies had embraced "ecology" in their advertisements and even made donations, when the issue seemed "moral" and a matter of changing thoughtless habits or of protecting the bald eagle (Arco's chairman contributed $80,000 to help found a study group linked to the Friends of the Earth) or the tiger (Exxon gave $50,000 to the World Wildlife Fund to help save the tiger from extinction). They were prepared to accept the generalization that "we are all at fault in that we have never had any concern about our energy uses"—as long as it was agreed that public government was the prime culprit.[85] But the industry insisted that a line be drawn against any "tampering" with the corporate judgments about private investments and profits which made America great. Gulf, for example, now playing Dr. Spock for the nation's growth, called for an energy policy which would neither destroy the environment "nor baby it to death."[86] Mobil reprinted the Declaration of Independence and also invoked the unlikely support of "Sam Adams: a radical for today." It admitted he couldn't dump tea in Boston harbor today because "he probably couldn't get past the first stage —the Environmental Impact Statement. But if he were a part of the U.S. petroleum industry, he'd still be a radical looking for that free market. And there would still be a reactionary government fighting him every step of the way."[87] One General Accounting Office study calculated that Exxon, Texaco, Gulf, Mobil, Standard (Indiana) and Shell spent $425 million on advertising from 1970 to 1972. To the companies such messages were primarily "informational" and rarely political—and thus generally tax deductible.[88]

But such efforts were not silencing the critics who now challenged their words as well as their deeds. "The soapbox is a lonely place," lamented Mobil from its favored Thursday corner on the New York Times "Op Ed" page.[89] And sponsored history was suspect. How salutary to have comparable balanced judgments articulated at the highest reaches of government. The council was in a strategic position to check zealous congressional and administrative environmentalists who might otherwise be carried away by the moral passions of the ecology movement. It could oppose proposals that no material from the industrial process be permitted to be released into the environment unless it could be shown to be harmless to people and their environment by pointing out that such restraints would curtail industrial innovation and "could be likened to a requirement of proof of innocence by the accused rather than proof of guilt by the accuser."[90] It also was a useful front for sending out literature bearing the seal of the U.S. Department of Commerce describing how the corporations were improving the landscape. On a somewhat less lofty plane the council provided a convenient fundraising setting for Secretary of Commerce Stans and his Committee to Re-elect the President. This industrial self-government thus has served as another device for the centralization of political control within the executive branch—to be shared with the forces of centralized economic power while shielded from congressional review and popular participation.

# 7

# Bureaucratic Wastelands

On the same day in November 1973 during the Arab embargo when President Nixon told the American people what they could do for their country and how with "discipline, self restraint and unity" they would successfully confront the "energy crisis" and by 1980 attain his vision of energy self-sufficiency, the White House also quietly announced that 250 oil and gas executives were being mobilized by the Interior Department. They were part of a national defense executive reserve and were to help plan and administer a fuel allocation program through an Emergency Petroleum and Gas Administration. This shadow government had been designed with the cooperation of the National Petroleum Council. It functioned as the emergency arm of the Office of Oil and Gas, a pattern reminiscent of previous national crises. Nominally, its chief administrator was the secretary of the interior; his alternate, who had the day-to-day responsibility was Stephen A. Wakefield, assistant secretary for energy and minerals, an oil lawyer who had succeeded Hollis M. Dole. Its cadre were already dominated by energy corporation executives, and the purpose now was to fill the remaining posts. The new recruits were to be paid by their companies. The familiar debate as to expertise and conflict-of-interest ensued. When the acting attorney general said the oilmen could not be guaranteed immunity from possible charges in the future that they might be involved in decisions involving their own companies, oilmen balked, and the Office of Oil and Gas postponed the draft "indefinitely."[1] There was no discussion, however, of the general orientation within the agency to industry definitions of the public good.

The larger patterns of industry control continued. In 1971 the corporations had sought permission to bargain collectively with the Organization of Petroleum Exporting Countries. The corporations had become concerned over Libya's encouragement of other producing countries to raise demands for participation and perhaps play them off against one another, while letting oil flow outside of the channels so carefully constructed and maintained by the private government of oil. United States government approval, without public disclosure of the exact terms of the pooled efforts, would show corporate deference to the laws and customs of the United States while conveying abroad the subtle support of the American flag. That the oilmen then were already meeting in the office of Chase Manhattan attorney John J. McCloy, who represented the seven sisters and many other oil companies, to coordinate strategy was a detail and presumably none of the public's business. McCloy recalled before a senate committee in 1974 that in discussions with President John F. Kennedy a decade earlier the latter's shock over his experiences with Premier Nikita Krushchev led him to anticipate the possibility of political confrontation with the Soviet Union in the Middle East. McCloy then suggested to Kennedy the need for the corporations to be ready to deal collectively with an emerging OPEC in protecting oil reserves and the desirability of obtaining such authority from the Justice Department. The president arranged for him to speak to Attorney General Robert Kennedy. Mindful of the great turnover in that agency, McCloy later testified, "I made it a point to call on each succeeding Attorney General just for the idea of keeping the thing fresh in his mind because any moment I was afraid we would have to do something."[2]

The State and Justice departments were amenable to the 1971 request by the corporations, and a "business review" letter from Justice gave assurance that it was not the agency's intent to invoke antitrust actions subsequently because of their cooperative behavior. With this encouragement the companies met at Teheran and Tripoli to negotiate with OPEC. They maintained a London Policy Group, composed of senior corporate executives, to establish the terms of reference for the negotiating teams. There was also a New York Group and various specialized back-up committees. No public officials attended these meetings. The corporate participants submitted oral reports to the State Department fuel officer. And McCloy, who represented the oil companies, also kept the Justice Department informed to assure that the consultations stayed within the framework of the business review letter. The Senate subcommittee investigating the oil multinationals noted that it was not until October 1973, after its staff had read some of the voluminous cable traffic in the company-OPEC negotiations and had begun to make inquiries of the department, that anyone from Justice "thought to read and evaluate this record."[3] The assistant attorney general expressed no regrets at the failure to have someone present at such meetings and indicated that the Antitrust Division had no evidence for questioning McCloy's good faith. Besides, "one always has to recognize that if a group of businessmen . . . have come to the conclusion that they want to fix prices or allocate markets they normally do not do it in the presence of lawyers, nor do they keep minutes of it, nor do they file reports of it."[4] Thus, private spokesmen functioned as surrogates for public government. Oil policy beyond the water's edge was obviously too important to be left in public hands.

A request to the Antitrust Division of the Justice Department for the terms approved evoked the reply that in the view of both departments release of this information during negotiations "would be contrary to the national interest." The promise was made to release the letter once negotiations were completed. The assistant attorney general in charge of antitrust further explained that his agency had no power to grant immunity for antitrust violations, but oil company arrangements, as represented to Justice, called for no limitations on the competitive freedom of the participants: there would be no price fixing, allocating of markets, limitations and allocation of production, sales imports, and the like.

> On the contrary, the reported activities of the companies involve a joint effort on the part of both large and small to assure that the concerted approach of the producing countries will not work to the greater prejudice of some competitors—especially the smaller ones— than to others. Faced with this combination of oil producing countries, demanding higher fees in the form of taxes or royalties, the

companies' actions of which we are aware represent no more than a countervailing force to minimize the adverse price effects on consumers.

The Department of Justice would not interpret earlier antitrust complaints and decrees in such fashion as "to leave individual companies helpless to cope with the concerted power of the governments of the oil producing countries, to the detriment not only of the companies themselves, but of consumers in many countries."[5]

Several years later, when asked for his interpretation of the still unreleased letter, J. K. Jamieson, chairman of Exxon, declined. He explained that the terms of the permission by the Nixon administration for the oil companies were classified because they dealt "in sensitive areas of sovereign governments."[6]

Once the 1973 Arab embargo appeared to be disrupting the American economy, the Foreign Petroleum Supply Committee, composed of the major importing companies, met (with nominal Oil and Gas Office leadership) to assess the supply situation and to prepare a plan of action. They recommended that the Emergency Petroleum Supply Committee, last activated during the 1967 Arab-Israeli war, be convened. This was the corporate meeting ground, authorized by the Defense Production Act of 1950, for "assisting the government" in coping with problems and coordinating worldwide shipments so as to minimize any adverse impact upon the United States and, incidentally, upon their own orderly production and marketing relationships. As in the past, the assumption was that an "emergency" condition invited a freer hand and less searching antitrust judgment. All the majors had served on the 1967 committee. Representing the United States government as chairman was John Ricca, the deputy director of the Office of Oil and Gas, who previously had been fifteen years with Aramco and was subsequently to head energy research for General Motors. The 1973 committee had virtually the same representation. Observers from British Petroleum and Shell were present. The chairman this time was Duke R. Ligon, formerly with Continental Oil and now director of the Office of Oil and Gas.[7]

There were some newly legislated limitations. Broader representation from all segments of the industry was required. This provision was ignored as was a suggestion from Senator Lee Metcalf that there be more balanced public representation from consumers, Rural Electrification Administration cooperatives, utilities, and oil jobbers. Among his suggestions were Charles F. Luce, a former Interior official and now chairman of Consolidated Edison, and Lee C. White, former chairman of the Federal Power Commission. The chief counsel of the National Oil Jobbers Council was accepted. But he was given "observer status" and not seated at the main table with the major oil company representatives. Convinced that a new subcommittee to determine the impact of the boycott on foreign petroleum supplies in the United States, whose staff was also drawn from the major importers, "would find it extremely difficult to collect and analyze the necessary data without some anticompetitive consequences for the independent sector," he applied, unsuccessfully, for membership.[8]

Under a general reform of all advisory mechanisms in the federal bureaucracy (there were over 1,500), meetings were to be announced ten days ahead of time in the *Federal Register* and to be open to the public. The State Department and the oil industry shared an unease about public attention. To the oil companies, there were technical and privileged matters involving the movement and "competitive arrangements" of their oil. As transnationals they were also wrestling with the dilemma of being good citizens in two regions in conflict. They were not certain how diplomatic it would appear in the eyes of the Arab world to be seen planning a cohesive policy with the United States government. While the State Department was generally sympathetic to the worries of the big oil companies, it also was reluctant to convey to the Arabs too great an air of anxiety about the embargo or to suggest that the United States was considering countermeasures while it was conducting "delicate negotiations." The solution was to announce meetings of the Foreign Petroleum Supply Committee, the Emergency Petroleum Supply Committee, and related subcommittees on the shortest possible notice—one day. A convenient ruling by the secretary of the interior denied the public access "in the interest of national defense or foreign policy," exemptions allowed under the Freedom of Information Act.[9] There was no evidence that participants were ever subject to security investigations.

Meetings of the EPSC were closed to the public because "trade secrets and commercial and financial information obtained from a person" were being considered by the assembled corporate executives.[10] "National security" and a discussion of "trade secrets" even provided justification for closing the doors to a meeting held in Exxon's headquarters in New York.[11] Another device to justify secrecy was to indicate that interagency business would be aired, again not appropriate for impressionable taxpayers. A simpler solution for evading the press, the public, and legal niceties was to fly to the Bahamas. Some fifty-five corporate energy executives and eleven government officials including Secretary of the Treasury George Shultz, William Simon, and White House energy adviser Charles DiBona did that five days before President Nixon's energy message in November 1973 in which he outlined his program to meet the emergency.[12] This program offered the energy industry just about everything it had sought, from opening up the naval reserves and temporary licensing of nuclear power plants without public hearings, to modest strip mining standards and the suspension of natural gas price regulation.

The National Petroleum Council circumvented the new Federal Advisory Committee Act by having most of its work done in "informal subgroups" of special study committees. These were not announced and were closed to the press and the public. For example, the chairman of the NPC would write to the director of the Office of Oil and Gas or to the deputy assistant secretary for mineral affairs in Interior to certify that a subcommittee of the NPC's Committee on Emergency Preparedness, co-chaired by a Sun Oil official and the Oil and Gas Office director, with top executives from Shell, Standard (Indiana), Exxon, Texas Pacific, Standard of California, the Edison Electric Institute, and Blythe Eastman Dillon and Company (brokers), were such a group and would be meeting in the NPC office. On other occasions they would meet in the home office of the Texas Pacific Oil Company, Standard of California, or Sun. Or the NPC chairman would make a similar determination about an Economic and Environmental Task Group meeting in the office of Marathon Oil or about a subcommittee of the NPC's Committee on U.S. Energy Outlook meeting in the board room of Continental Oil.[13]

Meanwhile, an Energy Research and Development Advisory Council, established by President Nixon in June 1973 to provide independent review of existing and proposed national energy programs and recommendations for new programs to the White House's Energy Policy Office, was also meeting in as much secrecy as it could muster. There was the now familiar one-day public announcement for its meetings. The staff director and the general counsel of the Senate committee which, by its activities, had led to the advisory reform had great difficulty before being admitted. But discussion of the president's proposed $10 billion energy research and development program was closed "for national security reasons," in violation of the Federal Advisory Committee Act of 1972. Chaired by the president's science advisor, who was also director of the National Science Foundation, its membership drew heavily from the ranks of research vice-presidents of such corporations as Exxon, Consolidation Coal, Consolidated Edison, General Motors, and International Business Machines. An outline of strategic issues for discussion included ways to meet the need "to maximize opportunities for cooperative effort between industry and government," and "to consider ways of 'pulling' technological innovation in energy system through adjustments in regulatory and marketplace incentives, rather than 'pushing' all of it through a federally managed R and D pipeline."[14]

There was an evident bias toward fossil fuels and uranium; the intruding Senate staff members reported that the council chortled over a scientist's presentation regarding the potential of solar power, wind power, and sewage conversion. Government spokesmen, including John C. Sawhill—the associate director of the Office of Management and Budget responsible for energy and science policy, and later to succeed William Simon as federal energy administrator—discussed antitrust and patent laws: "We really want to get industry's view of patent policy. . . . We can probably administer patent law in a flexible way." There was criticism of TVA-type government research corporations for energy in which "you lose the advantage of the kind of control we want to exercise in COMSAT-type corporations—which let industry in on decision-making." Mr. Sawhill also stated that "we are very anxious to get uranium enrichment [the one stage then not under industry control] into the private sector." In June 1975 President Ford proposed that future production and sale of enriched uranium, heretofore a government monopoly by law, be in private hands, with full guarantee for substantial profit (and against loss) for the oil and other corporate investors. It was this pattern which led Senator Lee Metcalf to conclude that "the major component of the energy crisis is the domineering role of the fossil fuel–uranium complex, which includes financial institutions behind them and the Government officials who implement their policies up front."[15]

The access and camaraderie of the oilmen in government, reinforced by the advisory system, result in control of the information ("the fuel of governmental machinery") upon which decisions about resource development and use, rationing, price controls, inflation, taxes, foreign policy, and literally war and peace are made. Accepting industry projections as to demand has meant also accepting unstated premises as to the direction of the economy. The United States government has lacked basic and complete figures about energy reserves, the relations between varying prices and production potentials, and about stocks held or controlled by individual corporations at home and abroad. It still has no firm picture about the costs of production of various energy forms. Nor does it possess reliable knowledge about industry's overall refinery construction plans, while the corporations have guarded specific breakdowns of refinery runs. Correlations between government investment incentives and productivity are almost nonexistent. In most cases it has relied upon the data provided by the American Petroleum Institute and the American Gas Association, which are gathered uncritically from company reports.[16]

The National Petroleum Council frequently serves to launder the information from the two trade associations before turning it over to Interior or the White House. These figures have often been too general to be of help in making independent appraisals. Interior's Bureau of Mines frequently reprints statistics and studies of the trade associations. There is little authorization or enthusiasm for verifying these studies. Nor is there any record of Interior's even challenging any American Petroleum Institute figures. "The API is staffed with competent people with many years experience in the oil business," the government agency explains.[17]

According to the comptroller general of the United States, Bureau of Mines officials "told us that they used these organizations' reserve statistics because they have been prepared on a basis consistent with prior years' statistics and that, if the Department also prepared them it would be a tremendous duplication of industries' effort." The Bureau of Mines had not determined the costs for computing its own reserve statistics. "BOM officials stated that BOM did not verify the organization's statistics because their [API and AGA] policies prohibit verification."[18]

Government figures are sometimes scrounged from annual corporate reports and data services, with no standardized definitions of categories of reserves and again no independent verification. Oil pipeline figures published by the Interstate Commerce Commission have been based upon nonaudited company reports of the common carriers. There are many omissions, and producers, refiners, and recipients are not identified.[19] Until the "energy crisis," deferential or housebroken public servants have rarely seen the need to develop autonomous figures. The issue is not simply that of dishonesty. These are often complex issues. Reserves, for example, are, at best, estimates about which honorable experts can differ. But refinery runs and fuel in storage are not inherently that elusive, especially with the advent of the computer.

In the past, Interior has not requested specific information on the location and quantities of oil or gas reserves from individual corporations, since that is "proprietary company information." It has dutifully recited the industry's claim that publicly revealing such information would give advantage to other firms and industries, upsetting the "competitive nature" of the energy industry, and would also violate its right to privacy and "our national philosophy."[20]

Comparable figures for reserves on *public* lands have also been respected by Interior as "proprietary." As John Ricca explained, the companies have bid and spent tremendous sums drilling based on what they think the reserves are. "They have no obligation to reveal these company secrets to anybody as far as what they have proven out underneath that land, because essentially that land under lease to them now is their land and those reserves are theirs and they are not Federal Government reserves."[21]

To Hollis M. Dole, the assistant secretary for mineral affairs, this was as it should be "in this government of ours, which is a private enterprise government." Autonomous studies would be ex-

pensive and require manpower which the Office of Oil and Gas
did not have or ask for, and the industry did not want it to have.
But Mr. Dole felt that the executive branch was getting precise
enough information upon which to make good judgment: it was
"Mother Nature" rather than corporations which set the limits
here.[22] Dole's commitment to private enterprise seemed total.
"Profits is the name of the game" in the United States, and "more
people want into this society than want out," he explained to a
Senate committee.[23] In the course of directing an Interior task
force for developing a prototype leasing program "to stimulate the
timely development of oil shale technology by private enterprise,"
he reported being most impressed with the plans of Colony Development and its attempts to reconcile economic and environmental
factors. (Colony Development was an oil shale project, jointly
sponsored by Shell, Ashland, Atlantic Richfield, and the Oil Shale
Corporation. It had successfully bid $117 million for shale lands
in western Colorado. It planned to build the first commercial oil
shale plant, with Atlantic Richfield as operator.) Dole cited its
approach as a reason for his opposition to any public development.[24] Working with Dole on the task force as Oil Shale Coordinator was Reid T. Stone, who had come to Interior from Atlantic
Richfield and was also co-chairman of the National Petroleum
Council's Oil Shale Task Group.

The admiration was obviously mutual. In 1973, Dole left government to head the consortium's project. The Department of the
Interior hailed the departing public servant as a vigorous advocate
of environmental legislation for mining and "an equally vigorous
critic of the actions of extremist groups which threaten continued
supply of energy and minerals." Secretary Rogers Morton said he
had done "more than anyone else" to alert the nation to the energy
crisis, and promptly appointed him to the National Petroleum
Council.[25]

The office of assistant secretary for energy and minerals remained
critical for industry surveillance over the Office of Oil and Gas,
the Bureau of Mines, and other Interior agencies dealing with oil,
gas, and coal. Dole's successor was Stephen A. Wakefield, an
attorney from a leading Texas law firm which had represented
some of the biggest oil and gas interests. Wakefield spoke for industry with a purity of dedication to profit-making that might even

have embarrassed oil executives. He hailed the integrated industry as the nation's principal asset for obtaining energy. "One of the remarkable things about it . . . is its lack of concentration," he explained, echoing the shopworn public relations claim of several hundred thousand "independent" small businesses. Profits would have brought forth the necessary fuel, had the industry not been "misled and hampered by Federal regulations" of natural gas prices and oil imports. In the face of an oil crisis it was imperative that government show a willingness "to let private industry proceed to do its job without hindrance and harassment." Responsible for developing a national energy policy, Wakefield warned against any "dismantling" of the integrated domestic structure. This "would so weaken the attractiveness of U.S. markets that this act in itself would assure that the United States stood at the end of the line of claimants in a world where energy scarcity is likely to be the normal condition for many years to come." Instead he favored every encouragement for the entry of petroleum corporations into synthetic fuels, oil shale, tar sands, and other organic forms.[26]

This network of privilege operates to forestall the gathering of necessary data for public use. Energy and advisory bodies within the Bureau of the Budget and its successor, the Office of Management and Budget, have been called to unpublicized meetings to review requests by regulatory agencies for informational studies about these industries. The original intent was to have the bureau coordinate the collection of information so as to lessen the burden upon small businessmen overwhelmed by government inquiries during World War II. To this end, an Advisory Council on Federal Reports was developed within the Budget Bureau, composed of and paid for by business groups. Special advisory panels on oil, gas, utilities, banking, railroads, and other businesses were created, composed of representatives of these industries. In their deliberations they have been able to decide whether proposals are justifiable, forcing the initiating agencies to placate and reassure the subjects of their studies. Proposals often have been "denied, delayed or diluted" with the result that agencies are discouraged from attempting to exercise much boldness.[27]

The minutes of a panel (membership from the American Petroleum Institute, coal, utilities, chemicals, mining, paper, steel and other users of the nation's waterways as sewers) reviewing a proposed U.S. Public Health Service survey of industrial waste water disposal reported critically on this study. It had been challenged and stalled for seven years as an intrusion into "trade secrets" and states' rights:

> Industry does not like to report effluents without some indication of the effect they will have, because the location of the discharge can make a difference. There is always pressure from the public to release Federal data, and the companies are afraid that the data may get into the hands of the news media. They feel that industry would have to assume that the data will be used against them and even be used in court. This would force industry to refuse to cooperate.[28]

The study was finally shifted to the Department of the Interior.

Searches by the Federal Trade Commission for authoritative figures on oil and gas reserves along with detailed information on the changing structure of the energy industry have to be cleared by a panel composed of representatives of the oil and gas industry and their trade associations. A survey of natural gas pipelines to determine the location, age and depth—there are over a million miles of pipeline in the United States, and until 1968 there were no federal safety standards—was challenged first by the industry advisory body in the fledgling Office of Pipeline Safety and then by the advisory panel of pipeline companies in the Office of Management and Budget. Inadequately funded and staffed and with limited data, the former agency's creation seemed more a public relations response to explosions and an industry tactic to preempt the field so as to preclude effective local regulation than a serious commitment to safety standards and enforcement.[29]

The Federal Power Commission has experienced similar frustration, as when Lee C. White, a consumer-oriented chairman, sought detailed data on the utilities. Legal and public relations fees have been another sensitive item, according to Senator Metcalf, "when we discovered that about half the members of certain legislatures were on the payroll of utilities."[30] Funds for independent surveys of gas reserves desired by professionals on the FPC's staff who have not been housebroken have also been denied by industry-oriented congressmen. Industry-screened or docile commissioners learn to accept the myth of "anticompetitive effects" and refrain from challenging the figures of the energy industry. In the same study in which the General Accounting Office found the FPC interpreting its authority to allow improper gas price increases which adversely affected millions of consumers, thus making "a sham of the regulatory process," it also charged that nineteen FPC officials, including seven administrative law judges, held stock in energy companies under their purview. Only seven of the 125 FPC officials required to file financial disclosure statements, including stock ownership, had done so properly in 1973. To the FPC these disclosures confirmed that there was a "lapse" in enforcing conflict of interest laws due to inadequate record keeping procedures. But no impropriety was seen.[31]

The Federal Power Commission has been crippled as an effective public instrument by its dependence upon gas industry data. American Gas Association reports of "dwindling reserves" are often the basis for the regulatory agency's determination of rates. The data have been gathered by producer company employees constituting a subcommittee of the AGA—each assigned fields in which his employer was the principal producer. As Charles F. Wheatley, Jr., the general manager of the American Public Gas Association, has observed, "it would be naive to assume that these men were unaware of the huge economic stake their producer-employers have in demonstrating a gas supply shortage, and this awareness presents a tremendous potential for abuse, both conscious and subconscious in their reporting."[32] Company records have been viewed as confidential and accepted at face value. There has been no will or way to verify or challenge the AGA findings and their FPC acceptance—or even be certain of the methods used in summarizing the data. A House of Representatives inquiry in 1971 concluded that such dependence derogated public confidence in "the regulatory process and in those who are sworn to protect the public's interest."[33]

A 1972 survey of gas reserves announced by the FPC in response to the pressures of its critics was not much more promising. The bulk of its information was to be supplied by the gas companies and a cluster of advisory panels. These were dominated by producer and pipeline officials. The executive advisory committee was composed of the heads of the major oil and gas companies, who were also on the National Petroleum Council. Most of them, or their companies, were also on the parent committee of the NPC's Committee on U.S. Energy Outlook, whose findings have generally made their way to the White House, the Secretary of the Interior, the Federal Energy Administration, and other offices nominally making public policy.

The spot checking of fields and other data were to be treated by the staff as confidential; presumably the factual basis of the aggregate findings could be disclosed neither to the commission nor the consumer public. "It is a curious anomaly," Mr. Wheatley mused, "that the companies are willing to allow competitors' employees in their roles as subcommittee members to examine data which producers withhold from public scrutiny."[34] And when figures emerged which suggested serious discrepancies between producer and pipeline company offshore estimates and between the sample survey and the American Gas Association estimates, attempts were made to ignore, suppress, or destroy them.

There is evidence that reserve figures have been seriously underestimated and totals manipulated by the industry. One FPC study of 168 offshore shut-in producible gas leases estimated that the reserves of these leases were two-and-one-half times the actual production and that there was also oil shut-in. FPC economist David Schwartz has described companies reporting no uncommitted proved reserves and then signing a long-term contract to provide gas from the same area, now reported as having significant reserves.

An investigation of the attempted destruction within the FPC of a detailed survey of corporate reserves suggested that there has been considerable gas and oil of commercial potential which has been shut-in by integrated producers holding offshore leases in the Gulf of Mexico. Only a faulty incinerator saved the already torn-up documents and their inconclusive findings. What was clear was the shoddy reporting, the discrepancies between what corporations recorded internally and reported, conflicting definitions of reserves, and public policy makers and experts working without adequate information.[35] As dissatisfaction among some staff and commissioners gained public attention, the FPC early in 1974, by a 3–2 vote, reversed earlier decisions and opened the door to the possibility of more effective regulation by announcing that the public right to information about natural gas reserves outweighs the "proprietary interest" of the corporations.[36]

In the aftermath of the Santa Barbara blowout, citizens found it somewhat difficult to penetrate the information barrier to assess damages, policies, and alternatives. The presidential panel of scientists and engineers recommending the resumption of drilling had relied upon oil and Interior witnesses, but Interior did not make their evidence or reasoning available, presumably because most of it came from the oil companies and was "proprietary." Skeptics recalled that the head of the panel, Dr. Lee A. DuBridge, was formerly president of the California Institute of Technology, of which Union Oil's president was a trustee. The deputy attorney general of California told of his inability to obtain help from petroleum experts at the state's universities since "they all seem to be working on grants from the oil industry. . . . The experts are afraid that if they assist us in our case in behalf of the people of California, they will lose their oil industry grants."[37] One professor of petroleum engineering was quoted as explaining that he could not testify "because my work depends on good relations with the petroleum industry. My interest is serving the petroleum industry. I view my obligation to the community as supplying it with well-trained petroleum engineers. We train the industry's engineers and they help us."[38]

Even the CIA, with its presumably fathomless resources, has claimed difficulty in penetrating the petroleum curtain. Director Richard Helms reported that although there was an overwhelming amount of literature, accuracy was at a premium. The companies had a great deal of information on reserves, production, pricing, and political directions in countries such as Venezuela, Saudi Arabia, and Iran. But getting such intelligence from them "is one of the hardest jobs we have."[39]

The energy industry continues to lobby and propagandize against all proposals for the development of independent and reliable data. It is most wary of legislation introduced by Senator Gaylord Nelson (Democrat, Wisconsin) to establish a National Energy Information System to collect comprehensive figures, employing uniform methods and set in historic and comparative frameworks.[40] Such efforts to inventory energy resources are designed to preclude another panic where once again no one would have reliable information. But to the corporations and their trade associations these are "unwarranted incursions" or "fishing expeditions" by a bureaucratic monster at loose in business territory. "Oilmen cut their teeth on competition," explained the chairman of Texaco, and public disclosure about energy supplies would constitute "expropriating a company's property" while imposing great burdens on the consumer.[41] The American Gas Association has advised any such office to "avoid getting into the business . . . of conducting its own inventory of resources and reserves. This agency must rely upon industry and other existing Government agencies."[42] Questions concerning reserves and production, crucial for public pricing policies but objectionable to the American Petroleum Institute, were deleted from a 1974 questionnaire designed by the Federal Energy Administration. The FEA had been given the responsibility, in the wake of the new skepticism about basic facts, for developing independent data.[43]

Meanwhile, the crude oil price regulations of the Federal Energy Administration—a function delegated to it by the Cost of Living Council in December 1973—continued to be based upon the oil industry's posted pricing system. Yet, as a staff report of the Federal Trade Commission had warned the previous year, these posted prices were artificially high and anticompetitive, set by the major oil companies, who were still operating "much like a cartel."[44]

Top Interior spokesmen have defended the integrated industry as the nation's "principal asset" for obtaining energy and have favored the entry of the petroleum companies into oil shale, tar sands, and synthetic fuels. Not surprisingly then, the federal government also lacks independent or publicly-oriented research. Indeed, it has abdicated its memory to the private sector. Thus, it is completely responsive to corporate definitions of "technological readiness" when considering alternative energy sources. Dramatic calls for technological crash programs to meet the new energy scare rip out of historical context the record of public and private research in shale and coal. They obscure the fact that the United States had federally-run experiments and pilot plants as far back as fifty years ago and that coal-oil laboratories were set up by the

Bureau of Mines during World War II. The shale oil pilot plant at Rifle, Colorado, and the Laramie, Wyoming, laboratory, along with coal-to-gas plants, were closed down in the fifties, not because of technological failures, but because the industry insisted and the government conceded that the next step toward introducing such fuels onto the market should be a private determination.[45] Yet the charade continues as once more shale experiments are closed down.

New federal loans and grants to stimulate research in the private sectors, proposed in a host of bills during the energy scare, have ignored completely the industry's behavior in these areas in the past. And they perpetuate the myth that the United States is still in Adam Smith's world of private initiative. There are no assurances of the possibility of entry by newcomers and "small" businesses who conceivably might introduce competitive fuels, technologies, and pricing. Nor is there recognition that belated coal research contracts have gone chiefly to the giant energy corporations.

Against this entrenched power, cabinet and other presidential appointees are transients with limited impact, even when they seek to exercise their authority. A tough and public-minded Harold E. Ickes was certain he could ride herd on the oil industry. Thus, he welcomed the integration of the economic with the political as providing what he assumed would be the more efficient handles for public control. His immediate successors simply drifted with the system, there always being "emergency" needs to rationalize such acquiescence.[46]

Stewart L. Udall, a passionate conservationist at the helm of Interior under presidents Kennedy and Johnson, relied upon the climate and constituency of the "new frontier" for support.[47] But decent and articulate sentiments were inadequate instruments of public policy in face of the staying power of those who viewed the department as an extension of the private domain. At critical points, such as in conflict with then Governor John Connally's insistence upon state prorationing control over the outer continental shelf, he found it easier to go along than fight.[48] The key decisions to develop oil in California's Santa Barbara channel were made during his regime. Dissident voices in Interior and California were ignored in the face of industry desires. When later reviewing his environmental "Bay of Pigs" (he cited several), Udall recalled the cocksureness of everyone involved that such a disaster could not happen. There were also "pressures from the Bureau of the Budget and the White House two years ago. The Vietnam war was at a high point . . . and the amount that could be realized on a sale [of oil leases] was significant. There was not sufficient attention given to the environmental risks that were being taken."[49]

Acutely aware that Interior functioned "under the shadow of Teapot Dome," Udall found it safer to be cautious than innovative. He recognized that oil shale could provide public leverage for a national policy on energy. But how to do this without stirring an industry watchful of his every move and working right within his own department to protect its private priorities for development? The familiar bureaucratic solution was to keep reassuring all that the problem was being studied. At one point preliminary leasing calls were announced, but on terms that the industry found easy to refuse. The focus on protection against predatory-speculative interests kept much of the public lands under public control, although the secretary had failed to withdraw all shale lands from other mineral claims.[50] Udall thus kept his integrity and the public held on to its lands. A secretary of the interior had been neutralized. And a chance to launch a battle for proposals such as a national energy corporation to develop shale as a yardstick and strategic reserve was lost. With it was abdicated an opportunity for public education on energy and on the realities of the power forces dominating its development.

The oil-sponsored appointment of Walter J. Hickel as secretary by President Nixon brought a searing nomination hearing of the kind infrequently undertaken in the Senate.[51] A frontier developer whose many interests had included oil leasing and natural gas distribution, he shared a common perspective with oilmen. Alaska was a challenge—overpowering, untamed. Yet there were few sources of income for settlers and the state. As governor, Hickel had opposed Secretary of the Interior Udall's freeze on federal lands to be taken under the statehood act until native claims were resolved. To Hickel, these could be settled without slowing up the exploration for oil or surrendering too much land. ("Just because somebody's grandfather chased a moose across the land doesn't mean he owns it.")[52] He had favored turning over the naval petroleum reserves to Interior and also was eager to see contiguous wildlife areas "inventoried" for their resources. He had followed an industry position and testified against the Machiasport refinery and free trade zone plan for Maine. Giving little thought to conflict-of-interest issues, he had not hesitated to appoint oilmen to public office, including the commissioner of natural resources. One special adviser was a United States Chamber of Commerce lobbyist who had opposed strict federal conservation regulations and water pollution controls. "It was just his natural willingness to help and probably a simple rapport," explained Hickel.

"Conservation just for conservation purposes" made little sense to those who saw worth in resources only when the market placed a price on them. "If we lived within the letter of the law," Hickel had said, "we'd be one big national park." Conservation should not stop the state's growth: "If the Federal Water Pollution Control Act affects our industry too much, we may have to tell the federal government to go fly a kite."[53]

Exposure to the relentless questioning of apprehensive senators may have alerted the aggressive governor from Alaska to the broader demands of national office—at least where the consequences were visible and dramatic. "Native claims" had become a test of America's belated willingness to respect the cultures and right of self-determination of people caught in its expansion and its technological rush. Hickel agreed not to lift the freeze without congressional consultation to assure that justice had been done. He supported land and cash payments through native development corporations. But he and Interior resisted the idea of royalty payments, claiming "this would place on our natives an uncertain element of risk."[54] To a spokesman for the business community, who had been the territory's first commissioner of natural resources, the proposed settlement gave the natives up to 50 percent of the land realistically available to the new state, a division "which could create a competitive sovereign power."[55] But to native spokesmen who saw their people after protracted negotiations surrendering aboriginal title in exchange for perhaps 10 percent of Alaska, such solicitude reflected the white fear of giving them a continuing voice in the new state's development.[56]

The new secretary showed anger over the lassitude and irresponsibility behind the Santa Barbara oil spill which occurred just after he took office. At first he assumed channel drilling, save for the offending Platform A, could continue. After viewing the debacle Hickel arranged pledges from the heads of other companies to suspend drilling in the channel until Interior could study the environmental damage and draft tighter regulations. It was now disclosed, in contrast to earlier claims, that leasing regulations had not been overhauled in fifteen years despite changes in drilling technology, gaps in geological knowledge of the area, and new environmental standards.[57] Then Hickel discovered, he later wrote, that Interior bureaucrats had authorized the resumption of drilling.[58] Literally overnight the industry and Interior had agreed to new drilling techniques and safeguards.[59] By the next day the moratorium, except for the Union platform, had been lifted. Many Californians were outraged by the cynical "tokenism," as the speedy resumption was labeled by one Santa Barbara County supervisor.[60] Under public pressure, Interior issued an absolute ban, while continuing to join the industry in minimizing the damage. But drilling soon received a go-ahead from a presidential panel which heard testimony for two days from Interior and oil officials. Its laconic report recommended that the best way to stop oil leaks caused by the pressures on the cracked ocean floor was to resume pumping in order to deplete the reservoirs as rapidly as possible.[61] This solution could take at least ten years. After he left office, Hickel said there was "some truth" to the recurring charge that Interior had been in "the pocket of big business." He recalled that some Interior staff "had worked so closely with oil men for so many years that they simply could not conceive of a Secretary of Interior doing something about an oil slick."[62]

Hickel exploded again when confronted with the statement of the president of a company planning a huge refinery complex on the coast of Georgia and South Carolina near wetlands and fishing waters, who had admitted that "we are going to pollute" by piping the worst effluent into the ocean. "It's only a question of how much. But, I think, with proper marketing and proper construction we're not going to pollute this area. What we are going to do is contribute to the pollution of the world." To the secretary, "it was an arrogant statement . . ., the kind of arrogance the industry does not need. If they want to challenge me, I'll find authority. . . . They ought to be ostracized for such a statement."[63]

In 1970 a Chevron platform in the Gulf of Mexico caught fire because of negligence and created a sizable oil slick. Subsequent inspections showed that hundreds of other offshore wells were also defective. Hickel moved to prosecute. "You've got to hit them with a two-by-four to make them believe you," he explained.[64] The outcome was a criminal indictment against nine companies for some 1,500 "willful" offenses. All pleaded nolo contendere, and the companies (not of course their officers) received substantial fines.

The intent of these actions was to put other producers on notice. At the same time, the Interior Department was forced to review its reliance on oil company self-policing as to pollution control safety, its own standards of regulation, and its own ability to regulate for safety. The "no contest," however, effectively shielded from the public much of the record about the performance of oil and Interior. But there was no escaping the consequences of an agency such as the United States Geological Survey, undermanned or not, operating without any apparent awareness of the conflict between its role as a promoter and celebrant of the frontier development of the outer continental shelf and its responsibility as a regulatory body enforcing environmental standards.

Hickel's stay as secretary was brief. The actions against oil brought cool winds from the White House. These became icy after, unable to gain an appointment, he wrote a letter to President Nixon, which became public, in which he deplored the insensitivity of the administration to protests over the Cambodian invasion and the polarizing impact of Vice-President Spiro Agnew's savage, self-righteous attacks upon youthful critics. With the killing of four Kent State University students by a National Guard intervention, encouraged by the White House, very much in mind, Hickel concluded that the critics were being afforded no opportunity to communicate with the government "other than through violent confrontations."[65] No contrast was made—or needed—with the opportunity of the oil industry for access.

The arrival of Hickel's replacement, Rogers C. B. Morton, a former congressman and chairman of the Republican National Committee, signaled that Interior was to be a refuge for the politically faithful as well as the spokesman for private industry. His general comments throughout the energy crisis were that prices

were too low and that the public was overcritical of the industry's
profits. Indeed, profits were not high enough. The best way to
develop new supplies, Morton argued, was to provide the corporations with a strong profit motive by allowing them to make large
increases in what they charged.[66]

In deference to the industry, the secretary refused to appraise
seriously an alternative Canadian route for Alaskan oil. His explanation for relying upon the involved oil companies to explore
with the Canadian government (and quickly reject) the possibilities
was that it was not within the legal province of Interior to study
the environmental consequences of a pipeline on foreign territory.
He had the backing of the president, who, despite pleas from
Midwesterners in his own party who wanted to see the oil flow to
their region, insisted that the route would have to be through
Alaska and the West Coast. The reason, Nixon was reported to
have said to Republican congressional leaders, was embedded in
foreign policy and national security: "You will just have to take
that on faith." Holding hearings on the department's final environmental impact statement was seen by Interior as not necessary;
there had been "ample opportunity for substantive comment" prior
to publication. (Critics noted that only seven copies of the nine-
volume study were made available for public inspection in the
"lower forty-eight" states; once available, sets could be purchased
for $42.50.) According to the undersecretary, Morton felt that "a
public hearing probably would be a circus."[67]

In 1974 California sought to delay lease sales on the outerconti-
nental shelf until its state environmental plans were completed, and
also sought full public hearings on Interior's program under Project Independence. Morton's responses were in harmony with the
long-standing response of Interior and the industry to such practices. He warned that such deference to state planning, which
California's Coastal Zone Conservation Commission sought in
accord with the federal Coastal Zone Management Act of 1972
and a California act of the same year, might "in an extreme case
give an important veto over an extremely important national decision to a very limited number of people."[68] When, in 1974, at a
special dinner (resplendent with the presence of President Ford and
Secretary of State Kissinger) designed to "sell" offshore drilling to

recalcitrant coastal state governors, the newly elected chief executive of Maine asked about state participation in such federal planning, Morton told him to sit down and await the question period.[69]

When replying on behalf of the president to a letter from twenty senators criticizing the 1975 goals as premature, Morton defended the leasing of the outer continental shelf as essential in reducing inflationary costs and the dependence upon imported oil. He reasoned that it would be much cheaper to produce the outer continental shelf petroleum. (Costs were estimated at $1.40 to $3.50 per barrel, as opposed to $11 for imported oil.) He added that "while this oil will sell within the United States at world prices, the difference between $11 and $1.40 to $3.50 will remain in the United States in the form of bonus payments for the leases and taxes (and hence lower U.S. taxes), higher wages and reinvestable profits." He did not offer any analysis of the premise of his rejoinder, including the rationale for accepting world prices (which had increased 400 percent) as the domestic guide—prices which on another occasion he had described as "unconscionably high." Nor did he break down the dollar flow to verify who would really be gaining what.[70]

Morton, who under Nixon's administration also headed the President's Energy Resources Council, insisted that the energy crisis was rooted in "government interference" with pricing and "a temporary situation which the American motivation, the American genius, and the free enterprise system can very well work itself out of if given the opportunity."[71] The need was for restructuring policies, and prices to bring up domestic production which had been allowed to lag behind rising demand. "I am going to turn you loose over all outdoors," he promised a meeting of the exploration and production industry.[72] And to petroleum executives assembled in the White House for a briefing, he gave repeated assurance—perhaps unnecessary given the record, but presumably comforting in the face of public outcry over shortages, prices and the priority of loyalties of international corporations who seemed more responsive to Arab than to American requirements—that

the Office of Oil and Gas is an institution which is designed to be your institution, and to help you in any way that it can. . . . Our mission is to serve you; not regulate you. We try to avoid it. I have tried to avoid regulation to the degree that I possibly can. . . . We want to be sure that we come up with guidelines and programs, where guidelines are necessary, that have a maximum of input by people who make their living in the marketplace. I pledge to you that the Department is at your service. We cannot be all things to all people. We cannot straddle issues. We have to do business today and tomorrow.[73]

FPC commissioners generally continue to be oil and gas lawyers with the proper political credentials. For example, Rush Moody, Jr., came in 1971 from a Texas law firm with powerful oil and gas clients, including Texaco and Mobil. Congressional critics charged that the post was first "offered" to Moody by William C. Liedtke, Jr., president of Pennzoil United, which had substantial natural gas-producing and pipeline holdings. Mr. Liedtke had secretly funneled $700,000 of oil and gas campaign contributions to the Committee to Re-Elect the President prior to Moody's nomination by President Nixon. Moody's subsequent opinion in a pivotal rate case opened the door to a major price increase and de facto deregulation. The FPC staff had documented the absence of competition in the industry, the collusive behavior of such giants as Texaco and Tenneco, and the resultant fallacy of dependence upon the "free play of the market" for the public's protection. According to Representative George E. Brown, Jr. (Democrat, California), who had watched and then contested the rate hearings, the commissioners "totally dismissed the critical evidence submitted by their own staff . . ., berating them for having attempted to present a strong, factually supported case concerned with consumer interests."[74]

"Good" commissioners generally have embraced the commitment to nonregulation—a far cry from the stereotype of power-mad bureaucrats. Extending federal regulation to the one-third of natural gas not now covered, so as to make regulation effective, is heresy. And an FPC ruling that it does not have jurisdiction over synthetic gas provided a clear signal for the energy corporations to move ahead with intensive stripmining and coal gasification and liquefaction, confident of the forthcoming higher prices for all energy. The day after one such opinion Exxon announced its plans to accelerate development in these areas. The FPC decision with its explanation for the dissimilarity of synthetic gas to natural gas was, according to one Senate staff member, "not only an insult to the intelligence, but might even be considered an act of gross malfeasance."[75]

Commissioner Pinkney Walker, a former business school dean and a consultant to pipeline interests, had no difficulty in accepting industry data. He consistently called for deregulation and higher profits, as did Chairman John N. Nassikas, a former utility lawyer and Nixon's first appointment to the FPC, and Commissioner Carl E. Bagge. The latter moved on to head the National Coal Association. There he continued to warn against the shackles of regulation and the rhetoric of antitrust. In their place he welcomed the emerging energy conglomerate of coal, oil, gas, and nuclear power as "the only way we can rationally go" to mobilize capital for the salvation of the coal industry and the resolution of a national energy crisis.[76] FPC general counsel R. Gordon Gooch came from the same law firm as Moody, where one of the senior partners was general counsel of Pennzoil. Gooch defended the secrecy of industry reserve data as well as other industry positions which so effectively emasculated his agency. He left the FPC after three years to become a fund raiser for the Committee to Re-Elect the President and to represent his law firm in Washington. Gooch's chief assistant at the FPC was Stephen A. Wakefield of the same law firm and later to move to Interior.

A general insensitivity to the ethical dimensions of public service allowed the appointment in 1972 of Claude S. Brinegar, a senior vice-president of Union Oil, to head the Department of Transportation. While there were no specific grievances against the executive's personal record, conservationists were troubled by his company's performance on pollution. The passion for lacing California with freeways, which it shared with Standard of California and automotive and trucking interests, led Union since the late sixties to support lobbies opposing proposals for earmarking a portion of the state's gasoline tax for mass transit. Union had also been part of the opposition to a coastline protection referendum seeking tight public control over coastal drilling and power plant siting. It had been charged with repeatedly dumping oily refinery waste into the Los Angeles harbor. In the courts, the company contested the authority of the state agency rather than the substance of the original cease and desist order of the generally impotent Los Angeles Regional Water Quality Control Board, on which Union's chief pollution officer sat as the industry representative.[77]

More disturbing was the nomination in 1972 of William P. Clements, Jr., as deputy secretary of defense. Clements had headed the largest overseas drilling company and along with his business associates was a Nixon campaign contributor in the April 1972 charade to beat the disclosure deadline. At the time of his appointment, Clements was a defendant in a civil suit which charged that he and his company had cheated an Argentine businessman on commissions for oil drilling contracts, had bribed high officials of the Argentine government, and then had destroyed many of the records. A legislative investigation in Argentina found "profound immorality and corruption." All these charges were denied by Clements. According to the White House, there was nothing in the case that "in any way disqualified Mr. Clements from assuming the position." He was confirmed without any requirement that he divest himself of his more than $100 million stock in the Southwest Drilling Company (SEDCO). Clements was then appointed as Pentagon representative to the President's Emergency Energy Action Group. He was also responsible for military programs concerning naval petroleum, and clients of his company were drilling near the boundaries of the giant reserve in Alaska. (It had long been believed that there was substantial oil to be found in NPR-4, but the navy's program did not allow for the kind of deep drilling which led to the Prudhoe Bay discoveries.) In response to critics, Clements insisted his duties were restricted to "technical matters." Yet Defense Department documents indicated that Clements supported the creation of a Defense Energy Policy Council "reporting directly to me for the purpose of approving major policies relating to energy matters."

He also backed a recommendation of a Defense task force, which he had created, calling for industry exploration and drilling of the Alaska naval petroleum reserves. Meanwhile, the President's Emergency Energy Action Group explored strategies for opening up to commercial development the neighboring Arctic National Wildlife Refuge. The secretary of defense finally assured the public that his deputy would withdraw from such policy areas.[78] But the tradition of placing oilmen in strategic administrative posts in the Department of the Navy heightens the odds against the emergence of any genuinely public policies.

On occasions the political system has generated resistance to such invasions. Thus the Senate successfully blocked the appointment of Robert H. Morris to the Federal Power Commission in 1973 because he had represented Standard Oil of California during most of his legal career, including natural gas cases before the commission. No challenges were raised about the nominee's ability or integrity. But the prevailing sentiment was that it was time for one clear consumer voice on a presumably independent regulatory body dominated by industry viewpoints.[79]

Policy makers need not be oilmen to embrace industry positions, as the record of William E. Simon demonstrated. A Wall Street bond trader whose company (Salomon Brothers) was a large underwriter for energy securities and a contributor on Rose Mary Wood's list, Simon headed energy efforts under Nixon. As deputy secretary of the Treasury and then as federal energy administrator during the 1973 alarm, he quickly created an aura of efficiency and purpose. Given his commitment to "private enterprise," he saw no reason to challenge industry-generated information and the technical input of corporate advisers and of the many former oil executives in the FEA. Oil cooperation with government was "outstanding." Indeed, he lobbied against provisions requiring detailed disclosures by the oil companies. As chairman of the President's Interagency Oil Policy Committee he wrote to the chairman of the Federal Trade Commission to express his "distress" over the FTC's suit charging eight major oil companies with monopolizing petroleum refining and manipulating shortages to the detriment of independents and consumers. "I find it difficult to accept the concept that the industry is not competitive." Rather than blame the oil corporations, Mr. Simon was certain that demand had outrun supply because of past public policies which offered inadequate financial incentives and were responsive to environmentalists who opposed new refinery sitings. Talk of divestiture would inhibit the industry and intensify the energy crisis. He sought a meeting with the FTC chairman to elaborate, a request denied on ethical and legal grounds since the case was then being adjudicated by the commission. Mr. Simon also released a Treasury Department critique of the FTC staff report; the former drew heavily upon Office of Oil and Gas data.[80]

Simon reflected the business community's hostility to what he labeled "total reliance" upon conservation: "it would lead to massive new interventions by the government in the private sector." Very much in mind were not speed limits for motorists, but construction standards for the automotive industry and comparable controls over other corporate sectors.

Simon was an advocate of accelerated development of the outer continental shelf by the major companies. He defended high oil prices, and in 1974 at his confirmation hearing for the post of secretary of the treasury he warned the senators against taking any "punitive" actions against the industry. (Once in office, he resisted pleas for loan guarantees from New York and other cities on the verge of bankruptcy, largely as a consequence of their efforts to compensate on a local level, with an inadequate income base, for a national government insensitive to unemployment, migration, welfare and public services. If there was to be any financial assistance, Simon admonished, the terms must be "so punitive, the overall experience be made so painful, that no city . . . would ever be tempted to go" beyond the pale of what he viewed as the proper role and fiscal integrity of government.)[81] Even "punitive comments" (regulation, public utility status, nationalization) had adverse consequences for the public good. For the captains of oil were sensitive to their primary obligations to shareholders, and if the future gave "great pause" they might diversify rather than return their profits to energy development. And if they did, as when Mobil invested in Marcor, this should be allowed, "as long as they are honestly earned profits." When the crude oil allocation program was inaugurated, Simon dismissed fears that the affected companies would divert supplies intended for the United States; he insisted that their patriotic responses would preclude such action and would obviate the necessity for more effective government enforcement. A subsequent Treasury memorandum conceded that "when the regulations were published in draft form without the compensatory measures, there was an immediate diversion of crude oil already in transit away from the United States to other destinations." Oil producing nations were told that their politics were "bad policies and bad economics." Given the ability of the United States to achieve energy independence by 1980 through conservation and new coal and nuclear technologies, even becoming an exporter once more, petroleum in the ground was a relatively poor investment. Prices would decline. Sell now and invest your money for a greater return was his business advice across the sea. And don't expect to avoid the consequences of the global disruption caused by the sharp price rises. Throughout his tenure Simon pledged to oil industry leaders continued efforts by the Ford administration to resist "surrender to a small band of [Arab] black-mailers." Nothing in all the disclosures as to the energy crisis and Middle Eastern policies justified stronger public intervention in corporate negotiations with producing countries. "It is proper for our government to provide advice to U.S. companies. But I do not believe the decision-making responsibility on the operation of their foreign trading activities and their foreign investments should be assumed by the U.S. government." Instead he would work to create "greater freedom in the energy marketplace" for the corporations. "Persuading the people will be a big job for both of us."[82]

His successor at the Federal Energy Administration in 1974 was John C. Sawhill, a business economist who opposed all proposals for a public energy corporation then being proposed and who campaigned vigorously for private development of western coal lands and all other fossil fuel resources. The marketplace was held to be the best way to allocate resources and bring the nation nearer to self-sufficiency. He found oil profits "reasonable" and concluded that "consumers are just going to have to live with these energy costs" without expectation of public subsidy. Natural gas had to be deregulated to remove uncertainty for developers. To help the electric utilities throughout the nation gain larger rate increases, he sponsored a meeting of state regulatory agencies and the Federal Power Commission to suggest ways to speed up automatic price increases—and thus destroy effective rate regulation. At this Washington conference—preempted by now Secretary of the Treasury Simon—FPC chairman Nassikas, Sawhill, and other federal officials warned the state representatives, many of whom resented what they felt was interference, that their failure to let private utilities gain a higher rate of return would lead to new brownouts and blackouts. "And worse," added Simon, "economic stagnation."[83]

Yet Sawhill was viewed suspiciously by the oil industry, Secretary of the Interior Morton, and Secretary of the Treasury Simon. To help set the tone for the FEA, he announced strict conflict-of-interest standards and indicated he would not go to work for the oil industry when he left. Lobbyists were required to register, and top management was to record and disclose the substance of conversations with people who had regulatory matters before the agency. He opposed the decontrol of "old oil" prices. He was skeptical about the original claims of Project Independence, doubting whether it was practical for the United States to become self sufficient in energy. He was against joint bidding for offshore leasing by the majors. He publicly expressed the belief that the administration under which he was serving had no plan for checking world oil prices—an admission upsetting to those who equated public relations with public policy. And he had explored monitoring negotiations between the international oil corporations and producing nations. He charged the major companies with "footdragging and calculated resistance" to the government's plan for them to share·their relatively cheaper crude oil with independent refineries who were dependent upon domestic "new oil" not under price controls and upon expensive imports. He was outspoken in his advocacy of a decisive conservation policy, including a refundable gasoline tax then opposed by President Ford, to bring energy demand and supply into balance by reducing the 30 percent of total energy use that was "pure waste." If such a target was taken seriously, many industrial practices and prerogatives would have had to be changed. It wasn't long before President Ford asked for his resignation. The White House explanation was "executive incompatibility." Reluctant to conclude that oil had "undue" or "excessive" power in the administration or Congress, Sawhill did concede that the industry "certainly does exercise a lot more influence than I realized when I came down here. . . . I was just surprised at the tremendous number of people here in Washington . . . connected one way or another with the oil industry."[84]

One person within the Federal Energy Administration who apparently was not surprised was Lee Richardson, director of the Office of Consumer Affairs. His eight-page letter of resignation in the middle of 1974 offered a savage critique of the FEA's "direct collision course with the best interests of consumers." The office had been created to appease mounting anger over the complete marriage of industry and government at the expense of the public. But the departing consumer advocate claimed that the office was given no policy function. The FEA accepted industry price increase and profit demands as necessary for increased energy supply without independent assembly or analysis of the information needed for such judgment. It was disinterested in its mandate to protect and promote the competitive sectors of the energy industry. It blamed rising energy costs on the environmentalists and raised few safety questions in its support of nuclear energy. The FEA treated consumer energy policy "as a welfare problem."

> FEA's attitude has been that some groups of consumers will complain when energy costs to them are higher than the average for other consumers. Therefore, a handful of New England homes with total electric dependence, a group of migrant families short of gasoline, or some few households cheated by a fuel oil dealer are but subjects for a little relief. Surely these and similar groups with special impact problems deserve attention, but the root cause of many such problems is the very structure and priorities which FEA builds into the system. A great deal of suffering could be prevented if consumer considerations were built directly into the formulation of basic price levels, allocation systems, resource development programs and other substantive policy matters.[85]

President Ford's nominee to replace Sawhill late in 1974 was Andrew E. Gibson, former administrator of the Maritime Administration and assistant secretary of commerce. Gibson had found it not at all troubling to serve public and private masters. After helping to design and gain adoption of a multimillion-dollar federal ship subsidy program during the Nixon regime, he became president of Interstate Oil Transport Company. The latter, half owned by Cities Service, hauled oil for oil utility corporations and was a chief beneficiary of the program. Cities Service also had a subsidy contract for transporting wheat to Russia in its tankers, an agreement which Gibson had helped negotiate. His termination arrangement, after a little over a year in the corporate fold, assured him almost a million dollars, to be paid out over ten years. He reasoned that since this severance agreement was ironclad it would not pose any conflict of interest in his duties as energy administrator. The White House had second thoughts. It did not relish the prospects of strong questioning in the Senate, including airing more details about the already awkward grain deal and the implications for natural gas regulation of plans to import expensive liquified natural gas.[86] The nomination was withdrawn. Watergate was presumably past history and standards of political morality were to be strengthened. But oil was to retain its accustomed immunity.

# 8

## Planning for New Beginnings

The cumulative record of the politics of oil cries out for fundamental reappraisal of the rules of the game that have shaped energy and growth policy. Organizing basic natural resources on premises of greed, whether individual, corporate, or national, remains destructive for the environment and for human solidarity. Accelerated "liberation" of the energies of nature, long equated with the liberation of human energies and spirit, becomes mindless looting of irreparable proportions when divorced from concern for the full social price for the living and the unborn. Comprehensive bookkeeping of a sort men have been reluctant to devise is required to assess the worth of immediate comforts and penetrate the disguise behind which energy-intensive techniques have increased, rather than decreased, the dependence of individuals and communities upon forces beyond their control. Spreading the benefits of industrialism a little more widely may mute criticisms. But it does not resolve the issues of power and of respect for the environment. And the use of rediscovered ecological wisdom as an argument against such broadened sharing becomes a convenient defense for existing structures of power and privilege within the United States and internationally.

In the main, American governmental efforts support "business as usual": risk is shifted to taxpayers, costs to consumers, and now blame to ecologists or to foreigners (Arabs, non-Arabs, Canadians, Venezuelans—whoever has acquired greater sophistication about the government of oil). Profits, of course, remain private. Public government in the United States retains the primary function of helping to keep supply down and prices up at levels wherein maxi-

mum gain accrues to the energy corporations. It is also expected
to serve as a relief agency when social costs become too glaring.
Then problems are labeled "emergency." The issues are quickly
coopted and formal administration placed in the hands of professional crisis managers. Fragmented responses to cohesive historical
forces are offered as public policies. Thoroughgoing solutions are
ruled out, and the structure of power over energy is preserved.

In such a setting, reliance upon the mythical free market sanctions the continued freedom of corporate forces to control and
allocate capital, resources, technology, and labor, as well as political power, in harmony with their private definitions of growth
and need. The claim that the planning of the modern corporation
has shifted from profit maximization to growth and security is a
deceptive way of reporting that the giants have the resources for
taking a somewhat longer view of their profit objectives than do
smaller enterprises. But the cash nexus remains; the corporation
cannot justify investing its internally generated capital or turning
to the money markets for projects which will not bring a return.
Neither the tough posturing of political leaders who call for regulation or even "breaking them up," nor the gentle cooing of business leaders as to their social awareness, however well-intentioned,
is a substitute for a responsible social system. They serve primarily
to forestall the development of the political mechanisms necessary
for energy programs responsive to broader human requirements
and possibilities.

There has been a rebirth of populist sentiment against concentrated economic power, and the continuing battles to place corporate political power within responsible bounds deserve support.
The work of committees headed by senators Lee Metcalf, Philip
A. Hart, and Frank Church to document the nature of corporate
power and then suggest ways to make the economic system more
accountable and lessen its political influence have provided valuable public education. More effectively administered laws on campaign financing and disclosure championed by groups such as Common Cause can be worthwhile reforms, as would the prohibition
against shifting political advertising and lobbying to the consumer
pocket and the public treasury as business expenditures. More

rigorous controls over lobbying activities, including stringent public disclosure requirements, applicable to dealings with the executive as well as the legislative branches, may help citizens gain a fuller picture as to who supports or opposes what public policies and how. Such scrutiny about the privilege of privacy may also lead to a redefinition of the legal claim to citizenship of the modern corporation. Senator William Proxmire and a vigorous corps from the House of Representatives have picked up from Paul H. Douglas to hammer against the tax privileges of the oil industry. Legislative actions to tighten the depletion allowance where it does not encourage desired domestic production (it has been cut to 22 percent, and giant corporations are to lose it entirely) and to eliminate overseas tax credits can help to make pricing and tax burdens more open, if not necessarily more just. (Facing the inevitable, the president of Atlantic Richfield took the corporate lead in 1973 by calling for the end of the depletion subsidy. He added the caveat that the consumer would be expected to compensate the industry for such "losses" of $2.5 to $3 billion annually through a 2 cents a gallon increase in the price of gasoline.)[1]

Removing—not simply making more representative—private advisory bodies now nesting cozily within the public bureaucracy would be a step toward visible and accountable government. The proposed requirement that decision-making sessions of regulatory agencies be opened to public scrutiny might help remind all participants that the deliberations are for defining the public interest rather than protecting the privileged and the bureaucratic. The revitalization of public service commissions in a number of states is another healthy trend toward implementing a public dimension in utility activities. A much-resisted "line of business" amendment, tagged onto the Trans-Alaska Pipeline Authorization Act and requiring from giant corporations a product breakdown of aggregate data about allocation of assets, sales, advertising, research, development, and profits, can help regulatory agencies such as the Federal Trade Commission become more effective in gauging business performance. Dissident stockholders organized against such practices as discrimination, subterranean politicking, and support for authoritarian regimes have offered ethical prodding to corporate boards and managers who have long assumed that the cash dividend is the ultimate test. Public interest law suits have reminded public agencies as to their legal responsibilities and their proper constituencies. In *Sierra Club et al. v. Rogers C. B. Morton et al.* (1973), for example, a cluster of environmental and civic groups, including the National Wildlife Federation, the Northern Plains Resource Council, the Montana Wilderness Association and state Leagues of Women Voters, sought to prevent the losing of the West by asking Interior to prepare thorough environmental analyses before further leasing coal lands, as they interpreted the requirements of the National Environmental Policy Act.[2] One basic admission smoked out in this action was that the Department of the Interior had no comprehensive plan for development. (Exxon, Shell, and other corporations directly involved have denounced such litigation and its objectives as a great waste of dollars and time.) Suits under the Freedom of Information Act (1967) have helped ferret out information indispensable for alternative approaches to public policy but which public bureaucracies have preferred to treat as privileged, so often a convenience for incompetence, private loyalty, or venality. Leasing requirements which reduce corporate speculation with public lands and give the greater return have been hard-fought and positive victories.

These measures remain inadequate for effective confrontation with the economic power of the private government of oil and for displacing its controls and its privileges. The corruption of the political economy and democratic life continues. Personal fulfillment is accepted as a substitute for a citizen's right to share in the shaping of public affairs. In the international arena, a search for codes of constraints upon international corporations evades the building of regional and national counterforces at home.

The primary need remains long-run energy planning that is in harmony with public goals of development and participation. Ideally, and ultimately, there must be a global dimension. But there is little in the record of international government or the charts of engineers and economists who think in terms of global systems to encourage the feeling that such planning, if undertaken presently, would be responsive to the complex needs and desires of the people of the world. Certainly American or European initiative would be suspect, coming just when "third world" oil producing nations feel it is time they were calling some of the shots through versions of national planning, socialism, or a new international economic order, and would be viewed as skeptically as the pressure by anxious Western industrial powers for international ecological standards or for ethical codes to govern the distribution of basic resources no longer under their thumbs. Ecological planning responsive to universal guidelines is necessary if billions of humans are to continue to inhabit the same planet. For example, the sea and its uncharted resources must be respected as a common holding for all members to share equitably while preserving the marine ecosystem. Otherwise it becomes a frontier for creeping seaward annexation by coastal and maritime nations and corporations with sophisticated ocean technology and insatiable thirsts. Cooperative research and regional and international authority to develop and enforce a law of the seas, whether over travel, armaments, pollution, fishing, farming, or oil drilling, are imperative. But the present priorities too rarely acknowledge the desperation of those whose very survival is in question daily and for whom a slowdown in the stripping of resources and a redress of basic imbalances would open the door to minimum economic security.

At the opposite end of the policy spectrum, a corollary ideal requires the implementation of what might be called "the case for the bicycle." That is, technological development and energy use are to be accepted only where they anticipate a minimum either of domination over or dependence upon others. Such commitment to live within one's means must be incorporated into the way the world learns to think. If this moral imperative is to take hold, economic growth and rebuilding must be to scales which maximize individual autonomy consistent with human brotherhood.

Backyard factories, rank-and-file participation in management, locally-controlled media, and neighborhood bakeries may have an irrelevant Gandhian or even Maoist ring to Americans grown accustomed to Standard Oil and International Business Machines and to palates cultivated by National Broadcasting and Continental Baking. But more satisfying work for individuals and a greater self-reliance for communities are unfulfilled needs for Americans who live as strangers in their own land.[3]

One cannot pretend that the American nation has the option to start afresh on its ravaged continent. But the people can make a new beginning for themselves and the rest of the world by placing on their own political agenda public ownership and democratic planning of all domestic energy resources. To this end Congress and the president should create a temporary national energy committee with the specific mandate to develop alternative approaches for public control and for the transition requirements for phasing out private control. Perhaps a two-year life span and membership drawn heavily from outside the formal political arena or the energy industry payroll might help keep the committee from becoming another device for obscuring needs and shelving innovation. It could then be replaced by a national energy planning board responsible for shaping and coordinating energy policy in harmony with economic and technological goals arrived at by related planning agencies also to be created. The successes and failures of the Temporary National Economic Committee, the National Resources Planning Board, the Tennessee Valley Authority, the Rural Electrification Administration, and the Council of Economic Advisers (as originally intended), limited as these experiences have been, might provide some guidelines here.

The time is long past for believing that intermediate steps for increasing accountability within the present private planning system will suffice. Trustbusting, despite the heroic imagery conjured up by the term, functions as timorous research or a common scold. The Antitrust Division, at its best, is painfully aware of ultimate limits and expects to be outwitted, outwaited, called off, or ignored. The Justice Department saw no threat to a free market in Continental Oil's takeover of Consolidation Coal since, it explained, the two marketed in different regions and were not likely to be in significant competition. Nor did Attorney General Mitchell let it pursue the implications for American energy supply of the domination of both the North Slope reserves and the Alaskan pipeline by three majors. Antitrust found its hands tied politically and diplomatically when it questioned British Petroleum's American invasion and mergers. (After all, the major United States oil combinations were dominant in the North Sea, although BP and Shell had sizable shares. And until 1974, when the Labor government moved for higher taxes, greater public control, and partial nationalization through majority public participation, leasing terms had been very generous.) The Justice Department has searched without success for an appropriate tack within the conventional antitrust frame for dealing with Mobil's takeover of Marcor. It instituted over two hundred investigations into petroleum and related industries from 1963 to 1973, filing some forty criminal and civil suits. Cases are often ended through inconclusive consent decrees. Or they suffer the fate of the investigation of the Colonial Pipeline joint venture, whose planned capacity, based upon existing markets of its owners, has in effect excluded competing refiners. This has been under what the Justice Department describes as "active study" for fifteen years.[4] Antitrust enforcement still awaits the right chance and backing to prove its efficacy. Unfortunately, the first condition for success appears to be the absence of corporate power.

Nevertheless, the temporary committee might also be asked to review the experience with and potentials of the familiar spectrum of ameliorative proposals, including more effective corporate disclosure about costs, pricing, tax calculations, profits, and actual ownership; regulation and antitrust actions including the holding of board members and management personally responsible for corporate offenses; breaking up of the integrated companies so as to outlaw ownership or control of more than one phase of the business; divestiture of control of competing energy sources; federal chartering to define directors' obligations, workers' and stockholders' rights, and community and national interest in corporate performance; and public representation on corporate boards. Would splitting up the oil industry into more units, hopefully competitive ones, diminish reliance on price and profit as determinants of the allocation of resources and the protection of the environment? Proponents who build good arguments against administered prices and withheld technologies seem less persuasive when dealing with the larger social and political consequences of private control over energy.

Would government ownership of minority or even majority stockholdings make any difference? The answer, from the British Petroleum model, where the crown has held controlling interest since 1914, is not encouraging. BP shows no evidence of any higher adherence to public objectives. The government possesses the right to nominate two board members with power to veto any resolution. But the government pledged itself not to interfere in "commercial affairs" and to reserve the veto for areas of general policy. As the holding company's annual report notes, "the right of veto has in fact never been exercised." When in 1975 the Bank of England took over most of Burmah Oil's interest in BP, it promised to respect such patterns and not to use the votes attached to its 20 percent share. In the political arena, BP went along with Shell and their American brethren in the payoffs to Italian politicians.[5]

Examining the case for the integrated operation—public or private—could be valuable. The seductive claim has long been that only big centralized systems harnessing big technology can effectively serve big publics. How valid is this technological determinism? To what extent are the astronomical "capital needs" proclaimed each year in institutional advertising and Chase Manhattan Bank studies—and echoed so solemnly in the financial sections of the press—based not on imperatives for service to the public but on corporate needs to protect their controls? By what tests are expensive marketing operations and forays into chemicals and other industries required investments? A fresh look, not at traditional energy theory or corporate public relations, but at the technological and economic practices of the industry set against social goals and costs, seems overdue. For example, what are the implications for the argument that only integration assures efficiency when some of the companies are organized internally along functional lines? Each department is judged separately as to performance and even has to compete within the parent organization for capital allocation. How different is this from what prevails in the Soviet Union's bureaucratic economy? And what does this feature do to the oil industry's insistence that the "free market" still rules and remains the best way to determine energy priorities?

Does the entire industry have to be taken over and operated along integrated lines? Or would maximum public benefit accrue from controlling the search for and development of energy and creating separate public corporations for refining and transportation? Is it much too late in history to look again to encourage the genuinely lone producer—who has taken most of the risk and found most of the oil—offering reasonable incentive but ensuring that these finds do not become the foundation for new economic extortion or empire? What would be the social gains for retaining a variety of means for distribution? Small private retailers freed from the coercions of the majors could offer genuine service to motorists and also careers to those attracted by the life. Cooperative marketing groups, such as now are run by farmers, and municipally-owned power companies, such as those already existing, are also worthwhile alternatives.

In Canada, the international oil companies, who dominate the country's industry, have been closing down provincial refineries and replacing them with larger, more centralized ones, as at Edmonton. The justifications have been economies of scale and also the relative expense of modifying old plants to meet new ecological requirements. No hard data have been offered to the Canadian public. And the government was not asked to share in the corporate deliberation as to alternatives. We consulted, insisted Imperial, the largest company, which is controlled by Exxon. "Consultation" turned out to mean a letter to the premier of Saskatchewan by the president of Imperial informing him of the decision to shut a Regina plant which had provided direct employment for several hundred workers and income for hundreds more.[6] The province, in familiar fashion, was given little time to appraise or dispute this decision or the cumulative phasing out of exploration. All this was in harmony with the workings of a free market, explained another Imperial executive: Saskatchewan was not an effective competitor, and so industry's investment capital and operations quite properly responded accordingly. Meanwhile, the social costs were transferred to the public ledger. Only belatedly did the nominally socialist government move to weigh the overall advantage of a regional refinery, the possible costs and benefits of moderate-size refinery technology, and the virtues of public ownership of some or all phases of the industry to minimize helplessness in the face of decisions made for the prairies by executives in Toronto and New York board rooms. The militant "Waffle" movement ("if we are always going to waffle, let's waffle to the left") of the New Democratic Party, successors to the Cooperative Commonwealth Federation which first brought elements of socialism to Canada, has been impatient with the caution of provincial action and the passivity of the federal government. It has called for a public corporation to take over the industry.[7]

In the United States, the focus of the Tennessee Valley Authority upon cheap power and the continuing necessity to defend itself from private utilities and their political allies left its directors insensitive to the full impact of its coal-buying policies (as the largest coal purchaser in the nation) upon the people and the land in Appalachia. What planning perspectives and mechanisms are needed to ensure that such experiments expand vision and accountability rather than empire and encrustation and preclude a TVA from becoming simply "another power company"?[8]

All the special privileges and subsidies which have protected the private energy industry from the exigencies of the market should be inventoried and reviewed. Who has gained and with what public justification? If current populist assaults upon such visible (and from the integrated corporation's perspective, relatively easily discardable) privileges as the depletion allowance and even overseas tax credits prevail, the industry's question where new investment money will come from must be met. Much of it has been from the public treasury or from levies upon the consumer through pricing based on replacement rather than production cost. If the energy industry becomes public, how will priorities be determined, costs allocated, and capital generated? What can be learned from societies that have accepted the premise that energy must be the public's business? There is much to be thought through about genuine costs and socially desirable pricing.

The committee should be wary of going overboard against what is now fashionable to deride as "cheap energy." Questions about waste and exploitation are certainly overdue. But what is to be learned from the TVA, the REA, and experiments in other countries? The TVA, with all its limitations as a vehicle for grassroots democracy and social planning, stimulated development in a depleted and depressed region. Through its low-cost power policies, the REA encouraged inexpensive public power for modernization in low-income and sparsely settled farm areas denied access to energy by private utilities who could not see adequate profit from such markets. Both the TVA and the REA fostered cooperatives and municipal power facilities as well as agricultural and conservation experiments. Nationalization of oil in Mexico was used to spur the strengthening of poverty-ridden sectors of the economy and to create a long-neglected domestic market in place of the previous corporate emphasis on crude oil exports. The 1938 date of expropriation remains a national holiday. Now new discoveries are enabling Petróleos Mexicanos (Pemex), the state company, to become self-sufficient and begin some export of refined products and petrochemicals without abandoning its commitment to balanced growth and a diversified economy. Yet the Mexican revolution is still incomplete. Millions of peasants are landless or in economic misery and without effective political voice for creating a more just political economy.

A blanket consignment of the "era of cheap energy" to history's dustbin may be one more device for keeping the poor at the bottom of the ladder of opportunity. The nation needs to ask in what sectors it wants low-cost energy and where it doesn't. Mass transit, detergents, and aluminum can-manufacturing each consumes energy. But they have very different consequences. The first needs every assistance. The latter two, which introduced intensified consumption of energy resources, justifiable by greater profit potential rather than by social contribution, should be discouraged. Then too, there is no simple correlation between high energy consumption and a high standard of living. On a per capita basis, countries such as Denmark, Sweden, and Germany have gross national products comparable to that of the United States, while consuming perhaps half the relative energy.

Such a review undertaken by the proposed committee should provide impetus for developing and placing in the public domain all the basic information about energy, resources, reserves, inventories, technological potentials, costs of production, and consumption patterns and projections. There is no reason for concealing such building blocks for public policy or for denying the public the right to create independent data. Ending corporate secrecy, whether masked as national security, proprietary rights, or technological readiness, becomes a step forward toward a responsible economy.

But it is not one to settle for. There is no need to exaggerate the factors of information and expertise. In a larger sense the issue is not privileged information. There have been abundant warnings over the years as to the consequences of spiraling demands upon ultimately finite fossil fuels and of the increasing economic, political, and social costs of such expectations. It has been no secret to the people of Appalachia that the quest for coal too often has left their land and their lives as slag heaps. It is no secret to Montanans who now fear a comparable fate. Nor is it a secret to the people of many oil producing regions that the great wealth generated can be badly distributed. It is no secret to the people of Latin America and the Middle East that oil companies have enjoyed the political support of the American government in the extraction of their wealth. And now millions of Americans are learning about their own vulnerabilities as consumers, workers, small business people, and taxpayers. They may not be able to decipher corporate reports or even their own monthly bills. But the message of the bottom line seems quite clear.

Knowledge about oil technology and oil policies is not as esoteric as corporate stewardship would have the citizenry believe. Industry errors in gauging demand may have been as important factors in the energy crisis as the planned withholding of production. In spite of this, corporate leadership is often arrogant, as Sister Jane Scully of Gulf's board noted after the upheaval there: "Management knows best for the corporation or for the nation or they know better than you. They don't see the validity of complaints from the outside. It's ridiculous for them to say the laws are strangling us. Government and law are the American people. When you assume the law of the land is your enemy, you're in trouble."[9]

There is no necessary correlation between high executive salaries and effective management in the public interest. In 1973 and 1974, just when corporate advertisements were emphasizing the imperative for a tightening of the national belt, some oil executives voted themselves substantial salary increases. Exxon's chairman received $677,000 in 1974, up from $597,000 in 1973; Gulf's chairman went to $544,000, from $490,000; Mobil's chairman to $596,000 from $500,000; Texaco's to $579,000 from $536,000; and Phillips's to $317,000 from $237,000, perhaps as compensation for the unaccustomed hazard of explaining profits and shortages to a skeptical public and to legislators not showing their customary deference.[10]

The incompetence and trained innocence that characterize so much of public energy leadership are not inherent in the nature of public policy. There have been and are experts in the government who know the score about energy, as technicians and as potential policy makers. More important, perhaps, there are those now in private industry and in the universities and laboratories who could respond to the challenge to develop and operate a publicly-oriented energy system, just as there are young people who would opt for such careers.

Centralizing public responsibility for energy appears to be the most likely administrative change to result from the energy crisis. Given the longtime fragmentation in some sixty federal agencies whose focus has rarely been national energy policy and whose activities are generally uncoordinated, save by private government, such reform is understandably tempting. Yet, Interior has long been a captive of industry. And in matters of economic regulation, the old Atomic Energy Commission was, in Senator George D. Aiken's (Republican, Vermont) phrase, "an agency of acquiescence."[11] Without transformations of the underlying structure and power of the energy industry or the present mandate of public government, such "logical" administrative reorganization conveniently parallels the emerging integration of the various energy sectors into the private government of oil. Reform simplifies the cooptation of the public bureaucracy into the expanded energy establishment. It eases the transition to a corporate state.

Energy policies determined at the local and regional as well as national and international levels thus become imperative. The committee must stimulate a network of representative planning bodies sensitive to communal resource and ecological concerns. It must also acknowledge the experiments underway, such as "lifeline service" pricing, which aims at relatively low, flat rates for basic residential usage of electricity and then scales rates upward to discourage excessive consumption—in effect, reversing the traditional practice which favors large users and leaves homeowners subject to discrimination and increases they often can ill afford. This proposal has been pioneered in Vermont through the initiative of a citizen's Public Interest Research Group rather than through governmental sponsorship. It has been modified and advocated in a number of other states.

Vermont and Maine activists have drafted model legislation for state energy planning. Their basic premises are that energy problems are not transitory, that dependence upon reasonably priced energy is critical, and that citizens have the right to be involved in decisions affecting their lives. A state energy board, selected by a network of local public energy districts, would have not only regulatory power over utilities but would develop long-range energy plans. It would also oversee a public authority for generating and transmitting electric power as well as a state fuel corporation for purchasing, stockpiling, and distributing fossil fuels. At the heart of the proposals is the public energy district, similar to the public utility district, a political subdivision whose directors are chosen at regular state elections. The device of the public utility districts as used in the state of Washington has enabled communities left wastelands by the lumber companies to exercise eminent domain, own land, sell revenue bonds, produce electricity, and then invest the returns in needed public services and redevelopment plans. Comparable transformations have been proposed for Appalachia through the creation of an Appalachian Mountain Authority whose policies would be shaped and held accountable through locally elected boards.[12] A primary goal is the retention of the remaining wealth within the region and the building of a political spirit which assumes that all decisions are not beyond the control of those whose lives have been so shaped by coal and its absentee corporate masters.

Municipally-owned power systems in a number of communities are taking imaginative leadership in the search for alternative energy sources. For example, Santa Clara, California, is concentrating on solar energy; Ames, Iowa, on garbage and sewage conversion; some northwestern towns are focusing upon wind power; Burbank, California, has invested in geothermal leases. The Canadian provinces of New Brunswick and Nova Scotia have studied a tidal power project at the Bay of Fundy, not far from the site of the aborted Passamaquoddy project off the Maine coast first begun in the thirties under the initiative of President Franklin D. Roosevelt. The New England states and eastern Canadian provinces have a task force appraising tidal power and other regional energy options. Those who, in bicentennial spirit, look for reaffirmation of earlier republican principles, should welcome the renewed meaning given to federalism by states acting as laboratories for a new social order. And those who still believe that a thoroughgoing democracy must include greater self-government in the workplace will encourage transformations which give scope to workers in basic management decision-making.

There is everything to be learned about how to attain flexible governance capable of coordinating such constituencies and agencies with larger goals. For local rule has its own built-in dangers. Unrelated to broader perspectives it can be exclusionary as well as susceptible to organized power forces. The challenge is far greater than the more publicized and reassuring searches for energy breakthroughs. Must the technocratic centralization identified with the corporate and the Soviet experiences be accepted as the last word in human possibility? Surely the concerns of the Yugoslav and Chinese Communists lest they fall into comparable planning molds and urban elitism are at least as worthy of dialogue as their approaches to Soviet might and acupuncture. To be so hopelessly weighed down by the conventional jeremiads against technology and bureaucracy is to concede the end of political imagination and the irrelevance of democracy for industrial life.

High among the projects deserving support are those which encourage systems based upon renewable rather than nonrenewable sources. Solar, geothermal, water, tidal and wind energy, and sewage conversion are each realistic supplements or alternatives for the present fossil fuels.[13] Solar energy, for example, is a potentially inexhaustible source of clean energy. It is technologically feasible and could meet most of the nation's heating and electricity needs. Yet a projected 1974 federal research and development budget allocated $15 million to solar, a fortieth of the amount for nuclear fission. Partisans of geothermal development point out that a number of countries (including Italy, Mexico, Japan, New Zealand, and Iceland) and some American communities have long had such power programs and that in the past it has been the lower price of conventional energy rather than technological hurdles which have explained the conservatism of federal research. Some $11 million were earmarked for such research and development in 1974.[14] Wherever possible first priorities should be given to small and intermediate-scale energy technologies which are clearly adaptable to regional needs and controls. Some of these ventures initially require substantial funding which undoubtedly will have to come from state and federal sources. But technologically they are adaptable to decentralized development. If any are to be postponed or rejected, it should be for clearly defined scientific and social reasons rather than because of the profit-timing motives of the present rulers of energy who haven't quite figured out yet how to brand the rays of the sun. To accelerate the development of a mass solar energy market, and break through the twin barriers of utility sloth and high bank interest, Senator James G. Abourezk (Democrat, South Dakota) has proposed an agency modeled after the REA which would offer low-interest loans to homeowner co-operatives.[15] More attention should be given to the fuel cell which could convert hydrogen and oxygen, rather than fossil fuels, directly into electricity. Space and military scientists have done considerable research here, and spacecraft have used electrochemical power technologies. The electric utilities and segments of the oil industry, including Exxon and Atlantic Richfield, have shown limited interest in adapting such findings to the commercial or industrial world.[16]

One need not be doctrinaire. Where it is demonstrable that technological integration advances public energy objectives without compounding the difficulty of control, then it should be accepted. A well-thought-out national power grid system, for example, which would coordinate regional power generation, could cut down on the number of new facilities required and be a rational and desirable step toward conserving energy. The utility industry's resistance is based on fear of a "federal presence" which might enforce a common carrier status requiring equal access to cooperatives and publicly-owned systems as well as to investor-owned utilities, thus shaping more just and economical transmission of energy. But private privilege should not be the ultimate determinant of public policy. Such integration, however, would not be without the irony so characteristic of much technological innovation: widening the pool of energy to preclude breakdown and local blackouts increases dependence upon remote sources and the vulnerability that it entails.

A critical appraisal of all nuclear experiments and their potential is essential. The projections of what now passes for government energy planning are based heavily upon hopes in this area. Yet there are many unresolved questions. The safety and control factors in the fission of uranium, including the long-term need to guard radioactive wastes and the mass production of plutonium (the raw material for nuclear bombs)—concerns dismissed by President Nixon as "old wives' tales"—are still frightening to many experts. Given the limits of public awareness and the closed character of the AEC–electric utility relationship, one could understand the frustration and the urgency of a young farmer who, on George Washington's birthday, 1974, sounded the alarm for the people of the Connecticut Valley by toppling a high steel tower in Montague, Massachusetts, intended for a giant nuclear plant.[17] By 1976 a number of top engineers in nuclear plants and agencies in the United States had resigned in protest against official soft-pedaling of hazards; a Swedish government had fallen—in large part because of mounting hostility to its faith in a nuclear future; and a British royal commission chaired by a leading physicist of the "nuclear establishment" had warned of the need to think through the implications of reliance upon nuclear power before it was too late. Fusion energy poses fewer threats, but its acceptable development appears to be far in the future. And from a planetary perspective, nuclear energy will be the least accessible to those most in need of energy, although they will share in the exposure to a poisoned atmosphere and nuclear destruction. The enthusiasm for nuclear solutions often sidesteps an energy cost accounting which asks whether the total energy investment in such facilities is likely to be greater than the ultimate energy product.

The waste in fossil fuel extraction can no longer be tolerated. Too much of the natural gas has been flared, too much of the oil and coal in developed fields has been bypassed in the race for easy profits. All engineering and pricing practices which encourage use of neglected resources deserve attention. For example, the methane gas which has been blown out of coal mines because of its explosive qualities can instead be collected from mines and from coal beds prior to mining. Advocates claim that such degasification would provide a valuable supplement to natural gas supplies while also reducing a major hazard in the mines.

Priorities for the development of the various energy forms and sources must be publicly set and controlled. One immediate asset for responsible planning is that over 50 percent of remaining fossil fuels—shale, coal, offshore oil, and gas—are believed to be on what are now public lands. (In 1970 some 6 percent of domestic oil production and under 5 percent of gas production came from federal lands; another 10 percent of oil and 11 percent of gas production came from the outer continental shelf.) To forestall further private expropriation, all private leasing sales should cease. These resources should immediately be placed under a network of public corporations. These corporations could serve as yardsticks for exploration, development, and conservation, working in harmony with guidelines hammered out at the newly created national energy planning board. This change by itself could end the scandalous leasing of public lands which has been carried out without adequate government knowledge and with minimum standards for the private holders. The present naval reserves, especially the large one at Elk Hills and the largely unexplored North Slope, should be included within this framework.

These public corporations could provide protection against a world producers' cartel and against a private industry whose power over technological development, price, and distribution has shaped the economic and national security options of the nation. The ability to rig prices charged the military during wartime, to cut off supplies to the armed forces at the behest of another nation, to be contractors and distributors for producer nations from whom the American government seeks independence, while at the same time serving as principal developers of energy at home, to make foreign policy decisions, to generate unemployment, and to control research on public as well as on private lands suggests power that people that call themselves sovereign cannot abandon to the profit calculations of corporate rulers.

Such public development would also add a genuine dimension to the fraudulent national security criteria that have so long prevailed. Draining American reserves first through import quotas was a strategy for profits and not security. And it backfired. Questions of which fields to set aside for emergency needs and which lands for future generations, ways and places for stockpiling strategic reserves (abandoned mines, salt caverns, and storage tanks are technologically feasible) to meet short-run supply interruptions without regional discrimination, and levels and sources of import needs might all become intelligible instruments for the public weal.[18] If there are serious national security dimensions to petroleum policy, why have decisions about the size and geographic concentration of refineries, about the use of tankers, and about the location of pipelines been left to corporate judgment? And if indeed the age of fossil fuels is drawing to a close, either because of relative costs or ultimate reserves, certainly there is minimum justification for private decisions allocating natural scarcity. Nor is there any conceivable requirement within the frame of capitalist theory for the public to provide the capital, the resources, and the risk so that the present industry can survive energy transitions and emerge supreme in new industrial pastures.

Blaming the "Arabs" for petroleum difficulties is a crude distraction. The United States is increasingly becoming an importer. In 1976 imports provided 40 percent of domestic requirements, as opposed to 33 percent in 1973. More than 10 percent now came from the Middle East, with Saudi Arabia replacing Venezuela as the leading overseas supplier. Domestic production was declining while consumption was rising. But tremendous energy sources remain within domestic boundaries—and under the control of a few corporations. Where energy is needed from beyond American borders such resources must be negotiated directly by the United States government and then allocated domestically—all in consultation with its national planning bodies. If substantial public funds were to be directed to the Middle East to keep energy flowing and sympathetic regimes in office, such aid should have been debated publicly. Slyly siphoning from the public treasury through overseas tax credits became one more mechanism for keeping foreign policy commitments away from political scrutiny and for preserving the power of the private corporations and their imperial arrangements.[19] And, as is now seen, such evasions of legislative review and democratic government have provided no long-run assurance of the desired petroleum or of the good will of the peoples of the producing regions. No private corporation should be allowed to represent national need, especially in light of the divided loyalties and consistent profit allegiances of the modern transnationals. Nor should the ability to gain favored access abroad provide the means for controlling the pricing and behavior of less advantaged companies at home, while the corporations perpetuate the twin myths of a competitive American industry and of a global economy at the mercy of politically motivated producing nations. Much of OPEC's success in escalating fourfold the price of crude oil has come from applying the economic teachings of their corporate mentors and from the continued coordination of information, output, and price by the latter who thus maintain their own market power, their profit margins on the higher price, and their crucial control over refinery flow and pricing.

Again, ideally the ultimate goal remains some publicly accountable international mechanism for ensuring stabilized prices, just distribution, and long-run conservation of a basic human necessity. The Western industrial nations failed to offer such visions when they and their corporate allies were in the driver's seat of global energy policy. To ask the producers to do so at this juncture is to ask for unilateral economic disarmament, removing from the producers' hands their greatest, however short-run, instrument for development and the redress of historic grievances. But to have the United States government replace the corporations simply as the exclusive overseas bargainer for "more and more" is to mobilize the unmasked might of the state for the familiar ends of national greed.

As an interim stage, until the temporary national energy committee has reported and its recommendations are adopted, all energy operations should be placed under rigorous controls as to price, profits, and supply allocations. Such regulation should include the intrastate production of natural gas. If there is to be rationing, it should be a public function, not a byproduct of corporate decision-making. In effect, the industry should be given a public utility status—not as any long-run solution but for the immediate emergency until more comprehensive public plans are developed.

Should the political parties or the Congress ignore the opportunity to create a temporary national energy committee, then state governments and citizens' groups should move independently. For the "energy crisis" of 1973 and its wake created a rare moment of widespread consciousness as to the meaning of the public interest. An indispensable function of such a committee would be to harness the momentum of that national experience to generate a great public dialogue about how best to implement the proposition that energy and resources are the people's business.

A debate over energy planning must document the bankruptcy of the prescription that production under the present market system is the cure for all economic ills. It must also illuminate alternative requirements for an ecologically sane society. The cry of "energy crisis" and the misleading slogans of "energy independence" have been used to justify a range of predatory projects of the old order—from massive strip mining and accelerated leasing of public lands to an unthought-out Alaskan pipeline and nuclear crash programs. These vitiate hard-earned ecological gains and undermine the beginnings of natural resources planning in a wider public perspective. Pleading against the acceptance of a developer mentality in the Interior Department which would sanction unthinking intervention in the natural environment of the Arctic Wildlife Range, the executive director of the Sierra Club has called upon the United States Congress "to concede that God has some management ability on earth."[20]

Fostering a genuine respect for the environment may take generations, given the unrestrained expansionism so closely identified with the national frontier experience and the character of the self-made individual. But the time for necessary transformation may be running out. It is not merely that fossil fuels are essentially irreplaceable. It is also that so many decisions, involving shifts in energy, technology, and landscape, are not reversible. Rather than simply urging maximum efficient recovery, especially where thinking in terms of the future may be more important than any present definitions of need, the nation must learn when to say "no" to the development of resources. By the late sixties, constituencies for such opposition were being mobilized in communities most directly affected. Californians stirred up by the Santa Barbara spill formed Get Oil Out (GOO) to monitor all efforts to develop offshore oil along their coastline. Court suits by towns, counties, and states on both the Pacific and the Atlantic have sought to block such leasing by the federal government, arguing that Washington was too remote or captive to understand the implications for the involved communities. In Delaware, an environmentally alert Republican governor, Russell W. Peterson, concluded that the time had come to protect his state's remaining recreational facilities. Despite the heavy opposition of oil and petrochemical corporations, the state AFC-CIO, and also the federal government, in 1971 the legislature banned new heavy installations along Delaware Bay and the Atlantic Ocean. Attracted by the deep natural channel and the proximity to markets, Shell had been planning a major refinery on its land, and a consortium of oil companies were interested in a port for supertankers and extensive storage facilities. Shell saw such coastal zoning as discriminatory and a spokesman was reported to have said that "we will be around a lot longer than Peterson will." Secretary of Commerce Maurice H. Stans warned the governor that he was interfering with national property and security. To Peterson, a former duPont chemist, "to trade our beaches and wetlands for a steel jungle and refineries and tank farms would be discrimination against the people of Delaware. . . . We must strike a balance between the right of the property owner and the right of the community. . . . If we can save our seashore playground, there is no greater legacy we can pass on to our children."[21] The governor had made powerful enemies who were to seek repeal and his defeat. But he had given direction to an issue for citizens who cared about the public realm.

In West Virginia, Kentucky, and Tennessee, young people— determined that their future no longer be betrayed by absentee corporate, union, and government forces interested only in the export of coal—have organized to instill a sense of pride in being Appalachian and to work for regional ownership of the mines.[22] In Montana and Wyoming, farmers, ranchers, and ecologists responded to plans for making their region an energy-generating base for the rest of the nation by creating in 1972 a Northern Plains Resource Council. This resistance group has sought to educate landowners and legislators as to the ways of the energy industry, including what to do when the coal company lawyers press them to sign. It has sought independent information to test corporate and Interior Department rhetoric about reclamation and "green pastures." And it has learned how to fight through the courts and the political arena.[23] In Maine, environmentalists and fishing and tourist interests have challenged plans for superports and refineries which they feel will desecrate their landscape and lives. Puerto Rican nationalists have viewed superports as the export of pollution and other social costs of industrialization. In Alaska, the Federation of Natives has mobilized conscience and legal talent to force recognition of aboriginal claims not as dole but as basic right.

Often ignored in developing an energy balance sheet is the appalling "silent violence" against human life in the production of energy.[24] A "black lung" movement among coal miners and health workers has achieved some reform through state legislatures. It also helped to challenge a moribund and corrupt United Mine Workers union which had maintained a close relationship with the coal industry, uncritically accepting technological innovations which brought wholesale unemployment while opposing air pollution and other environmental controls on the grounds that they would throw thousands of miners out of work. A fresh leadership has demanded strict safety enforcement. There is also awareness that strip mining is becoming as dangerous per man hour, although not per ton, as underground mining. The union speaks savagely against the takeover of coal by the oil industry and the attendant political corruption in such economic power.

A consumer movement concerned about labeling or banning deleterious ingredients in household use opened larger questions about the vulnerability of workers exposed daily to vats and plants of toxic chemicals and vapors. The Oil, Chemical, and Atomic Workers International Union has mounted a national battle for health and safety standards in refineries, one of the most hazardous of working places in terms of accidents and long-run health conditions. A landmark strike was called in 1973 against Shell Oil, which is also a leading petrochemical and pesticide producer. The international company has resisted joint union-management committees for monitoring and improving the workplace environment under the provisions of the Occupational Safety and Health Act (OSHA) of 1970, arguing that such responsibility was managerial and could not be shared. The strike brought the union into alliance with environmental groups who heretofore had been viewed as elitists (not unlike their predecessors in the conservation movement) and unconcerned about the impact of their causes upon employment.[25] Some trade unionists are now finding common ground with ecologists in the proposition that solar, wind, and other benign energy technologies, along with labor-intensive recycling, may create more jobs in their communities than the huge nuclear and offshore projects.

Consumer groups around the country have developed the curiosity to ask questions and the will to organize around such presumably private and technical matters as plant siting and pricing decisions of their "local" utilities, which they soon discover are the offspring of remote holding companies.[26] In Georgia a group has developed a militant watchdog role over all policies of the Georgia Power Company and the state public service commission which appear inimical to local needs. Most of these movements have focused on immediate villains and objectives, although the Georgia Power Project is frankly committed to direct control by workers and consumers.[27] Saying "not here" is far short of a national ecological ethic. But each stand is important for opening a larger perspective.

The United States remains without a significant conservation program. Where there is official acceptance of the worth of slowing down the growth rate of per capita energy consumption, the burden is generally placed upon the individual. Such appeals cynically manipulate the liberal ethic with the implication that if each person would refrain from tossing beer cans, would drive a little slower and install exhaust devices on his car's tailpipe, would bring old newspapers to salvage centers, would exercise caution on the job, and would take the pledge to have fewer children, then people, machines, and nature would once more be in harmony. And that if corporations would lower the sulphur content of the fuels in their furnaces and put filters on their chimneys, if Consolidated Edison would urge restraint in the use of air conditioners, and if Consolidation Coal would plant hardy grass after strip mining, then the nation would be binding up the wounds of development successfully.

The critical issue remains untouched. Fundamental ecological thinking must go beyond the end products of the industrial system —its garbage, sewage, exhaust, and resource depletion. Thorough-going energy planning requires end-use planning which defines communally desirable and undesirable uses of energy. There has been scandalous waste in present industrial practices, whether in the production of aluminum cans, automobiles, or energy itself. The energy industry is the largest single user of natural gas. Refineries have been powered by natural gas, a convenient but certainly shortsighted practice. Utilities have burned oil and gas to produce electricity, an extraordinarily inefficient conversion which becomes even more wasteful of the energy content when the electricity is ultimately converted back to heat. Perhaps two-thirds of natural gas energy content is dissipated.

The internal combustion engine remains a prime culprit.[28] In 1973 the automobile consumed approximately 20 percent of all the energy in the United States. Legal minimum standards for fuel economy, including more efficient engines and smaller and lighter cars, might cut such usage in half while reducing costs for motorists and the dollar drain for the nation.[29] In the past, sporadic proposals for federally sponsored research on alternatives were resisted or treated gingerly. The oil industry reaffirmed its commitment to improving the internal combustion engine, which it knowingly predicted would win out as the form of propulsion for the future mass market car.[30] Yet battery-powered electric vehicles are feasible and attractive possibilities for the short trips which constitute a large part of motoring.

Completely eliminating the Highway Trust Fund, which has annually earmarked some $5 billion of federal gasoline taxes for road construction, would be a move toward more balanced transportation policy. Some reform has been made, and a portion of this money can now go for more efficient public transportation. There is revived interest in the once-scorned electric trolley car. Experts, who now refer to it as light rail transit, see modernized versions providing relatively inexpensive and pollution-free transport appropriate for many communities. Massive experiments in public transit must be encouraged, and not necessarily the gimmicky ones whose major attraction seems to be the elimination of jobs. Lip service has been paid to improved mass transit, even in the advertisements of at least one oil company. But actual investment, public and private, remains paltry. At a time when productive capacity and workers are idle and mass transit needs largely unfilled, the best the automotive industry can come up with are "rebates" to revive the sharp decline in buying occasioned by the energy crisis and ensuing recession. For as the chairman of General Motors has explained, Americans do not need "empty austerity"; new cars are more efficient than old ones, hence their purchase "is the common sense conservation we need."[31] In the face of such business thinking, the case for public planning for industrial conversion and the rebuilding of the railroads is incontestable.

The cities at present tolerate vast energy waste. New York City's Pan Am Building and its World Trade Center—one glorifying the corporation, the other the state—are crowning commentaries on the absence of an effective public voice to call into question such energy-hungry architecture, which misallocated capital while blocking sunlight and perspective. Human-scale urban planning that includes ecologically stringent building codes is a must.

The move toward chemically based, capital-intensive agriculture and the concentrated corporate control to marshal these resources and integrate them into processing, marketing, and energy empires must be challenged. Less developed peoples are beginning to ask about the costs of a "green revolution." Can the United States do less? Much of the centralization of agriculture becomes less justifiable when one adds up the costs of forcing people off the land. The loss to community life has long been documented. Now the social price of factories in the field must be calculated to include the high energy demands of agribusiness, including the heavy energy investment in packaging and then transporting vegetables and other foods grown thousands of miles from the population centers where they are needed and where they often could be raised.[32] A rural renaissance will not provide the answers for all or even most of social ills. But fundamental land reform which would make farm land accessible, especially to those interested in a more natural farming, could be a valuable component of regional energy planning.[33] It will require regional land banks and trusts to prevent remaining farm lands from being turned over to oil corporate developers and other absentee owners.

Thus, the technological review to be sought must extend far beyond the immediate arena of alternative energy sources if there is to be a successful challenge to corporate socialism and the pervasive human malaise of modern industrial life. Ultimately, all major technological innovations must be appraised in terms of their likely social impact. One can reasonably argue that nineteenth-century Americans had little incentive to predict the darker results of their race to develop a continent.[34] But surely there is now abundant painful evidence to suggest that all technological advances do not automatically mean human progress.

The present technological incentives for insatiable and inequitable consumption must be challenged. That ventures are technically feasible is an inadequate reason for embarking upon them, unless one succumbs totally to the principle that the means should determine the end. If proposed technological changes seem too threatening to democratic values or to ecological capabilities, the society must learn to muster the political will to say "no," or "not now." Such technological review must be related to energy and overall planning for economic directions and common necessities. Otherwise those who have not yet shared in the benefits of development will properly be skeptical of any suggestions of a simpler life which still leaves them without hope or, at least the illusion of economic betterment.

If it is to be democratic, planning must develop and reconcile alternatives through national and regional planning bodies which maximize citizen participation while involving fully the executive and the legislative branches. Reliable information and projections are critical here. Once agreed upon, such planning must be supported through controls which will protect the communal priorities and through checks and balances which will sustain personal and local freedom. Responsible planning thus requires a thorough overhaul of the American political apparatus to create the channels for maintaining democratic involvement. It will also require a scaling down of energy-intensive technologies so as to lessen the necessity for centralization and for the social controls that remorselessly follow.

Basic to the effectiveness of such planning is the willingness to challenge the concept of the freedom of private investment. What too often has been profitable private management has turned out to be gross mismanagement for the public interest. Witness the "energy crisis" of 1973–74 and its ripple effect on every area of life. Given the economic and the political power that flows out of an oil barrel, national planning will not be responsible to the public if energy is left in corporate hands. Energy development, distribution, and use thus become fundamental starting points for effective national economic planning. As Thornton Bradshaw, president of Atlantic Richfield, expressed it, "the whole energy situation is too important to be left to the oil and energy industries, the same as war is too important to be left to the generals."[35]

It is a somewhat ironic measure of corporate evolution that business leaders are moving to accept and even advocate governmental national and international economic planning they once so strenuously opposed. They do this, presumably, not because of any eagerness to become accessories to their own democratic socialization. But they do recognize the disjointed and unpredictable character of the international economy and the limits of the private planning of disparate special interests. "We must end the adversary relationship which destroys our ability to cooperate," declared the chairman of Texaco. "It is only by government and industry working together that we can solve our problems." To develop more domestic energy for a strong economy will require a comprehensive and coordinated national energy program, a senior official of Gulf told top oil colleagues appearing before the Texas Railroad Commission. "Goals will have to be set, priorities established and funding provided" through legislative and executive action. Senator Jacob K. Javits (Republican, New York), a co-sponsor of legislation for long-term national economic planning backed by a broad spectrum of liberal economists, businessmen, and labor leaders, has assured the wary that "planning has nothing whatsoever to do with greater governmental interference in the private sector." He sees it as "a neutral tool that adapts to the character of a country." If planning is socialist in Russia, it is because of the Marxist social structure. In the United States as in France, the proposed economic planning board he favors would rely upon debate and persuasion and be supportive of capital formation, growth, competition, and the abolition of "outdated" government regulation.[36]

Some oilmen are confident in the ability of their private governments to shape the quality and boundaries of public planning likely to emerge under such auspices. One now finds coal and oil spokesmen endorsing, in principle, "national" land use planning. Sponsors of this legislation cautiously have sought to encourage the individual states to save the last coastal wetlands and the last forest stand from the developers' bulldozer, without adding a heavy federal presence. Behind the prudent enlightenment of the energy industry is the hope that national guidelines can be included which will provide safeguards against "irrational" citizen action at the revitalized state level cantankerously blocking strip mining, gasification plants, refineries, and deep-water terminals for supertankers. National planning, judiciously applied, can restore the larger perspective by withholding grants from those states which "ignore the need for energy facility siting and other beneficial development."[37] In the international arena the corporations foresee such measures helping to make the world safe for capitalism by sanctioning the new cartelization patterns for the control of basic energy resources. Meanwhile, their support of codes of environmental and multinational corporation behavior through the United Nations and other international agencies is reminiscent of their sophisticated preemption of domestic regulatory approaches.

Until recently, the haves of the world assured the have-nots (and themselves) that increased private development of energy and production would realize "rising expectations." But taken to its logical conclusion, with the highly developed sectors continuing to get "theirs" and the definition of need always scaled upward, the global corporate system as we know it reduces the likelihood that much of the world will ever experience a livable economy. An industrial society which views other regions primarily as reservoirs for filling its own wants while unabashedly devouring a third of the total daily usage of fossil fuels to sustain its 6 percent of the world population must be seen for its inefficiency and immorality as well as for its vulnerability. And a corporate and political leadership whose finest vision is to pledge the search for more and "the use of all we can get" must be challenged for its vacuity. The theme of "more," sustained by the presumed magic of technology and the myth of limitless resources, too long has been used to evade the tougher questions about just distribution at home and abroad. Supersonic speed for the well-heeled and for warfare, contrasted with limping subways for urban majorities and starvation for third world peoples, mirror the prevailing class-income patterns and priorities. (Noting that 200 million Americans use more energy for air conditioning alone than China's population of 700 million use for all purposes, Maurice F. Strong, executive director of the United Nations Environmental Program, has questioned "whether any country has a permanent right to a disproportionate share of the world's resources.")[38] Thus, "the case for the bicycle" becomes more than a metaphor for a healthy self-sufficiency. It is a way of saying that if machines require much of mankind to serve a minority master technocratic race, and if more equitable and ecologically sane alternatives cannot be developed, then such "progress" must not be allowed. At its heart, then, technological planning involves the moral quest to renew the essential humanity of humans. In the absence of concerted efforts to develop and share economic minimums for sustaining life for all, the gratuitous message of population control has the ring of genocide—as ugly as, if less honest than, the covert argument that it would be an act of kindness to let those who "spawn like codfish" leave the earth. (As long as they go quietly, biologist George Wald has added.)[39] Thus, more efficient burning of wood and ingenious conversion of cow dung for energy and fertilizer have greater relevance for the immediate survival of great numbers of people who are still rural than do blueprints for multibillion dollar nuclear installations, however accident-free they may be made.

Global thinking must be sensitive to the impact of present corporate-governmental arrangements with the new producer cartel upon the truly deprived of the world—the great numbers to whom shortages or rigged prices mean not fewer air-conditioned hours but no kerosene for warmth or fertilizer for survival. Forgotten has been the pressure by the United States and some international agencies upon the poorer nations, who often pay the highest prices for petroleum, against developing independent or regional energy sources. Also obscured is the general refusal to assist in developing more viable economies where the energy would become the basis for new and needed local industries. There is scant discussion in official circles of how high energy prices set by the corporations and their governmental allies have canceled out foreign aid and hamstrung growth. The United States has expended more in the search for oil in Latin America than in aid for the continent's overall development. Corporations have taken out in profits their investments many times over. Meanwhile, local investment capital has been absorbed to support these operations, thus further narrowing the presumed advantage of the foreign presence. And the legacy to future generations in these producing areas is scarcer and more expensive-to-get-at petroleum. Should these resources ultimately be nationalized, as appears to be the likely pattern, the corporations and their industrialized parent nations then will be able to emphasize most virtuously how costly are such activities when undertaken publicly.

For the United States, "self-sufficiency by 1980," by 1985, or any equivalent target date is public relations, not public planning. Although the nation retains an extraordinarily rich energy base which can minimize foreign dependence, self-sufficiency is an unfeasible objective unless accompanied by the most profound reappraisal of the total industrial system and the levels of energy consumption at the core of the present "American way." And there is no evidence of any leadership in this direction. The present notions of self-sufficiency are also inconsistent with minimum ecological safeguards, given the state of knowledge about the environmental hazards of nuclear production, strip mining, continental shelf drilling, and oil shale production. Corporate enthusiasm for lifting of natural gas price regulation and the accelerated leasing of all remaining public lands seem more clearly related to profit planning than to the resolving of any growing dependence upon overseas sources of energy. Industry's warning to the public of growing shortages of natural gas and attendant loss of jobs if price controls are not removed becomes prophecy. For it is a measure of the power to withhold—what Thorstein Veblen described as sabotage.

The search for self-sufficiency also seems inconsistent with the official anger at countries such as Canada and Venezuela for "behaving like Arabs" in rejecting United States–sponsored continental and hemispheric resource planning in favor of a rising nationalist concern with holding resources for their own futures. United States and Canadian positions were being reversed. Venezuelan and Middle Eastern oil, directly linked to the escalating OPEC prices and to the unpredictable sources affecting United States imports, was no longer cheap for Canadians. Once eager to develop the market south of the border but spurned by the United States, Canada now shifted its debate to the phasing out of exports. Canadians found little justification for shipping their western crude oil to the United States at corporate-controlled prices (and with limited opportunity for additional revenue and employment through refining), instead of building a pipeline to the eastern metropolis of Canada. In effect they were shipping capital. An export tax on crude going southward was tripled, bringing Canadian prices in the United States up to the new world level. The intention was to balance the higher prices being paid for imports, giving Canada protection and profit, with the windfall accruing to the provinces and the federal government rather than to the corporations. Production in Alberta and Saskatchewan had peaked, and there was concern as to whether this meant dwindling reserves or simply lessened corporate interest. Meanwhile, over 40 percent of Canada's natural gas was flowing to the United States, and the Canadian National Energy Board began to deny export licenses for new discoveries. These searches had been financed through interest-free loans of over $700 million from United States pipelines to producers (generally American) in Canada. The pipelines received options on the gas, and the cost of the advances were put into the rates paid by American consumers until the Federal Power Commission was pressed to question such generous corporate shifting of risk, which was often going into exploratory as well as development drilling. Canadians, in turn, began to question whether their own short-run profits meant they were bequeathing higher costs and scarce energy to their children and to a possibly expanded population. "We'll be as helpful as we can with their energy problems," commented the Canadian minister of energy, mines, and resources, "but if anybody's lights are going to have to be turned out, why should it be ours?"[40] The Canadian public and politicians were also beginning to awaken to the impact of intensive exploration upon the lives of their often-ignored Eskimo and Indian peoples as well as upon the environment of the hinterlands and the Arctic.[41] And underlying the specifics of oil policy was a wariness about a presumed shared destiny, whether in relation to continental defense and the premises of American foreign policy, the prospects of a branch plant economy deferential to the decisions of global corporations based in the United States, or the more elusive matter of "cultural penetration."

A thoroughgoing reappraisal of the present energy system thus demands a careful examination of its relations to the ongoing objectives of American foreign policy. If imports of oil and gas are to be accepted, their rate and prices must be attuned to public needs rather than corporate profitability. Banding together with other consumer nations, however understandable a defense against producer cartel attempts at what may be seen as economic blackmail or political reprisals, is a shortsighted strategy. It invites self-defeating military and diplomatic intrigue to widen fissures among the producer nations. This paradigm of economic sufficiency and security fuels the presumably abandoned cold war positions abroad. The United States still arms and finances racketeering ruling cliques who promise to deliver energy, markets, anticommunism, and populaces which ask few questions.

The producer nations, primarily in the Middle East, understand that previous collaboration with Western interests resulted in the draining of their energy and even their scarce capital, while distorting their own growth. Their growing response has been, first to enlarge their share of the profits from the lifting of crude oil; then to develop some participation, in profits and then decision-making, in all stages of the integrated process; then to recognize points of common bond with others caught up in colonialism and to search for effective common strategies; and ultimately to control the basic resources with greater focus upon their own long-run needs—whether through nationalization, limiting production so as to protect prices and reserves while lessening dependence upon one crop, or the creation of an industrial base wherein the people of their own region might gain greater material benefit through processing the crude oil and using the energy for their own domestic production of finished goods.

There may have been a time when the United States could have shown leadership in joint development of energy and its more just allocation. Now its righteous anger at the Arab OPEC for adopting the ways of the Western cartel for their own members is suspect. Nor does the United States' eagerness to secure advantage in the battle over defining legal and development patterns for the potential resources of the ocean beds suggest any belated global enlightenment in this newer arena.

Meanwhile, despite all the official hysteria over inflated crude prices, negotiations by corporations and diplomats continue with a central objective being to ensure that the American industry remains insulated from the more haunting nightmare of *lowered* foreign prices. And the industry works fervidly in domestic political vineyards for authorization to raise all energy price levels to the new overseas peaks, always claiming and never proving that such parity will produce new technologies and new supplies.

American diplomacy contributes to the heightening rather than the defusing of Middle Eastern tensions. Iran and Saudi Arabia are courted through heavy military and nuclear aid. As regional police, they are expected to keep oil flowing, more radical native and neighboring forces (including maverick oil-producing sheikhdoms) in check, and Soviet influence at bay. A secretary of state (William B. Rogers), who was soon to be on retainer to the shah's investment vehicle, the Pahlevi Foundation, and also on the board of Standard Oil (Ohio), termed such sales a "stabilizing influence" for peace while Russian arms to Iraq and other Middle Eastern countries were "an invitation to trouble."[42] The senior member and former director of the Central Intelligence Agency, Richard Helms, who had "been studying Iran . . . from the CIA point of view for a long time" (he rose through what is known as the "department of dirty tricks" and was deputy director at the time of the CIA-organized overthrow of the Mossadegh regime in 1953) was in 1973 appointed ambassador to that country.[43] This political bias toward the two authoritarian nations reflects the almost universally antidemocratic and antirevolutionary allegiances shown by the United States in its policies toward the "developing" world. It feeds the fear that energy calculations increasingly determine its dealings with Israel.

It has become fashionable to discuss strangulation theories and strategies. At what point, it is asked, must the United States and/or the more vulnerable western European nations decide that, to forestall an embargo which might cripple their economies, there is justification for a prior "surgical strike" (directly or by a client state or group) into one or more of the culpable producing countries. (The imagery of "surgical," suggesting the absence of blood, is reminiscent of the fantasies behind the tragic incursion into Southeast Asia). President Ford and Secretary of State Kissinger raised such trial balloons (while denying the likelihood of implementation), as if to test public reactions: "When you are being strangled it is a question of either dying or living and when you use the word 'strangulation' in relation to the existence of the United States or its non-existence, I think the public has to have a reassurance . . . that we are not going to permit America to be strangled to death."[44] Scholars and journalists pick up the cues, rushing into print and prominence with speculation; meanwhile, the United States army engages in desert warfare maneuvers, the air force trains for "limited" nuclear bombing, and naval strategy (more acceptable at home since sailors are supposed to be away at sea someplace) encompasses the Indian Ocean and the Persian Gulf as well as the Pacific.

The violence against nature inherent in the unthinking grabbing of all that is gettable easily spills over to become violence against other humans who may stand in the way. Arms to ensure a supportive energy flow in turn require guaranteed energy sources. United States "defense"—arms production and the armed forces —now account for at least 10 percent of national energy consumption. And the role of the United States as arms merchant and drill sergeant, selling a minimum of $11 billion of hardware in 1974, heavily to the Middle East, is defended as necessary for balancing the flow of payments for foreign petroleum.[45]

Defeat in Indochina of the world's largest military power by "gooks on bikes" and the equally devastating inroads upon democratic freedom by a supporting national surveillance apparatus at home increasingly have brought into public question the wisdom and durability of America's imperial reach. The illusion that the nation can engage in covert operations abroad, whether intervening in civil wars, overthrowing legitimate governments or planning assassinations, while itself remaining democratic, gets further shaken by each accompanying revelation about the cold war deceits against the American people. Yet the national security establishment remains and the heavy energy drain in fueling the military goes unchallenged. A garrison approach to protect the greed and the power of the more industrialized nations furthers the permanent mobilization for war. It frustrates a world planning which might respect the longrun needs and fellowship of all mankind, producers and consumers.

Criticisms of this foreign policy and its architects and investigations of the accompanying subordination of constitutional liberties at home have been denounced by Secretary of State Kissinger as self-destructive and isolationist, more endangering than any overseas adversaries.

> An effective foreign policy requires a strong national government which can act with assurance and speak with confidence on behalf of all Americans. But when the executive is disavowed repeatedly and publicly other governments wonder who speaks for America and what an American commitment means. Our Government is in danger of progressively losing the ability to shape events, and a great nation that does not shape history eventually becomes its victim.

He saw the government "systematically" demoralized and deprived of the ability to secure its economy and deal with communist rivals. Its very legitimacy was at stake. If the "domestic divisions" were not to end, the nation's only option was to retreat—"to become an isolated fortress island in a hostile and turbulent global sea, awaiting the ultimate confrontation with the only response we will not have denied ourselves—massive retaliation."[46]

As argued in *The Politics of Oil*, there is no magic in public planning. Nor in public ownership. State capitalism may be no more efficient than its private counterpart. And public authorities may be equally insulated from democratic accountability. The question of power is not resolved by labels. Everyone is now aware of the curse of big bureaucracy, private or public, military or civilian, "democratic" or "authoritarian." (Sinclair Oil's use of the dinosaur as its symbol may have been uncomfortably prescient.) The American economic system, like its political system, may be ungovernable, toppling under the weight of big technology.

But surely there is no social gain in extending the power of the already rapacious and corrupting private government of energy. And there is ample experience with the failure of regulation, where the regulated remain more powerful than the regulators and the presumed tribunes of the people serve to exact tribute from them for their corporate constituents. The time is long past for presuming that the right mix of governmental controls and subsidies will be successful in keeping the activities of the energy industry in harmony with the public interest.

Corporate control on this scale is wrong, not because individual businessmen are evil, but because the profit perspective is inappropriate. The assumption that the missing key is a more encompassing synchronization of all the parts of one global energy system, whether through multinational corporation or superstate, places a premium on managerial cleverness operating the ultimate machine. The scurryings of a secretary of state in shuttle diplomacy and the computerized calculations of corporate men to eliminate the last uncertainty in support of some ultimate plan which will keep the system going, at least a little longer, are the frenetic motions of overextended jugglers. The glamorized labors of each impose constraints and directions upon mankind which seem remote from the simpler questions as to the necessary conditions for keeping life human.

There are many exciting frontier areas of energy research and experimentation. One familiar temptation to be shed, however, is the continued illusion that science will always come to the rescue with new techniques but without new social prices. Rather than reappraise or scale down human demands upon the environment, all that is needed, if one reads much of the now conventional rhetoric and the emerging legislative proposals, is a redoubling of technological effort. Yet crash programs to maintain present industrial patterns have their own built-in dangers. Giant science, whether public or private, accelerates the growth of giant institutions and their remote elites. An already politically passive public is reinforced in its conclusion that integration into one bureaucratic system is inevitable. It is further discouraged from contemplating, let alone attempting, democratic reconstruction.

An Energy Independence Authority proposed in 1975 by the Ford administration suggested the ultimate in "thinking big." Sired by Vice-President Nelson Rockefeller (most appropriate historic symmetry, when one reflects on origins), this federal corporation was to provide over the next ten years $100 billion in loans and loan guarantees to underwrite energy industry ventures for emerging new technologies (such as synthetic fuels and shale oil), nuclear development, and costly traditional projects such as pipelines. The agency was also to guarantee prices to shelter the private sector against the "considerable risk if world oil prices drop." Such unprecedented largess was to do for the faltering economic system what the corporate successors to John D. Rockefeller seemed incapable or unwilling to do for the nation. No reservations were expressed about the existing power of the oil industry or its part in shaping policies which steered the United States into its difficulties. Indeed the call for independence insisted that "the private sector must play the primary role." It pledged not to disrupt "competitive forces" and solemnly disavowed any bent toward public ownership, control or operation.[47] There was no assurance to consumers that they would receive fuel. Nor was there any intimation that the already grossly inequitable cost burden upon lower-income people, who pay a greater percentage of their earnings for fuel, would be lessened. No concern was shown over the further distortion of public priorities by such capital infusion.

Genuinely democratic planning and public ownership do not offer "final solutions." They suggest beginnings. They introduce the passion of convictions about economic and political alternatives and the tension of balancing social needs with individual freedoms. Such planning and public control cannot be imposed from the top by administrator kings. Nor can they be expected to emerge full-blown from legislative halls. For they involve the re-distribution of economic and political power, matters of social con-tract which formal political procedures assume have already been resolved. The prior requirement for such transformation is the emergence of new social forces sufficiently potent to insist on re-sponsiveness. The issue of national energy planning provides one focal point. And the developments of the last two decades, from the consumer and ecology movements and the emergence of "third world" perspectives at home and abroad to a revitalized United Mine Workers of America, "whistle-blowing" in public agencies, and even an underground newspaper of oil employees, indicate the potential support.

A fight for national energy planning and public ownership will provoke the full weight of the oil industry and its business allies, ever ready to play upon the widespread disenchantment with pub-lic government. Partisans will be targets for political ridicule and denunciation. The corruption of the political process will intensify. Scares and threats about shortages, unemployment, the destruction of small business and individual initiative, and the breakdown of the economy will mount. Tied to their own image-building activi-ties (largely paid for by taxpayers), which saturate the media, are savage denunciations of proposals for full disclosure of energy in-formation as the undercutting of the market economy; regulation is labeled "the first resort of the demagogue"; injecting competi-tion through divestiture of multibillion dollar energy empires is equated with a cottage industry mentality; a proposed public energy corporation is deplored as both unfair competition and an-other useless, self-perpetuating bureaucracy; public ownership is the subversion of freedom and national survival.[48] The manipula-tion of political language and discussion will continue. At the out-set of the "energy crisis," Continental Oil offered to help maga-zine writers prepare articles: "We have an excellent editorial staff" ready to provide "ideas, data, documentation, interviews, photos . . . relating to the decontrol of natural gas, moderating environ-mental requirements, and encouraging the integration of competing fuels under one roof."[49] There is even the rewriting of history on such issues as shale oil and synthetic rubber. In a discussion of energy needs, Chase Manhattan, having noted that nearly two-thirds of the United States population is not old enough to have a meaningful recollection of shortage conditions in 1941, then manages to recount the story of how the United States entered World War II cut off from natural rubber without mentioning the part played by its friends at Jersey Standard in frustrating the development of a synthetic substitute.[50]

Oilmen present themselves as an international "peace corps," business managers for the emerging "global society." "We are accused of raping emerging nations of their natural resources when, in fact, the *nation* reaps the major share of the benefit it *could not* unlock without us. We are labeled the source of the world's pollution when, in fact, all mankind is contributing and it is our technology which is the vital key to its eventual elimination." The international coporations, concludes Gulf's B. R. Dorsey, "are the neutral force entwining nations, contributing to the economies of the haves, increasing the productive powers of the have-nots . . . and forming . . . bridges between nations."[51] Americans can thus take pride in bringing progress and enlightenment while assured as to their shared innocence in the face of worldwide upheavals. Meanwhile, the major oil companies underwrite on educational television a stream of classic theater and other programs in the performing arts and science to convince a discerning public of the urbane highmindedness behind their technical dedication.

The fear of political democracy may be the most effective constraint upon the corporation and perhaps democracy's greatest immediate asset. But there is nothing self-operative about such defense. The sustained mustering of knowledge and conviction by determined constituencies will be required if onslaughts against honest discussion and appeals to the most selfish side of public concerns are to be withstood and the quest for the common good kept in focus. "One ecological world" requires unprecedented cooperation and, some will add, unattainable human goodness. Yet the easier solutions, including those which assume inherent self-centeredness and the survival of the strongest, come with totalitarian coercions whose disguise as free choices becomes more apparent with each crisis. Great numbers of citizens now acknowledge that something is morally wrong and politically ominous in the disproportionate control and use of the world's resources.[52] But if lethargy or stake, reinforced by all the persuasive talents of the business system, should lead them to conclude, in the absence of alternatives, "not yet," then they accept themselves as powerless. They thus default in the struggle to have this society identify with the best of human expectation. Creating a sense of the politically possible may yet liberate the generous energies within people and also their will to self-discipline. This is the primary resource question. Rather than depoliticize oil, the requirement is to place energy planning within the arena of democratic politics.

In contrast, the shoddy debate over oil price controls and policies between the Democratic and Republican parties and between the president and the Congress suggest how little has been learned and how fatigued and myopic are most contemporary political practitioners. The election year pieties of presidential candidates concerning conservation and energy industry accountability underscore how alien remains the concept of public initiative for social resources. It is too late for them to claim there are no fundamental energy issues to be resolved or that these will fade away. Nor are they now able to accept openly the industry's heavily-financed siren call to "take oil out of politics" when its translation so clearly is to "keep policies in profitmaking hands." But there is minimum eagerness to capitalize on the shared public experience of the energy crisis and launch a continuing national forum over coherent positions on energy planning and the related issues of full employment, administered inflation, ecology, and foreign policy. Meanwhile, opinion polls record sharply declining public confidence in the corporation and indeed in all giant bureaucratic institutions, including the Congress, and an accompanying suspicion that much of the "game of politics" is tilted permanently by corporate hands, an erosion of commitment to the party system, and a widespread sense of personal alienation.[53]

Time is short, not necessarily because resource depletion and human extinction are inevitable. More troubling is the likelihood of continued adaptation to the present systems of power. One can envision 1985: landscaped energy parks, glowing towers and stacks amidst a national wasteland of stripped countryside, decaying cities, unemployed citizens, and neglected public services—monuments to corporate planning and political mindlessness. Unable to think outside of the framework of profit, the sponsored "fuel for thought" messages urge, as always, more of the same.

To restore from exile the ideal of the public interest and governance based upon the consent of the governed remains the underlying challenge of the recent energy crisis and of the political economy which produced it.

# Notes

CHAPTER 1. *Crude Awakenings*

1. Transcript, *New York Times*, November 2, 1966.

2. Release, The White House, November 26, 1973. The Seafarers International Union contributed $100,000 to the president's 1972 campaign shortly after the Justice Department abandoned a case involving the 1970 indictment of the union and its officers for violating the Federal Corrupt Practices Act. See William A. Dobriver, Joseph D. Gebhardt, Samuel J. Buffone, and Andra N. Oakes, *The Offenses of Richard M. Nixon: A Guide for the People of the United States of America* (New York: Quadrangle, 1973), pp. 8, 81.

3. "We have the police power to regulate where our fuel goes, and I predict that unless something is done soon, we may use those powers," Governor Edwin W. Edwards of Louisiana told fellow governors at the Southern Governors Conference. To which Governor Dolph Briscoe added, "Texas will decide who gets Texas oil." *New York Times*, September 26, 1973.

4. *Report*, Special Subcommittee on Department of Defense Energy Resources and Requirements of the Committee on Armed Services, U.S. House of Representatives, 93d Congress, 2d Session (Washington, 1974), pp. 3, 18–22 and passim.

5. *Presidential Energy Statements*, reprinted for National Fuels and Energy Policy Study by Committee on Interior and Insular Affairs, U.S. Senate, 93d Congress, 1st Session (Washington, 1973). See, for example, statement, June 29, 1973, at which time the president spoke of the energy situation as a "challenge" which could be met by "making very small alterations in our present living habits." Also, remarks at White House, September 8, 1973; "Message to the Congress," September 10, 1973; "Address on the Energy Emergency," November 7, 1973. Also, Remarks before Seafarers International Union (above, n. 2).

6. *Presidential Energy Statements*, "Message to the Congress," November 8, 1973; and "Address on the National Energy Policy," November 25, 1973.

7. *New York Times*, March 12, 1974.

8. Robert Engler, *The Politics of Oil: A Study of Private Power and Democratic Directions* (New York: Macmillan, 1961; Chicago: University of Chicago Press, Phoenix ed., 1967), pp. 202, 217–20, 236, 253, 259.

9. *New York Times*, November 4, 1975.

10. Senator Percy. [Charles H. Percy, Republican, Illinois] Who did make the decisions to divert oil to the United States?

Dr. Sawhill. [John C. Sawhill, Administrator, Federal Energy Office] The companies did.

Senator Percy. What criteria were used by the international companies in determining how much oil to divert and to whom to divert it?

Dr. Sawhill. I do not think I have a good answer to that question.

Senator Percy. Did the FEO or any other organ of Government instruct the companies as to the amount of oil they should bring to the United States?

Dr. Sawhill. No we did not set specific targets for them to bring in. We continued to urge them to bring as much as possible.

*Multinational Corporations and United States Foreign Policy*, Hearings before the Subcommittee on Multinational Corporations of the Committe on Foreign Relations, U.S. Senate, 93d Congress, 2d Session (Washington, 1974), part 9, p. 33. Hereafter cited as *Multinational Corporations, Hearings*.

11. Transcript of news conference, *New York Times*, September 6, 1973.

12. Ibid.

13. Ibid. For background concerning the overthrow of the Mossadegh regime, see *The Politics of Oil*, op. cit., pp. 69, 73, 202–12, 237, 265, 303, 310–12. Also, *The International Petroleum Cartel, the Iranian Consortium, and U.S. National Security*, Subcommittee on Multinational Corporations of the Committee on Foreign Relations, U.S. Senate, 93d Congress, 2d Session (Washington, 1974) contains heretofore secret documents from the files of the National Security Council, the Department of State, and the Department of Justice concerning American policy relating to the Iranian oil dispute. See also David Wise and Thomas B. Ross, *The Invisible Government* (New York: Random, 1964), pp. 110–14.

14. *New York Times*, January 7, 1974. Yet as late as April 1975 Assistant Secretary of State Thomas O. Enders, second-in-command in the American delegation to a producer-consumer nation conference in Paris designed to moderate the emerging conflict, said in a television

interview that the consumer countries were seeking to get enough power to "hasten OPEC's demise." *New York Times*, April 8, 1975.

15. *Report*, Special Subcommittee on Department of Defense Energy Resources and Requirements, *op. cit.*, p. 23; *New York Times*, December 14, 1973; also, *Wall Street Journal*, February 21, 1974.

16. *New York Times*, January 7, 1974. See also testimony of Attorney General Robert K. Killian concerning efforts of his state to deal with the industry or to get help from the federal government in alleviating shortages and controlling prices. "I hate to say that big oil is bigger than the United States Government; but its favored treatment at the hands of our government certainly leads to that conclusion." *Competition in the Energy Industry*, Hearings before the Subcommittee on the Judiciary, U.S. Senate, 93d Congress, 1st Session (Washington, 1973), pp. 15 ff.

17. *Oversight-Mandatory Petroleum Allocation Programs*, Hearings before the Committee on Interior and Insular Affairs, U.S. Senate, 93d Congress, 2d Session (Washington, 1974), Part 1. See, for example, testimony of Texaco, pp. 85 ff., and of Gulf, pp. 125 ff. In contrast, see testimony of Ashland, pp. 102 ff., claiming independents would cease to be viable operators without the mandatory crude allocations program. Also, *The Prospects for Gasoline Availability: 1974*, paper prepared by Congressional Research Service for National Fuels and Energy Policy Study, Committee on the Interior, U.S. Senate, 93d Congress, 2d Session (Washington 1974), pp. 47–51 and passim. Also, *New York Times*, February 22, 1974, and June 30, 1974. For critical and comprehensive reportage on the contrived aspects of the energy crisis, contrasting industry's overseas expansion with domestic "scarcity," see Donald L. Burlett and James B. Steele's two series of articles in the *Philadelphia Inquirer* during 1973. These have been reprinted by the newspaper under the titles "Oil, the Created Crisis" and "Oil: the Crisis and the Facts."

18. The statement by Senator Magnuson is in *Oversight-Mandatory Petroleum Allocation Programs, op. cit.*, p. 21. The comment by Thomas H. Kean, minority leader of the New Jersey Assembly, is in a roundup by Frank Lynn of local official reactions, *New York Times*, February 12, 1974.

19. *Current Energy Shortages Oversight Series—The Major Oil Companies*, Hearings before the Permanent Subcommittee on Investigations of the Committee on Government Operations, 93d Congress, 2d Session (Washington, 1974), Parts 2, 3, and 4. Also, *Current Energy Shortages Oversight Series—Cutoff of Petroleum Products to U.S. Military Forces*, ibid. (Washington, 1974), Part 8. See also *Business Week*, December 1, 1973, pp. 18–19, and April 27, 1974, pp. 45–46.

20. Cables from Aramco president Frank Jungers to the four American shareholders, October 14, 1973. *Multinational Corporations,* op. cit., Hearings, Part 7, pp. 544–45. Also, *Multinational Oil Corporations and United States Foreign Policy,* Report (Washington, 1975), p. 144. Hereafter cited as *Multinational Oil Corporations,* Report.

21. *New York Times,* January 24 and 26, 1974.

22. See, for example, Aramco cable to its four shareholders, June 1, 1973, *Multinational Corporations,* Hearings, op. cit., Part 7, p. 509. Also, briefing papers for American policy makers visiting Dhahran, ibid., pp. 517–28.

23. Memorandum to President Nixon, October 12, 1974, ibid., pp. 546–47.

24. *A Documentary History of the Petroleum Reserves Corporation 1943–1944,* Subcommittee on Multinational Corporations of the Committee on Foreign Relations, U.S. Senate, 93d Congress, 2d Session (Washington, 1974), pp. 63, 118 and passim. Also, *The Politics of Oil,* op. cit., chapters 8, 9. Within Caltex (the joint venture of Standard of California and Texaco) there was some resistance to admitting Jersey into Aramco. A major argument was that Caltex could expand its markets by making oil available to the many large companies in the United States looking for foreign sources of crude; joining with Jersey would lock Caltex into the former's restrictive agreements. See *Multinational Corporations,* op. cit., Hearings, Parts 7 and 8, and Report, pp. 45–55.

25. *Current Energy Shortages Oversight Series—The Major Oil Companies,* op. cit., Part 3, pp. 421–22. Also, *New York Times,* January 25, 1974.

26. *New York Times,* January 25, 1974, February 22, 1974.

27. *New York Times,* January 28, 1974.

28. See, for example, address to United Nations General Assembly, September 18, 1974; also, to World Energy Conference, Detroit, September 23, 1974. *New York Times,* September 19 and 24, 1974.

29. Interview with Henry Kissinger, *Business Week,* January 13. 1975.

30. *Business Week,* February 2, October 5, 1974.

31. President Monroe J. Rathbone, *Business Week,* October 1, 1954.

32. *United States Energy Outlook,* A Report of the National Petroleum Council's Committee on U.S. Energy Outlook (Washington, 1972).

33. Testimony of Charles E. Spahr, chairman, Standard Oil Company of Ohio, and also chairman of the board, American Petroleum Institute, *Market Performance and Competition in the Petroleum Industry,* Hearings before the Committee on Interior and Insular Affairs, U.S. Senate, 93d Congress. 1st Session, (Washington, 1973), Part 1, p. 310. Also, Richard C. Sparling, Norma J. Anderson, Richard S.

Dobias, *Annual Financial Analysis of a Group of Petroleum Companies, 1972*, Economic Energy Division, Chase Manhattan Bank (New York, 1973), p. 18. By the following year the bank reported that the funds generated internally had risen to 73 percent and remained at that level during 1974. *Annual Financial Analysis of a Group of Petroleum Companies, 1973*, p. 16; *1974*, p. 16.

34. *New York Times*, November 19, 1975.

35. *New York Times*, August 26 and November 13, 1975.

36. Testimony of Jack W. Carlson, assistant secretary of the interior, *The Utilities Act of 1975*, Hearings before Subcommittee on Intergovernmental Relations and the Subcommittee on Reports, Accounting, and Management of the Committee on Government Operations, U.S. Senate, 94th Congress, 1st session (Washington, 1975), pp. 6–7.

CHAPTER 2. *Traces of Oil*

1. For a documented study, focusing primarily upon the automobile industry's efforts to reshape all ground transport for its own advantage, see testimony of Bradford C. Snell, *The Industrial Reorganization Act*, Hearings before the Subcommittee on Antitrust and Monopoly of the Committee on the Judiciary, U.S. Senate, 93d Congress, 2d Session (Washington, 1974), Parts 3, 4 and 4A, especially Mr. Snell's document "American Ground Transport", in Part 4A, pp. A-1 to A-103. Mr. Snell was assistant counsel to the subcommittee.

See also discussion by other scholars and officials. Also rejoinder by General Motors in Part 4A, pp. 105–27.

2. Of the many studies, Barry Commoner's *The Closing Circle* (New York, Alfred A. Knopf, 1971) remains one of the most telling.

3. *Standard Oil Co. of Indiana–Occidental Petroleum Corp. Merger*, Hearing before the Special Subcommittee on Integrated Oil Operations of the Committee on Interior and Insular Affairs, U.S. Senate (Washington, 1974), p. 9.

Also, *An Analysis of the Proposed Standard–Occidental Merger*, prepared by the chairman of the Special Subcommittee (Washington, 1975). The chairman, Senator Floyd K. Haskell (Democrat, Colorado) concluded that the raid on Occidental was blocked, not because of a basic fear of federal antitrust action, but because of the determined resistance of the Hammer corporation.

4. *Standard Oil Co. of Indiana–Occidental Petroleum Corp. Merger*, Hearing, testimony of Armand Hammer and of John Swearinger, chairman of the board, Standard (Indiana). For details of the Iran–Occidental negotiations and their last minute breakdown, see *New York*

*Times,* June 22 and August 28, 1976; and *Business Week,* July 5, 1976, pp. 15–16.

5. See Robert Engler, *The Politics of Oil,* op. cit., chapters 3–5.

6. "The Fortune Directory," *Fortune,* May 1975; also August 1975.

7. *Capital Investments of the World Petroleum Industry—1972,* Chase Manhattan Bank (New York, 1973), pp. 4–5.

8. "Preliminary Federal Trade Commission Staff Report on its Investigation of the Petroleum Industry," in *Investigation of the Petroleum Industry,* Permanent Subcommittee on Investigations of the Committee on Government Operations, U.S. Senate, 93d Congress, 1st Session (Washington, 1973).

9. See testimony of Shirley Ward, supervisory auditor, U.S. General Accounting Office, *Multinational Corporations,* Hearings, op. cit., Part 7, pp. 173 ff. Also, Joseph J. Johnston, senior vice-president, Arabian-American Oil Co., pp. 192 ff; George T. Piercy, senior vice-president, Exxon, pp. 222 ff.

10. "For a long time our foreign profits were on crude oil because our taxes in the Middle East were so low. Now those profits are going to have to shift downstream for the simple reason that the Middle East governments now control prices and our profits on crude." Rawleigh Warner, Jr., chairman, Mobil, *Business Week,* February 2, 1974.

11. See, for example, "How the Multinationals Play the Money Game," *Fortune,* August 1973, pp. 59 ff. Calculating what companies should be allowed to carry on their books as a cost for crude oil purchased from one of its own affiliates has been a major problem in enforcing federal petroleum pricing regulations. "In some cases, but by no means all, the transfer prices are inflated," FEA administrator John C. Sawhill noted. See *New York Times,* April 27, May 9, May 17, 1974; *Wall Street Journal,* December 19, 1974. The following year the FEA notified a dozen international oil companies that it believed they had overpaid their affiliates $170 million for oil imported into the United States during the 1973–74 embargo. *New York Times,* June 24, 1975. Also testimony of Sawhill, *Multinational Corporations,* op. cit., Hearings, Part 9, pp. 1–44.

12. "Preliminary Federal Trade Commission Staff Report on its Investigation of the Petroleum Industry," op. cit., p. 27. For two somewhat varying analyses of the industry's structure and control, see Thomas D. Duchesneau, *Competition in the U.S. Energy Industry* (Cambridge: Ballinger, 1975) and Stanley H. Ruttenberg and Associates, *The American Oil Industry, A Failure of Antitrust Policy,* (New York: Marine Engineers' Beneficial Association, 1973).

13. See the statement of Senator Frank E. Moss (Democrat, Utah), *Market Performance and Competition in the Petroleum Industry,* op. cit., Part 1, pp. 5–15.

14. For useful summary, see Muriel Allen and Richard Levy,

"Whose Alaskan Oil?" *New Republic*, July 28 and August 4, 1973, pp. 14–16. For a discussion of the antitrust issues and the calling off of the study by Attorney General Mitchell, see letter to Senator Floyd K. Haskell (Democrat, Colorado) from William J. Lamont, formerly with Enforcement Division of Justice Department, April 18, 1973, in *Congressional Record*, July 12, 1973, pp. 23568–69.

Pertinent data and inconclusive interpretations about the degree of control by the majors in the western states and about the possible impact of Alaskan oil upon competitive patterns are found in *Report to the Federal Trade Commission on the Structure, Conduct and Performance of the Western States Petroleum Industry*, a staff report of the Bureau of Competition and the Bureau of Economics of the Federal Trade Commission (Washington, 1975).

15. *U.S. Energy Resources, A Review as of 1972*, Background paper prepared for National Fuels and Energy Policy Study, Committee on Interior and Insular Affairs, U.S. Senate, 93d Congress, 2d Session (Washington, 1974), Part 1, pp. 153–56 and passim. The document, prepared by geophysicist M. King Hubbert, offers useful data and interpretations concerning overall national reserves. It also presents conflicting and higher estimates, based on different methods of estimating reserves, by the U.S. Geological Survey. See also Hubbert's "The Energy Resources of the Earth," *Scientific American*, September 1971, pp. 60–70. Physicist Leonard Rodberg has a defense of Hubbert's computations concerning the declining rate of discovery in a sympathetic interview with the geophysicist in *The Elements*, a monthly newsletter by the Institute for Policy Studies (Washington, April 1976). For criticism of Hubbert's methods and conclusions concerning the peaking of domestic oil production and an insistence instead that there is no immediate danger of shortage because of geological limits— that the shortage is rooted in profit-based corporate decision-making to reduce exploratory efforts—see Barry Commoner, "Energy," *The New Yorker*, February 2, 1976, pp. 38–66. This and succeeding articles, February 9 and 16, are expanded in his book *The Poverty of Power* (New York: Knopf, 1976).

16. *Disclosure of Corporate Ownership*, Subcommittees on Intergovernmental Relations, and Budgeting, Management and Expenditure of the Committee on Government Operations, U.S. Senate, 93d Congress, 1st Session (Washington, 1973). Especially, introduction and pp. 29–33.

17. Ibid., p. 242. The president of Exxon had explained that "normally, of course, third party inquiries arise out of marital difficulties, creditors' claims, or just plain curiosity of say a relative or a newspaper columnist. I fully appreciate that your inquiry must have a substantial purpose. Unfortunately, we have been unable to establish any satisfactory dividing line between "good" inquiries and "bad" inquiries and this has forced us to decline to make any voluntary disclosures."

18. Ibid., p. 243.

19. *Congressional Record*, May 5, 1971, pp. 13530–32. See also, *Corporate Disclosure*, Hearings before the two subcommittees, op. cit., Parts 1 and 2 (Washington, 1974).

20. See *Governmental Intervention in the Market Mechanism*, Hearings before the Subcommittee on Antitrust and Monopoly of the Committee on the Judiciary, U.S. Senate, 91st Congress, 1st and 2d Sessions (Washington, 1969 and 1970), "The Petroleum Industry" (Parts 1–5). Especially, testimony of George Shultz, chairman, Cabinet Task Force on Oil Import Control, Part 4, pp. 1691 ff. Also, J. J. Simmons III, administrator of Oil Import Administration, pp. 1743 ff. Also, testimony of economist Joel Dirlam, Part 1, pp. 249 ff, and as an appendix on pp. 448–49, *Oil and Gas Journal*, vol. 67, no. 9 (March 3, 1969), p. 91, the secret agreement with Canada. Also, testimony of Robert Engler, Part 1, pp. 364 ff. which brought up to date the relevant section in *The Politics of Oil*, especially pp. 230–247. The hearings, organized by John M. Blair, chief economist of the subcommittee, provided a thoroughly documented picture of the imports issue and its relation to oil supply and public policy. See also, "U.S. Establishes Formal Limitation on Oil Imports from Canada," White House announcement and proclamation, March 10, 1970, in U.S. Department of State *Bulletin*, April 13, 1970, pp. 494–95. Edward H. Shaffer, *The Oil Import Program of the United States, An Evaluation* (New York: Praeger 1968), presents useful basic data about the workings of the program.

21. *The Politics of Oil*, op. cit., pp. 65–79. *The International Petroleum Cartel*, Staff Report to the Federal Trade Commission, released through subcommittee on Monopoly of Select Committee on Small Business, U.S. Senate, 83d Congress, 2d Session (Washington, 1952) remains an invaluable source. It was reissued in 1975 by the committee.

22. The Senate hearings on *Multinational Corporations*, op. cit., Hearings, especially Parts 4–9, provide rich documentation and illustration, chiefly from industry and State Department sources, of the various efforts to preserve worldwide industry order while dealing with Iraq, Iran, Saudi Arabia, Libya, and the other producing nations. Part 8 also presents behind-the-scenes documents from the National Security Council, the State Department, and the industry concerning the International Petroleum Cartel case, the 1950 Aramco tax decision, the Iranian consortium, and industry activities in the Middle East. Generally not available, either classified or in corporate files at the time of the writing of *The Politics of Oil*, op. cit., these support the discussion of these issues in that study. See especially pp. 65–79, 146–48, 182–229. For useful background concerning the financial pro-

visions of the concessions, see Zuhayr Mikdashi, *A Financial Analysis of Middle Eastern Oil Concessions: 1901–1965* (New York: Praeger, 1966). For discussion of profits, see Charles Issawi and Mohammed Yeganeh, *The Economics of Middle East Oil* (New York, Praeger, 1962). For a description and analysis of the economic activities of the international companies, see Edith T. Penrose, *The Large International Firm in Developing Countries, The International Petroleum Industry* (London: George Allen and Unwin, 1968).

23. Fuad Rouhani *A History of O.P.E.C.* (New York: Praeger, 1971) offers very useful background. Also, George W. Stocking, *Middle East Oil* (Kingsport, Tennessee: Vanderbilt University Press, 1970). The *Annual Review and Record*, published by OPEC in Vienna, offers a chronological summary of its activities and resolutions. *The Middle East Economic Survey*, Beirut, Lebanon, often provides pertinent documentation and speeches. For an analysis of world oil pricing, see M. A. Adelman, *The World Petroleum Market* (Baltimore: Johns Hopkins University Press, 1972). Joe Stork, *Middle East Oil and the Energy Crisis* (New York: Monthly Review, 1975), places oil diplomacy and the energy crisis within the perspective of the internal political conflicts and nationalist movements of the Middle East. See also *MERIP Reports*, monthly bulletin of the Middle East Research and Information Project, Washington.

24. For a State Department defense of these arrangements, see testimony of George McGhee, *Multinational Corporations*, op. cit., Hearings, Part 4, pp. 83 ff. Also, Part 8, especially pp. 341–79 and passim. Also, Report, op. cit., pp. 77–93, and *The Politics of Oil*, op. cit., pp. 222–29. McGhee had been assistant secretary of state for Near Eastern, South Asian and African Affairs from 1949–1951; he had also held many other diplomatic posts. By training he was a geologist, headed an independent oil producing firm and was a director of Mobil Oil.

25. There are a number of versions and translations of his exact words, but the meaning is not in doubt. See, for example, *New York Times*, June 12, August 8, 1973; also, *Washington Post*, June 12, 1973; also statement by George Henry Mayer Schuler, chief London Policy Group representative for Bunker Hunt Company, *Multinational Corporations*, Hearings, op. cit., Part 6, p. 56. Colonel Qaddafi went on to say: "American arrogance is symbolized in the support of the monopolistic oil companies. It is high time the Arabs take serious steps to undermine American interests in our region."

26. See, for example, *The Politics of Oil*, op. cit., pp. 236–37.

27. For example, testimony of E. L. Shafer, vice-president in charge of production, Eastern Hemisphere Petroleum Division, Con-

tinental Oil Co., *Multinational Corporations*, op. cit., Hearings, Part 7, pp. 244 ff. Also, Report, op. cit., pp. 95–118.

28. For documented analysis of the industry's planning for a stable growth rate for global supply, see testimony of John M. Blair, *Multinational Corporations*, op. cit., Hearings, Part 9, pp. 192 ff. Late in 1974 the four American partners in Aramco announced that negotiations over their rights were far enough along to prepare to turn over full title to the Saudi Arabian government. *New York Times*, November 30, and *Wall Street Journal*, December 6, 1974.

29. Exxon Corporation *1973 Annual Report,* pp. 5–6.

30. John K. Jamieson, speaking to Japanese and other businessmen in Tokyo, *New York Times*, April 25, 1973.

31. International oil executives openly expressed less concern about ownership of assets in the producing areas than about access. "What we're concerned about," said an executive of a major international oil company, "is whether we have to pay the same price as every Tom, Dick and Harry"—referring to oil companies that had been buying from the Aramco partners. *New York Times*, December 8, 1974.

32. For a discussion of economic impact of oil and alternative routes for producer nation participation, see Kamal S. Sayegh, *Oil and Arab Regional Development* (New York: Praeger, 1968).

33. For a suggestive discussion, see Michael Tanzer, *The Political Economy of International Oil and the Underdeveloped Countries* (Boston: Beacon, 1969), pp. 90–106, 117–35, and passim.

34. *Multinational Corporations*, op. cit., Hearings, Part 7, especially pp. 173–92. For Aramco records, see Part 8, 379–494.

35. "We are a cartel and I'm not ashamed to say it," said one Kuwaiti oil official. Dispatch from Vienna meeting of OPEC, *New York Times*, September 17, 1974.

36. See "Venezuela, Its Oil Within Grasp, Needs Foreign Concerns' Refining Technology," *New York Times*, November 3, 1975. For a statement of Venezuelan epectations about oil prices, the global redistribution of wealth, and interdependence, see interview with President Carlos André Pérez, *Business Week*, October 13, 1975, pp. 56–60. For background see Edwin Lieuwen, *Petroleum in Venezuela, History* (Berkeley: University of California Press, 1955). Also, Harvey O'Connor, *World Crisis in Oil* (New York: Monthly Review, 1962), chapters 10–12 and passim. A. A. Berle, Jr., *The 20th Century Capitalist Revolution,* (New York, Harcourt, Brace, 1954). Mr. Berle had argued that the live-and-let-live arrangements of the oil corporations represented a successful experiment in world economic government. See, for example, p. 157.

37. *Current Energy Shortage Oversight Series—The Major Oil Companies,* op. cit., Part 3, especially pp. 414–22. Summary of internal

documents of Cost of Living Council, released at request of consumer advocate Ralph Nader under Freedom of Information Act, *New York Times*, June 8, 1974. Also, Nader testimony, *Energy Information Act*, Hearings before the Committee on Interior and Insular Affairs, U.S. Senate, 93d Congress, 2d Session (Washington, 1974), Part 1, pp. 309–50 and passim. Also "Financial Impact of Oil Pricing Policies," memorandum to Representative John E. Moss (Democrat, California) from Economics Division, Congressional Research Service, Library of Congress, October 3, 1974. For a survey of oil price increases, the jump in the amount of uncontrolled oil being produced, and a discussion of the failure to spur overall increased production, see *New York Times*, April 12, 1974. Critics pointed out the inconsistency of the United States government's claim that it would like foreign oil prices to be lowered while it was encouraging the rise of its own domestic prices. As part of the announcement of the dollar a barrel increase John T. Dunlop, director of the Cost of Living Council, said: "The increased ceiling price for domestic crude can be expected to generate only marginal increments to crude supply in the short run. Some increase, however small, is, of course, desirable in the current energy crisis. However, the announced increase will create additional incentive for the petroleum industry to pursue further research and development efforts, new exploration and new technology to augment our energy resources." Cost of Living Council *News*, Release, December 19, 1973. See, also its *Economic Stabilization Program Quarterly Report* (October 1–December 31, 1973).

38. "An Atlantic-Japanese Energy Policy," presented before the Europe-America Conference sponsored by The European Movement, Amsterdam, March 27, 1973. A modified version appears in *Foreign Policy*, no. 11, Summer 1973, pp. 159–92.

39. *New York Times*, August 16, 1975. See also *Implications of Recent Organization of Petroleum Exporting Countries (OPEC) Oil Price Increases*, for National Fuels and Energy Policy Study, Commitee on Interior and Insular Affairs, U.S. Senate, 93d Congress, 2d Session (Washington, 1974).

40. For a revealing narrative of government policy-making (or non-policy-making) reflecting the president's Oil Policy Committee's dependence upon the industry for predictions and judgments about supply, refinery capacity, and public needs, and its respect for the industry's reluctance to have public hearings or discussion about pricing policies, see *Staff Study of the Oversight and Efficiency of Executive Agencies with Respect to the Petroleum Industry, Especially as it Relates to Recent Fuel Shortages*, Permanent Subcommittee on Investigations of the Committee on Government Operations, U.S. Senate, 93d Congress, 1st Session (Washington, 1973). Also in ibid., Hearings,

Part 1, see testimony of George A. Lincoln, pp. 201–22 and passim. General George A. Lincoln, director of the Office of Emergency Preparedness and chairman of the Oil Policy Committee, repeatedly told questioners that "we didn't know there was going to be a shortage. We had the refinery capacity and the crude oil necessary. . . . We had industry assurances that it wouldn't happen." Report, *Emergency Petroleum Allocation Act of 1973*, Committee on Interior and Insular Affairs, U.S. Senate, 93d Congress, 1st Session (Washington, 1973), pp. 7–8 and passim.

A summary analysis of the unworkability of the then existing mandatory imports program is found in *Toward a Rational Policy for Oil and Gas Imports*, a policy background paper prepared for the Interior Committee (Washington, 1973).

41. For illustration of the "paper projects," see *Business Week*, December 15, 1973. For discussion of surplus refining capacity, see *Business Week*, November 9, 1974, and *New York Times*, December 9, 1974. *Oversight-Mandatory Petroleum Allocation Programs*, op. cit., Hearings, Part 1, passim. Also, *Problems in the Federal Energy Administration's Compliance and Enforcement Effort*, U.S. General Accounting Office (Washington, 1974). Also, *Market Performance and Competition in the Petroleum Industry, Hearings*, op. cit., Part 1. Also "Staff Report to the Federal Trade Commission," March 15, 1974; and "Evaluation of the Mandatory Petroleum Allocation Program," *Oversight-Mandatory Petroleum Allocation Programs*, op. cit., Appendix, 1974. Also, "Comments on Staff Report on the Emergency Petroleum Allocation Program," Federal Trade Commission (Washington, 1974). Z. D. Bonner, executive vice-president of Gulf, saw the allocation orders as "unlawful taking of private property. By allocating crude oil supplies on a percentage of capacity basis, many inefficient, antiquated and obsolete plants will be processing more crude oil but making less total produce." *New York Times*, February 12, 1974. See also *New York Times*, January 30, 1975. Exxon also sought redress through the courts; *New York Times*, June 18 and July 2, 1974. For Secretary of the Treasury George F. Shultz's reservations about the likely success of such legislation, which asked companies to "act against their self interest," see *The Trade Reform Act*, Hearings before the Committee on Finance, U.S. Senate, 93d Congress, 2d Session (Washington, 1974) pp. 208–10 and passim. *New York Times*, February 22, and June 30, 1974. Also, *Oversight-Federal Energy Administration Programs*, Hearings before the Committee on Interior and Insular Affairs, U.S. Senate, 94th Congress, 1st Session (Washington, 1975). For the indictment of Gulf and the reaction of the company, see *New York Times*, August 6, 1975.

42. Alvin J. Moore, vice-president Giant Service Stations, Inc. (Arizona) and member of legislative committee, Society of Independent

Gasoline Marketers, *Market Performance and Competition in the Petroleum Industry*, Hearings, op. cit., p. 62.

43. "We underestimated the pace of economic activity and failed to anticipate the new need for energy to clean up the environment,' J. K. Jamieson, chairman of Exxon, told the Economics Club of Detroit. "We made an even bigger error in our forecast of oil consumption. This we underestimated by about 10 percent." (In the period 1968–69, when decisions were made that were affecting supply in 1973–74, he conceded an underestimation of energy consumption of about 5 percent. *New York Times*, January 29, 1974.) For a Senate committee conclusion about an industry underestimation of demand right after World War II and its relation to a "shortage" then, see *The Politics of Oil*, op. cit., pp. 149–50.

44. G. T. Piercy, senior vice-president and chief negotiator for Exxon, reporting on discussions with Sheikh Zaki Yamani, from cable, January 20, 1971, appearing as part of testimony of George Henry Mayer Schuler, chief London Policy Group representative for Bunker Hunt Oil Co., *Multinational Corporations*, op. cit., Hearings, Part 6, p. 70. Yamani, who had been on the board of Aramco, and was considered a friend of the Western interests, favored "participation" as a device for keeping the special relationship with the United States mutually profitable and for forestalling the outright nationalization favored by the more militant producer states. "Who are the so-called moderates?" he asked in a report to Aramco after a tour of the OPEC states. "There is only Saudi Arabia, Kuwait and a handful of small Gulf states. There is a worldwide trend toward nationalization and Saudis cannot stand against it alone. The industry should realize this and come to terms so that they can save as much as possible under the circumstances" (March 1, 1972). Ibid., p. 50. Earlier, he had described the majors as a "sort of buffer between us and the consumers." Even when they had cut crude prices to protect their profits from newcomers, they knew the value of a floor under prices. Thus, posted prices served the companies and the producing countries. See discussion with Yamani in *Middle East Economic Survey*, June 7, 1968.

45. *New York Times*, July 1, 1974.

46. *Concentration by Competing Raw Fuel Industries in the Energy Market and its Impact on Small Business*, Hearings before the Subcommittee on Special Small Business Problems of the Select Committee on Small Business, U.S. House of Representatives, 92d Congress, 1st Session (Washington, 1971), vols. 1 and 2; also Report (Washington, 1971). Also, *Competitive Aspects of the Energy Industry*, Hearings before the Subcommittee on Antitrust and Monopoly of the Committee on the Judiciary, U.S. Senate, 91st Congress, 2d Session (Washington, 1971), Part 1. For a useful analysis of coal costs and the possible sources for the sharp price increases since 1969, see James R. Barth and James T. Bennett, "An Economic Analysis of Price In-

creases in the U.S. Coal Industry," October 1, 1974, monograph prepared for American Public Power Association, Emergency Committee for the Tennessee Valley, National Rural Electric Cooperative Association and Tennessee Valley Public Power Association, Washington, D.C.

47. James Cannon has written a succinct and valuable summary analysis. See *Leased and Lost, A Study of Public and Indian Coal Leasing in the West*, Council on Economic Priorities (New York, 1974). See also, *Federal Coal Leasing Program*, Hearings before the Subcommittee on Minerals, Materials and Fuels of the Committee on Interior and Insular Affairs, U.S. Senate, 93d Congress, 2d Session (Washington, 1974), Part 1. On Sun Oil lease sale, see *New York Times*, August 22, 1971. Also, *U.S. Energy Outlook*, op. cit., pp. 135–71, and *Project Independence*, Project Independence Report of Federal Energy Administration (Washington, 1974), pp. 98–108 and passim.

48. Testimony of George H. Lawrence, vice-president and director, American Gas Association, *Review of the Developments in Coal Gasification*, Hearings before the Subcommittee on Minerals, Materials, and Fuels and the Full Committee on Interior and Insular Affairs, U.S. Senate, 92d Congress, 1st Session (Washington, 1972), pp. 49–56 and passim. Also, *Coal Policy Issues*, Hearings before the Committee on Interior and Insular Affairs, U.S. Senate, 93d Congress, 1st Session (Washington, 1973). Also, *New York Times*, August 22, 1971.

49. See *The Politics of Oil*, op. cit., pp. vii, 8, 11–33, 383, 390, 395, 414.

50. Governor William L. Guy, *Surface Mining*, Hearings before the Subcommittee on Minerals, Materials, and Fuels of the Committee on Interior and Insular Affairs, U.S. Senate, 92d Congress, 1st Session (Washington, 1972), Part 3, p. 952. See also, testimony of spokesmen from other states and environmental interests; also, director, U.S. Bureau of Mines, pp. 955 ff.

51. "An Initial Appraisal by the Oil Shale Task Force," Subcommittee, Committee on U.S. Energy Outlook, National Petroleum Council (Washington, 1972); also, *U.S. Energy Outlook*, op. cit., pp. 205–23; *Project Independence*, op. cit., pp. 129–34. Also, Chris Welles, *The Elusive Bonanza, The Story of Oil Shale—America's Richest and Most Neglected Natural Resource* (New York: E. P. Dutton and Co., 1970); also, *The Politics of Oil*, op. cit., pp. 96–100, 450, 489.

52. *Competitive Aspects of Oil Shale Development*, Hearings before the Subcommittee on Antitrust and Monopoly of the Committee on the Judiciary, U.S. Senate, 90th Congress, 1st Session (Washington, 1967), Part 1. A valuable source for basic data, positions held by a range of citizens, economists, and public officials. For report of the Department of the Interior's Oil Shale Advisory Board, see pp. 444–63. For testimony of Orlo E. Childs, president of the Colorado School of Mines, see pp. 230–52; quotation is on p. 235.

53. *Water and Energy Self-Sufficiency*, Staff Analysis and Selected Materials on Water Use in Energy Production, Committee on Interior and Insular Affairs, U.S. Senate, 93d Congress, 2d Session (Washington, 1974), pp. 9–10, 16, 37–38, 725–828, and passim. For an optimistic progress report conceding that "Oxy may be onto something big," see *Business Week*, March 29, 1976, pp. 36–37.

54. Testimony of Reid T. Stone, oil shale and geothermal coordinator, Department of Interior, *Energy Data Requirements of the Federal Government* (Part II, *Oil Shale*), Hearing before the Subcommittee on Activities of Regulatory Agencies of the Permanent Select Committee on Small Business, U.S. House of Representatives, 93d Congress, 2d Session (Washington, 1974), p. 24. Also, *New York Times*, January 18, 19, 1974.

55. See testimony of Morton Winston, vice-president, Oil Shale Corporation, *Competitive Aspects of Oil Shale Development*, Hearings, Part 1, op. cit., pp. 308–46. Also, Professor Morris Garnsey, economist, University of Colorado, pp. 34–66.

56. For a useful source of documents describing the oil shale regions, assessing the technological approaches and problems, and airing concerns of oilmen, environmentalists, and citizens of the involved areas, see *Final Environmental Statement for the Prototype Oil Shale Leasing Program*, United States Department of the Interior (Washington, 1973), 6 vols. This review was undertaken in compliance with the National Environmental Policy Act of 1969. The correspondence (vol. V) and the public hearings (vol. VI) are particularly rich; it is unfortunate that the pages of vol. V were not numbered for easier reference.

57. News release, October 4, 1974, through Atlantic Richfield Company, Denver, Colorado.

58. The Arco executive was Thornton F. Bradshaw, and the Union Oil executive was John M. Hopkins, at the annual meeting of American Petroleum Institute, New York, *Wall Street Journal*, November 14, 1974.

59. *Commentary*, November 1974. The advertisement also ran again in the January 1975 issue, where there was an article by Robert W. Tucker, "Oil: The Issue of American Intervention," pp. 21–31, which explored the question when there might be justification for military action in the Middle East. For report of the suspension of the prototype oil shale development program in Colorado, see *New York Times*, August 24, 1976.

60. *New York Times*, January 31, 1975; also *Wall Street Journal*, December 9, 1974.

61. See, for example, *Competitive Aspects of the Energy Industry*, Hearings, op. cit., pp. 156–278 and passim; *Concentration by Competing Raw Fuel Industries in the Energy Market and Its Impact on Small Business*, Report, especially pages 12–13, and Hearings, op. cit. Also, testimony and documents, U.S. Atomic Energy Commission,

*Energy Information Act,* Hearings before the Committee on Interior and Insular Affairs, U.S. Senate, 93d Congress, 2d Session, (Washington, 1974), Part 2, pp. 545–784 and passim. Also, testimony of Dixy Lee Ray, chairman, U.S. Atomic Energy Commission, *Market Performance and Competition in the Petroleum Industry,* Hearings, op. cit., Part 2, pp. 595–680; oil corporation testimony on their activities in nuclear development, pp. 680–718. Also, *New York Times,* December 18, 1973. In 1975, the Royal Dutch/Shell group and Gulf each reported substantial losses on the joint venture; later in the year, General Atomic, the joint venture, announced it was quitting production of high-temperature nuclear gas reactors in order to become competitive with liquid water reactors. *New York Times,* April 19, October 25, 1975. For a discussion of the management difficulties, see *Wall Street Journal,* February 25, 1976.

62. See *Geothermal Energy Resources and Research,* Hearings before Committee on Interior and Insular Affairs, U.S. Senate, 92d Congress, 2d Session (Washington, 1972). For a discussion of energy resources "in the future," see Wilson Clark, *Energy for Survival, The Alternative to Extinction* (New York, Anchor, 1974), especially chapters 5–8.

63. For basic documents, data, and interpretations, see *The Natural Gas Industry,* Hearing before the Subcommittee on Antitrust and Monopoly and the Subcommittee on Administrative Practice and Procedure of the Committee on the Judiciary, U.S. Senate, 93d Congress, 1st Session (Washington, 1973), Parts 1 and 2.

64. For background, see *The Politics of Oil,* pp. 115–31, 313–14, 319–22, 324–29, 338–39, 386–89, 392, 397–418, 452–58, 479.

65. *Energy Information Act,* Hearings, op. cit., Part 2. Also, *New York Times,* October 7, 1973.

66. See *The Natural Gas Industry,* op. cit., Part 1. See for example, testimony of Representative George E. Brown, Jr. (Democrat, California), pp. 15–36 and passim. The FPC quotation is from *New York Times,* December 5, 1974.

67. *The Need for Improving the Regulation of the Natural Gas Industry and Management of Internal Operations, Federal Power Commission,* Comptroller General of the United States (Washington, 1974).

68. "Conservation—a Marketing Dilemma, a Research Challenge," Leonard W. Fish, senior vice-president, American Gas Association, speech before Third Conference on Natural Gas Research and Technology, Dallas, Texas, March 6, 1974.

69. Robert K. Killian, *Market Performance and Competition in the Petroleum Industry,* Hearings, op. cit., Part 1, p. 343.

70. *The Utilities Act of 1975,* Hearings, op. cit., see pp. 1–3, 131–35, and passim.

71. Aubrey J. Wagner, chairman, Tennessee Valley Authority, before Tennessee Valley Public Power Association Annual Meeting, Gulf Shores, Alabama, April 16, 1975. Also, his testimony, *Concentration by Competing Raw Fuel Industries in the Energy Market and its Impact on Small Business*, Hearings, op. cit., vol. 2, pp. 5–25 and passim; also vol. 1, passim.

72. "Letter to Shareholders," Rawleigh Warner, Jr., June 28, 1974. See, also, correspondence with Senator Edward W. Brooke (Republican, Massachusetts), reprinted in *Congressional Record*, July 18, 1974, pp. S 12885–86; also, *New York Times*, June 19, August 7, 1974. In 1976, Mobil moved to gain complete control over Marcor, increasing its holdings from the 54 percent acquired in 1974. The merger placed Mobil third on *Fortune's* list of the 500 largest companies. From Washington came hints that such actions would accelerate divestiture legislation; there was also word that the Justice Department was "still investigating" Mobil's initial investment in Marcor. *New York Times*, March 13, 19, and 27, 1976. For Arco's interest in Anaconda, see interview with President Thornton F. Bradshaw, *New York Times*, April 4, 1976; also April 2, 1976.

73. United Nations Economic Commission for Asia and the Far East *Report of the Sixth Session of the Committee for Co-ordination of Joint Prospecting for Mineral Resources in Asian Offshore Areas (CCOP) and Report of the Fifth Session of its Technical Advisory Group* (Appendix 4 of the Report of the Committee) *with Part 2—Technical Documentation*, held at Bangkok, Thailand, June 26, 1969. Also, *Congressional Record*, March 11, 1971, pp. S 2911–15; March 15, 1971, pp. H 1525–32. For useful chronology and bibliographic citations, see "Vietnam and Oil—No. 1," American Friends Service Committee, Philadelphia, Pennsylvania, April 19, 1971.

74. Harry S. Schimmel, "A Discussion on Oil Exploration in the Southeast Asian Offshore," April 1, 1969, published by the investment banking firm of F. S. Smithers and Co., New York. Also, Wise and Ross, *The Invisible Government*, op. cit., pp. 136–46.

75. "Green Light for Oil Men," *Vietnam Economic Report*, The Vietnam Council on Foreign Relations, Saigon, Viet Nam, January 1971. The oil companies, which had begun what appeared to be promising exploratory work in 1973, pulled out in 1975, presumably because of the politically insecure climate. *New York Times*, November 27, 1975. For a critical roundup see Leon Howell and Michael Morrow, *Asia, Oil Politics, and the Energy Crisis* (New York: IDOC/North America, 1974).

76. For a discussion of overseas refinery construction, see testimony of James M. Patterson, professor of marketing, Indiana University, coauthor with Fred C. Allvine of *Competition, Ltd.: The Marketing of Gasoline* (Bloomington, Indiana University Press, 1972), in *Mar-*

*keting Performance and Competition in the Petroleum Industry,*
Hearings, op. cit., Part 2, pp. 530–57. Also, testimony of John W.
Wilson, chief, Division of Economic Studies, Office of Economics,
Federal Power Commission, *The Natural Gas Industry,* Hearings,
op. cit., Part 1, pp. 456–504, offers useful data on joint overseas ven-
tures as well as on concentration in the industry. Also, Harry Magdoff,
*The Age of Imperialism, The Economics of U.S. Foreign Policy* (New
York: Monthly Review, 1969), and Richard J. Barnet and Ronald E.
Müller, *Global Reach: The Power of the Multinational Corporations*
(New York: Simon and Schuster, 1974). *The Multinational Corpora-
tion, Studies in U.S. Foreign Investment,* Office of International Investment, U.S. Department of Commerce (Washington, 1972) vol. 1.

77. *New York Times,* April 15, May 28, 1974. Also, *Annual Financial Analysis of a Group of Petroleum Companies, 1973,* op. cit. For
a critical breakdown of the industry's effective tax rate, see *Congressional Record,* January 23, 1974, p. H 169. Also, Phillip M. Stern *The
Rape of the Taxpayer* (New York: Vintage, 1974), chapter 11 and
passim. Also, *Analysis of Tax Data of Seven Major Oil Companies,*
Permanent Subcommittee on Investigations of the Committee on Government Operations, U.S. Senate, 93d Congress, 2d Session (Washington, 1974).

78. For an analysis and discussion of Aramco profits, see *Multinational Corporations,* op. cit., Hearings, Part 7, especially pp. 173–
243. For materials on Aramco tax decisions, see Part 8, pp. 341–494.
Also, *New York Times,* March 28, 1974. See *The Politics of Oil,* op.
cit., especially pp. 37–39, 67, 129, and 181–261, for background on
oil profits, tax arrangements, and privileges.

79. Presented to House Ways and Means Committee by Secretary
of the Treasury George P. Shultz. *New York Times,* February 5,
1974.

80. *New York Times,* January 24 and March 15, 1974. Also, "The
Profit Situation," Special Petroleum Report of Energy Economics Di-
vision of Chase Manhattan Bank, New York, April, 1974. Also, *Energy
Windfall Profits* and *Profitability of Domestic Energy Company Op-
erations,* Hearings before the Committee on Finance, U.S. Senate, 93d
Congress, 2d Session (Washington 1974).

81. *Annual Fiscal Analysis of a Group of Petroleum Companies,*
op. cit., pp. 14–15.

82. *New York Post,* April 26, 1974; *New York Times,* April 27,
1974.

CHAPTER 3. *Political Explorations*

1. Ronnie Dugger, "Oil and Politics," *The Atlantic,* September
1969, p. 75.

2. "Trade Investments and United States Foreign Policy," address to National Business Advisory Council at Hot Springs, Virginia, October 19, 1962, in U.S. Department of State *Bulletin*, November 5, 1962, p. 684.

3. See *The Politics of Oil*, op. cit., p. 402.

4. Ibid., pp. 147, 319, 380, 399–408, 412, 453.

5. Bernard D. Nossiter in *Washington Post*, July 16, 1970.

6. *The Politics of Oil*, op. cit., pp. 358, 408–9, 477.

7. Transcript of April 21, 1971 meeting, in *Statement of Information*, Book V, Part 1, *Department of Justice Litigation—Richard Kleindienst Nomination Hearings*, Hearings before the Committee on the Judiciary, House of Representatives, 93d Congress, 2d Session (Washington, 1974), p. 372.

8. Memorandum, August 7, 1970, in *Multinational Corporations*, op. cit., Hearings, Part 2, pp. 551–52.

9. *Statement of Information*, Transcript of April 19, 1971 conversation, pp. 318–19, 347. Richard W. McLaren, a Republican corporate lawyer who was appointed by Mitchell as assistant attorney general in charge of the antitrust division, was a special target for presidential and corporate wrath because of initial zeal in spelling out the price implications of imports control and in pursuing cases such as the expansion of the ITT empire. See *Investigation of Conglomerate Corporations*, A Report by the Staff of the Antitrust Committee (Subcommittee No. 5) of the Committee on the Judiciary, House of Representatives, 92d Congress, 1st Session (Washington, 1971), chapter 2 and passim; also, ibid., Hearings, Part 3. The hearings on the nomination of Richard G. Kleindienst as attorney general provided devastating if not always conclusive documentation about the behavior of the ITT conglomerate, antitrust, and political responses to corporate power: *Richard G. Kleindienst*, Hearings before Committee on Justice, U.S. Senate, 92d Congress, 2d Session (Washington, 1972), Parts 1, 2, 3. Also, Anthony Sampson *The Sovereign State of ITT* (New York: Stein and Day, 1973). In a searing analysis of the political intrigue in the ITT case, journalist I. F. Stone noted that McLaren "came in like a lion . . . and has gone out—a judge," the appointment coming after a consent settlement prior to a Supreme Court ruling which presumably McLaren had been seeking. "Behind the ITT Scandal," *The New York Review of Books*, April 6, 1972.

10. Clyde La Motte, remarks before the Gas Men's Roundtable, December 5, 1972, Washington. For the squelching of the antitrust inquiry into the Alyeskan pipeline consortium, see letter, William J. Lamont (chapter 2, note 14, above).

11. The White House, February 17, 1969, reprinted as Exhibit 15, *Presidential Campaign Activities of 1972*, Appendix to the Hughes-Rebozo Investigation of the Select Committee on Presidential Campaign Activities of the U.S. Senate, 93d Congress, 2d Session (Wash-

ington, 1974), Book 26, p. 12469. See also, *The Final Report* (Washington, 1974), pp. 940 ff.

12. Baruch Korff, *The Personal Nixon: Staying on the Summit*, (Washington: Fairness Publishers, 1974), p. 63. Rabbi Korff founded a National Citizens Committee for Fairness to the Presidency. For a discussion of this "disinterest" in profit, see William V. Shannon, "A Man of Property," *New York Times*, July 13, 1974.

13. *Congressional Record*, January 22, 1974, pp. E 87–88; January 23, 1974, pp. E 141–42; January 24, 1974, pp. E 175–76. Also, *The Final Report of the Select Committee on Presidential Campaign Activities*, op. cit., especially chapters 4 and 8; Hearings, Book 13. Also, *New York Times*, August 24, September 30, 1973; *Washington Post*, September 30, 1973. Also, *The Offenses of Richard M. Nixon*, op. cit., p. 78. And "News From Common Cause", Campaign Finance Monitoring Project, Washington, November 1, 1973.

14. *The Politics of Oil*, op. cit., especially chapters 12 and 13. Also, *Congressional Quarterly*, November 29, 1968; Erwin Knoll, "The Oil Lobby is Not Defeated," *New York Times* Magazine, March 8, 1970; Murray Seeger, "The Oilmen and Politics", *Washington Post*, January 17, 1971; Morton Mintz and Jerry S. Cohen, *America Inc.: Who Owns and Operates the United States* (New York: Dial, 1971), chapters 4, 6, and passim.

15. For an analysis of Long's income, see *New York Times*, October 5, 1969. The call for protecting oil prices is in his newsletter, "Senator Russell B. Long Reports from Washington," January 1974. And the speculation about a war with Canada was in a floor debate with Senator William Proxmire (Democrat, Wisconsin) over oil imports, profits, and taxes: "The Senator talks about Canadian oil being available and Mexican oil being available. The Senator does not know what he is talking about. How does the Senator know whether a war would not break out between the United States and Canada, and if so, why would Canada give us its oil to fight a war with Canada? That could happen. Has the Senator ever heard of the War of 1812?" *Congressional Record*, April 15, 1969, p. 3742.

16. "News from Common Cause," Washington, March 11, 1975. The press release noted that the Senate Finance Committee agreed to support Chairman Long in striking from the House-passed tax cut bill the repeal of the oil depletion allowance.

17. For Gravel's view, repeated in numerous hearings and debates, see, for example, *Congressional Record*, July 29, 1975, pp. S 14144–48. The address by Stevens was at the 20th Alaska Science Conference, Alaska Division of American Association for the Advancement of Science, University of Alaska, College, Alaska, August 27, 1969. For environmentalist concern over the road sought by the oil companies

and approved by Secretary of the Interior Walter J. Hickel, see *New York Times*, August 14, 1969, and April 14, 1970; also May 28, 1970.

18. *New York Times*, July 18, November 14, 1973; also May 26, 1974. See also, *Draft, Environmental Impact Statement for the Trans-Alaska Pipeline*, U.S. Department of the Interior (Washington, 1971). For a critical appraisal of the pipeline, which suggests why the companies and its allies in Interior favored the socially questionable but very profitable trans-Alaskan route, see Charles J. Cichetti, *Alaskan Oil: Alternative Routes and Markets* (Baltimore: Johns Hopkins University Press, 1972). For examples of discussion as to Canadian interest in an alternative route and industry-Interior attitudes, see *House of Commons' Debates*, vol. 115, no. 95, 3d Session, 28th Parliament, March 12, 1971, Ottawa, pp. 4207, 4212–38. Also *Congressional Record*, September 21, 1971, pp. E 9832–38; April 4, 1972, pp. E 3414–15; June 20, 1972, pp. E 6329–31.

For careful documentation of the Canadian government's criticisms of the Alaskan pipeline, its preference for a pipeline system through the MacKenzie Valley of Canada, and distortions of the Canadian position by the American State and Interior departments and oil companies, see presentations by Senator Walter Mondale (Democrat, Minnesota), *Congressional Record*, July 10, 1973, pp. 22981–23002; July 11, 1973, pp. 23330–42; July 12, 1973, pp. 23554–79; July 13, 1973, pp. 23748–65. Also, *New York Times*, June 10, 1972. And letter to Congress from Secretary of the Interior Rogers C. B. Morton summarizing Interior's thinking and ultimate conclusion, U.S. Department of the Interior, April 4, 1973.

19. Morton Mintz, a tireless reporter, put together many of the data for the *Washington Post*, February 24 and June 28, 1969. For a more detailed account see his "A Colonial Heritage," in Robert L. Heilbroner and others, *In the Name of Profit* (New York: Doubleday, 1972), pp. 60–105.

20. For the pre-April 7 list, see *Presidential Campaign Activities of 1972*, op. cit., Book 22, pp. 10284–338. The Hess contributions are listed on p. 10318. For Woods's testimony about her understanding as to the nature of the funds, see testimony, pp. 10193–283; also *The Final Report*, op. cit., p. 692.

21. See *Governmental Intervention in the Market Mechanism*, op. cit., Hearings, passim; also Kenneth W. Dam, "Implementation of Import Quotas: The Case of Oil," reprinted from *The Journal of Law and Economics*, April 1971 (Washington, Brookings, 1971); also *U.S. Oil Week*, January 15, 1973.

22. *Business Week*, September 21, 1974, pp. 84–87.

23. A top official at Union Oil, whose executives had given campaign contributions in twenty-two states in 1970, offered a similar ex-

planation: "We're not trying to buy votes. We're trying to buy an entree to talk about our problems." *New York Times*, April 11, 1971. The letter to the Ashland stockholder, July 28, 1973, is reprinted in *Presidential Campaign Activities of 1972*, op. cit., Hearings, Book 13, p. 5802. The Atkins testimony is on pp. 5439–59.

24. Ibid., p. 5444.

25. *The Final Report*, op. cit., p. 460.

26. *Securities and Exchange Commission v. Ashland Oil, Inc.*, Civil Action no. 75–0794, United States District Court for the District of Columbia, May 16, 1975, including pleadings and judgment; also, *Report of the Special Committee to the Board of Directors of Ashland Oil, Inc.* filed with SEC pursuant to the judgment, vols. 1 and 2, June 26, 1975. This special committee of Ashland board members was created to meet one of the conditions for a plea of nolo contendere and a consent decree. A breakdown of the domestic political contributions showed payments to congressional and gubernatorial candidates in both parties; $100,000 to candidate Richard M. Nixon's campaign for the presidency in 1968; $30,000 for the 1968 Democratic presidential campaign as well as a number of small gifts directly to campaigns of Hubert Humphrey (Democrat, Minnesota) for the Senate and the presidency; $100,000 to the Finance Committee to Re-elect the President (Nixon) in 1972; $50,000 between June 1970 and February 1972 to Robert Strauss, treasurer of the Democratic National Committee. Schedule 1, *Report of the Special Committee*, August 8, 1975. Accountants for the special committee noted in their review of flight logs maintained with respect to corporate aircraft "numerous instances of flights that included as passengers various federal and state government officials. In addition, we noticed names of people who have been candidates for public office." See vol. 2, op. cit., Exhibit 21, p. 28. One disturbing question emerging from a reading of the corporate maneuvers concerns the role of the corporation's accountants and outside auditors in accepting responsibility for presumably accurate financial statements. Another question raised concerns the vigilance of the United States Internal Revenue Service. See also *New York Times*, July 10, 1975, and *Business Week*, July 21, 1975. The overseas recipients included Libya's minister of petroleum in 1969 and Gabon's president and several ministers from that state.

27. *Presidential Campaign Activities of 1972*, Hearings, op. cit., Book 13, pp. 5460–81; also, Book 25, pp. 1209–32; Book 2, p. 714; *The Final Report*, op. cit., pp. 923–25; also, Schedule 1, *Report of the Special Committee*, op. cit., p. 5; also, *New York Times*, August 8, 1974, and November 26, 1975.

28. *Presidential Campaign Activities of 1972*, op. cit., Book 13, p. 5808.

29. *Securities and Exchange Commission v. Gulf Oil Corporation et al.*, Civil Action no. 75–0324, United States District Court for the District of Columbia, March 11, 1975.

30. *Multinational Corporations*, op. cit., Hearings, Part 6, pp. 289–290.

31. *Report of the Special Committee of the Board of Directors of Gulf Oil Corporation*, filed with SEC, December 30, 1975, p. 4.

32. Ibid., pp. 2, 64, 68–79, 82, 231, 234, 236, and passim. With regard to Senator Scott, "Wild apparently told the Senator that he could not provide money any longer, but the Senator seemed unable to understand why" (p. 74). Representative H. John Heinz 3d (Republican, Pennsylvania), having announced he would seek his party's nomination to succeed Senator Scott, who had indicated he would not run again, was also a recipient of Gulf funds; he explained that he had never reported these contributions since they had gone to his campaign committees and not to him personally. *New York Times*, December 19, 1975.

33. *Report of the Special Committee of the Board of Directors of Gulf Oil Corporation*, op. cit., pp. 247–48.

34. Ibid., pp. 86–89.

35. *Business Week*, April 1, 1972, pp. 48–49.

36. *Report of the Special Committee of the Board of Directors of Gulf Oil Corporation*, op. cit., pp. 83–85. For a discussion of the critical role of the Texas Railroad Commission in the private planning of the oil industry, see *The Politics of Oil*, op. cit., pp. 130, 141–46, 231, 238–41, 384, 392, 400, 409, and passim. For Texas civil suits, seeking total damages of over $1.4 million, see *New York Times*, February 5, 1976.

37. "The Corporation," CBS Reports, Columbia Broadcasting System Television Network, December 6, 1973.

38. *The Final Report*, op. cit., pp. 489–92; also *New York Times*, November 22 and December 5, 1973.

39. *Securities and Exchange Commission v. Phillips Petroleum Company, et al.*, Civil Action no. 75–0308, United States District Court for the District of Columbia, March 6, 1975.

40. *Special Report by Phillips Petroleum Company to the Securities and Exchange Commission*, filed September 26, 1975, passim; also, *New York Times*, October 27, 1973, July 19, 1974, and February 19, 1976.

41. *Report of the Special Review Committee of the Board of Directors of Gulf Oil Corporation*, op. cit., pp. 279–85. The *Report* does not include the diaries.

42. Ibid., pp. 281–84; also, *1974 Annual Report*, Gulf Oil Corporation (Pittsburgh, 1975), p. 41; and *New York Times*, March 28, 1974,

November 5 and 11, 1975 and March 13, 1976. The Symington exchange with Dorsey is in *Multinational Corporations and United States Foreign Policy*, op. cit., Hearings, Part 12, pp. 20–21.

43. *Report of the Special Review Committee of the Board of Directors of Gulf Oil Corporation*, op. cit., pp. 277–79. See also, *Presidential Campaign Activities of 1972*, Hearings, op. cit., Book 13, pp. 5460–81, and *The Final Report*, op. cit., pp. 469–473.

44. *New York Times*, January 13 and 15, March 7, 1976; *Wall Street Journal*, January 15, 1976. For a summary of the financial terms on which Dorsey departed, and also the subsequent restitution forced through stockholder suits, see chapter 8, note 10.

45. *Report of the Special Review Committee of the Board of Directors of Gulf Oil Corporation*, op. cit., pp. 177–79.

46. "Interim Report" to Stockholders, September 1, 1974 (Attachment 9); "Notice and Proxy Statement, Annual Meeting," April 29, 1975 (Attachment 11); "Special Report to Stockholders on Political Contributions by Phillips Petroleum Company," March 31, 1975 (Attachment 12). These are in *Attachments to Special Report by Phillips Petroleum Company to the Securities and Exchange Commission*, September 26, 1975. Also, *New York Times*, account of stockholders meeting, April 30, 1975.

47. "Special Report to Stockholders on Political Contributions by Phillips Petroleum Company," op. cit., Attachment 12, pp. 5–6.

48. *New York Times*, February 19, 1976. In a message to stockholders in March 1976, chief executive officer W. F. Martin spoke of economic adversity for the company during 1975 but made no mention of the company's and his own political difficulties. All the familiar phrases about public interference appeared. For example, a new price control law allowed for gradual domestic price increases. "But it should be recognized that these administered price increases will be subject to congressional review and therefore vulnerable to unforeseen political influences." Also: "Continued assaults on the oil industry's ability to perform are anticipated in 1976," including increased taxes and divestiture, *1975 Annual Report*, Phillips Petroleum Company, 1976.

For a summary of the federal grand jury indictment and the response of Phillips, see *New York Times*, September 3 and 14, 1976.

49. *Report of the Special Committee of the Board of Directors of Ashland Oil, Inc.*, op. cit., vol. 1, pp. 162, 166–67, 176–77, and passim. Also, "Summary of Report of Special Committee and the Action of the Board of Directors Thereon," Ashland Oil Co. Inc., 1975. Chairman Atkins of Ashland reiterated that "these contributions were made with the genuine belief that they were necessary and in the best interest of the company, given the political environment which existed." "Proceedings of the January 30, 1975, Meeting of Shareholders," p. 6.

"I felt I was doing what was being done generally." *New York Times,* August 22, 1975.

50. *New York Times,* December 5, 1973.

51. For a picture of Stans's fundraising style, see *Minneapolis Tribune,* November 25, 1973, reprinted in *Advisory Committees,* Oversight Hearings before the Subcommittee on Budgeting, Management, and Expenditures of the Committee on Government Operations, U.S. Senate, 93d Congress, 1st and 2d Sessions (Washington, 1974), pp. 146–69. Also, Stans's testimony, *Presidential Campaign Activities of 1972,* Hearings, op. cit., Book 2, pp. 687–782 and passim. The statements about "technical violations" and "privacy" are on pp. 689 and 691. Also, *The Final Report,* op. cit., pp. 544–50. Also, *New York Times,* March 13 and May 15, 1975.

52. *Report of the Special Review Committee of the Board of Directors of Gulf Oil Corporation,* op. cit., pp. 31–35, 44, 54–55, 60–63, 223–28, 271, and passim. For the Gulf program announced in 1958 and the letter by senior vice-president Archie D. Gray, see *The Politics of Oil,* op. cit., pp. 369–71, 388.

53. See Michael C. Jensen, "The New Corporate Presence in Politics" and "Business Builds its Political War Chest—Legally," *New York Times,* December 14, 1975, and March 28, 1976. Mr. Jensen's earlier reporting of the corporate giving disclosed by the SEC was solid and pointed. The Sun comments are by Samuel K. White, vice-president and general counsel, *Philadelphia Inquirer,* August 22, 1975. The Phillips Petroleum statement is from "The Corporation," CBS Reports, op. cit.

Late in 1975 the Justice Department gave a green light to corporate political action committees which solicited and then turned over contributions from employees to candidates designated by the corporate managers of the fund. *New York Times,* November 8, 1975. This ruling encouraged the formation of such groups. For a roundup of these political action committees, including some twenty in coal, oil, and gas, see "News from Common Cause," Campaign Finance Monitoring Project, Washington, March 10, 1976.

54. "Notice of Annual Meeting of Stockholders," Standard Oil Company of California, March 16, 1972, and March 15, 1973. A letter to the author from H. L. Severance, secretary of the company, adds that, while political giving is legal in some states, "it is not legally possible for corporate funds to flow to any federal elections, and Standard of California complies meticulously with the law." July 3, 1972.

The shareholder proposal was offered by James B. Hoy of Hamden, Connecticut, who was seeking to build a shareholder alliance, Project Standard Oil, to mobilize individual stockholders for effective participation in Socal decisions.

55. "Why Nixon Fears to Resign," *New York Review of Books*, November 29, 1973. Quoted with permission of I. F. Stone.

56. *New York Times*, March 5, 1976.

57. "Basically, the Senators were not wild about going beyond the narrowest scope of inquiry," explained a former staff member of the Senate Watergate committee. *Washington Post*, January 6, 1975. For the McCloy reactions, see *New York Times*, March 5, 1976. For Ervin's comments about Ford's role, see *New York Post*, March 24, 1976; also correspondence with author.

58. *Washington Post*, September 22, 1976.

59. *The Final Report of the Select Committee on Presidential Campaign Activities*, op. cit., chapter 5, "Mills Fund," pp. 579–867 and passim; also testimony of John B. Connally, *Presidential Campaign Activities of 1972*, Hearings, op. cit., Book 14, pp. 6051–6104 and passim; also Books 15, 16, 17, passim. Also, *New York Times*, July 30 and August 8, 1974.

60. *New York Times*, April 18, 1975.

61. Confidential Memorandum, August 16, 1971, *Presidential Campaign Activities of 1972*, Hearings, op. cit., Book 4, pp. 1689–90; also, testimony of Dean, Books 3 and 4, passim.


CHAPTER 4. *The Rites of Government*

1. For background on the role of state and federal "conservation" machinery in protecting price, see *The Politics of Oil*, op. cit., pp. 132–50 and passim; on imports, see pp. 230–47 and passim.

2. *Governmental Intervention in the Market Mechanism*, op. cit. See for example, testimony and discussion, M. A. Adelman, economist, Part 1, pp. 6–14; Edith Penrose, economist, pp. 156–81; George P. Shultz, chairman, Cabinet Task Force on Oil Import Control, Part 4, pp. 1694–1742. See also, chapter 2, note 20, above.

3. Ibid. For complaints of independents, see Part 3; for example, testimony of Arthur T. Soule, president of the Independent Fuel Terminal Operators Association, and John A. Kareb, president of Northeast Petroleum Corporation, pp. 1202–17. The M. A. Wright statement is in his testimony, Part 2, p. 798. A summary of the criticisms of oil import controls by the petrochemical industry can be found in "The Petrochemical Industry and Oil Import Controls" published by Celanese, Dow, E. I. Dupont de Nemours, Monsanto, and other affected corporations (Washington, 1969).

4. George P. Shultz, *Governmental Intervention in the Market Mechanism*, op. cit., Part 4, p. 1707 and passim. For a succinct history and analysis, see Walter S. Measday, committee economist, "A History of Federal Cooperation with the Petroleum Industry," Part 1, pp. 578–99.

5. The hearings cited in *Governmental Intervention in the Market Mechanism*, op. cit., are a good starting point for understanding the Machiasport controversy. See testimony of Armand Hammer, chairman of the board of Occidental, Part 3, pp. 1419–29, 1645–73.

6. Ibid. See testimony of Maine's Governor Kenneth M. Curtis, a Democrat, pp. 1406–19, 1641–44.

7. *Congressional Record*, October 14, 1968, pp. H 10007–22, for statement by Boggs; his legal memorandum before the examiners' committee, and news accounts in the *Washington Post*, the *Boston Herald Traveler*, the *New Orleans Times-Picayune*, the *Wall Street Journal*, the *New York Times,* the *Portland (Maine) Press Herald*, and the *Portland (Maine) Evening Express* tracing the events.

8. McIntyre's analysis appeared in the *Boston Globe*, November 2, 1969, and is reprinted in the *Congressional Record*, November 4, 1969, pp. S 13713–15.

9. For a discussion of the relation of the oil industry and the U.S. Department of the Interior, see chapters 6 and 7 of the present work; also, *The Politics of Oil*, op. cit., chapters 5, 10, and passim.

10. *New York Times*, February 26, 1969. For a lively and authoritative account of the Maine case, see Peter Amory Bradford, *Fragile Structure: A Story of Oil Refineries, National Security, and the Coast of Maine* (New York: Harper's Magazine Press, 1975). Bradford writes as insider, having served on the staff of Governor Curtis before becoming Public Utilities Commissioner in Maine. For perspectives on the environmental issues involved, see *The Relationship of Economic Development to Environmental Quality*, Hearings before the Subcommittee on Air and Water Pollution of the Committee on Public Works, U.S. Senate, 91st Congress, 2d Session (Washington 1971). There are documents, studies, reprints of pamphlets as well as pertinent testimony by a range of environmentalists, public officials, citizens, scientists, and oil spokesmen.

11. *See Governmental Intervention in the Market Mechanism*, op. cit., Part 4, pp. 1727, 1887, and passim. For a discussion of Interstate Oil Compact Commission, see *The Politics of Oil*, op. cit., pp. 140–49, 286, 290, 392, 401, 424.

12. Cabinet Task Force on Oil Import Controls, *The Oil Import Question: A Report on the Relationship of Oil Imports to the National Security* (Washington, 1970).

13. Ibid.; see also testimony of George P. Shultz, *Governmental Intervention in the Market Mechanism*, op. cit., Part 4, pp. 1694–1742; also Appendix to his statement, pp. 1783–92.

14. *Governmental Intervention in the Market Mechanism*, op. cit., p. 1719.

15. Ibid.; see testimony and discussion, J. J. Simmons III, Administrator, Oil Import Administration, pp. 1743–69. For insights into jurisdictional controversy between Texas Railroad Commission and the

U.S. Department of the Interior, see memoranda, correspondence, special orders, *Oil and Gas Journal* articles, pp. 1793–1848.

16. For a discussion and interpretation of the difficulties of getting public government in such contexts, see Theodore J. Lowi, *The End of Liberalism: Ideology, Policy and the Crisis of Public Authority* (New York: W. W. Norton, 1969).

17. "Statement by the President," and press conference of Peter M. Flanigan, assistant to the president, February 20, 1970, reprinted in *Governmental Intervention in the Market Mechanism*, op. cit., Part 4, pp. 1771–80. For a good example of an oil state attack, see speech by Senator Clifford P. Hansen (Republican, Wyoming) March 6, 1970, ibid., pp. 1878–81. For some suggestion as to the industry's appreciation of Mr. Nixon's actions, see *New York Times*, February 21, 1970.

18. Bernard Nossiter, *Washington Post*, August 19, 1970. For summary accounts of the low-level political machinations behind the high-level justifications for public policy, see Erwin Knoll "The Oil Lobby is Not Defeated," op. cit., and Morton Mintz and Jerry S. Cohen, *America, Inc.*, op. cit., especially pp. 195–98.

19. "Message to the Congress on A Program to Insure an Adequate Supply of Clean Energy in the Future," June 4, 1971, reprinted in *Presidential Energy Statements*, op. cit., pp. 1–12.

20. "U.S. Establishes Formal Limitation on Oil Imports from Canada," White House announcement and Proclamation, March 10, 1970, op. cit. See also chapter 2, note 20, above.

21. *U.S. Energy Outlook, A Report on the National Petroleum Council's Committee on U.S. Energy Outlook*, op. cit. passim.

22. *New York Times*, April 4, 1973.

23. *U.S. Oil Week*, April 23, 1973.


CHAPTER 5. *Imperial Energies*

1. The Kennedy statement, *New York Times*, September 18, 1963, is quoted in Harry Magdoff, *The Age of Imperialism* (New York: Monthly Review, 1969), p. 133, from John D. Montgomery, *Foreign Aid in International Politics* (Englewood Cliffs, New Jersey: Prentice-Hall, 1967), p. 20.

2. See, for example, E. F. Schumacher, "Roots of Economic Growth," (Varanasi, India: Gandhian Institute of Studies, 1962); "The Death of the Green Revolution," North London Haslemere Group (London: Haslemere Declaration Group and Third World First, 1973); also *Rural Development*, Sector Policy Paper (Washington: World Bank, 1975) gives a sense of the changing recognition about the limits of big technology.

3. *United States Security Agreements and Commitments Abroad: Kingdom of Thailand*, Hearings before the Subcommittee on United

States Security Agreements and Commitments Abroad of the Committee on Foreign Relations, U.S. Senate, 91st Congress, 1st Session (Washington, 1970), Part 3, pp. 741–42 and passim.

4. News conference, *New York Times*, March 17, 1971. For some of the critical documents, correspondence between J. W. Fulbright (Democrat, Arkansas), chairman of the Senate Foreign Relations Committee, and the State Department; and articles (as for example by historian Gabriel Kolko, "Oiling the Escalator," in the *New Republic*, March 13, 1971) see *Congressional Record*, March 11, 1971, pp. S 2911–15, and March 15, 1971, pp. H 1525–32. Also, see chapter 2, notes 72–74, above. Also, *New York Times*, April 2, 1971, for statements by oil economist Michael Tanzer and others.

5. Correspondence, State Department, *Congressional Record*, March 15, 1971, p. H 1532.

6. Interview with Marylin Bender, *New York Times*, November 7, 1971.

7. David W. Ewing, "The Corporation as Peacemonger," *Aramco World*, March–April, 1972.

8. See *The Age of Imperialism*, op. cit., pp. 54, 121, 128, for specific references. The entire tightly argued book deserves careful reading. Also, William Appleman Williams, *The Tragedy of American Diplomacy* (Cleveland: World, 1959).

9. *Congressional Record*, March 11, 1971, pp. S 2911–13, and March 15, 1971, pp. H 1531–32; also *New York Times*, April 2, 1971.

10. "A Review of Progress and Problems in Viet-Nam," U.S. Department of State *Bulletin*, February 15, 1971.

11. *New York Times*, November 7, 1971.

12. *New York Times*, November 26 and 27 and December 31, 1975; April 25, 1976.

13. See, for example, testimony of Barry J. Shillito, assistant secretary of defense, installations, and logistics; also, of Admiral Elmo R. Zumwalt, Jr., chief of naval operations, *Oil and Gas Imports Issues*, Hearings before the Committee on Interior and Insular Affairs, U.S. Senate, 93d Congress, 1st Session (Washington, 1973), Part 3, pp. 738–828. Also, transcript of testimony of Admiral Zumwalt before Committee on Armed Services, U.S. House of Representatives (Washington, February 21, 1974). The reference to the Mediterranean as "an American lake" is in Schlesinger's article "A Testing Time for America," *Fortune*, February 1976.

14. *The Economics of Middle Eastern Oil*, op. cit., p. 108. See, for example, the studies by Harry Magdoff, Michael Tanzer, Ronald E. Müller and Richard Barnet cited earlier.

15. *USIA Appropriations Authorization, Fiscal Year 1973*, Hearings before the Committee on Foreign Relations, U.S. Senate, 92d Congress, 2d Session (Washington 1972), pp. 48, 232–33, 331–34, and passim.

16. For background on the linkage between food shipments and fertilizer, see *The Political Economy of International Oil and the Underdeveloped Countries*, op. cit., pp. 243–56. For background and discussion of the dispute between IPC and Peru, and also of the "Hickenlooper" amendment to the Foreign Assistance Act of 1961, which was designed to minimize presidential discretion over invoking this prohibition of aid when properties were nationalized without the payment of what the owners or the State Department felt was adequate compensation, see *United States Relations with Peru*, Hearings before the Subcommittee on Western Hemisphere Affairs of the Committee on Foreign Relations, U.S. Senate, 91st Congress, 1st Session (Washington, 1969), passim. The quotation is from Richard Goodwin and is on p. 91. The view that developing nations must create their own energy industries is a central conclusion in the study by Michael Tanzer, cited previously. The general discussion and the notes for chapter 7 of *Global Reach*, op. cit., offer relevant illustrations and research citations.

17. Robert A. Hurwitch, deputy assistant secretary of state, Bureau of Inter-American Affairs, testimony, *U.S. Policy Toward Cuba*, Hearings before the Subcommittee on Western Hemisphere Affairs of the Committee on Foreign Relations, U.S. Senate, 93d Congress, 1st Session (Washington, 1974), p. 11 and passim.

18. See, for example, *The Political Economy of International Oil and the Underdeveloped Countries*, op. cit., pp. 327–30 and passim.

19. Philip W. Bonsal, *Cuba, Castro, and the United States* (Pittsburgh: University of Pittsburgh Press, 1971), p. 149. Quoted with permission of the publisher.

20. Speech by George W. Ball, under secretary of state, Roanoke, Virginia, April 23, 1964.

21. Paul Sheldon, Gulf Statement to Trustees, Ohio Conference, The United Church of Christ, Columbus, Ohio, September 10, 1970.

22. Remarks by Paul Sheldon, vice-president, Gulf Oil Corporation, to Eastern/Southeastern Institutional Investors Study Group on Corporate Responsibility in Southern Africa, African-American Institute, New York, April 12, 1972.

A "Gulf Boycott Coalition," with headquarters in Dayton, Ohio, was formed in 1971 and sought to publicize the political dimensions of the Gulf empire and develop opposition to its products and policies. See testimony of Patricia Roach, chairwoman, *U.S. Business Involvement in Southern Africa*, Hearings before the Subcommittee on Africa of the Committee on Foreign Affairs, House of Representatives, 92d Congress, 1st Session (Washington, 1973), Part 3, pp. 76–81 and passim.

23. Remarks by E. D. Brockett, chairman of the board and chief executive officer, Gulf Corporation, at the Annual Meeting of Share-

holders, Pittsburgh, Pennsylvania, April 28, 1970.

24. Interview with B. R. Dorsey, who was replacing E. D. Brockett as chief executive officer of Gulf, *New York Times*, November 7, 1971.

25. Paul Sheldon (see notes 21 and 22 above).

26. Ibid.

27. E. D. Brockett, op. cit.

28. Paul Sheldon (note 22).

29. Paul Sheldon, testimony, *U.S. Business Involvement in Southern Africa*, Hearings, op. cit. Part 1 (1972), pp. 94, 97.

30. "Notice of Annual Meeting of Shareholders," Gulf Oil Corporation, March 23, 1972. For examples of the critical literature against Gulf and the text of the church resolution, see *Background Information Re: Resolution Passed at the Seventh Annual Meeting of the Ohio Conference, United Church of Christ*, Columbus, Ohio, 1970. Also, *Gulf Oil—Portuguese Ally in Angola*, Brief issued by the Corporate Information Center of the National Council of Churches, New York, 1972.

31. Letter from B. R. Dorsey to the Reverend Reuben J. Schroer, immediate past president of the Ohio Conference of the United Church of Christ, *Washington Post*, August 8, 1970.

32. *Report of the Special Committee of the Board of Directors* of Gulf Oil Corporation, op. cit. Also, testimony of B. R. Dorsey, chairman of the board of Gulf Oil, *Multinational Corporations*, op. cit., Hearings, Part 12, pp. 1–58.

33. *New York Times*, November 7, 1971. Also, *Report of the Special Review Committee of the Board of Directors of Gulf Corporation*, op. cit., pp. 23, 93–122. Dorsey also headed the U.S.-Korea Economic Council, which was intended to promote trade and attract U.S. investments.

34. *New York Times* July 13, 17, 1975; *Wall Street Journal*, November 15, 1975. Also, *Report of the Special Review Committee of the Board of Directors of Gulf Oil Corporation*, op. cit., pp. 160–76 on Bolivia; pp. 80 and 193–96 on the Arab public relations; pp. 122–60 on Italy. Also testimony of B. R. Dorsey, *Multinational Corporations*, op. cit., Hearings, Part 12, pp. 1–58. The Communist Party denied ever having received the money and saw the revelation as a cheap trick to discredit it: "Not only our hands, but also the coffers . . . are clean." *New York Times*, July 15, 1975. The Bolivian military government suggested that the late president, General René Barrientos, never received such support and that Gulf officials might have used the money "for their own benefit." *New York Times*, January 16, 1976.

A useful starting point for tracing Exxon's Italian political activities and its relation to Esso Italiana is the testimony of Archie L. Munroe, controller of Exxon, *Multinational Corporations*, op. cit., Hearings

Part 12, pp. 239–314. Included are sections of the *Report to Board Audit Committee*, Report on Special Audit and Investigation in Italy, Standard Oil Company (New Jersey), October 17, 1972, and also the Internal Audit Report on Esso Italiana's Special Budget by Esso Europe. In its defense, Exxon has reiterated that these practices, rooted in an admitted "failure of management and financial controls," and deviations from its pride in its "reputation for lawful ethical conduct worldwide," were curtailed on its own initiative in pre-Watergate 1972 when the subsidiary's chief executive, an Italian national, was removed. A 1972 policy statement by Exxon's chairman emphasized that the company expected managers to follow the course of highest integrity in all dealings: "An overly-ambitious manager, who is not aware of our policy and our views, might have the mistaken idea that we do not care how results are obtained, as long as he gets results. He might think it best not to tell higher management all that he is doing, not to record all transactions accurately in his books and records, and to deceive the company's internal and external auditors. He would be wrong on all counts." J. K. Jamieson, "Morality and Management," October 16, 1972, reprinted in *Determination and Report of the Special Committee on Litigation*, Exxon Corporation, January 23, 1976.

The company's printed version of the 1975 shareholders' meeting has the chairman saying he did not know how much Imperial in Canada contributed: "it is not our business what they do as long as the contributions are legal." As for Italian contributions, they were "done by management at a level below ours. . . . We give our management wide discretion and wide latitude. We run a decentralized operation . . . and cannot take care of all the really minor details in New York. It would be an impossible job and would keep us from doing other important things." "Report of the 93d Annual Meeting of Shareholders," New Orleans, Louisiana, May 15, 1975, pp. 12–13.

Exxon's board created a Special Committee on Litigation in September 1975 to appraise a shareholder demand that Exxon sue its board because of the waste and misuse of $59 million for Italian politics. The committee, after reviewing the events and the internal operations, recommended against any such action. There were "errors of business judgment," but not through "lack of devotion to duty or breach of faith." Top management of Exxon "operated in the belief that Exxon was a company of unusual integrity and high principles— that Exxon was above unethical practices. While this appears to have been true in the United States and most other locations, this attitude seems to have created at the top of the corporation a trusting nature, which in the case of Italy was not justified. As the record shows, Exxon was vulnerable to unauthorized activity by a remotely located, under-supervised affiliate manager." The committee repeated the now familiar theme about Italian political involvement: that "it was in the interest of all people of goodwill to see that the democratic element in society continued to flourish." It deplored the inability to pinpoint payments. It exonerated the Exxon officers and directors, while making occasionally intriguing references to the role of experts within the corporation. For example: "Jamieson, while he was President of Exxon in 1968, was told about the existence of the contributions . . . but was assured that they were legal and were being phased down by Esso Europe. He was told by the General Counsel he should not become involved in the details and accepted that advice." The committee also warned that any such suit would stir up resentment against Exxon among Italian political figures. And internally, it "could damage the company by undermining the willingness of the employees in the future to assume responsibility and make decisions in what is inevitably a risk-taking business." *Determination and Report of the Special Committee on Litigation*, op. cit., pp. 15, 17, 39, 50, 80, and passim.

According to Jerome Levinson, chief counsel of the Senate subcommittee investigating the multinationals, the American embassy people in Rome who had been informed of Esso Italiana's contribution had shown neither surprise nor disapproval. "The reaction reported to me was it was a 'nice slice of the pie' that the parties were getting and, therefore, the parties were not as bad off as they represented to the Embassy." Hearings, op. cit., Part 12, p. 265. By CIA standards, the corporate giving was modest. For discussion of recent CIA activities in Italy, see *New York Times*, January 7, 1976.

35. *New York Times*, May 17 and July 16, 1975. For Gulf's Canadian gifts, considered legal, see *Report of the Special Commitee of the Board of Directors of Gulf Oil Corporation*, op. cit., pp. 177–79, 220. For a discussion of Mobil's overseas contributions, see testimony of Everett S. Checket, executive vice-president, International Division, *Multinational Corporations*, op. cit., Hearings, Part 12, pp. 315–40.

36. *New York Times*, October 9, 1975; February 18, 1976. When W. Alton Jones, chairman of Cities Service and one of the oilmen who paid for the upkeep of Dwight Eisenhower's farm, was killed in a plane crash en route to see his friend, now retired from the presidency, $61,000 was found in his briefcase. For a summary of the reporting on the Eisenhower farm and its upkeep, see Drew Pearson and Jack Anderson, *The Case against Congress* (New York: Simon and Schuster, 1968), pp. 438–40. In *The Politics of Oil*, op. cit., I had insisted and still hold, although with more awareness of the continuing cruder sides of oil politics, that "the spotlight belongs more on lawmakers and respectable men with bulging brown cases entering the portals of government rather than on lawbreakers and furtive men with little black bags using side entrances of hotels" (p. 419).

37. *New York Times*, May 17, 1975. Testimony of B. R. Dorsey, *Multinational Corporations*, op. cit., Hearings, Part 12, pp. 1–58.

38. Ibid., p. 7.

39. Ibid., p. 34. Senator William Proxmire subsequently announced he would introduce a bill making it a federal crime, enforced through the SEC, to bribe foreign officials; companies would be required to disclose periodically all foreign sales agents and their fees. If such practices were not stopped, "they will corrupt the domestic economic system, too," New York Times, March 13, 1976.

40. U.S. Department of Commerce, Survey of Current Business, September, 1973.

41. Amilcar Cabral, former leader of the liberation movement in Guinea-Bissau, related a conversation with a secretary in the American embassy concerning the offshore presence of Continental and Exxon: "I told him that we considered this an unfriendly attitude of the United States toward our people. And he said, 'Oh, no, we can do nothing at all through our government, because these are private companies and you see, Mr. Cabral, they would very much like to be the first, because when you'll be independent, they will be the first there.' I told him, 'You are a Christian. You must remember that Christ said that maybe the first will be last.' He was not too happy with that." George M. Houser, "U.S. Policy and Southern Africa," in Frederick S. Arkhurst, ed., U.S. Policy toward Africa (New York: Praeger, 1975), p. 124. Houser has been executive director of the American Committee on Africa.

42. "U.S. and Africa in the 70s," Submitted to President Nixon by Secretary of State William Rogers, U.S. Department of State Bulletin, April 20, 1970, pp. 513–21. Also, U.S. Policy toward Africa, op. cit., passim.

43. See, for example, "Background paper on U.S. bases in Spain and Portugal," United States Security Agreements and Commitments Abroad: Spain and Portugal, Hearings before the Subcommittee on United States Security and Commitments Abroad of the Committee on Foreign Relations, U.S. Senate, 91st Congress, 2d Session (Washington, 1970), Part II, pp. 2404–12 and passim. Also, "Allies in Empire," Africa Today, vol. 17, No. 4 (July–August 1970).

44. "Foreign Economic Interests and Decolonization, a Report," United Nations (New York, 1969), p. 27 and passim.

45. Wall Street Journal, March 7, 1974. New York Post, December 15, 1975.

46. New York Times, December 21, 23, 1975; February 22, March 27, April 3, 1976. The Gulf statement about "working with any government" was made by its president, James E. Lee, Business Week, March 1, 1976.

47. Timothy Smith, "The American Corporation in South Africa: An Analysis," Council for Christian Social Action, United Church of Christ, New York, 1970; also, "Apartheid and Imperialism: A Study

of U.S. Corporate Involvement in South Africa," *Africa Today*, vol. 17, No. 5 (September–October 1970). Also, "U.S. Investment in Southern Africa—A Focus for Church Concern and Action," a report by an ecumenical church team visiting South Africa, Southern Africa Task Force, United Presbyterian Church, New York, February, 1972; and *U.S. Business Investment in Southern Africa*, Hearings, op. cit., Part 3, passim.

48. *New York Times*, January 29, 1969. For background, see Scott R. Pearson *Petroleum and the Nigerian Economy* (Stanford: Stanford University Press, 1970). Also Robert Fitch and Mary Oppenheimer, "Let Them Eat Oil," *Ramparts*, September 1968, pp. 34–38.

49. *The Politics of Oil*, op. cit., pp. 182–309 and passim.

50. Memorandum, *Multinational Corporations*, op. cit., Hearings, Part 8, p. 299; also, *The Politics of Oil*, op. cit., pp. 222–29.

51. "Middle East Oil" (Used as Background Paper for September 11, 1950 Meeting with Oil Executives), State Department Policy Paper, September 10, 1950, *Multinational Corporations*, op. cit., Hearings, Part 7, pp. 122–23; also Report, op. cit., p. 81 and passim.

52. Report, *Multinational Oil Corporations*, op. cit., p. 92; also *Multinational Corporations*, op. cit., Hearings, Part 4, pp. 83–128, and Part 8, pp. 341–78.

53. Ibid., Part 9, pp. 115–16, letter to Dean Rusk, January 11, 1967. Also, Report, op. cit., pp. 12, 92–93.

54. Ambassador David Newsome in Report, op. cit., p. 16.

55. Richard J. Barnet *Roots of War* (New York: Atheneum, 1972), p. 56; see his discussion of "The Education of a Governing Class," chapter 3 (pp. 48–75).

56. *Multinational Oil Corporations*, op. cit., Report, pp. 83–84.

57. For discussion of ECA action against company pricing under the Marshall Plan, see *The Politics of Oil*, op. cit., pp. 218–21.

58. George Piercy, *Multinational Corporations*, op. cit., Hearings, Part 5, p. 217.

59. "Middle East Oil," op. cit., Hearings, Part 7, p. 130.

60. *Multinational Oil Corporations*, op. cit., Report, pp. 111–14, 117. For oil and State Department memoranda and correspondence concerning the possibility of information being leaked by companies not in the consortium or otherwise discovered by Iran, see ibid., Hearings, Part 8, pp. 557–90 and passim.

61. "Iranian Demands on Oil Consortium," Department of State Memorandum of Conversation, October 24, 1966, ibid., Hearings, Part 8, pp. 571–74.

62. Ibid. The memorandum concludes (p. 574): "As the visitors started to leave, Ambassador Hare asked if his understanding was correct that the companies did not wish the U.S. Government to become involved in the substance of the problem at this time. He was assured

that the companies desired only that the U.S. Government do its best to dissuade the Iranians from rash actions and discreetly probe Iranian intentions." Also, pp. 532–90. See, also, Report, op. cit., pp. 107–9, 114, 117, and passim.

63. Ibid., p. 100; also Hearings, Part 7, pp. 310–14.

64. Report, op. cit., p. 102.

65. Hearings, op. cit., Part 8, pp. 532–55. Also, *Wall Street Journal*, February 15, 1974. The State Department documents reveal direct pleas to such companies as Sinclair, Standard (Indiana), Union, Continental, and Getty in its efforts "to deter poachers" from making offers to Iraq which might weaken the bargaining position of the majors in Iraq. Countries such as Germany, France, and Italy were also asked not to intervene. One State Department telegram to the American embassy in Tokyo, dated September 10, 1968, reported that "Esso asked Department to try persuade Japanese to suspend efforts to enter Iraq" (p. 549). Another State memorandum concluded that there was nothing improper in the United States government's support of IPC, but the company had few legal remedies and "we have no firm legal basis for telling independent American companies—let alone foreign companies—to stay out of Iraq." The best leverage which IPC had "is the fact that Iraq would find it very difficult by itself to market the large amounts of oil it produces. Obviously, the leverage would be reduced greatly if other Western companies were to become deeply engaged in Iraq" (p. 541).

66. See discussion, chapter 3, above.

67. *Multinational Corporations*, op. cit., Hearings, Part 4, "Chronology of the Libyan Oil Negotiations, 1970–1971" (prepared for the Subcommittee by the Foreign Affairs Division, Congressional Research Service, Library of Congress, 1974), pp. 155–83; Part 5, especially testimony of James E. Akins, Office of Fuels and Energy, Department of State, pp. 1–28; John J. McCloy, counsel for Exxon and other major oil companies, pp. 59–73 and 247–87 (the quotation from McCloy is on p. 266); George Henry Mayer Schuler and Norman Rooney, Bunker Hunt Oil Co., pp. 75–143; John N. Irwin, State Department, 145–73; George T. Piercy, senior vice-president, Exxon, pp. 175–246; Part 6, passim, documents and statements related to testimony in Part 5, especially Schuler chronology of Libyan negotiations and cable traffic among London Policy Group, New York Advisory Group, and Teheran and Tripoli negotiating teams; also McCloy correspondence with State and Justice departments; Part 9, testimony of William P. Tavoulareas, president, Mobil Oil Corporation, pp. 73–118; Julius Katz, acting assistant secretary of state for economic and business affairs, pp. 146–66. Also, Report, "1970–73 Price and Participation Negotiations," chap. VI, pp. 121–40.

68. See testimony of Edward M. Carey, president, New England Petroleum Corporation, ibid., Hearings, Part 5, pp. 29–58; also, statement by the Department of State on policy on "hot" Libyan oil, Part 6, pp. 316–25. Also, response of Standard Oil of California, Part 8, pp. 682–87; also *Wall Street Journal*, February 15, 1974.

69. Transcript of news conference, *New York Times*, September 6, 1973.

70. "Address on the National Energy Policy," November 25, 1973, op. cit. (see chapter 1, note 6).

71. Harold J. Haynes, *New York Times*, December 8, 1974.

72. Testimony of Julius Katz, acting assistant secretary of state for economic and business affairs, and Gerald L. Parsky, assistant secretary of the treasury, *Multinational Corporations*, op. cit., Hearings, Part 9, pp. 150, 159, 166, and 273; also Report, op. cit., "The October Revolution," chap. VII, pp. 141–63. See also Walter J. Levy, oil consultant, *New York Times*, February 26, 1973.

73. Testimony of John C. Sawhill, administrator, Federal Energy Office, *Multinational Corporations*, op. cit., Hearings, Part 9, p. 33; also, Report, op. cit., pp. 141–63.

74. Cable, October 21, 1973 (obtained from files of Standard of California by Jerome Levinson, chief counsel, and Jack Blum, associate counsel, Subcommittee on Multinational Corporations), reprinted in *Multinational Corporations*, op. cit., Hearings, Part 7, pp. 515–17.

75. Ibid., p. 418, testimony of George Keller, vice-chairman of the board of Standard of California and a director of Aramco.

76. Ibid., pp. 401–39, 445–56, and documents, pp. 470–594.

77. Ibid., pp. 504–5: confidential report of meeting of oilmen with King Faisal, May 23, 1973.

78. Ibid., pp. 439–45: testimony of W. W. Messick; see also pp. 403–5, 407–11.

79. *New York Times*, December 22, 1974.

80. "Principles of Relations and Cooperation between Egypt and the United States," *New York Times*, June 15, 1974. Also, *Wall Street Journal*, December 16, 1974. President Anwar Sadat has assured American oil and business executives of an "economic open door" policy with "unlimited opportunities" for investments. *New York Times*, October 30 and November 2, 1975. He also sought to assure critics at home that such liberalization did not mean abandonment of socialist principles. *New York Times*, January 7, 1974.

81. Statement by President Nixon, May 23, 1970, on United States Oceans Policy: "At issue is whether the oceans will be used rationally and equitably and for the benefit of mankind or whether they will become an arena of unrestrained exploitation and conflicting jurisdictional claims in which even the most advantaged states will be losers."

The integrity of investments was also assured. Weekly Compilation of *Presidential Documents*, Washington, May 25, 1970, pp. 677–78.

A speech by Arvid Pardo, representing Malta, before the United Nations General Assembly on August 17, 1967, was a basic catalyst in the search for peaceful international development (United Nations Document A/6695, August 18, 1967). There is a growing body of literature dealing with the regulation of the uses of the sea. See, for example, Wolfgang Friedmann, *The Future of the Oceans* (London: Dennis Dobson, 1971). Norman J. Padelford, ed., *Public Policy for the Seas* (Cambridge, Massachusetts: M.I.T. Press, 1970); John J. Logue, ed., *The Fate of the Oceans* (Villanova: Villanova University Press, 1972). Robert B. Krueger, "An Evaluation of United States Ocean Policy," *McGill Law Journal*, vol. 17, no. 4 (1971), pp. 603–98, provides an insightful analysis.

82. Senator Claiborne Pell (Democrat, Rhode Island), member of U.S. delegation to 25th Session of U.N. General Assembly, *The United Nations: The World as a Developing Nation*, Report to the Committee on Foreign Relations, U.S. Senate, 92d Congress, 1st Session (Washington, 1971), p. 11.

83. See, for example, testimony of Cecil J. Olmstead, assistant to chairman, Texaco, and member of the National Petroleum Council's technical subcommittee drafting its report on resources on the seabed; also, summary and recommendations of the National Petroleum Council; and testimony of Carl A. Auerback, professor of law at University of Minnesota, and Clark M. Eichelberger, executive director, Commission to Study the Organization of the Peace, *Activities of Nations in Ocean Space*, Hearings before the Subcommittee on Ocean Space of the Committee on Foreign Relations, U.S. Senate, 91st Congress, 1st Session (Washington, 1969), pp. 119–212. The reference to geology is on page 141. The position of the American Petroleum Institute, along with the Mid-Continent Oil and Gas Association, the Rocky Mountain Oil and Gas Association, and the Western Oil and Gas Association, can be found in *Federal Leasing and Disposal Policies*, Hearing before the Committee on Interior and Insular Affairs. U.S. Senate, 92d Congress, 2d Session (Washington, 1972), pp. 512–50; specific conclusion of the UN drafts are on pp. 541–43. The president of the 15,000-member American Association of Geologists displayed even less professional restraint in discussing the seabed: "Giving all of the ocean bottoms to the United Nations . . . would stifle the United States in its race to secure minerals from the sea and the underlying strata in order to feed and clothe an ever-increasing population. . . . The United States should not relinquish its advantage" and should "review thoroughly the issues at stake before giving away its share of seven-tenths of the earth's surface to a political body over which we have very little control and which might not always serve our best interests." J.

Ben Carsey, "Who Should Own the Ocean Bottom," excerpted in *Washington Evening Star*, March 11, 1968.

84. Testimony of Robert A. Frosch, assistant secretary of the navy for research and development, and G. Warren Nutter, assistant secretary of defense for international security affairs, *Activities of Nations in Ocean Space*, op. cit., pp. 30–42 and 233–48. The quotation is on p. 245. See also Sam Baker and Kerry Gruson, "The Coming Arms Race under the Sea," in Leonard Rodberg and Derek Shearer, eds., *The Pentagon Watchers* (New York: Doubleday, 1970), pp. 335–69.

85. Testimony of U. Alexis Johnson, under secretary of state for political affairs, pp. 214–33; the call for continuing exploitation of the resources is on p. 219 of *Activities of Nations in Ocean Space*, op. cit.

86. Statement by Leigh S. Ratiner, alternate U.S. representative, the Third United Nations Law of the Sea Conference (Caracas, Venezuela, August 9, 1974), in *The Third U.N. Law of the Sea Conference*, Report to the Senate by Senators Claiborne Pell et al., 94th Congress, 1st Session (Washington, 1975), pp. 29–52 and passim.

87. *The Politics of Oil*, op. cit., pp. 100–108, 199–200. For a discussion and denial of General Motors involvement in the Axis war effort, see *The Industrial Reorganization Act*, op. cit., especially Part 4A. See chapter 2, note 1, above.

88. Carl A. Gerstacker, chairman, Dow Chemical Corporation, speaking at White House Conference on the Industrial World Ahead. *New York Times*, February 13, 1972.

89. *New York Times*, April 10, 1971.

90. Some observers have been convinced that access for American oil companies was a major item on the American agenda in the missions of President Nixon to Peking. For intriguing speculation, also about the role of then Secretary of the Treasury John B. Connally, see report from Tokyo by Selig S. Harrison, *Washington Post*, February 18, 1972. See also his article "Time Bomb in East Asia," *Foreign Policy*, Fall 1975, pp. 3–27. The Gulf quotation is on page 14 of this preliminary report on a year-long investigation. In the same issue, see also Choonho Park and Jerome Alan Cohen, "The Politics of China's Oil Weapon," pp. 28–49. The authors speculate on Chinese alternatives, including the joining of OPEC. Also, *New York Times*, January 3, March 3, 1974, and September 5, 1975. Also, see appraisal by Senator Mike Mansfield (Democrat, Montana) of Chinese oil development and use, and China's potential for emerging as the world's next great oil producer, in *Winds of Change*, U.S. Senate, 94th Congress. 1st Session (Washington, October 1975), pp. 18–21.

91. See, for example, *Report of the Special Study Mission to the Middle East*, Committee on Foreign Affairs, House of Representatives. 93d Congress, 2d Session (Washington, 1974), p. 6; also "Oil Lobby Influence Reaches Midwest." *Washington Post*, January 9, 1975.

92. Confidential Aramco report on meeting with King Faisal, May 23, 1973, and Aramco cable, June 1, 1973, in *Multinational Corporations*, op. cit., Hearings, Part 7, pp. 504–5 and 509.

93. Otto N. Miller, "To Our Stockholders," July 26, 1973.

94. *Multinational Corporations*, op. cit., Hearings, Aramco cable, June 1, 1973, p. 509.

95. Ibid., Aramco cable, October 26, 1973, p. 517, and memorandum from the chairmen of Exxon, Mobil, Texaco, and Standard of California to President Nixon, October 12, 1973, pp. 546–47; also testimony of O. N. Miller, chairman, Socal, pp. 446–56.

96. Ibid., Aramco (Frank Jungers) cable, June 19, 1974, pp. 536–37.

97. *New York Times*, February 18, 1974. Also, "Fact and Fiction about the Oil Crisis," The Commission on International Affairs, American Jewish Congress (New York, 1974). Criticism of his letter to the stockholders prompted the Socal chairman to circulate a new letter he had subsequently written to a Jewish leader: "Some people have indicated that they thought I meant to imply in my statement that peace and stability in the area could be established without regard to the existence of Israel or its legitimate interests. This is simply not true, and no such implication can or should be read into what I have said." *New York Times*, March 3, 1974. For a list of firms on the Arab League's boycott list, the guidelines for the boycott, and explanations by the U.S. departments of State and Treasury, and also the Army Corps of Engineers which screened out alleged Zionist companies from construction projects in Saudi Arabia, see *Multinational Corporations*, op. cit., Hearings, Part 11, pp. 195–476. Also, *The Politics of Oil*, op. cit., pp. 256–59.

98. General George S. Brown at Duke University October 10, 1974, disclosed by *Washington Post*, November 13, 1974, reported in *Wall Street Journal*, November 14, 1974.

99. *New York Times*, December 5, 1972.

100. *The International Telephone and Telegraph Company and Chile, 1970–71*, Report to the Committee on Foreign Relations, U.S. Senate by the Subcommittee on Multinational Corporations, 93d Congress, 1st Session (Washington, 1973), p. 18.

101. *Washington Evening Star*, July 12, 1971; also *Washington Post*, July 12, 1971.

102. *The International Telephone and Telegraph Company and Chile, 1970–71*, Report, op. cit., passim. Also, Hearings, Parts 1 and 2; see testimony of John A. McCone and John D. Neal, international relations director, ITT, Part 1, pp. 93–125 and pp. 59–86. The comment about Cuba is on page 80. When asked about his dual role as former director and present consultant to the CIA while also being on the

board of ITT, McCone explained that "when I was asked to go on the board of ITT there was not a single word mentioned about CIA and ITT did not know, nobody in ITT knew, that I was a consultant to CIA. As a matter of fact, I cannot remember mentioning CIA to anybody in ITT in anything other than a casual way until this question of the Chile election came up. Furthermore, in the countless meetings I had with Mr. Helms and members of his staff from 1965, when I left CIA, until 1970, I never discussed ITT matters with him except to say that it was a great company and was operating in 70 countries and it was a pleasant association" (p. 125).

103. Tad Szulc, "Exporting Revolution," *New Republic*, September 21, 1974; Godfrey Hodgson and William Shawcroft, "Destabilization," *Sunday Times* (London), October 27, 1974. Also, testimony of Richard Helms, former director of CIA, *CIA Foreign and Domestic Actvities*, Hearing before the Committee on Foreign Relations, U.S. Senate, 94th Congress, 1st Session (Washington, 1975).

104. *New York Times*, September 17 and 18, 1974.

105. *The Multinational Corporation and the World Economy*, Committee on Finance, U.S. Senate, 93d Congress, 1st Session (Washington, 1973), pp. 5–15, 30–41, and passim. Also, J. J. Servan-Schreiber, *The American Challenge* (New York: Atheneum, 1968).

106. *The Impact of Multinational Corporations on Development and on International Relations*, Report of the Secretary General and Report of the Group of Eminent Persons to Study the Impact of Multinational Corporations on Development and on International Relations, United Nations, Department of Economics and Social Affairs (New York, 1974). See also background document, *Multinational Corporations in World Development*, United Nations, Department of Economic and Social Affairs (New York, 1973). Transcript of oral statement to the Group of Eminent Persons by G. A. Wagner, who was also senior managing director of the Royal Dutch/Shell Group of Companies, Geneva, November 5, 1973.

107. Views of United States on the report, *Addendum, The Impact of Transnational Corporations on the Development Process and on International Relations*, "Views of States on the Report of the Group of Eminent Persons," Report of the Secretary General, United Nations, November 14, 1974.

108. *Multinational Corporations*, op. cit., Hearings, Part 3, on Overseas Private Investment Corporation, passim. Also, *Annual Reports*, 1974 and 1975, Overseas Private Investment Corporation.

109. *Multinational Corporations*, op. cit., Hearings, Part 3, testimony of Jacob K. Javits, pp. 311–23. Also, comments by Javits, *The Impact of Multinational Corporations on Development and on International Relations*, op. cit., pp. 104–15.

CHAPTER 6. *Partners in Development*

1. Senator Claiborne Pell, *The United Nations: The World as a Developing Country*, op. cit., p. 7.

2. *Activities of Nations in Ocean Space*, op. cit., p. 227.

3. *Programmatic PDOP* [Program Decision Option Document] *on the OCS Accelerated Leasing Program*, Office of the OCS Program Coordination, U.S. Department of the Interior (Washington, 1975), p. 10.

4. *Congressional Record*, February 4, 1969, pp. H 661–64.

5. Testimony of George Clyde, member Santa Barbara County Board of Supervisors and Santa Barbara Channel Oil Advisory Committee, and Richard S. Whitehead, director of Planning, County of Santa Barbara, *Water Pollution—1969*, Part 2, Hearings before the Subcommittee on Air and Water Pollution of the Committee on Public Works, U.S. Senate, 91st Congress, 1st Session (Washington, 1969), pp. 268–306. The assistant secretary of the interior was J. Cordell Moore, addressing state, county, city, and university officials before the February 6, 1968, awarding of the leases, as reported in a series in *Santa Barbara News Press*, pp. 310–11.

6. Ibid., Fred Hartley, president of Union Oil Company, pp. 320–66. For a description of the spill and of the cleanup efforts but with no attempt to appraise the causes behind "the incident," see *Review of Santa Barbara Channel Oil Pollution Incident*, a research report prepared under contract for the Department of Interior Federal Water Pollution Control Administration and the Department of Transportation, United States Coast Guard, by the Pacific Northwest Laboratories of the Battelle Memorial Institute (Richland, Washington, 1969). For an on-the-scene narrative of the events and the political responses, see Robert Easton, *Black Tide* (New York: Delacorte, 1972).

7. Henry Wright, executive secretary of Western Oil and Gas Association, "Oil and Troubled Waters," an address given in 1962 before the Pacific Coast Division of the American Petroleum Institute, excerpted in Lawrence L. Brundall (chairman, Environmental Quality Advisory Board, Santa Barbara), "Platform A: The Oil Spill that Spread around the World," in *Outer Continental Shelf Policy Issues*, Hearings before the Committee on Interior and Insular Affairs, U.S. Senate, 92d Congress, 2d Session (Washington, 1972), Part 2, pp. 1272–73.

8. Jerry McAfee, vice president, Gulf Oil, "Industrial Statesmanhip in Air Pollution Control," National Conference on Air Pollution Proceedings, December 10–12, 1962, Department of Health, Education, and Welfare, Public Health Services, Division of Air Pollution (Washington, 1963), pp. 25–29.

9. John M. Houchin, deputy chairman, Phillips Petroleum Company, on behalf of the American Petroleum Institute, *Outer Continen-*

*tal Shelf Policy Issues,* op. cit., Part 2, pp. 707–49. For a bibliography and a summary of the research, see statement by Dale Straughan, marine biologist who headed the research at the University of Southern California and concluded that a retrospective look at Santa Barbara "would suggest that much of the 'environmental damage' was really inconvenience, economic and aesthetic issues," while pointing out that much more basic biological research was needed to learn how much oil the environment can tolerate and yet maintain a stable ecosystem (pp. 1020–22; also, Part 3, pp. 1775–84). For an example of the oil industry's feeling that the spill at Santa Barbara was an incident exaggerated by the unknowing, see Robert L. Klause, "In the Case of Santa Barbara," *Our Sun,* Sun Oil Company, Summer 1969, pp. 3–17. A major conclusion of this review of Santa Barbara was a remark by Stanley C. Lowry, general manager of Santa Barbara's Chamber of Commerce, in response to the question from the editor of *Our Sun* whether the spill was really a disaster: "No, I guess it wasn't. Disaster is a word we probably picked up from the press. I guess what it was was just one hell of a mess" (p. 15).

10. Mr. Lowry, who conceded that he, along with the majority of the community, wanted oil operations removed from the channel, described "emotional" critics who "questioned our ethics in accepting oil company money to pay for the ads until I pointed out that the oil companies had not only cleaned up the oil on the beach but in the process had cleaned up the massive drifts of debris after the winter floods. Had the county and the city had to clean up the debris . . . it would have cost them a great deal of money. How, I asked them, did accepting oil company money in the form of cleaning up beaches differ from oil company money used to restore our image? . . . I may be the only head of a Chamber of Commerce anywhere in the country who was picketed for trying to help his community's image and for trying to help local business." Interview, "In the Case of Santa Barbara," op. cit., p. 14.

11. Max Blumer, senior scientist, Woods Hole Oceanographic Institution, Woods Hole, Massachusetts, "Oil Contamination and the Living Resources of the Sea," reprinted in *Outer Continental Shelf Policy Issues,* op. cit., Part 1, pp. 38–48. For discussion of these findings, by Department of the Interior officials among others, see pp. 1–38. For Blumer's appraisal of the reports by Dale Straughan at the University of Southern California, see his ten-page letter to Gardiner S. Hunt, chemist, Maine Environmental Improvement Commission, March 29, 1971 (mimeographed). Also, *Outer Continental Shelf Policy Issue,* Part 3, pp. 1449–1552; and Max Blumer et al., "A Small Oil Spill," *Environment,* vol. 13, no. 2, March 1971.

12. American Petroleum Institute, Western Oil and Gas Association and Mid-Continental Oil and Gas Association, responses submitted to prepared questions by Senate Committee on Interior and Insular

Affairs. *Outer Continental Shelf Policy Issues*, op. cit., Part 2, pp. 849–921; the quotations are from page 917.

13. Ibid., Thomas D. Barrow, president, Humble Oil and Refining Company (Exxon), pp. 673–749, the testimonial to competition in the American oil industry is on page 731.

14. *New York Times*, July 14, 1974; also, March 23, 1976. For useful background to the California conflict, the federal Coastal Zone Management Act, and the California Coastal Zone Conservation Commission, see *Outer Continental Shelf Oil and Gas Leasing Off Southern California: Analysis of Issues*, National Ocean Policy Study, Committee on Commerce, U.S. Senate, 93d Congress, 2d Session (Washington 1974).

15. Memo by Eugene Standley, Department of the Interior, to J. Cordell Moore, assistant secretary of the interior for mineral resources, commenting on a meeting with Army Corps of Engineers personnel on the Santa Barbara channel issue: "I pointed out that we had handled our own public relations business in Santa Barbara through City, County and State people and we had chosen not to go the public hearing route. That we had tried to warn L.A. Dist. Engr. of Corps. [sic] of what he faced and we preferred not to stir the natives up any more than possible," in "Platform A: The Oil Spill that Spread around the World," op. cit., p. 1270.

16. E. L. Petree, Gulf Oil, responding to Secretary of Interior Walter J. Hickel's call for tightening of federal offshore oil leasing controls, *New York Times*, August 3, 1969.

17. Ibid.

18. George Clyde, Board of Supervisors, and Marvin Levine, deputy county counsel, Santa Barbara, *Outer Continental Shelf Policy Issues*, op. cit., Part 2, especially pp. 1093–1107.

19. *Outer Continental Shelf Oil and Gas Leasing Off Southern California*, op. cit., p. 27.

20. Complaint, *State of California v. Morton*, filed August 15, 1974, United States District Court, Central District of California, Civ. no. 74–2374–AAH, and Complaint, *County of Suffolk, County of Nassau, et al. v. Department of the Interior, Rogers C. B. Morton, individually and as Secretary of the Interior et al.*, filed February 10, 1975, United States District Court, Eastern District of New York, Civ. no. 75–C–208.

21. *Project Independence*, Federal Energy Administration (Washington, 1974), passim, and *U.S. Energy Outlook*, National Petroleum Council, op. cit.

22. American Petroleum Institute, *Trends in Oil and Gas Exploration*, Hearings before the Committee on Interior and Insular Affairs, 92d Congress, 2d Session (Washington, 1972), pp. 208–49, 415–540; the specific comment on the newer restraints on leasing is on page 518.

23. *New York Times*, March 16, 1972, November 13, 1973, March 27 and December 1, 1974, and March 11, 1976; *New York Post*, December 6, 1974.

24. See testimony of Robert C. Sharp, member, Environmental Quality Advisory Board, Santa Barbara. Sharp had been engineering vice-president of a contracting company which had drilled many offshore wells in the Santa Barbara channel for major oil companies; he was also a member of the board of directors of the American Association of Oilwell Drilling Contractors; see also his written exchanges with J. C. Posgate, Humble Oil's vice-president for production. In his discussion of the hazards of drilling and the role of insurance companies, Sharp quoted the corporate secretary for Union Oil as saying in 1970 that "if the Santa Barbara Channel spill would happen today, we would not be covered for the liability—today it is not possible to buy pollution insurance for offshore operations." Sharp, who saw himself as a lifetime oilman and said he liked that group, said that since his retirement he had come to see that the industry "has one unwritten rule that is self defeating . . .: any outside criticism . . . is unjustified. It's all right to be critical of our industry within the confines of the petroleum club, but you must never voice that criticism to the public." *Outer Continental Shelf Policy Issues*, op. cit., Part 2, pp. 1117–45. For an example of API literature, see its booklet "Operation Rescue—Cleaning and Caring of Oiled Waterfowl" (Washington, 1972).

25. The $9 million settlement was the largest ever for offshore oil damages, according to the office of California's attorney general. The state had also filed suit against the federal government, charging negligence in supervising the drilling, but this suit ended with the company settlement. *New York Times*, July 24, 1974. See also *New York Times*, November 26, 1971. In the criminal action, the judge was a retired Los Angeles municipal judge who had been called in to hear the case after all three Santa Barbara municipal judges disqualified themselves because of prejudice against the oil companies. *Wall Street Journal*, January 12, 1972.

26. See *OCS Oil and Gas—An Environmental Assessment*, A Report to the President by the Council on Environmental Quality (Washington, 1974), chapter 6. Howard L. Sanders (biologist), Max Blumer (geochemist), John M. Hunt (chemist), Woods Hole Oceanographic Institution, testimony, *Governmental Intervention in the Market Mechanism*, op. cit., Hearings, Part 5, pp. 1961–94.

27. Statements of Herbert A. Steyn, Jr., Mobil Oil, speaking for American Petroleum Institute; James J. Reynold, president, American Institute of Merchant Shipping; Roland C. Clement, vice-president for biology, National Audubon Society; Eugene V. Coan, marine biologist, Sierra Club; L. F. E. Goldie, Naval War College, in *Conventions and Amendments Relating to Pollution of the Sea by Oil*, Hearings before

the Subcommittee on Oceans and International Environment of the Committee on Foreign Relations, U.S. Senate, 92d Congress, 1st Session (Washington, 1971), passim. See also, Marvin Zeldin, "Oil Pollution," Audubon Black Paper No. 1, *The Audubon Cause*, May 1971. For a fascinating informative appraisal of the supertankers, "technological audacities" built for quick profit rather than seaworthiness, along with a discussion of oil pollution and the nightmare of the seas becoming "a wasting asset," see Noël Mostert, *Supership* (New York: Alfred A. Knopf, 1974). The description by Thor Heyerdahl is from the *San Francisco Chronicle*, June 14, 1970, as quoted by Eugene Coan, "Oil Pollution," *The Sierra Club Bulletin*, March 1971. See also Heyerdahl, *The Ra Expedition* (New York: New American Library, 1972); the clots of oil in the sea were found far more widespread than on the Kon Tiki expedition. One could not safely dip a toothbrush in the water, an experience which shipowners and industrial and political leaders were spared as they crossed with greater speed and not at nose level, Heyerdahl observed (pp. 231–32). For background on U.S. subsidies for tanker construction and policies regarding "flag of convenience" ships, see *The Politics of Oil*, op. cit., pp. 166–67, 172–73, 176–81.

28. Testimony of Department of Interior officials, *Energy Data Requirements of the Federal Government*, Part III, *Federal Offshore Oil and Gas Leasing Policies*, Hearings before the Subcommittee on Activities of Regulatory Agencies of the Permanent Select Committee on Small Business, House of Representatives, 93d Congress, 2d Session (Washington, 1974) pp. 194–270.

29. Memorandum, U.S. Department of the Interior, September 18, 1974, reprinted in *Outer Continental Shelf Oil and Gas Leasing Off Southern California: Analysis of Issues*, op. cit., p. 69.

30. *Draft Environmental Statement*, Prepared by the Bureau of Land Management, U.S. Department of the Interior (Washington, October 18, 1974) 2 vols.

31. Ibid., vol. 2, p. 169. The conclusions about recovery, stated in a letter from James I. Jones, Research Coordinator of the Coastal Coordinating Council of the Florida Department of Natural Resources, are quoted and accepted by the report.

32. "Now, if you read each of these impact statements separately, they always tend to conclude that the impact of the proposed projects is negligible and, therefore, the projects should go ahead. The question is what happens when you add up all these impacts?"—Robert Solomon of California Energy Commission at Hearings on Draft Environmental Impact Statement, Los Angeles, as quoted in *Analysis of Draft Environmental Impact Statement for Proposed 1975 Outer Continental Shelf Oil and Gas Lease Sale Offshore Southern California*, presented on behalf of Southern California Council of Local Govern-

ments by Tom Bradley, mayor, and Burt Pines, city attorney (Los Angeles, 1975).

33. This warning was a basic theme of the Report to the President by the Council on Environmental Quality, *OCS Oil and Gas—An Environmental Assessment*, earlier that year. See note 24 above. Paul Yevich, a pathologist on the staff of the National Marine Water Quality Laboratory in Narragansett, Rhode Island, pointed out that the damage to marine animals may also affect adversely humans eating fish and clams: "We are dealing with a world of unknowns." *Analysis of Draft Environmental Impact Statement*, op. cit., pp. 42–44.

34. *Project Independence*, op. cit.

35. *Draft Environmental Statement*, op. cit., vol. 1, p. 144.

36. Robert C. Sharp at hearings held by Bureau of Land Management, Beverly Hills, California, February 7, 1975, in *Analysis of Draft Environmental Impact Statement Regarding "Proposed Increase in Acreage to be offered for Oil and Gas Leasing on the Outer Continental Shelf,"* Prepared and Submitted on Behalf of the Southern California Council of Local Governments (Los Angeles, 1975), Section II, pp. 125–35. Also see note 23 above.

37. Dr. William T. Pecora, head of Interior's Geological Survey, which oversees offshore oil development, *New York Times*, January 27, 1971.

38. Ibid., "Offshore Oil is the Answer," *Los Angeles Times*, January 8, 1975, Section I, p. 328. Also, *Programmation PDOP on the OCS Accelerated Leasing Program*, op. cit., pp. 29–30.

39. William Grant, manager of the Pacific OCS Office of the Bureau of Land Management, to Frank Edwards, assistant director of Minerals Management of the Department of the Interior, July 3, 1974. *Memorandum of Plaintiffs*, September, 1975, Docket no. 75 C 208, pp. 17–18, see note 20.

40. "Offshore Oil: Channel Blowout Points up Information Gap," *Science*, May 2, 1969, p. 530.

41. William A. Vogely, acting deputy assistant secretary for energy and minerals, *Energy Data Requirements of the Federal Government*, Part III, op. cit., p. 206.

42. Ibid., Monte Canfield, Jr., deputy director, Ford Foundation Energy Policy Project, observed that "these estimates have been significantly revised without additional evidence, and we have no information to indicate the basis of that revision. . . . This wide divergence in estimates results from the fact that there has been virtually no geological or detailed geophysical exploratory activity on the Atlantic Outer Continental Shelf" (pp. 149–76).

43. Ibid., pp. 1–2, 189–94. The second quotation is from Senator John V. Tunney (Democrat, California), after reviewing leasing policies and plans, *New York Times*, November 26, 1974.

44. *New York Times*, March 5, 1975.

45. *New York Times*, September 28, 1975.

46. See discussion of leasing policies by Keith I. Clearwaters, deputy assistant attorney general, Antitrust Division, *Energy Data Requirements of the Federal Government*, Part III, op. cit., pp. 464–505.

47. Ibid., statement of Assemblyman Kenneth Cory, chairman, on findings of the Joint Committee on Public Domain of California State Legislature, read and discussed by Richard Newman, the California committee's special counsel, and William J. Lamont, consultant, pp. 277–303. See also responses of major oil companies, passim. Also, *The Administration of State Owned Tidelands*, A Report of the Joint Committee on Public Domain (Sacramento, California, 1974).

48. *Energy Data Requirements of the Federal Government*, Part III, op. cit., pp. 189–94.

49. Otto N. Miller, in deposition for the California State Legislative Joint Committee on Public Domain, January 4, 1974, *New York Times*, February 20, 1974. For discussion of this statement by oil company officials, as well as defense of joint bidding as "essential to vigorous competition" and increased receipts for the U.S. government, see *Energy Data Requirements of the Federal Government*, Part III, op. cit., pp. 401, 432–58, and passim.

50. *Improved Inspection and Regulation Could Reduce the Possibility of Oil Spills on the Outer Continental Shelf*, General Accounting Office, Report to the Conservation and Natural Resources Subcommittee, Committee on Government Operations, U.S. Senate, June 1973. Also, see *OCS Oil and Gas, An Environmental Assessment*, op. cit.

51. *Offshore Investigation: Producible Shut-In Leases*, First Phase and Second Phase, as of January 1974, staff report, Bureau of Natural Gas, Federal Power Commission (Washington, 1974). Also, Paul Davidson, Lawrence H. Falk, Hoesung Lee, "Oil: Its Time Allocation and Project Independence," in Arthur M. Okun and George L. Perry, eds. *Brookings Papers on Economic Activity—2* (Washington: The Brookings Institution, 1974), pp. 411–48. Also, *The Accelerated Development of the Outer Continental Shelf: Its Problems and Costs*, Report by Ad Hoc Committee on the Domestic and International Monetary Effect of Energy and Other Natural Resources Pricing, Committee on Banking and Currency, U.S. House of Representatives, 93d Congress, 2d Session (Washington, 1974). The committee report concluded that outer continental shelf production could be significantly increased by utilizing shut-in wells and existing leases.

52. *Improvements Needed in Administration of Federal Coal Leasing Program*, Comptroller General of the United States, March 29, 1972, reprinted in *Surface Mining*, op. cit., Part 3, pp. 1095–1143.

53. "Preliminary Report on the Analysis of Coal Leases," Bureau of Land Management, in *Federal Coal Leasing Program*, op. cit., Part I, pp. 90–121.

54. Letter from Assistant Secretary of the Interior Richard Bodman to Senator Henry Jackson, quoted in *Leased and Lost*, op. cit., p. 22.

55. *Improvements Needed in Administration of Federal Coal Leasing Programs*, op. cit., pp. 1123–26.

56. Ibid., pp. 1119–26, and *Leased and Lost*, op. cit., pp. 7, 27–28.

57. Harrison Loesch, assistant secretary for public land management, Department of the Interior, *Federal Leasing and Disposal Policies*, op. cit., p. 84.

58. *Further Action Needed on Recommendations for Improving the Administration of Federal Coal-Leasing Program*, Comptroller General of the United States, April 28, 1975. On December 31, Interior announced new regulation for "diligent development and continuous operation" of mines; leaseholders would be required to produce one-fortieth of their estimated recoverable reserves within ten years and to mine continuously at least 1 percent of those reserves each year. If these provisions were not met, the secretary could initiate court proceedings to cancel the leases. *New York Times*, January 1, 1976. President Ford and the coal industry saw this environmental victory in the congress as providing "administrative roadblocks" to coal development and energy independence. *New York Times*, August 5, 1976.

59. See, for example, *Production of Oil and Gas on Public Lands*, Hearings before the Subcommittee on Public Lands of the Committee on Interior and Insular Affairs, U.S. House of Representatives, 93d Congress, 1st and 2d Sessions (Washington, 1974). Early in 1975, Standard of California informed the navy of its desire to withdraw as operator of Elk Hills, claiming a desire to assign its personnel and rigs to its own leases elsewhere and also to end congressional criticism of the company's behavior as operator. *New York Times*, January 19, 1975. Meanwhile, President Ford in his State of the Union Message called for the designation of the naval reserve as a national strategic reserve, part of it to be earmarked for the navy but the rest available for commercial production, with revenues to go to the development of the Alaskan naval reserve. *New York Times*, January 16, 1975.

60. See *The Politics of Oil*, op. cit., pp. 80–86, 311–12, 396.

61. Lt. Comdr. Kirby Brant, U.S. Navy, Deputy Director, Naval Petroleum and Oil Shale Reserves, Department of Defense, in *Production of Oil and Gas on Public Lands*, op. cit., p. 338.

62. Ibid., pp. 348, 487–88, 491–92, and passim. Also, *Alaska Native Land Claims*, Hearings before the Subcommittee on Indian Affairs of the Committee on Interior and Insular Affairs, U.S. House of Representatives, 92d Congress, 1st Session (Washington, 1971). Also, *Alaska Native Land Claims*, Hearings before the Committee on Interior and Insular Affairs, U.S. Senate, 91st Congress, 1st Session (Washington 1969), Parts 1 and 2, and 92d Congress, 1st Session.

1971, Parts 1, 2, and 3; and *Alaska Native Claims Settlement Act of 1971*, Report, 1971. See also *Alaska Natives and the Land*, Federal Field Committee for Development Planning in Alaska (Anchorage, Alaska, 1968).

63. Testimony of Lt. Comdr. Kirby Brant, *Production of Oil and Gas on Public Lands*, op. cit., pp. 278–84, 303, 338, and passim.

64. For example, letter of Hollis M. Dole, assistant secretary of the interior, November 12, 1971, in *Surface Mining*, op. cit., Part 1, pp. 33–35. In contrast, see testimony of Representative Ken Heckler (Democrat, West Virginia), pp. 167–83; James Branscome, director of Save Our Kentucky, pp. 223–33; and Malcomb Baldwin, staff attorney, Conservation Foundation, pp. 501–40.

65. Ibid., Elburt F. Osborn, Part 3, p. 960. In 1973 safety enforcement was placed within a Mining Enforcement and Safety Administration in Interior. Secretary Morton explained that "because of its mission to encourage development of the industry and of mining technologies, [Bureau of Mines] policies have sometimes run at tangent with requirements under mine health and safety laws." News release, Department of the Interior, July 12, 1973.

66. Ibid., Part 1, pp. 150–61; the quotation is on page 151.

67. "Environmental Effects," from *Surface Mining and Our Environment*, U.S. Department of the Interior, 1967, reprinted in *The Issues Related to Surface Mining*, A Summary Review, with Selected Readings, Committee on the Interior and Insular Affairs, U.S. Senate, 92d Congress, 1st Session (Washington, 1971), pp. 91–93.

68. *North Central Power Study*, Report of Phase I, prepared under direction of Coordinating Committee, North Central Power Study, Vols. 1 and 2 (printed for U.S. Bureau of Reclamation, Billings, Montana), October 1971. See also Alvin M. Josephy, Jr., "Plundered West: Coal is the Prize," *Washington Post*, August 26, 1973. Also, for criticisms and discussion of court actions against Interior's "laissez-faire" role when dealing with industry planning in this area, as well as the department's defense of its position, see *Federal Coal Leasing Program*, op. cit., Part I, passim.

69. John Corcoran, testimony, *Coal Policy Issues*, op. cit., Part I, pp. 358–63. For examples of criticisms of the niggardly research funds for coal, see Senator Robert C. Byrd (Democrat, West Virginia), pp. 6–21; Arnold Miller, president, United Mine Workers, pp. 106–29; Senator Adlai E. Stevenson (Democrat, Illinois), pp. 320–28.

70. Ibid.; see, for example, testimony of John McCormick, Environmental Policy Center, pp. 69–106.

71. Ibid., cited in testimony of Senator Robert C. Byrd, p. 12. For a study of land reclamation, see *Rehabilitation Potential of Western Coal Lands*, National Academy of Sciences (Cambridge, Mass.: Ballinger, 1974).

72. *Review of the Developments in Coal Gasification*, op. cit., p. 23; See also Dole's letter, p. 11, and his full testimony, pp. 18–37.

This volume also contains the texts of the proposed legislation and of the Interior-AGA agreement as well as the statements of gas industry officials.

73. *Washington Post*, December 11, 1968; also *Congressional Quarterly*, Weekly Report, December 20, 1968, p. 3309.

74. *Department of the Interior and Related Agencies Appropriations for Fiscal Year 1970*, Hearings before a Subcommittee of the Committee on Appropriations, U.S. Senate, 91st Congress, 1st Session (Washington, 1969), Part 1, p. 680.

75. See *The Politics of Oil*, op. cit., chapters 10 ("Oilmen in Government") and 11 ("Corporate Statesmanship and Public Policy") and passim.

76. See testimony of Hollis M. Dole and John Ricca, Department of the Interior, *Advisory Committees*, Hearings before the Subcommittee on Intergovernmental Relations of the Committee on Government Operations, 92d Congress, 1st Session (Washington, 1971), Part 2, pp. 467–71.

77. For background concerning Brooks's career, see David Sanford, "Uncivil Servants," *New Republic*, May 16, 1970, and Tom Bethel, *The Hurricane Creek Massacre* (New York: Harper and Row, 1972), pp. 95–96 and passim.

78. The quotations from O'Leary are from *New York Times* ("U.S. Mine Director will be Replaced"), February 17, 1969; see also *New York Times* ("Nixon Ousts Head of Mines Bureau"), March 1, 1970. O'Leary had submitted the standard resignation to incoming President Nixon, but it was not until thirteen months later that the rumors of dismissal were translated into an acceptance of the resignation by the president and a twenty-four hour notice to clear out. For background, see Bethel, op. cit., pp. 91–96, 140, and passim. Hickel later explained that his delay in implementing the White House orders was because of a subsequent call to "hold off for a while" until the administration could be assured of two more votes for its position on the antiballistic missile. "I thought to myself, 'Okay, so I'll be a team player.' But I wondered: 'What about the miners?' " Hickel's reminiscences about the bureau's "silent partnership" with industry are in his *Who Owns America*? (New York, Paperback Library, 1972), pp. 124–26 and passim. For further discussion of the reorganization along commodity lnes, see David Sanford, "Uncivil Servants," op. cit. A detailed discussion of the reorganization "to foster a close and confidential relationship" is in correspondence of Representative Henry S. Reuss (Democrat, Wisconsin) with Hollis M. Dole, April 20, 1970; also letter of Interior Undersecretary Fred J. Russell to Representative Julia B. Hansen (Democrat, Wisconsin), May 26, 1970.

79. Testimony of Hollis M. Dole and also of John Ricca, *Advisory Committees*, op. cit., Hearings, Part 2 (1971), pp. 443–90. For discussion of API, NPC, and Oil and Gas Office, see *The Politics of Oil*, op. cit., chapters 6, 10, 15, and passim.

80. John Ricca, *Advisory Committees,* op. cit., pp. 487–88.

81. Correspondence, Representative Henry S. Reuss (Democrat, Wisconsin) and Vincent E. McKelvey, director, Geological Survey, U.S. Department of the Interior, August 13, 1973, January 9 and 21, 1974, April 3 and 19, 1974; also *New York Times,* April 26, 1974.

82. *Congressional Record,* February 13, 1974, p. E 614.

83. There was special concern about these regulations since they would have a major impact upon the shipping of Alaskan oil from Valdez to the west coast. Many experts feel that double hulls provide even more spill protection in case of accident than the double bottom. Segregated ballast compartments are intended to preclude flushing out oil compartments when taking on water ballast, thus cutting back on an operational source of oil pollution. Senator Lee Metcalf noted that while a first version of the report mentioned the origins on the cover, a final draft, dated the same day, omitted mention on the cover of the American Petroleum Institute and the American Institute of Merchant Shipping. Metcalf saw the Coast Guard circumventing legislation requiring advisory committees in the federal government to be representative, and their deliberations publicized. See *Congressional Record,* September 5, 1975, pp. E. 4522–27 and March 18, 1976, pp. S 3751–55.

84. "Statement by the President on Establishing the National Industrial Pollution Control Council," April 9, 1970; also *Executive Order,* and list of members appointed by the president, in *Advisory Committees,* op. cit., Hearings, Part 3 (1970), pp. 501–4 and passim. Also, *Congressional Record,* April 21, 1971, statement by Senator Lee Metcalf, pp. S 5405. A comparable pattern of industry-dominated antipollution boards has held among the states. See, for example, survey by Gladwin Hill in *New York Times,* December 7, 1970.

85. See interview with Frank Ikard, head of the American Petroleum Institute, in *Detroit Sunday News,* January 13, 1974, reprinted as full-page advertisement by the API, *New York Times,* February 13, 1974.

86. Also in *New York Times* for February 13, 1974.

87. *New York Times,* July 3, 1974, and April 24, 1975.

88. Figures released through office of Representative Charles B. Rangel (Democrat, New York), January 31, 1974. It was further charged that this total was greater than the expenditures of the six leading companies (Standard of California figures were unavailable) for research and development activities. For a critical roundup of the debate as to whether many of these "corporate image" advertisements were educational rather than political and hence legitimate tax deductible business expenses, see Joseph J. Selden, "Corporate Advertising: Who Pays for the Image?" *The Nation,* December 20, 1975.

89. *New York Times,* May 8, 1975.

90. First Report of the Council to President Nixon, *New York Times*, February 11, 1971.


CHAPTER 7. *Bureaucratic Wastelands*

1. "Address on the National Energy Policy," November 25, 1973, op. cit. Also, *Washington Post*, November 29, 1973; correspondence between Acting Attorney General Robert H. Bork and Secretary of the Interior Rogers C. B. Morton, together with testimony of Bruce B. Wilson, deputy assistant attorney general, Antitrust Division, November 29, 1973, in *Market Performance and Competition in the Petroleum Industry*, op. cit., pp. 398–404. For the table of organization of the Emergency Petroleum and Gas Administration and the oil affiliations of its key personnel, see Senator Lee Metcalf, "Calling up Oil's Shadow Government," *Congressional Record*, November 27, 1973, pp. 38142–54. For the announcement of the shelving of these plans, see *New York Times*, December 22, 1973.

2. Testimony, *Multinational Corporations*, op. cit., Hearings, Part 5, pp. 255–57.

3. *Multinational Oil Corporations,* op. cit., Report, p. 17; also pp. 126–30. See also in Hearings, Part 5, testimony of James E. Akins, Office of Fuels and Energy, Department of State, pp. 1–28; John N. Irwin II, former under secretary of state, pp. 145–73; and John J. McCloy pp. 247–87. Also, correspondence between McCloy and Antitrust Division, in Hearings, Part 6, pp. 223–70; McCloy and Senator Church, pp. 289–96; McCloy and State Department, pp. 297–309; statement of former Attorney General John M. Mitchell, pp. 311–14. Also, Thomas E. Kauper, assistant attorney general, Antitrust Division, in Hearings, Part 9, pp. 45–72, and Julius Katz, acting assistant secretary of state for economics and business affairs, pp. 146–66.

4. Thomas E. Kauper, ibid., Hearings, Part 9, p. 69.

5. Letters, Richard W. McLaren, assistant attorney general, to Senator William Proxmire, March 5, 1971, and Walker B. Comegys, acting assistant attorney general, to author, February 10, 1972.

6. *New York Times*, January 29, 1974.

7. For background, see *The Politics of Oil*, op. cit., pp. 236–39, 290, 303–9. and passim; also "Oil Plan of Action Approved: Emergency Supply Committee Appointed," News Release, Office of the Secretary, U.S. Department of the Interior, July 6, 1967; also, annual reports, including membership rosters with company affiliation of Federal Petroleum Supply Committee and Emergency Petroleum Supply Committee, 1972, in *Federal Advisory Committees, First Annual Report of the President to the Congress, Including Data on Individual Committees*, March 1973, released by Subcommittee on Budgeting, Manage-

ment, and Expenditures of the Committee on Government Management, U.S. Senate (Washington, 1973 and 1974), Part 3, pp. 3415–22 and 3552–55. See also subsequent annual reports. The initial and huge five-volume report from the president provided information on over 1,400 advisory committees operating within the federal bureaucracy. It was one of the requirements of the Federal Advisory Committee Act of 1972 which emerged from the investigations into the functioning and accountability of such bodies conducted by senators Lee Metcalf (Democrat, Montana) and Edmund S. Muskie (Democrat, Maine), Vic Reinemer, staff director of the subcommittee, and E. Winslow Turner, the chief counsel. See *Advisory Committees*, Hearings, 1970–74, op. cit.

8. Discussion between Frederic V. Malek, deputy director, Office of Management and Budget, and Senator Metcalf; also correspondence, Doug Mitchell, chief counsel, National Oil Jobbers in *Advisory Committees*, Hearings, 1974, op. cit., pp. 104–6; also, Stephen A. Wakefield, assistant secretary for energy and minerals, U.S. Department of the Interior, in *Market Performance and Competition in the Petroleum Industry*, Hearings, op. cit., Part 1, p. 263.

9. Memorandum to Duke R. Ligon, director, Office of Oil and Gas, from Secretary of the Interior Rogers C. B. Morton, October 29, 1973; also, notice of meetings of Emergency Petroleum Supply Committee and its Supply and Distribution Subcommittee, *Federal Register*, November 7, 1973; *Wall Street Journal* October 30 and 31, 1973; *Congressional Record*, November 7, 1973, pp. 36172–74; and *Advisory Committees*, Oversight Hearings, op. cit., 1974, p. 74.

10. Memorandum on Advisory Committee Use of the National Defense and Foreign Policy Exemption of the Freedom of Information Act, prepared by Martha Crewshaw Hutchinson, analyst in international relations, Library of Congress Congressional Research Service, December 11, 1973, reprinted in *Advisory Committees*, Oversight Hearings, op. cit., pp. 179–82.

11. Ibid., E. Winslow Turner, chief counsel, p. 75.

12. Mark J. Green of the Corporate Accountability Research Group, along with members of the press, were denied admittance. See *Market Performance and Competition in the Petroleum Industry*, Hearings, op. cit., Part 1, p. 385.

13. For texts of the letters and discussion by Ronald L. Plesser, staff attorney, Center for Study of Responsive Law, *Advisory Committees*, Oversight Hearings, op. cit., p. 62–74.

14. President Nixon, Statement on Energy, June 29, 1973, in *Presidential Energy Statements*, op. cit., p. 53. White House press release concerning duties of Energy Research and Development Advisory Council, October 11, 1973; also membership, agenda, outline of strategic issues prepared for the meeting by Mr. Sawhill, and Senator Met-

calf's account of the experiences of his staff associates, Vic Reinemer and E. Winslow Turner, in *Congressional Record*, October 18, 1973, pp. S 19370–73; also statement by Representative David R. Obey (Democrat, Wisconsin), October 10, 1973, p. E. 6373; and Metcalf, November 7, 1973, pp. 36138–39; and *Advisory Committees*, Oversight Hearings, op. cit., pp. 22, 91.

15. *Congressional Record*, October 18, 1973, pp. S 19370–73. Also, *New York Times*, June 19 and December 8, 1975. The General Accounting Office was highly critical of the proposal because of its giveaway features. See *New York Times*, November 3, 1975.

16. For documentation and illustrations, see *Energy Data Requirements of the Federal Government*, Hearings, op. cit., Part 1; also, memorandum by E. W. Browne, Jr., economist, April 28, 1969, *Governmental Intervention in the Market Mechanism*, Hearings, op. cit., Part 2, pp. 1021–26.

17. *Energy Data Requirements of the Federal Government*, Hearings, op. cit., Part 1, pp. 448–49.

18. *Information on Certain Oil and Gas Industry Oversight Responsibilities—Department of the Interior*, Comptroller General of the United States, June 17, 1974, pp. 1–2 and passim.

19. Testimony of James T. Halverson, director, Bureau of Competition, Federal Trade Commission, *Energy Data Requirements of the Federal Government*, Hearings, op. cit., Part 1, pp. 485–93.

20. Ibid., testimony and subsequent written statement, John B. Riggs, acting assistant secretary for energy and minerals, U.S. Department of the Interior, pp. 459–60.

21. John Ricca, acting director, Office of Oil and Gas, accompanying Assistant Secretary for Mineral Resources Hollis M. Dole, *Advisory Committees*, Hearings, op. cit., Part 2 (1971), pp. 473–74; 479, and passim. Several years later the department, through Assistant Secretary Riggs, answered no, without any elaboration, when asked in writing by Ralph Nader if it agreed with Ricca's formulation. See *Energy Data Requirements of the Federal Government*, Hearings, op. cit., Part 1, p. 447.

22. *Advisory Committees*, Hearings, op. cit., Part 2, pp. 476–77.

23. Testimony, *Review of the Developments in Coal Gasification*, Hearing, op. cit., p. 32.

24. Statement, *Oil Shale*, Hearing before the Subcommittee on Minerals, Materials and Fuels of the Committee on Interior and Insular Affairs, U.S. Senate, 92d Congress, 1st Session, (Washington, 1971), pp. 29–56. For materials relating to the work of the task force, see *Final Environmental Statement for the Prototype Oil Shale Leasing Program*, op. cit.

25. The press release from the office of the Secretary of the Interior also said Dole "has been a vigorous advocate of legislation designed

to limit adverse environmental effects from both surface and underground mining, and an equally vigorous critic of the action of extremist groups which threaten continued supplies of energy and minerals." March 12, 1973. Santa Barbara environmentalists could understand the latter category; they viewed Dole as instrumental in Interior's opposition to legislation banning drilling in federal waters of the Santa Barbara channel.

26. *Market Performance and Competition in the Petroleum Industry, Hearings,* op. cit., Part 1, pp. 95–101, 264, and passim. Also "News Release," Office of the Secretary, Department of the Interior, March 2, 1973.

27. *Advisory Committees,* Hearings, op. cit., Parts 1 and 2, (1970), passim; also testimony of Frederic V. Malek, deputy director, Office of Management and Budget, *Advisory Committees,* Oversight Hearings, op. cit., pp. 97–130. The quoted phrase is from the introduction to *Disclosure of Corporate Ownership,* op. cit., p. 2.

28. Minutes, Panel on Proposed Survey of Industrial Waste Water Disposal, April 13, 1968, reprinted in *Advisory Committees,* Hearings, op. cit., Part 1 (1970), pp. 67–70.

29. Ibid., pp. 81 and passim. See also for names and corporate affiliates of members of these advisory bodies. Also, testimony of Ralph Nader, *Advisory Committees,* Hearings, op. cit., Part 2 (1970), pp. 209–33, 263–391. Also, "Pipeline Safety Act Amendments," *Congressional Record,* June 6, 1972, pp. S 8813–15. Some 200,000 miles of oil pipeline were policed by one full-time federal engineer in 1973; a study in 1971 indicated that eight federal engineers were responsible for 1.4 million miles of natural gas pipelines. The industry pushed through a federal "regulatory" statute in 1965 designed to preserve the regulatory void. Christopher J. Matthews, "Oil Pipeline Safety: Slippery Regulation," *The Washington Post,* September 2, 1973.

30. Discussion with John N. Nassikas, chairman of Federal Power Commission, *Advisory Committees,* Hearings, op. cit., Part 3 (1970), pp. 522–23.

31. *The Need for Improving the Regulation of the Natural Gas Industry and Management of Internal Operations, Federal Power Commission,* op. cit. See also, *New York Times,* September 15, 1974, for FPC reactions.

32. Statement, Hearings on S. 2405 and S. 2467, Committee on Commerce. U.S. Senate, 92d Congress, 2d Session (Washington, 1972), p. 13 of transcript of Mr. Wheatley's testimony, March 22, 1972. Wheatley also served as general counsel of the American Public Gas Association, which is composed of over 225 publicly owned gas distribution systems. He has been a source of critical documentation of the structure of the natural gas industry, problems of public regulation, and the myth about the natural gas "shortage." See, for ex-

ample, testimony, *Natural Gas Policy Issues*, Hearings before Committee on Interim and Insular Affairs, U.S. Senate, 92d Congress, 2d Session (Washington, 1972), pp. 716–97; also, *Fuel and Energy Resources, 1972*, Hearings before the Committee on Interior and Insular Affairs, U.S. House of Representatives, 92d Congress, 2d Session (Washington, 1972), pp. 411–48. The APGA *Newsletter*, published in Washington, is also a useful source of information about the energy industry and its impact upon consumers.

33. *Concentration by Competing Raw Fuel Industries in the Energy Market and Its Impact on Small Business, a Report*, op. cit., p. 14 and passim. Also, Wheatley on the problem of data, *Advisory Committees*, Hearings, op. cit., Part 3 (1970), pp. 583–97.

34. Statement, Hearings on S. 2405 and S. 2467, op. cit., p. 16.

35. *Offshore Investigation: Producible Shut-in Leases*, op. cit.; also, "Oil: Its Time, Allocation, and Project Independence," op. cit.; and Morton Mintz, "FPC Official Ordered Gas Data Burned," *Washington Post*, June 10, 1973. David S. Schwartz, assistant chief economist, Office of Economics, John W. Wilson, chief, Division of Economic Studies, and John N. Nassikas, chairman, FPC, *The Natural Gas Industry*, Hearing, op. cit., Part 2, pp. 855–63, 1037–64, 1107–34. The latter volume is also very useful in appraising the data and the controversy over natural gas reserves.

36. *New York Times*, February 6, 1974.

37. Charles A. O'Brien, speech before Channel City Club of Santa Barbara, *Santa Barbara News Press*, August 8, 1969, in Harvey Molotch, "Oil in Santa Barbara and Power in America," *Sociological Inquiry*, Winter 1970, p. 137 (also, Warner Modular Publication reprint).

38. *Santa Barbara News Press*, April 12, 1969, quoting from a *San Francisco Chronicle* interview, in the revealing article by Molotch cited above, p. 137.

39. *Nomination of Richard Helms to be Ambassador to Iran and CIA International and Domestic Activities*, op. cit., p. 52. During the energy crisis, Federal Energy Administrator William E. Simon reported that the CIA was "extraordinarily helpful" in collecting information on oil shipments from foreign ports, reporting cargo and destinations. *New York Times*, January 10, 1974. Ex-CIA agent Philip Agee said that one of his routine jobs as an intelligence agent had been to screen prospective employees of large corporations such as Creole (Exxon subsidiary) in Venezuela to ensure against "bad guys," that is, those with left-wing associations. See *Inside the Company: C.I.A. Diary* (Penguin Books, 1975), pp. 103 and passim.

40. See *Energy Information Act*, Hearings, op. cit.

41. Maurice F. Granville, *Texaco Star*, Winter, 1974, pp. 10–11.

42. *Energy Information Act*, Hearings, op. cit., Part 2, p. 801.

43. Statement, Senator William Proxmire (Democrat, Wisconsin), November 19, 1974, reprinted in APGA *Newsletter*, December 4, 1974, pp. 11–13.

44. *Investigation of the Petroleum Industry*, op. cit., p. 27.

45. *The Politics of Oil*, op. cit., pp. 85, 96–100, 156, 359, 424, 450.

46. Ibid., pp. 139–40, 248–51, 273–79, 285–90, 292, and passim.

47. In his book *The Quiet Crisis* (New York: Holt, Rinehart and Winston, 1963), Stewart S. Udall displayed a sense of the history of his office, including awareness of its pitfalls in a social climate which so often viewed public lands as a source for private profit and of the desperate need to develop a national conservation conscience.

48. See correspondence with Connally, also with Texas Railroad Commission, Louisiana's governor and its Department of Conservation, the U.S. attorney general, and the director of the budget; also memoranda and releases from files of Department of the Interior, *Governmental Intervention in the Market Mechanism*, Hearings, op. cit., Part 4, pp. 1793–1848. Also, *The Oil and Gas Journal*, January 2, 16, and 30, March 20, July 17, 1967, reprinted in the same hearings, pp. 1818–23, 1827–28 and 1835–36.

49. "Platform A: The Oil Spill that Spread around the World," op. cit. "If there was one decision I made in all my tenure as Secretary of the Interior that I regret, and if I had the chance, that I would retract, it would be the offshore oil leases in the Pacific." Udall, quoted in *New York Times*, March 19, 1972.

50. Stewart L. Udall, statement and discussion with Senator Philip A. Hart, *Competitive Aspects of Oil Shale Development*, op. cit., Part 1, pp. 288 and passim. J. Wiley Bowers, executive director of the Tennessee Valley Public Power Association, which represents most of the 160 municipal and rural cooperative power distributors of TVA-generated electricity, who was also a member of the American Public Power Association Advisory Committee, has described efforts to get Secretary Udall to move Interior to go into developing shale oil, "but we have not gotten anywhere." *Concentration By Competing Raw Fuel Industries in the Energy Market and its Impact on Small Business*, Hearings, op. cit., vol. 2, p. 34.

51. *Interior Nomination*, Hearings, Committee on Interior and Insular Affairs, U.S. Senate, 91st Congress, 1st Session (Washington, 1969), Parts 1 and 2, passim.

52. Radio address by Hickel on Alaska radio stations, February 7, 1967, as recounted by Emil Notti, president the Alaska Federation of Natives, in Daniel Jack Chasan, *Klondike '70: The Alaskan Oil Boom* (New York: Praeger, 1971), p. 92.

53. The senators, led by Gaylord Nelson, who were questioning the fitness of Hickel to hold the post, were armed with devastating ac-

counts of Hickel's career and more devastating reports from environmentalists, from native groups, and from Hickel's own press conferences in Alaska and Washington. *Interior Nomination*, op. cit., for example, pp. 82, 152–53, 269, 274. Freshman Senator Ted Stevens (Republican, Alaska) made spirited defenses of the governor who had appointed him to his seat less than a month earlier.

54. *Alaska Native Land Claims*, Hearing on S. 1830, Committee on Interior and Insular Affairs, U.S. Senate, 91st Congress, 1st Session (Washington, 1969), Part 1, p. 65.

55. Phil R. Holdsworth, chairman of Native Land Claims Task Force of the Alaska State Chamber of Commerce and mineral exploration manager for Inexco Mining Co., *Alaska Native Land Claims*, Hearings on S. 35, S. 835, and S. 1571, Committee on Interior and Insular Affairs, U.S. Senate, 92d Congress, 1st Session (Washington 1971), Part 2, p. 502.

56. Ibid., passim.

57. Walter J. Hickel, *Washington Post*, February 5, 1969; also *Science*, May 2, 1969, p. 530.

58. Walter J. Hickel, *Who Owns America* (New York: Paperback Library Edition, 1972), pp. 87–96.

59. *Outer Continental Shelf Oil and Gas Leasing Off Southern California*, op. cit., pp. 13 and passim.

60. George Clyde, *Water Pollution—1969*, Hearings, op. cit., Part 2, pp. 291 and passim.

61. "Special Panel on the Future of the Union Oil Lease," Memorandum for the President, chaired by John C. Calhoun, Jr., vice-president, Texas A and M University, May 27, 1969, and released through Lee A. DuBridge, Office of Science and Technology, Executive Office of the President, June 2, 1969. In 1971, the Environmental Protection Agency suggested that pumping from existing wells in the Santa Barbara channel should be increased to lessen the pressures and the likelihood of new spills, rather than authorize the new drilling sought by oil companies. *New York Times*, July 24, 1971. An earlier panel on the Santa Barbara oil spill, also under DuBridge, had warned that the nation still lacked an adequate oil spill technology and was not yet providing the means for bringing one into existence. It emphasized the need to balance public and private uses of resources. See *Congressional Record*, September 12, 1969, pp. S 10467–69, and December 19, 1969, pp. S 17344–45.

62. *Who Owns America*, op. cit., pp. 84, 88.

63. Hickel was commenting on a statement made by R. P. Clinton, president of Clinton Oil Company, which appeared in the *Florida Times-Union* (Jacksonville), April 28, 1970 and was confirmed by Clinton. *New York Times*, May 5, 1970.

64. *Who Owns America*, op. cit. ,pp. 104–6.

65. Vice President Agnew, who subsequently was to resign rather than face charges of receiving cash payoffs while in public office, had been traveling throughout the country delivering attacks upon dissidents and any sympathetic press. For example: "America cannot afford to write off a whole generation for the decadent thinking of a few. America cannot afford to divide over their demagoguery . . . or to be deceived by their duplicity . . . or to let their license destroy liberty. We can, however, afford to separate them from our society— with no more regret than we should feel over discarding rotten apples from a barrel." Address, Pennsylvania Republican Dinner, Harrisburg, Pa., October 30, 1969. For Hickel's account of his decision to write the letter and the immediate events surrounding his action, see *Who Owns America*, op. cit., pp. 215–27 and 244–60.

66. For example, *New York Times*, April 11, 1972, and December 7, 1973; also, *New York Post*, April 26, 1974.

67. *New York Times*, March 21, 1972; a collection of articles and comments inserted by Representative John D. Dingell (Democrat, Michigan) *Congressional Record*, May 15, 1972, pp. E 5213–18; also, Representative Les Aspin (Democrat, Wisconsin), "Why the Trans-Alaskan Pipeline Should be Stopped," *Sierra Club Bulletin*, June 1971. The report on President Nixon's meeting with Republican congressional leaders is from Rowland Evans and Robert Novak, *Washington Post*, June 1, 1973.

68. Letter to Senator Ernest F. Hollings (Democrat, South Carolina) and nineteen other senators who had written President Gerald R. Ford on October 7, 1974, about what they felt was the hasty action to lease ten million acres of the outer continental shelf, October 25, 1974. Correspondence appears in *Outer Continental Shelf Oil and Gas Leasing Off Southern California*, op. cit., pp. 69–74. The quotation is on page 73.

69. Eliot Marshall, "Offshore Drilling," *New Republic*, December 28, 1974.

70. Letter to Senator Ernest F. Hollings, op. cit., p. 73. The reference to "unconscionably high prices" for imported foreign oil was in an address, "How Did We Get into This Mess and How Do We Get out of It?" before oil drillers, manufacturers, and engineers at a meeting in Houston, Texas of the Society of Petroleum Engineers, October 8, 1974, as reported in *Journal of Petroleum Technology*, November 1974, pp. 1254–55. The version subsequently released by the Department of the Interior omitted some of the more colorful and controversial phrases.

71. Transcript, "Petroleum Industry Briefing," The White House, August 16, 1973, page 6.

72. "How Did We Get into This Mess and How Do We Get out of It?" op. cit.

73. "Petroleum Industry Briefing," op. cit., pp. 6, 8.

74. Testimony, *The Natural Gas Industry*, Hearings, op. cit., Part 1, pp. 15–36. The quotation is on p. 34. Also, Morton Mintz, *Washington Post*, September 30, 1972, and May 13, 1973.

75. *New York Times*, September 5, 1973, and *APGA Newsletter*, September 17, 1973, pp. 19–22.

76. Testimony, *Greater Coal Utilization*, Joint Hearings, Committees on Interior and Insular Affairs and Public Works, U.S. Senate, 94th Congress, 1st Session (Washington, 1975), pp. 135–36 and passim.

77. Brinegar saw himself as a professional economist and manager—"I by no means consider myself an oilman, whatever that term means." A business associate agreed that he was capable of implementing long-range plans and directing large organizations, and was not "what is generally referred to as an idea man who creates public policy." *New York Times*, Dec. 24, 1972; also December 8, 1972, and February 9, 1969.

78. *Nominations of Elliot L. Richardson and William P. Clements*, Hearings, Committee on Armed Services, U.S. Senate, 93d Congress, 1st Session (Washington, 1973), pp. 135–84; also, testimony of Representative John E. Moss (Democrat, California), *Production of Oil and Gas on Public Lands*, Hearings, op. cit., pp. 90–98; also, *New York Times*, December 18 and 19, 1972. Subsequent questions concerning possible conflict of interest were raised in the Senate a year later because of the renewed interest in Alaskan naval petroleum reserves to meet national needs and the activities of SEDCO, of which Clements's son was now chairman. Clements continued to insist that his duties were technical and resisted appearing before a Senate Commerce subcommittee. Asked why he thought the Armed Services had approved and then the full Senate had confirmed Clements without requiring that he divest himself of his stock, Senator Adlai E. Stevenson III (Democrat, Illinois), who had not voted but was recorded as "positioned against" confirmation, speculated that "no one was thinking in terms of an energy shortage" then. *New York Post*, January 4 and 14, 1974.

79. *Congressional Record*, June 13, 1974, pp. S. 11094–11110; also *New York Times*, June 14, 1974.

80. Texts of the correspondence, *The Natural Gas Industry*, Hearings, op. cit., Part 2, pp. 1063–66; also testimony of Ralph Nader, *Energy Data Requirements of the Federal Government*, Hearings, op. cit., Part 1, pp. 222–24. Ending natural gas regulation, building the Alaskan pipeline and "reappraising" environmental policies where they

hindered energy development, were just a few of Simon's priorities for energy self-sufficiency. See, for example, *Competition in the Energy Industry*, Hearings before Subcommittee on Antitrust and Monopoly, Committee on the Judiciary, 93d Congress, 1st Session (Washington, 1973), pp. 311–49.

A controversy over the activities of a Phillips official working for a year under the executive interchange program in the Treasury's Office of the Energy Advisor (and later to move with Mr. Simon on loan to the FEA) provided a revealing study of how a position was defined as "technical," only to have questions arise later as to the policy dimensions of the executive's activities and the possibility of a conflict of interest. A memorandum to Mr. Simon, then deputy secretary of the treasury, from his special assistant described the work of the Phillips petroleum specialist as "primarily to collect and analyze factual data and provide technical calculations and studies where subjective judgment and advice are not required." Among the tasks listed were the development of data pertaining to present and future foreign oil operations, the oil import control program and energy conservation, and the preparation of background papers on the U.S. petroleum industry. Once in the FEA, he prepared studies dealing with such topics as the effects of regulation on the oil and gas industry, capital investment patterns, imports, price controls, and marketing. At first his superiors insisted that throughout he was insulated from any policy making. But then specific questions arose about any part he may have had in the writing of crude oil allocation regulations which allowed some oil companies selling oil to other refiners under the mandatory allocation program to charge far more than the original cost of obtaining the crude. At one point John Sawhill, Simon's successor at the helm of the FEA, estimated that such "double dipping" may have resulted in a $100 million overcharge to consumers in 1974. See *Interim Report on the Use of Presidential Executive Interchange Personnel with Oil Industry Backgrounds by the Federal Energy Office*, United States General Accounting Office, Washington, May 3, 1974. Also, *Energy Data Requirements of the Federal Government*, op. cit., Hearing, also Report (Washington, 1974).

81. Address to the American Petroleum Institute, New York City, November 12, 1974. *New York City Financial Crisis*, Hearings, Committee on Banking, Housing and Urban Affairs, U.S. Senate, 94th Congress, 1st Session (Washington, 1975), p. 67.

82. Address to the American Petroleum Institute, New York City, op. cit.; also, *New York Times*, February 12, 1974; and testimony, *Multinational Corporations and United States Foreign Policy*, Hearings, op. cit., Part 9, p. 235, 275 and passim. *Energy Data Requirements of the Federal Government*, op. cit. *A Report*, pp. 81–82 and passim.

83. The faith in the market and the message to consumers were voiced in response to a complaint by one governor at the Western Governors Conference that many people could not afford the new energy prices. Sawhill's plea for support of the administration's energy program, including western coal development, was countered by questions about the fate of the west in such "eastern" planning. *New York Times*, July 30, 1974; also, April 23, 1974. The proposal for automatic price increases for utilities was not simply for fuel costs but presumably all operating costs, an arrangement which would completely undercut the regulatory bodies. There was also considerable protest from consumer groups over the biased character of such action and the obvious conflict with calls from newly-elevated President Ford for a halt to inflation. For a while it appeared that the meeting, originally intended to be closed to the public, had been canceled. Separate news item, *New York Times*, July 30, 1974; also August 14, and September 12, 1974, and *Congressional Record*, September 24, 1974, p. E 6049.

84. Just as Sawhill was leaving, the FEA issued a comprehensive report *Project Independence* (Washington 1974) which provided careful data for appraising the nation's energy picture and then spelled out four alternative options. No formal policy recommendation was offered, but the inescapable importance of Sawhill's belief in mandatory conservation and energy demand management was quite explicit. See *New York Times*, October 23, 1974, for preliminary reactions, and also Sawhill's testimony, *Project Independence*, Hearing before the Committee on Interior and Insular Affairs, U.S. Senate, 93d Congress, 2d Session (Washington, 1974), passim. For a discussion with Senator William Proxmire of his policies as an administrator, see *The Economic Impact of Environmental Regulations*, Joint Economic Committee, Congress of the U.S., 93d Congress, 2d Session (Washington, 1974), pp. 3–34. For his charge about footdragging, Sawhill's first open criticism of big oil, see *New York Times*, June 30, 1974. For his cautious discussion of the need to have the United States government somewhat more involved in the overseas regulation of the companies, see *Multinational Corporations*, op. cit, Hearings, Part 9, pp. 5, 11–12, 17–19, 31–33, and passim. Sawhill was subsequently appointed president of New York University. For an earlier discussion of three energy scenarios: historical growth, which would emphasize vigorous effort to enlarge supplies; technical fix, which would temper growth and use energy more efficiently; and zero energy growth, which would focus on activities requiring less energy, see *A Time to Choose, America's Energy Future*, final report of the Energy Policy Project of the Ford Foundation (Cambridge: Ballinger, 1974). The report concluded that energy growth could be sustained in the economy without increasing annual energy consumption.

85. "Resignation," memorandum from Richardson to Sawhill, October 8, 1974. Sawhill's response in an interview was that Richardson had discussed the points of the memo before it was released, and he "didn't make a case." According to the *New York Times*, "Sawhill adhered to his position that the oil industry had not until recently had a return on its investment equal to the average of the rest of American industry, a situation that inhibited production." But the head of the FEA announced he was acting to strengthen consumer protection. *New York Times*, August 14, 18, and 21, 1974, also *Congressional Record*, August 14, 1974, pp. E 5507–8.

86. *New York Times*, November 7, 8, 9, 12, and 13, 1974.


CHAPTER 8. *Planning for New Beginnings*

1. *Washington Post*, December 25, 1973; also, Thornton Bradshaw, president of Arco, Congressional Conference on "Energy and Government: Toward a Sound Oil Policy," Fund for New Priorities, Washington, March 20, 1975, transcript, pp. 4–7. For congressional actions and reactions concerning the removal of the depletion allowance, see *New York Times*, February 28 and March 19, 1975. "The historic vote to repeal the depletion allowance, which was said by the advocates of repeal to be the first on the issue ever taken in the House of Representatives, was 248 to 163. There was applause from members of the House, a rare happening, when the vote was over," reported Eileen Shanahan.

2. Case filed in U.S. District Court, District of Columbia, June 13, 1973. For discussion, see *Federal Coal Leasing Program*, Hearings, op. cit., passim.

3. For examples of such approaches, each with a somewhat different emphasis, see E. F. Schumacher, *Small is Beautiful: Economics as if People Mattered* (New York: Harper and Row, 1973); Peter van Dresser, *A Landscape for Humans* (Albuquerque, New Mexico: Biotechnic Press, 1972); Murray Bookchin, *Post-Scarcity Anarchism* (Berkeley, California: Ramparts Press, 1971); Ivan D. Illich, *Celebration of Awareness: A Call for Institutional Revolution* (New York: Doubleday, 1970); also his *Tools for Conviviality* (New York: Harper and Row, 1973); and *Energy and Equity* (London: Calder and Boyars, 1974). Also, David Morris and Karl Hess, *Neighborhood Power: The New Localism* (Boston: Beacon, 1975).

4. For two revealing summaries of the tragedy of antitrust in the energy area, see Leonard J. Emmerglich, former special assistant to the attorney general, discussing actions against the oil cartel in the 1950s, *Multinational Corporations*, Hearings, op. cit., Part 7, pp. 99–121, and Part 8, documents, passim; and Bruce B. Wilson, deputy as-

sistant attorney general for antitrust, *Market Performance and Competition in the Petroleum Industry*, Hearings, op. cit., Part 1, pp. 398–439. Also, *The Politics of Oil*, op. cit., pp. 210–17 and passim.

5. *Annual Report and Accounts for 1973*, The British Petroleum Company, Limited, 1974, p. 2. Also, *New York Times*, January 24, 1975. For a documented discussion of BP's involvement in Italian politics, see *The Sunday Times* (London), April 11, 1976.

6. Press release, Imperial Oil, 1971, and statement in response by Premier Allan Blakeney, September 30, 1971; also, remarks by Premier Blakeney before Canadian Petroleum Association, Regina, January 11, 1973.

7. For a history of the CCF, see S. M. Lipset, *Agrarian Socialism* (New York: Doubleday, 1968), updated edition. For illustrations of Canadian nationalism and the growing hostility to the presence of American corporations, see Kari Levitt, *Silent Surrender: The American Economic Empire in Canada*, (Toronto: Macmillan, 1970); Dave Godfrey and Mel Watkins, eds., *Gordon to Watkins to You, Documentary: The Battle for Control of our Economy* (Toronto: New Press, 1970); James Laxer, *The Energy Poker Game: The Politics of the Continental Resources Deal* (Toronto: New Press, 1970). For a critique of the New Democratic Party's Blakeney administration by the Saskatchewan Waffle Movement, published by the latter in a pamphlet, see *The Blakeney Government—One Year After*" (Regina, 1972). The proposal for Sask Oil, an integrated publicly owned company to run the entire provincial industry, was made in the Saskatchewan legislature on February 1, 1973, by John G. Richards, member from Saskatoon.

8. The literature on TVA, sympathetic and critical, continues to expand. For a sympathetic general account by a former director, see Frank E. Smith, *The Politics of Conservation* (New York: Pantheon, 1966). The general warnings of Philip Selznick, *TVA and the Grass Roots: A Study in the Sociology of Formal Organization* (Berkeley: University of California Press, 1949), remain relevant and should be read with the review by Rexford G. Tugwell and Edward C. Banfield, "Grass Roots Democracy—Myth or Reality," in *Public Administration Review*, Winter 1950, pp. 47–55. A useful summary essay is by Peter Barnes, "TVA After 40 Years," *New Republic*, November 10, 1973.

9. Some oil executives now admit that the original Alaskan pipeline would have been an ecological disaster. (In 1970, William T. Pecora, director of the Geological Survey, had told Alaskans that the consortium's plan to bury a hot oil pipeline in the permafrost was unsafe and that its engineers had conceded a 50-50 chance that it would break. *New York Times*, April 28, 1970). "The conservationists are one of the best things that could have happened to us," one oil com-

pany executive, who refused to be identified, was quoted as saying. "We would never be taking the precautions we are if it weren't for the attention focused on us. After all, oil companies are very competitive. We like to think we're socially responsible, but in the long run our aim is to make money. Until recently it was to our advantage to run a sloppy operation because no one was enforcing the rules. Anyone who wanted to be a good citizen did so at his economic disadvantage." *New York Times*, August 23, 1970. Four years later Walter J. Hickel offered a similar judgment. *New York Times*, May 26, 1974. By 1976, there was substantial evidence to support the recurring claim of critics that Alaskan oil was not needed on the West Coast. *Congressional Record*, March 18, 1976, pp. S 3734–35. The comments by Sister Jane Scully, are from an interview, *New York Times*, March 7, 1976.

10. For breakdown of oil executives' compensation, see *Business Week*, May 12, 1975. In 1966, a shareholder asked the chairman of Jersey Standard: "Now, what makes you worth $350,000 a year, three and a half times the salary of the President of the United States? . . . I think this is very excessive, Mr. Chairman. What is it based on?" The reply was: "It is based on consideration of the board of directors of the value of this job compared with competition, with comparable jobs in the industry." "Report of the 84th Annual Meeting of Shareholders," Standard Oil Company (New Jersey), Cleveland, Ohio. May 18, 1966, p. 8. Asked a similar question in 1975, when his salary was nearly $677,000, the chairman explained: "It is necessary to pay salaries comparable to the salaries paid by other large industrial companies if we are to attract and keep the large number of executives needed to run the Corporation. Unless the salary of the chairman is at the level indicated by the market, the salaries of these other executives will be depressed." "Report of the 93rd Annual Meeting of Shareholders," New Orleans, Louisiana, May 15, 1975, p. 17. In 1975, B. R. Dorsey, the Gulf chairman who was removed because of the political payoffs, had his total pay cut from $544,000 to $360,000. Gulf did not give him a bonus as it did its other executives, but it agreed to pay him $1.6 million in exchange for lowering his annual pension from $244,400 to $48,200. He also had stock options worth $1.4 million. *Business Week*, April 12, 1976. Gulf subsequently worked out a plan, as part of its settlement of stockholder suits, requiring Dorsey and five other ousted officials to make some restitution by surrender of some stock and stock options and the payment of cash. *New York Times*, September 24, 1976.

11. *Competitive Aspects of the Energy Industry*, Hearings, op. cit., Part 1, p. 6.

12. Geoffrey Faux and Lee Webb, "An Act to Provide for the Public Ownership of the Energy Industry within the State," March 31, 1974; also, "Lifeline Service," prepared by Vermont Public Interest Research Group, Montpelier, Vermont. Also, James Ridgeway and

Bettina Conner, "Public Energy, Notes toward a New System," in *Working Papers*, Winter, 1975; also see their book *New Energy: Understanding the Crisis and a Guide to an Alternative Energy System* (Boston: Beacon, 1975), and Ridgeway's earlier roundup of the energy world, *The Last Play* (New York: E. P. Dutton, 1973). And *Congressional Record*, December 18, 1974, pp. S 22059–65, and December 19, 1975, pp. S 22913–17. Also, Harry M. Caudill, "Appalachia," in Peter Barnes, ed., *The People's Land* (Emmaus, Pennsylvania: Rodale Press, 1975), pp. 33–37. Caudill's *Night Comes to the Cumberlands* (Boston: Little, Brown, 1963) remains a shattering biography of a depressed region.

13. A considerable literature has developed. See, for example, *Energy for Survival*, op. cit.

14. *Geothermal Energy Resources and Research*, op. cit., is a useful source.

15. *Congressional Record*, July 23, 1975, pp. S 13412–14.

16. See, for example, *Electric Vehicles and Other Alternatives to the Internal Combustion Engine*, Joint Hearings before the Committee on Commerce and the Subcommittee on Air and Water Pollution of the Committee on Public Works, U.S. Senate, 90th Congress, 1st Session (Washington, 1967), passim.

17. Harvey Wasserman, "Nuke Developers on the Defensive," *WIN* (Rifton, New York), December 5, 1974, pp. 4–9; also "Up against the Nukes," *WIN*, June 27, 1974. A film on the toppling of the tower, *Lovejoy's Nuclear War*, 1975 (Green Mountain Post Films, Montague, Massachusetts), offers a stimulating debate over means and ends. For an example of President Nixon's discussion of "old wives' tales and horror stories," see "Remarks on the Nation's Energy Policy," September 8, 1973, in *Presidential Energy Statements*, op. cit., p. 70. For a strong brief against nuclear power plants, see John W. Gofman and Arthur R. Tamplin, *Poisoned Power* (Emmaus, Pennsylvania: Rodale Press, 1971; Signet edition, 1974). For a summary of the report of the royal commission, chaired by Sir Brian Flowers, see *New York Times*, September 23, 1976.

18. See *Strategic Petroleum Reserves*, Hearings before the Committee on Interior and Insular Affairs, U.S. Senate, 93d Congress, 1st Session (Washington, 1973), passim.

19. Letter, John J. McCloy to Secretary of State Dean Rusk, January 11, 1967, *Multinational Corporations*, Hearings, op. cit., Part 9, pp. 115–16.

20. David Brower, *Interior Nomination*, op. cit., p. 280.

21. *New York Times*, July 16, 1972.

22. One such group has been the Peoples' Appalachian Research Collective (PARC). See, for example, such issues of *People's Appalachia* (Morgantown, West Virginia) as "Regional Knowledge for Whom," March 1970; "Rediscovering our Struggle History," June–

July 1970; "The Developers: Partners in Colonization," August–September 1970; "Last Stand to Save the Land," September–October 1971; "Urban Migrants," July, 1972; "Getting from here to there—together," Spring 1973.

23. See its newsletter *The Plains Truth*, published in Billings, Montana.

24. The phrase is used by Anthony Mazzocchi, legislative director of Oil, Chemical and Atomic Workers International Union, AFL-CIO, *The Relationship of Economic Development to Environmental Quality*, op. cit., p. 128.

25. *Oil and Gas Journal*, February 5, 1973, p. 28; also, *Environmental Action*, March 3, 1973, pp. 3–6, and Richard Engler, *Oil Refinery Health and Safety Standards: Their Causes and the Struggle to End Them* (Philadelphia: Philadelphia Area Project on Occupational Safety and Health, Ramazzini Library, 1975). Also, Ray Davidson, *Peril on the Job* (Washington: Public Affairs Press, 1970), and Jeanne M. Stellman and Susan M. Daum, *Work Is Dangerous to Your Health* (New York: Pantheon, 1973).

26. See Richard Morgan and Sandra Jerabek, *How to Challenge Your Local Electric Utility: A Citizen's Guide to the Power Industry* (Washington: Environmental Action Foundation, 1974); also *The Price of Power* (New York: Council of Economic Priorities, 1972). For background, Lee Metcalf and Vic Reinemer, *Overcharge* (New York: David McKay, 1967).

27. *Power Politics*, newsletter, Atlanta, Georgia.

28. "American Ground Transport," in *The Industrial Reorganization Act*, Hearings, op. cit., Part 4A, pp. A 1–103; also, Ralph Nader, *Unsafe at Any Speed* (New York: Pocket Books, 1965); Emma Rothschild, *Paradise Lost: The Decline of the Auto-Industrial Age* (New York, Random, 1973). Sections of the discussion in this chapter on ecology have previously appeared in the *Forum for Contemporary History*, November/December, 1973 ("Energy and Public Policy"), pp. 4–8.

29. For an example of legislation setting standards for automobile fuel efficiency, championed by Senator Gaylord Nelson and opposed by industry, see *Congressional Record*, February 11, 1975, pp. S 1775–76.

30. Testimony of Robert Dunlop, president of Sun Oil and chairman of the board of the American Petroleum Institute, *Electric Vehicles and Other Alternatives to the Internal Combustion Engine*, op. cit., pp. 316–42.

31. R. C. Gerstenberg, "A message to America's car buyers . . .," advertisement, *Newsday*, November 8, 1974.

32. Eric Hurst, *Energy Use for Food in the United States*, Oak Ridge National Laboratory, for the U.S. Atomic Energy Commission,

Oak Ridge, Tennessee, 1973. Also, Arjun Makhijani, *Energy and Agriculture in the Third World* (Cambridge, Mass.: Ballinger, 1975).

33. See Peter Barnes, ed., *The People's Land: A Reader on Land Reform in the United States*, op. cit.; also, Charles L. Smith, *Land Reform in Rural America*, a bibliography, Center for Rural Studies, San Francisco, California, 1975.

34. See Leo Marx, *The Machine in the Garden: Technology and the Pastoral Ideal in America* (New York: Oxford University Press, 1964), for a discussion of the views and premonitions of such figures as Jefferson, Thoreau and Melville; also "American Institutions and Ecological Ideals," *Science*, November 27, 1970, pp. 945–52. Also, Henry Nash Smith, *Virgin Land, The American West as Symbol and Myth*, (Cambridge: Harvard University Press, 1950); Samuel P. Hays, *Conservation and the Gospel of Efficiency* (Cambridge: Harvard University Press, 1959); Lewis Mumford, *Technics and Civilization* (New York: Harcourt, Brace and World, 1934), and his *The Myth of the Machine* (New York: Harcourt Brace Jovanovich, 1967, 1970), 2 vols.; also, James Willard Hurst, *Law and the Conditions of Freedom in the Nineteenth Century United States* (Madison: University of Wisconsin Press, 1956).

35. Congressional Conference on "Energy and Government," op. cit., p. 141.

36. The Texaco statement was by Maurice F. Granville before the annual stockholders' meeting, Miami, Florida, April 23, 1974. The Gulf statement was by executive vice-president James K. Warne. *New York Times*, March 14, 1973. "Javits/Humphrey Propose Legislation for Long-Term Economic Planning," release from office of Senator Javits, May 12, 1975; also "For a National Economic Planning System," statement by the Initiative Committee for National Economic Planning, White Plains, New York, May 6, 1975.

37. See, for example, views of National Coal Association, represented by former FPC commissioner Carl E. Bagge, and of the American Petroleum Institute and the Rocky Mountain Oil and Gas Association, *Land Use Policy and Planning Assistance Act*, Hearings before Committee on Interior and Insular Affairs, U.S. Senate, 93d Congress, 1st Session (Washington, 1973), Part 3, pp. 160–73 and 433–42.

38. *New York Times*, November 22, 1973.

39. From an address delivered before the Twentieth World Conference Against Atomic and Hydrogen Bombs, Tokyo, August 2, 1974, *New York Times*, August 17, 1974.

40. Donald S. McDonald, *New York Times*, June 25, 1973. Canada subsequently announced that it would reduce the flow of oil southward by a third in 1976 and that it expected to terminate exports entirely by 1981. *New York Times*, November 21, 1975.

41. See, for example, Peter J. Usher, *The Bankslanders: Economy and Ecology of a Frontier Trapping Community*, Northern Science Research Group, Department of Indian Affairs and Northern Development (Ottawa, 1971), especially vol. 3, *The Community*, which discusses the conflict between economic development and the welfare of the indigenous northern people whom the study sees as being hurt by oil exploration. Economic well-being was threatened and the trappers "found themselves at an enormous disadvantage" in trying to deal with the oil companies and their representatives (p. 59). Canadian environmentalists have also begun to question the Mackenzie valley proposals.

42. William B. Rogers, news conference, *New York Times*, June 12, 1973; also, *Business Week*, June 22, 1974, and *New York Times*, January 29, 1975.

43. Senator J. W. Fulbright (Democrat, Arkansas) at hearing on *Nomination of Richard Helms to be Ambassador to Iran and CIA International and Domestic Activities*, op. cit., p. 3.

44. *Interview with President Ford*, NBC News, as reported in *New York Times*, January 25, 1975.

45. See, for example, *Intelligence Activities and the Rights of Americans*, Final Report of the Select Committee to Study Governmental Operations with Respect to Intelligence Activities, U.S. Senate, 94th Congress, 2d Session (Washington, 1976), Books I–III; also Hearings, vols. 1–7. *World Military Expenditures and Arms Trade, 1963–1973*, U.S. Arms Control and Disarmament Agency, Department of State (Washington, 1975). These agency studies were stopped after the Secretary of Defense protested that their release and the comparisons with social spending complicated the Pentagon's mission in gaining appropriations. For a comparable analysis for 1974–75, see report of study, "World Military and Social Expenditures," in *New York Times*, March 1, 1976. Also, Statement by Senator William V. Roth, Jr. (Republican, Delaware) and others on "World Arms Trade," news release, November 3, 1975.

For a defense of the aggressive pushing of the sale of arms, including modern sophisticated weapons and aircraft in fierce competition with European "merchants of death," see discussion by State, Treasury, Commerce, and military officials in *The Persian Gulf: Money, Politics, Arms and Power*, Hearings before the Subcommittee on the Near East and South Asia of the Committee on Foreign Relations, House of Representatives, 93d Congress, 2d Session (Washington, 1975). The Defense Department has also conceded that it has technical assistance and training programs for troops in thirty-four countries, the largest ones being in Saudi Arabia and Iran. These arrangements, sometimes with kickbacks and bribes, are increasingly made through private corporations, presumably to lessen criticisms at home and abroad of America's imperial reach and to blur the issue as to whether such "advisers" are mercenaries. Under one Defense Department contract, a U.S. construction corporation (Vinnell) has recruited several hundred American veterans to train Saudi Arabian combat troops to protect the oil facilities. *New York Times*, February 9 and 20, April 14, 1975.

46. "America's Destiny: The Global Context," address, February 4, 1976. University of Laramie, Wyoming.

47. Fact Sheet; Letters from the President to the Speaker of the House of Representatives and the President of the Senate; and text of the bill to establish an Energy Independence Authority, Office of the White House, October 10, 1975.

48. The illustrations are endless; for example, "Are You Being Railroaded?" Phillips Petroleum pamphlet, no date; Texaco advertisement, *Washington Post*, January 18, 1974; Gulf, *New York Times*, January 24, 1974; Mobil, *New York Times*, May 2, 1974. The Mobil "op ed" advertisements have run across the nation in numerous papers since 1970 and appear weekly in the *Chicago Sun-Times, Los Angeles Times, Boston Globe, Wall Street Journal, Washington Post* and *New York Times*. Some of the corporations, such as Mobil, now seek to answer those who suggest interpretations of energy policy at variance with corporate handouts. Herbert Schmertz, vice-president of Mobil, explains that there is a crisis of free speech in the country; many are denied access to the public, and "energy is simply too profound a subject to be left to the overdramatizations of the new journalism, so bright in its style, so careless with its facts." Letter to the editor, *Village Voice* (New York), October 6, 1975. Also, full-page advertisement, *More*, April 1976, and news story, *New York Times*, June 7, 1974. Meanwhile, critics unkindly have labeled much of the advertising on energy, pricing, profits, and governmental policies as propaganda which should be substantiated in the same way as product claims. See, for example, petition before the Federal Trade Commission filed by Media Access Project of Washington, D.C., and supported by a number of members of Congress, press release, January 9, 1974; also *New York Times*, January 10 and May 7, 1974. Also, *Wall Street Journal*, May 14, 1975; Leonard C. Lewin, "Public TV's Corporate Angels," *The Nation*, November 22, 1975; Joseph J. Seldin, "Who Pays for the Image?" op. cit.; and Gerald Astor, "The Gospel According to Mobil," *More*, April 1976. Meanwhile, the Public Media Center, a nonprofit advertising agency (in San Francisco) circulated radio commercials critical of the oil industry. It discovered that Shell had been deviously monitoring these activities and then telephoning some of the offending stations, an action which led Representative Benjamin S. Rosenthal (Democrat, New York) to ask the Justice Department to determine whether any intimidation was involved. *New York Times*, September 13, 1974.

49. Morton Mintz, *Washington Post*, May 25, 1972.

50. "The Petroleum Situation," Chase Manhattan Bank, July 1969.

51. B. R. Dorsey, "Business Responsibility to Society," National Association of Accountants, Pittsburgh chapter, April 15, 1970.

52. Louis Harris Survey, *New York Post*, December 1, 1975.

53. For example, Louis Harris Survey, *New York Post*, December 6, 1973, and October 6, 1975.

# Index

Abourezk, James G., 224
Abu Dhabi, 11
Acheson, Dean, 120–21
advertising. *See* public relations
advisory bodies, 3, 173–75, 180–84, 187–90, 211. *See also* oilmen in government
Africa, 12, 70, 113–14, 115, 155. *See also* specific countries
Agnew, Spiro T., 60, 64, 197, 310
agriculture, 17, 18, 50, 98, 218–19, 234–35, 238
AID (Agency for International Development), 103, 112, 117. *See also* Overseas Private Investment Corporation
Aiken, George D., 221
air conditioning, 16–17, 233, 238
airlines, 2, 6
Akins, James E., 123, 124, 139
Alaska, 18, 23, 39, 51, 59, 64, 71, 93, 156, 163–66, 194–95, 198, 229, 316
Alaskan naval reserves (NPR–4), 59, 64, 164–65, 202, 299. *See also* naval reserves
Alaska pipeline, 5, 14, 23, 39, 61, 64, 164–66, 198, 214, 229, 315–16
Alberta, 240
Algeria, 26, 27, 60
Allende, Salvador, 141–42
allocation program, 7, 38–39, 72, 204, 312
Allott, Gordon, 88
"alternate" energy, 11, 21, 40, 46–47, 50, 183, 223–24, 232. *See also* specific forms

Amerada Hess Corporation (merger of Hess Oil and Chemical Corp. and Amerada Petroleum Corp.), 17, 23, 54, 62, 65, 86, 115
American Gas Association, 41, 49, 169, 184–85, 189–90, 192
American Institute of Merchant Shipping, 174
American Jewish Congress, 140
American Near East Refugee Aid, 137
American Petroleum Institute, 1, 45, 48, 62–63, 68, 70, 90, 95, 149, 153–54, 171, 173, 174, 184–85, 187, 192
American Public Gas Association, 189, 306–7
Americans for Middle East Understanding, 137
Amoco. *See* Standard Oil Company (Indiana)
Anaconda Company, 51
Anderson, Robert B., 58–59, 84, 85, 108, 164
Anderson, Robert O., 59
Angola, 109–10, 113–15
Antarctic, 51
anti-Semitism, 140–41
antitrust actions, 7, 10, 23, 40, 59, 60–61, 69, 108, 117, 123, 160, 178–80, 183, 201, 210, 214–15
Antitrust and Monopoly Subcommittee, U.S. Senate (Hart committee), 92, 210
anti-Zionism, 140–41
apartheid, 116

Appalachia, 41, 168, 172, 218, 220, 222, 230
Appalachian Mountain Authority, 222
Arab boycott, 140
Arab common market, 32
Arab-Israeli conflict, 1, 5, 8–9, 30, 38, 114, 129–30, 137, 139–40, 180
Arab oil, 1, 4, 85, 122–23, 138, 140, 205, 227. See also OPEC; embargo; Middle East; North Africa; and specific countries
Arab OPEC, 30, 32, 242
Aramco, 8, 30, 33, 54, 118, 120, 129–30, 137–40, 170, 171, 180
Arco. See Atlantic Richfield Company
Arctic National Wildlife Refuge, 202
Arctic North Slope, 23, 61, 164–65, 214, 226, 241
Arctic Wildlife Range, 229
Argentina, 106, 202
Arizona, 41
arms merchants, 123, 241, 242, 243–44
Army, United States, 105. See also military; Navy
Ashland Oil, Inc., 22, 31, 62, 66–68, 72, 76–77, 82, 186, 272
Asia, 12, 20, 52–53, 102–3, 126, 136, 243. See also specific countries
Aspin, Les, 63
Atkins, Orin E., 66, 77
Athabasca River Basin. See tar sands
Atlantic Ocean, 155–56, 158, 230. See also offshore lands; continental shelf
Atlantic Refining Company, 18, 171
Atlantic Richfield Company (Arco), 18, 22, 23, 24, 28, 38, 41, 43, 45, 46, 47, 51, 52, 59, 60, 79, 126, 131, 150, 160, 164, 165, 171, 174, 175, 186, 211, 224, 236
Atomic Energy Commission (AEC), 46, 142, 221, 225
Attorney General, 178
Australia, 53
automobile industry, 2, 6, 16, 175, 180, 183, 201, 204, 232–34

Babcock, Tim M., 63, 72
Bagge, Carl E., 201, 319
Bahamas Exploration Ltd., 67, 69, 78–79
Baker, Howard H., Jr., 69
Baker, Robert G. (Bobby), 63
Bangladesh, 12, 33
Bank of England, 18, 216
Bankers Trust Company, 24
Banking and Currency Committee, U.S. House of Representatives, 81
banks, 13, 22, 23–24, 57, 101, 131, 141–42, 143, 144, 187, 224
Barnet, Richard J., 120
Bechtel Corporation, 65, 104, 131, 174
Bentsen, Lloyd, 64, 69
Berle, A. A. Jr., 34
Biafra, 116–17
black community, 70, 83
"black lung" movement, 231
Blair, John M., 92, 258
Blythe Eastman Dillon and Company, 182
Boggs, Hale, 88
Bolivia, 111
Bonsal, Philip W., 107–8
Bounds, Joseph E., 78
Bradshaw, Thornton, 236
Brant, Kirby, 166
Brazil, 106
Brinegar, Claude S., 201
British Petroleum Company, Ltd. (BP), 18, 19, 23, 28, 29, 31, 51, 53, 54, 82, 116, 154–55, 164, 180, 214, 215–16
Brockett, E. D., 109
Brooke, Edward W., 81–82
Brooks, David B., 171–72
Brown, George E., Jr., 200
Brown, George S., 141
Brown and Root, Inc., 62, 82, 116, 131
Bunker, Ellsworth, 102
Burmah Oil Company, 18, 216
Bush, George, 64, 88, 94
business review letter, 178–80

Cabinda Gulf Oil, 114
Cabinet Task Force on Oil Import Control, 90–94

California, 147–58, 160, 191, 193, 198, 201, 230

California Institute of Technology, 191

Caltex (California-Texas Oil Company, Ltd.), 52, 53, 115, 116, 121, 135, 171, 254

Cambodia, 197

campaign contributions. See political payments

Campaign Spending Act, 82

Canada, 3, 20, 25, 45–46, 52, 53, 63, 67, 74, 92, 95–96, 105, 112, 143, 166, 172, 198, 217, 222–23, 240–41, 319

Canadian National Emergency Board, 95–96, 240

Canadian pipeline, 61, 64, 166, 198, 320

Cannon, Howard, 81

capital investment, 13, 20, 22, 32, 36, 38, 43, 48, 49, 50, 51, 53–56, 85, 92–93, 101, 105, 113, 144, 150, 155, 201, 210, 216, 218, 225, 227, 237, 239, 246

cartel, corporate, 7, 22, 25, 26, 84–85, 192, 226, 237–38, 242

cartel, producer, 7, 33, 226, 241, 242. See also OPEC

Case, Francis, 59

Castro, Fidel, 107–8

Central Intelligence Agency, U.S. (CIA), 29–30, 52, 67, 111, 115, 117, 127, 135, 142, 171, 191, 242–43, 290–91, 307

Ceylon, 106

Champlin Petroleum Company (Union Pacific Corporation), 22

Chase Manhattan Bank, 20, 24, 53, 56, 57, 69, 178, 216, 248

Chevron. See Standard Oil Company of California

Chile, 141–42, 144

China, 12, 52, 102–3, 104, 111, 115, 135, 136–37, 223, 238

Church, Frank, 8, 10, 210. See also Multinational Corporations

Cities Service Company, 24, 45, 52, 57, 207–8, 283

Clark, Richard C., 113

Clements, William P., Jr., 202–3, 311

CNA Financial Corporation, 50

coal, 4, 39, 42, 96, 137, 171–72, 187, 205, 218, 220, 222, 225–26, 230–31, 237

coal, deep mining, 167, 168, 169, 231

coal gasification, 41, 95, 168–70, 200, 237

coal industry, oil takeover, 18, 40–42, 50, 60, 201. See also specific corporations

coal lands, leasing, 41, 161–63, 167, 212

coal prices, 36, 41, 50

coal research, 5, 169, 192–93, 205

coal, strip mining, 41, 50, 163, 167–68, 182, 200, 229, 231, 233, 237, 239

coastal planning, 87, 148–54, 156–57, 201, 230

Coastal Zone Conservation Commission, California, 150, 198

Coastal Zone Management Act, 152, 198

coast guard, 174

cold war, 3–4, 17, 35, 98, 101, 102–5, 107, 111, 113, 115, 117–18, 120, 178, 241–42, 244

Collado, Emilio, 111

Colonial Pipeline Company, 22, 65, 70, 215

Colony Development Corporation, 43, 44, 45, 186

Colorado, 22, 41, 44, 162, 186

Colorado School of Mines Research Foundation, 43

Commerce, Department of, 174, 176

Committee to Re-elect the President (CRP), 62–63, 66, 77–79, 113, 176, 200, 201

Common Cause, 210

Common Market, 3

Commonwealth Oil Refinery Co. Inc., 86

communism, 3, 9, 101, 105, 115, 118, 137, 142, 223, 244

Comptroller General, U.S. See General Accounting Office

Congress, U.S., 5, 6, 7–8, 10, 14, 51, 58–59, 63–65, 69, 71, 81–82, 94, 133, 141, 170, 176, 211, 229, 249

Connally, John B., 57, 59–60, 82, 193, 289
Connally, Tom, 63
conservation, 6, 49, 146, 147–48, 151, 156, 195, 204, 206, 218–19, 225–26, 230–33, 234, 237, 249
conservation as price mechanism, 84, 93
Consolidated Edison Company of New York, 126, 153, 181, 183, 233
Consolidation Coal Company, 40, 168, 174, 183, 214, 233
consumer, 13, 34, 47–48, 49, 50, 53–54, 84–85, 170, 171, 188, 189, 200, 203, 205, 209, 210, 220, 231–32, 246, 247
consumer as investor, 13, 92–93, 218, 240
consumer nations, 3, 4, 12, 27, 28, 31, 32, 121, 131, 241
consumer representation, 173, 175, 181, 203, 207
consumption, energy, 1, 2, 13, 16–17, 47–49, 95, 99, 127, 219–20, 227, 237–38, 243; constraints, 6, 36–37, 96, 206, 232, 313; reappraisals, 206, 235, 238, 239, 248–49
Container Corporation, 51
Continental Oil Company, 40, 41, 43, 46, 47, 53, 124, 168, 171, 180, 182, 214, 247
continental shelf, 22, 51–53, 93, 132–34, 136, 147, 150–61, 193, 198–99, 204, 226, 239. See also law of the sea; ocean beds; offshore lands
Cooperative Commonwealth Federation (CCF), 217
cooperatives, 181, 217, 218–19, 224
corporate responsibility, 4, 13–14, 58, 79, 151, 175, 210, 211, 236, 248, 316; and citizenship, 8, 12–13, 100, 108–10, 112–13, 115–16, 135–37, 143, 178, 181, 204, 215–16, 228; and executives, 73–77, 112, 215, 220
Cost of Living Council, 9, 36, 192
Council of Economic Advisers, 214

Council on Environmental Quality, 154, 174
Cuba, 52, 59, 65, 107–8, 115, 142

Daimler Benz AG, 11
Dayton (Ohio), 70
Dean, Arthur H., 120, 124
Dean, John W., III, 83
deep-water ports, 51, 86, 230, 231, 237
Defense, Department of, 2, 5–6, 17, 102, 139, 202–3. See also military
Defense Production Act of 1950, 180
Delaware, 230
Democratic National Committee, 82, 272
Democrats, 68, 249
Denmark, 219
depletion allowance, 7, 34, 44, 54, 56, 57, 59, 63, 68, 72, 211, 218. See also income tax
detergents, 17, 219
"developing" world, 11, 12, 14–15, 25, 27, 32–33, 37, 101, 106, 109–10, 114, 134–35, 141–45, 156–57, 212–13, 220, 237–39, 241–42, 247. See also specific countries and regions
DiBona, Charles J., 171, 182
Dillon, C. Douglas, 57
Dillon, Read and Company, 57, 59
Dingell, John D., 159
divestiture, 14, 215, 247
Dole, Hollis M., 169–70, 171, 172, 173, 177, 185–86, 305–6
Dole, Robert, 64
Dominican Republic, 67
Dorsey, B. R., 68, 70, 73–74, 78, 99, 102–3, 109, 110, 112–13, 248, 281, 316
Douglas, Paul H., 211
Dow Chemical Corporation, 136
DuBridge, Lee A., 191, 309
Dulles, John Foster, 120

East Coast, 60, 91, 95, 96, 153
Eastern Europe, 125, 127
Ecuador, 26, 105
Edison Electric Institute, 182

Egypt, 29, 131
Ehrlichman, John D., 61
Eisenhower, Dwight D., 57, 58, 84, 283
electric utilities, 39, 47, 126, 168, 218, 233; and government advisory agencies, 174, 181, 187; rates, 12, 14, 17, 50, 87; regulation, 188, 205–6, 211, 222, 224–25, 232
electric vehicles, 233
Elk Hills, 66, 163–64, 166, 226, 299. *See also* naval reserves
El Paso Natural Gas Company, 41, 60, 104, 131
embargo, oil (1973), 1–8, 12, 31, 34, 91, 122, 127, 129–30, 139–40, 177, 180, 181
Emergency Petroleum and Gas Administration, 177
Emergency Petroleum Supply Committee, 180–81
Emergency Preparedness, Office of, 67, 94, 262
Enders, Thomas O., 252–53
"energy crisis" 1973–74, 1–15, 21, 30, 33, 38, 39, 85, 94–95, 96, 106, 122, 140, 153, 163, 166, 177, 184, 185, 186, 192, 197–98, 201, 203, 205, 220, 229, 236, 247, 249, 250
Energy Independence Authority, 246
Energy Policy Office, White House, 182–83
Energy Research and Development Advisory Council, 182–83
Energy Resources Council, 199
ENI (Ente Nazionale Idrocarburi), 125
environmental controls, 2, 5, 6, 85, 87, 95, 143, 146, 149–53, 163, 167, 168, 174, 194–95, 209, 212–13, 221, 229, 234
environmental impact studies, 44, 150, 152, 156–59, 198
environmentalists, 39, 44–45, 64, 149, 175–76, 186, 203, 230–32, 247, 315–16
Environmental Protection Agency, 77, 167

ERAP (Entreprise de Recherches et d'Activités Pétrolières), 125
Ervin, Sam J., Jr. (Select Committee on Presidential Campaign Activities, U.S. Senate), 66, 67, 70–71, 81
Esso Italiana, 111–12, 281–83
Ethics Committee, Senate, 81
Europe, 3, 4, 11, 25, 28, 53, 87, 116, 118, 120–21, 125–26, 138, 139, 140, 243
European Cooperation Administration (ECA), 120–21
European Economic Community, 53, 143
executive salaries, 220–21, 316
Export-Import Bank, 19, 104
Exxon Corporation, formerly Esso (Standard Oil Company [New Jersey]), 8, 9, 13, 19, 20, 22, 23, 24, 27, 30–31, 33, 39, 40, 43, 45, 46, 47, 53, 54, 56, 85, 87, 88, 91, 92, 97, 106, 107, 111–12, 115, 118, 119, 121, 123, 124, 125, 126, 129, 131, 135, 150, 152, 154, 160, 164, 171, 174, 175, 180, 182, 183, 200, 212, 217, 220, 224, 248

Faisal, 8, 9, 130, 137, 139
Farbenindustrie, I.G., 135
Federal Advisory Committee Act, 182–83
Federal chartering, 10
Federal Election Commission, 79
Federal Energy Office (FEO), later changed to Federal Energy Administration (FEA), 6, 35, 39, 156, 183, 190, 192, 203–8, 252, 312
Federal Field Committee for Development Planning in Alaska, 165
federalism, 221, 223, 235–36
Federal Power Commission (FPC), 47, 48, 49, 60, 91, 171, 181, 188–91, 200–201, 203, 205, 240
Federal Trade Commission (FTC), 22, 188, 192, 203–4, 211
Federal Water Pollution Control Act, 195

Federation of Natives, Alaska, 231
fertilizer, 12, 17, 19, 50, 104, 106,
    131, 238, 239
Finance Committee, Senate, 63–64
First National City Bank, 24, 67
fishing industry, 87, 133, 148, 196,
    213, 231
FitzGerald, Joseph H., 165
Flanigan, Peter M., 59, 94
Florida, 22
food, 2, 5, 12, 106, 132, 234–35, 238
Ford, Gerald R., 69, 71, 81
Ford administration, 12, 49, 74, 142,
    163, 166, 183, 198, 205, 206, 243,
    299
Ford Foundation, 69
foreign aid, 12, 32–33, 98, 106,
    110–11, 112, 114, 117, 119, 145,
    227, 239
Foreign Petroleum Supply
    Committee, 180–81
Foreign Relations, Committee on,
    U.S. Senate, 101, 147
foreign trade zone, 86–90, 195
Foreign Trade Zones Board, 87–89
France, 3, 116, 131, 237
Freedom of Information Act, 152,
    181, 212
Friends of the Earth, 175
fuel adjustment clauses, 50
fuel cell, 224
Fulbright, J. W., 101, 106
Fund for Arab Economic Develop-
    ment (Kuwait), 32–33
Fundy, Bay of, 222

Gabon, 26, 67
garbage and sewage, 222–23, 233
Geneen, Harold S., 60–61
General Accounting Office, 49, 159,
    162, 163, 175, 184, 189
General Motors Corporation, 180,
    183, 234
Geological Survey, U.S., 155–59,
    161–62, 167, 174, 197
Georgia, 87, 196, 232
Georgia Power Company, 232
Georgia Power Project, 232
geothermal energy, 40, 46–47,
    222–24

Germany, 135, 219
Gerstacker, Carl A., 136
Get Oil Out (GOO), 230
Getty, J. Paul, 61–62
Getty Oil Company, 24, 46, 47, 62
Gibson, Andrew E., 207–8
Gooch, R. Gordon, 201
Gravel, Mike, 64–65
Gray, Archie D., 78
Great Britain, 3, 4, 18, 116, 135,
    154, 214, 225
"green revolution," 98, 234
Guinea, 114
Gulf boycott, 109–10, 280
Gulf Marine and Services Company
    Ltd., 79
Gulf Oil Corporation, 10, 19, 22,
    24, 38, 40, 41, 43, 44, 45, 46, 47,
    50, 51, 52, 53, 54, 62, 67–70,
    72–74, 78–79, 81, 87, 97, 99–100,
    102–3, 104, 105, 109–10, 111,
    112–15, 119, 123, 137, 144,
    147–48, 151, 154, 162, 175, 220,
    236, 248, 316

Haldeman, H. R., 61–62
Hammer, Armand, 18–19, 63, 72,
    82, 87, 112. See also Occidental
    Petroleum Corporation
Hamon, Jake L., 62–63
Harriman, Averill, 124
Harris, Fred R., 69, 88
Hart, Philip A., 210. See also
    Antitrust and Monopoly
    Subcommittee
Hatfield, Mark O., 69
Hawaii, 86
heating fuel, 22, 38, 95
Heinz, H. John 3d, 273
helium, 171
Helms, Richard, 191, 242–43, 291
Hess, Leon, 65, 68. See also
    Amerada Hess Corporation
Heyerdahl, Thor, 155
Hickel, Walter J., 23, 59, 88, 89,
    91, 172, 194–97
highways, 16, 98, 201, 233
Highway Trust Fund, 233
Hooker Chemical Corporation, 18,
    88

Hughes, Howard E., 61
Humble Oil. *See* Exxon
Humphrey, Hubert H., 69, 272
Hunt, Bunker (Hunt International Petroleum Company, affiliated with Hunt Oil Company), 26, 28, 82
Hunt, H. L., 28, 82

Iceland, 223
Ickes, Harold E., 193
Ikard, Frank, 171
Imperial Oil Ltd., 112, 217
imports, 1–3, 6–7, 11, 21, 25, 36–37, 38, 43, 45, 59, 61, 63, 66, 84–97, 126, 132, 138, 146, 170, 171, 187, 199, 226–27, 240, 241
income tax, federal, 14, 17, 18–19, 21, 25, 28, 34, 54–55, 119. *See also* depletion allowance; tax credits
independents, 9, 17, 19, 21, 26, 30, 31, 36, 38, 39, 62–63, 66, 85, 87, 92, 97, 115, 125, 161, 169, 173, 181, 203, 206, 216–17
indexing, 27
India, 12, 33, 52, 106
Indian lands, 41, 46, 162, 165
Indian Ocean, 104
Indonesia, 4, 5, 26, 29, 52, 53, 99, 106, 117
information, 3, 8, 106, 146, 158, 173, 181, 200–201, 226, 228, 231–32, 235, 247; "proprietary," 6, 10, 24, 135, 152, 184–92, 203, 219–20
Information Agency, U.S. (USIA), 105–6, 117
Inouye, Daniel K., 69
Interior and Insular Affairs Committee, U.S. Senate, 64, 68, 69
Interior, Department of the, 14, 22, 42–45, 58, 59, 64, 65–66, 68, 86, 89, 90, 93, 133, 146–53, 155–73, 177, 181–82, 184–88, 190, 191–200, 201, 212, 221, 229, 231
International Bank for Reconstruction and Development (World Bank), 32–33, 69, 106

International Business Machines (IBM), 183
International Monetary Fund, 32–33, 106
International Petroleum Company (IPC), 106
International Telephone and Telegraph Company (ITT), 60, 141, 144
Interstate Commerce Commission, 185
Interstate Oil Compact Commission, 89, 90
Interstate Oil Transport Company, 207
Iran, 4, 5, 9, 11, 19, 26, 29–30, 31, 32, 33, 59, 117, 120, 122–23, 126, 127, 131, 138, 140, 191, 242–43
Iraq, 26, 27, 29, 117, 124–25, 131, 242
Iraq National Oil Company, 124
Iraq Petroleum Company, 124–25
Irvis, K. Leroy, 70
Island Creek Coal Company, 18, 40
Israel, 1, 4, 5, 8–9, 12, 52, 130, 137–41, 243, 290
Italy, 111–12, 116, 125, 216, 223

Jackson, Henry M., 8, 10, 68, 69
Jamieson, J. K., 31, 180, 260, 282–83
Japan, 3, 4, 11–12, 23, 31, 52–53, 85, 98, 102, 103, 104, 111, 118, 120, 125, 135, 136, 137, 138, 139, 223
Javits, Jacob K., 144–45, 236–37
"Jewish lobby," 141
Johnson, Lyndon B., 57, 58, 63, 69–70
Johnson administration, 1, 58, 65, 84, 85–86, 88–89, 106, 172, 193
Joint Chiefs of Staff, 141
Jones, W. Alton, 57, 283
Jungers, Frank, 129
Justice, Department of, 35, 40, 60, 93, 126, 160, 178–80, 214–15, 267

Kalmbach, Herbert W., 62
Keeler, W. W., 70–71, 75–76
Keller, George, 129–30
Kelley, Thomas E., 23

Kennecott Copper Corporation, 141
Kennedy, John F., administration, 57–58, 84, 98, 178, 193
Kent State University, 197
Kentucky, 230
Kern County Land Company, 18
Kerr, Robert S., 63
Kerr-McGee Corporation, 41, 46
Killian, Robert K., 6, 49–50, 253
Kissinger, Henry A., 3, 12, 142, 198, 243, 244
Korea, 52, 102, 110–11. *See also* South Korea
Krupp, house of, 11
Kuwait, 11, 26, 30, 32–33, 69, 97, 117, 140

Land Management, Bureau of, 155–56, 162–63, 167
land use planning, 162, 237
Laos, 98
Latin America, 12, 20, 91, 92, 105, 106, 220, 239
law firms, 25, 57, 101, 120, 171, 186, 188, 200–201
law of the sea, 132–35, 213. *See also* continental shelf; ocean beds; offshore lands
Leagues of Women Voters, state, 212
Levy, Walter J., 37, 53
Libya, 18, 25–29, 30, 33, 34, 67, 82, 86, 117, 125–27, 178
Liedtke, William, 63, 200
lifeline service pricing, 221–22
Ligon, Duke R., 180
Lincoln, George A., 94, 262
"line of business" amendment, 211
liquified natural gas, 48, 59, 60, 66, 131, 208
lobbying, 66–69, 74, 85, 88, 94, 133, 140, 141, 167, 171, 191, 195, 201, 206, 210–11
London Policy Group, 126, 178
Lone Star Gas Company, 171
Long Island (New York), 153
Long, Russell B., 63–64, 69
Louisiana, 2, 47, 63, 87, 90, 93
Luce, Charles F., 181

Machiasport (Maine), 86–90, 94, 195
Mackenzie River valley. *See* Canadian pipeline
Magnuson, Warren G., 7
Maine, 86–90, 95, 195, 198–99, 222, 231
Management and Budget, Office of (formerly Bureau of the Budget), 172, 183, 187–88, 194
Marathon Oil Company, 62, 182
Marcor Corporation, 51, 204, 214–15, 267
Maritime Administration, 207
marketing, 17, 18, 19, 20, 21–22, 25, 29–32, 53, 92, 101, 107, 122, 129, 180, 215–17
Marshall Plan, 3, 53, 120
Martin, W. F., 75–76
Maryland, 87
mass transportation, 16, 201, 219, 233–34
Mazzocchi, Anthony, 231, 318
McCall, Tom, 10
McCloy, John J., 69, 73–74, 78, 81, 119, 120, 126, 139, 178–79
McCone, John, 142, 290–91
McGovern, George, 77
McIntyre, Thomas, 88–89
Mediterranean, 105
Mellon family, 59, 74, 78
mergers, 17–19, 60, 85, 214
Metcalf, Lee, 23–24, 180–81, 184, 188, 210
Mexico, 117, 219, 223
Mexico, Gulf of, 22, 156, 190, 197
Michigan, 87
Midcaribbean Investments Limited, 78–79
Mid-Continent Oil and Gas Association, 67
Middle East, 3–5, 7–11, 20–21, 25–35, 84–85, 87, 91–92, 122–32, 137–41, 227, 241–44. *See also* *individual countries*; Persian Gulf; OPEC
Middle East Institute, 137
Midwest, 19, 22, 61, 166, 198
military, 2, 3–4, 5–6, 8, 9, 12, 14, 17, 35, 64, 99–100, 104, 115, 130, 133,

141, 202, 226, 243–44. *See also* Defense; Navy

military aid, 98, 110–11, 112, 114, 139–41, 243

Military Petroleum Advisory Board, 70

Miller, Otto N., 138, 160, 290

Mills, Wilbur D., 68, 82, 90–91, 171

Mineral Leasing Act of 1920, 44

Mines, Bureau of, 167, 171–72, 184–85, 186, 192–93, 300

Mining Enforcement and Safety Administration, 300

Mitchell, John N., 60, 61, 62, 67, 81, 91, 94, 214

Mobil Oil Corporation, 9, 13–14, 19, 22, 23, 24, 33, 43, 47, 50–51, 53, 54, 87, 111–12, 114, 115–17, 118, 119, 123, 124, 126, 129, 131, 147–48, 153, 154, 162, 171, 175–76, 200, 204, 214–15, 220, 267

Mobil Oil Italiana, 111

Montana, 41, 220, 230

Montana Wilderness Association, 212

Montgomery Ward and Company, 51

Moody, Rush, Jr., 200

Morgan Guaranty Trust Company of New York, 24

Morris, Robert H., 203

Morton, Rogers C.B., 157, 186, 197–200, 206, 300

Mossadegh, Mohammed, 5, 35, 243

Moynihan, Daniel P., 115

Mozambique, 114

Multinational Corporations, Subcommittee on, U.S. Senate (Senator Church), 8, 10, 73, 113, 119, 124–25, 178–79

municipally-owned power companies, 217–19, 222

Murchison, Clint W., Jr., 62, 72

Murchison, John, 62

Muskie, Edmund S., 24, 77

Nader, Ralph, 305

Nassikas, John N., 91, 201, 205

National Association of Manufacturers, 70

National Coal Association, 169, 201

National Energy Information System, 191–92

national energy planning board, 214, 221–24, 226, 235–36

national energy policy: prevailing patterns, 2–5, 14–15, 45, 120–22, 128–29, 131, 146, 156, 158–59, 161, 162–63, 167, 168, 170, 173, 179, 182–83, 187, 190, 207; planning for new beginnings, 209–50. *See also* planning

National Environmental Policy Act, 64, 152–53, 157, 159, 167, 212

National Industrial Pollution Control Council, 174–75, 176

National Iranian Oil Company, 31–32

nationalization: U.S., 14, 161, 204; world, 20, 27–29, 31, 33, 34, 53, 60, 106, 107, 116, 120, 126–27, 130, 142, 145, 214, 219, 239, 241–42, 263

National Oil Jobbers Council, 181

National Petroleum Council (NPC), 13, 70, 90, 95, 96, 133, 158, 170, 173, 177, 182, 184, 186, 189–90

national power grid, 224

National Resources Planning Board, 214

National Science Foundation, 51, 183

"national security," 6, 9, 12, 35, 84, 90–91, 96, 102, 117, 118, 124, 131, 151, 153, 156–57, 181–82, 183, 198, 219, 226–27

National Security Council, 118

National Wildlife Federation, 212

native claims (Alaska), 39, 165–66, 194–95, 231

NATO, 114

natural gas, 17, 36, 40, 41, 47–50, 59, 60, 104, 153, 169, 187–91, 200–201, 208, 225–26, 228, 233; deregulation, 5, 14, 37, 47–49, 182, 200–201, 205, 239–40, 247

Natural Gas Act of 1938, 49

Natural Resources, Department of, 170

Naval Petroleum and Oil Shale Reserves, Office of, 163–64

naval reserves, 5, 59, 66, 163–66, 182, 194–95, 202, 226, 299

Navy, United States, 64, 104–5, 134, 136, 163–65, 203

Nelson, Gaylord, 167–68, 191

Netherlands, 4

Netherlands East Indies, 52

New Brunswick (Canada), 222

New Democratic Party (Canada), 217–18

New England, 86–90, 95, 223

New England Marine Resources Foundation, 86

New England Petroleum Corporation (Nepco), 126–27

new international economic order, 213

New Jersey Turnpike Authority, 70

New Mexico, 41

New York "financial crisis," 204

New York Group, 178

New Zealand, 223

Nigeria, 5, 26, 52, 67, 116–17

Nixon, Richard M., administration, 1–3, 5–6, 9, 49, 58–63, 71–72, 80–83, 89–91, 94, 114, 127, 132, 150, 155, 166, 169–70, 173–74, 177, 182, 194–205

Nixon, Mudge, Rose, Guthrie, Alexander and Mitchell, 60

North Africa, 4, 19, 20, 25, 84, 87, 91, 92, 95, 122, 126. See also specific countries

North Atlantic Treaty Organization (NATO), 114

North Carolina, 87

North Dakota, 17, 41–42

Northern Plains Resource Council, 212, 230–31

North Sea, 4, 11, 214

Nova Scotia, 222

nuclear power, 46, 87, 95, 131, 169, 182, 201, 205, 225, 229, 232, 238, 239, 246

Occidental Petroleum Corporation (Oxy), 18–19, 24, 26, 28–29, 40, 43, 47, 54, 63, 66, 72, 82, 86–89, 104, 112, 125

Occupational Safety and Health Act (OSHA) of 1970, 232

ocean beds, 51–52, 242. See also continental shelf; law of the sea

offshore lands, 93, 99, 147–50, 152, 155–58, 161, 162, 174, 190, 206, 230, 232. See also continental shelf; law of the sea

Offshore Operations Advisory Committee, 174

Offshore Operators Committee, 174

Oil, Chemical, and Atomic Workers International Union, 231–32

Oil and Gas, Office of, 170-71, 173, 177, 180, 182, 186, 199–200, 204

Oil Import Administration, 94, 170

oilmen in government, 3, 159, 171, 177, 180, 184, 186, 195, 202–3, 312. See also advisory bodies

Oil Shale Advisory Board (Interior Department), 43

Oil Shale Corporation (Tosco), 22, 43, 186

oil spills, 87, 147–49, 153–57, 195–97

Okinawa, 102, 136

Oklahoma, 2, 71

Old Ben Coal Company, 40

O'Leary, John F., 172

OPEC (Organization of Petroleum Exporting Countries), 4–5, 12, 26–28, 30–37, 104, 112, 122, 125–29, 139, 178, 228, 240, 252–53

Overseas Private Investment Corporation (OPIC), U.S., 103, 142, 144. See also AID

Oxy. See Occidental Petroleum Company

Pacific Gas and Electric Company, 47

Pahlevi Foundation, 242

Palestinian movement, 12, 130, 137

Pardo, Arvid, 288

Park, Chong-huii, 110

participation, 9, 21, 28–29, 106, 127, 178, 214–16, 241, 263

Passamaquoddy project, 222
Patman, Wright, 81
Pauley, Edwin, 62
Peabody Coal Company, 174
Pell, Claiborne, 147
Pennzoil United, Inc., 62, 63, 200, 201
Peoples' Appalachian Research Collective (PARC), 317–18
Percy, Charles H., 252
Persian Gulf, 3, 9, 25–26, 39, 52, 100, 104, 115, 126–27, 243. *See also individual countries*; Middle East; OPEC
Pertamina, 52
Peru, 106, 117
pesticides, 17, 50, 231–32
Peterson, Russell W., 230
petrochemicals, 2, 17, 85, 89, 131, 230–32
petrodollars, 7, 11
Petróleos Mexicanos (Pemex), 219
Petroleum Reserves Corporation, 9
Petromin, 30
Pew family, 59
Philippines, 52
Phillips Petroleum Company, 23, 24, 43, 44, 47, 53, 62, 70–72, 75–76, 79, 86, 116, 220, 312
Piercy, G.T., 39, 263
pipelines, 9, 17, 20, 22–23, 31, 37, 48, 49, 51, 53, 58, 60, 65, 104, 159, 185, 188, 190, 201, 227, 240, 246
Pipeline Safety, Office of, 188
Pittsburgh and Midway Coal Mining Company, 40
planning: corporate, 19–56, 84–85, 100–101, 121–22, 135–36, 145, 146–47, 161, 178, 209–10, 236–37; democratic, 209–50. *See also* national energy policy
political contributions: within U.S., 57–83, 88–89, 102, 200–202, 203, 210, 251, 271–72, 273, 275, 316; overseas, 19, 67, 68–69, 74, 110–13, 216, 284
*Politics of Oil, The,* 245
pollution, 2, 16, 42, 45, 134, 148–57, 168, 174–75, 187–88, 196–97, 201, 213, 231, 233, 248
population control, 238

Portugal, 114–15
Portuguese Africa, 109–10, 114
President's Emergency Energy Action Group, 202
President's Interagency Oil Policy Committee, 203, 261–62
press, 10–11, 33, 51, 83, 139, 182, 188, 247
pricing, oil, 1, 4–5, 9–10, 12–13, 20–21, 24–40, 119–21, 125–31, 139, 170, 179–80, 184, 192, 197–98, 218–19, 223–24, 226, 228, 238–42, 246; and coal, 36, 45, 50; and continental shelf, 147, 155, 199; and Cost of Living Council, 9–10, 35–36, 192; and import controls, 84–87, 90–97; and natural gas, 47–50, 189, 200–201 (*see also* natural gas, deregulation); and shale, 44–45; and tar sands, 46; and transfer prices, 21, 256
profits, 3, 7, 11, 13, 14, 17, 21, 28, 33, 34, 48, 49, 53–56, 84, 105, 126, 131, 147, 209–10, 226–28, 239, 245, 250
profit-sharing, 29, 118
Project on Corporate Responsibility, 72
"Project Independence," 2–3, 127, 155, 156, 177, 206, 229, 239
prorationing, 84, 85, 90, 93, 193
Proxmire, William, 211, 284
Prudhoe Bay, 11, 23, 164, 202
public energy corporations, 9, 14, 150, 161, 183, 186, 194, 205, 222, 226, 247
public energy districts, 222
Public Interest Research Group (Vermont), 221–22
public lands, 5, 22, 23, 41–47, 64, 93, 95, 146–47, 152, 155, 158–65, 170, 185, 194, 212, 226, 229, 239
public ownership, 9, 161, 214–15, 217–18, 230, 246, 247
public relations, 12–14, 40, 50, 51, 56, 61, 70, 87, 93, 111, 118, 122, 139–40, 149, 153, 175–76, 187, 188, 210, 220, 239, 247–49
public utility district, 222
public utility status, 204, 228–29

Puerto Rico, 52, 86, 231
Pure Oil Company, 18, 171

Qaddafi, Muammar el, 28
Qatar, 26

railroads, 16, 187, 234
rationing, 5, 184, 228
Rayburn, Sam, 63
Rebozo, Charles G. ("Bebe"), 62
reclamation, 41, 163, 166–68, 231, 233
Reclamation, Bureau of, 168
recycling, 232
refineries, 6–7, 9, 17, 20–22, 47, 85–87, 91, 95–97, 184, 185, 203, 215, 227–28, 233; construction of, 2, 3, 37–38, 53, 86–87, 92, 184, 196, 217, 230–31, 237
regulatory activities, 59, 77, 167, 187–89, 197, 199–200, 203, 205–6, 210, 211, 215, 221, 228, 232, 237, 245, 247; by states, 167, 205–6, 222, 232. See also specific agencies
Republican National Committee, 62, 88, 197
Republican party, 62, 63, 68, 82, 249
research and development, 42–43, 169–70, 183, 192–93, 223–24, 226, 233, 245–46
reserves, United States, 3, 6, 20, 23, 36, 39–40, 64, 85, 90, 96–97, 153, 158, 161, 184–85, 191–92, 219, 227, 257. See also coal; continental shelf; natural gas; naval reserves; shale
Ricca, John, 170, 173, 180, 185, 305
Richardson, Lee, 207
Richardson, Sid W., 59
Richfield Oil Corporation, 18
Ringling Brothers–Barnum and Bailey Combined Shows, 51
Rockefeller, David, 53
Rockefeller, John D., 37, 246
Rockefeller, Nelson, 246
Rockefeller family, 59
Rogers, William P., 99, 114, 242
Roosevelt, Franklin D., 222–23
Royal Dutch Petroleum Company, 143

Royal Dutch/Shell Group of Companies, 19, 31–32, 52, 54. See also Shell
royalty payments, federal lands, 44, 148–49, 150, 155, 159, 163, 194, 195
royalty payments, overseas, 25–28, 34, 54–55, 86, 115, 118–19, 179–80. See also tax credits
rubber, 247–48
Rural Electrification Administration (REA), 181, 214, 218, 224
Rusk, Dean, 58, 119

Sakhalin, 104
Samoa, 52
Santa Barbara (Channel), 147–52, 154, 155, 158, 160, 164, 166, 191, 193–94, 195–96, 230
Saskatchewan, 217–18, 240
Saudi Arabia, 4, 7, 8–9, 21, 26, 30–31, 39, 54–55, 82, 117, 118, 120, 122–23, 129–32, 138–40, 191, 227, 242
Sawhill, John C., 183, 205–7, 252
Schlesinger, James R., 104–5
Schwartz, David, 190
Scott, Hugh, 69, 81, 273
Scottish nationalism, 52
Scully, Sister Jane, 74, 220
seabed. See law of the sea; ocean beds
Seafarers International Union, 1, 251
Securities and Exchange Commission, 19, 66, 67, 68, 71, 73, 75–77, 110, 112, 113
SEDCO, 202, 311
Select Committee on Presidential Campaign Activities, U.S. Senate (Watergate Committee), 66–67, 70–71, 81
seven sisters, 12, 19, 28, 32, 69, 178
severance tax, 44
shale oil, 19, 22, 40, 42–45, 95, 96, 159, 164, 171, 186, 187, 192–94, 226, 239, 246, 248
Shapp, Milton, 69
Sheldon, Paul, 109–10
Shell Oil Company, 13, 22, 28, 41, 42, 46, 47, 53, 54, 87, 92, 107–8,

116, 126, 131, 171, 175, 180, 182, 186, 212, 214, 216, 230, 231–32. *See also* Royal Dutch/Shell Group of Companies
Shultz, George P., 10, 90–92, 94, 182
shut-in wells, 93, 124, 161, 190
Sierra Club, 229
*Sierra Club et al. v. Rogers C. B. Morton et al.* (1973), 212
Signal Oil and Gas Company, 18, 24, 47
Simon, William E., 35, 49, 182, 183, 203–6
Sinclair Oil Corporation, 18, 43, 60, 87, 124–25, 171, 245
Singapore, 53
Snedeker, T. C., 170
Socal. *See* Standard Oil Company of California
solar energy, 11, 40, 46–47, 222–24, 232
South Africa, 115–16
South African Foundation, 116
South Carolina, 196
South Dakota, 41
Southern California, University of, Allan Hancock Foundation, 149, 153
South Korea, 1, 53, 110, 112–13. *See also* Korea
Southwest Drilling Company (SEDCO), 202, 311
southwestern oil interests, 57–58, 63
Soviet Union, 9, 12, 18–19, 29, 34, 52, 65, 66, 82, 104–5, 107–8, 111, 115, 117–18, 123, 125, 133–34, 139, 178, 216, 223, 237, 242
Standard Oil Company of California (Chevron, Socal), 9, 17–18, 19, 24, 28, 33, 47, 53, 54, 66, 79–80, 114, 116, 119, 123, 126–28, 129–30, 138, 142, 160, 163–64, 182, 197, 201, 203, 299
Standard Oil Company (Indiana) [Amoco], 19, 22, 24, 43, 44–45, 47, 53, 54, 59, 106, 124, 131, 162, 175, 182
Standard Oil Company (Kentucky), 17–18

Standard Oil Company (New Jersey). *See* Exxon
Standard Oil Company (Ohio), [Sohio], 18, 40, 46, 171, 242
Stans, Maurice H., 62, 67–68, 70–71, 77–78, 81, 89–91, 176, 230
Stanvac (Standard-Vacuum Oil Company), 52
State, Department of, 3, 12, 35, 58, 78, 99, 101–2, 106, 107–8, 111, 113, 114, 117–29, 131, 132–33, 135, 139, 141, 142, 166, 178–79, 181, 242, 243, 244
Stevens, Ted, 64
Stevenson, Adlai E., III, 311
stockholders, 23–24, 55, 72–76, 79–81, 109–11, 138, 142, 204, 211–12, 215
stockpiling strategic reserves, 90, 194, 227
Stone, I. F., 80–81
Stone, Reid T., 186
strangulation, 5–6, 12, 243
Strauss, Robert, 82, 272
Strong, Maurice F., 238
Suez Canal, 28, 29, 51, 91, 116
Sukarno, 52
Sun Oil Company, 18, 22, 41, 44, 46, 47, 79, 114, 115, 116, 182
Sunray DX Oil Company, 18
supply, 2, 7, 8, 9, 29–31, 36–39, 46, 84–85, 93, 96–97, 121, 124, 127, 129–30, 153, 164. *See also* imports; reserves
Supreme Court, U.S., 47, 49, 93
Sweden, 219, 225
Symington, Stuart, 73
Synacrude, 45
synthetics, 17, 50

Taiwan, 53, 102, 136
tankers, 20, 31, 59, 60, 127, 134, 151, 154–55, 164, 174, 207–8, 227, 237; supertankers, 17, 51, 86–87, 104, 154, 230, 237
tariff, 90–92, 97
tar sands, 11, 40, 45–46, 187, 192
tax credits, overseas, 21, 28, 34, 54–56, 86, 118–19, 121, 211, 218,

227. *See also* income tax; royalty
  payments, overseas
tax privileges, 54, 56, 63, 68, 84, 176,
  209–11, 218. *See also* depletion
  allowance; income tax; tax credits
Teapot Dome, 163, 164, 194
technical assistance, 34, 144
technology, 41, 95, 100, 104, 131,
  135, 144, 192, 210, 213, 216,
  219–20, 223, 235–36, 238, 245–46
Temporary National Economic
  Committee (TNEC), 214
temporary national energy
  committee, 214–21, 228–29
Tennessee, 230
Tennessee Gas and Transmission
  Company (Tenneco), 18, 53, 104,
  114, 200
Tennessee Valley Authority (TVA),
  50, 214, 218
Texaco Inc. (The Texas Company),
  9, 13, 19, 24, 28, 33, 38, 47, 53, 54,
  79, 97, 105, 107, 114, 116, 119,
  123, 126, 129, 135, 147–48, 154,
  174, 175, 192, 200, 220, 236
Texas, 2, 71, 90, 93
Texas Company. *See* Texaco Inc.
Texas Eastern Transmission
  Corporation, 62, 66
Texas Pacific Oil Company, 182
Texas Railroad Commission, 70, 97,
  236, 277–78
Thailand, 53, 98–99, 103
Thieu, Nguyen van, 53
tidal energy, 87, 222–23
*Torrey Canyon*, 154–55
Tosco. *See* Oil Shale Corporation
Tower, John G., 88
trade unions, 16, 167, 175, 231–32,
  247
Trans-Alaska Pipeline
  Authorization Act, 211
Trans-Arabian pipeline, (Tapline),
  28
transfer pricing, 21, 256. *See also*
  income tax; pricing
Transportation, Department of, 201
Treasury, Department of the, 55, 57,

58–59, 82, 84, 85, 108, 118–19,
  128, 132, 147–48, 182, 203–6
trolley car, 16, 233–34
trucking industry, 2, 6, 16, 201
Truman doctrine, 4

Udall, Stewart L., 65, 89, 193–94
Unger, Leonard, 98
Union Oil Company of California,
  18, 23, 24, 43, 45, 47, 52, 53, 87,
  124, 147–48, 154–55, 191, 196,
  201–2, 271–72
United Church of Christ, Council
  for Christian Social Action, 72,
  109–10, 280–81
United Emirates, 26
United Mine Workers of America
  (UMW), 167, 231, 247
United Nations, 115–16, 132–33,
  141, 144, 147, 237
United Nations Economic Commis-
  sion for Asia and the Far East, 52
United Nations Economic and Social
  Council, "Group of Eminent
  Persons," 142–45
United Nations Environmental
  Program, 238
United Nations General Assembly,
  114, 135, 141
Uranium, 40, 46, 50, 96, 131,
  183–84, 225
urban planning, 234, 238
USIA. *See* Information Agency
Utah, 41

Venezuela, 3, 5, 19, 25, 26–27, 33,
  34, 86, 92, 95, 107, 112, 117, 118,
  191, 227, 240
Vermont, 222
Vietnam, 14, 17, 52, 53, 89, 98,
  99–104, 119, 136, 194, 244
Virgin Islands refinery, 65–66, 85–86
Virginia, 87

Wagner, G. A., 143, 291
Wakefield, Stephen A., 177, 186–87,
  201
Wald, George, 238
Walker, Pinkney, 201

Washington (state of), 222
Watergate break-in and cover-up, 5,
    14, 61–63, 65–68, 73, 81–83, 208
water power, 223
water requirements and rights, 40,
    42, 43, 44–45, 168
Ways and Means Committee, U.S.
    House of Representatives, 68, 171
west coast, 23, 60, 198, 230
Western Oil and Gas Association,
    149
western plains, 41–42, 162–63, 168,
    212, 313
West Virginia, 230
Wheatley, Charles F., Jr., 189–90
White, Lee C., 181, 188
Whiteford, William K., 78
Wild, Claude C., Jr., 67–68, 70,
    72–74, 78, 81–82

Wilson, Harold, 4
wind power, 11, 46, 87, 222–23,
    232
wood, 238
Woodridge (New Jersey), 65
Woods, Rose Mary, 65, 72
worker health and safety, 41, 167,
    171–72, 197, 231–32, 300
workers' rights, 215, 220, 223
World War II, 120, 135, 164, 187,
    248
World Wildlife Fund, 175
Wright, M. A., 85
Wyoming, 41, 42, 162, 230

Yamani, Zaki, 39, 263
Yarborough, Ralph, 64
Yugoslavia, 223